Contents

Promoting Adolescent Sexual and Reproductive Health in East and Southern Africa

Edited by
Knut-Inge Klepp, Alan J. Flisher
and Sylvia F. Kaaya

NORDISKA AFRIKAINSTITUTET, SWEDEN
HSRC PRESS, CAPE TOWN
2008

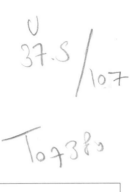

Indexing terms:
  Adolescents
  Reproductive health
  Sexual behaviour
  Sex education
  Health programmes
  Health service
  AIDS prevention
  Social change
  Case studies
  East Africa
  Southern Africa

Language checking: Elaine Almén
Index: Jane Coulter
Cover: FUEL Design, Cape Town

© The authors and Nordiska Afrikainstitutet 2008
P.O. Box 1703, SE-751 47 Uppsala, Sweden
www.nai.uu.se
ISBN 978-91-7106-599-5

Published in South Africa by HSRC Press
Private Bag X9182, Cape Town, 8000, South Africa
www.hsrcpress.ac.za
ISBN 978-0-7969-2210-6

Printed in Sweden by Alfa Print 2008

Preface

The basis for this volume emerged out of the extensive collaboration born out of the Adolescent Reproductive Health Network (ARHNe), which lasted from 1997–2001. This was a European Union-funded concerted action project which developed the competence and capacity of researchers in East and Southern Africa to engage in health promotion activities (particularly in the area of reproductive health).

Specifically, the main objectives of the ARHNe were to:

–   strengthen and further develop research and practice related to the design and delivery of sexual and reproductive health-related services and programs targeting adolescents

–   foster the development and application of trans-disciplinary theories, conceptual models and research methods relevant to the study of adolescent health, and ultimately develop culturally appropriate intervention programs to modify adolescent health-related behaviors

–   facilitate technical co-operations between African researchers and between African researchers and their European colleagues in order to stimulate a productive scientific context for ongoing programs and to reduce the risk of costly, uncoordinated duplication of research

In response to the need to articulate new perspectives and strategies on promoting adolescent sexual and reproductive health, the network researchers working in East and Southern Africa represented a unique and comprehensive attempt to bring together the social and biomedical sciences in an effort to disseminate concrete empirical evidence from diverse vantage points. This book ultimately represents a tool that may be utilized not only by academics in the field, but also by practitioners, governments, policy makers and students interested in the future research agenda, priorities and challenges of sexual and reproductive health in the wake of several international commitments.

We would like to thank all of our colleagues who over the years participated in the ARHNe project workshops and who contributed to the scientific discussions that stimulated the writing of this volume. Furthermore, we would like to thank the European Commission for their generous support through the ARHNe grant (Contract no. ERBIC18CT970232) and the University of Oslo which supported this work through the Centre for Prevention of Global Infections (GLOBINF), a thematic research area at the Faculty of Medicine. Finally, our grateful appreciation goes to Ms. Sheri Bastien for her editorial assistance during the final stages of this book project.

Oslo, Cape Town and Dar es Salaam, October 2005

Knut-Inge Klepp   Alan J. Flisher   Sylvia F. Kaaya

Introduction

Knut-Inge Klepp, Alan J. Flisher and Sylvia F. Kaaya

Primary prevention and health promotion: A focus on adolescents

In the realm of global health research, adolescent sexual and reproductive health has emerged as an area of key concern, particularly in developing nations and regions such as sub-Saharan Africa where HIV and AIDS account for the second highest number of deaths. Globally, one-fourth of these cases represent people under the age of 25 years, with 63 per cent residing in sub-Saharan Africa (UNAIDS, 2004). Young women are three times as likely as young men to be infected. Adolescents in East and Southern Africa are also faced with a host of potential sexual and reproductive health problems in addition to HIV/AIDS, such as sexually transmitted infections, unwanted pregnancies, unsafe abortions, contraception, sexual abuse and rape, female genital mutilation and circumcision, and maternal and child mortality.

Young people under the age of 25 constitute an important group given that they comprise approximately half of the global population and are ultimately the future adult citizenry. Indeed, the health of a nation's young people and its vulnerability serve as a barometer for the health of wider society. In recognition that the sexual and reproductive health needs of adolescents differ markedly from those of adults, nations are now increasingly placing the issue firmly on their development agendas. Yet despite being at the center of the HIV epidemic in terms of transmission, vulnerability and impact, the vast majority of adolescents encounter significant barriers to maintaining their sexual and reproductive health, such as stigma and discrimination, lack of access to youth-friendly services, critical information, and programs which are designed to equip them with the skills and services they need for prevention, treatment and care. Moreover, the period of adolescence and the transition to adulthood varies widely from society to society and is marked in different ways and at different ages. Consequently, adolescents may face different challenges and have different opportunities which may impact their sexual and reproductive health.

The research agenda

The widely recognized 10/90 imbalance, whereby 10 per cent of funding worldwide is spent on diseases which afflict 90 per cent of the population makes collaborative research, capacity building and dissemination efforts by networks such as ARHNe critical to achieving the substantial progress necessary for narrowing the gap. A number of international agreements and initiatives have been made in the last decade which also underpin the network's activities and form the core of this volume's efforts in the field of sexual and reproductive health. The International Conference on Population and Development (ICPD) in Cairo, has been instrumental in affirming the status of reproductive rights as basic human rights to be enjoyed by all and the importance of gender equality in facilitating development and alleviating poverty, while at the same time acknowledging the need to address the underlying mechanisms which perpetuate ill health and stand in the way of the realization of those rights. Two additional international commitments underpinning the network's activities are the UN Convention on the Rights of the Child (1989) and the UN's Millennium Development Goals (MDGs), as reflected in a number of the chapters in this volume. These instruments, which are built on an understanding that the rights, safety, health and well-being of children and young people, are imperative to the development process of nations and are intrinsically linked, reinforced, and complemented by each other.

Our understandings of sexual and reproductive health have matured to the point that it is now widely acknowledged that personal, social, structural and environmental factors often beyond the scope of individual control are instrumental in making sense of the diversity of factors which combine to shape sexual behavior. Understanding the complex interplay of these factors, which may simultaneously work to constrain or facilitate individuals in negotiating any given behavior, has become a focal point for researchers engaged in prevention and health promotion activities. The contributions in this volume are built on this premise that sexual and reproductive health behavior is multifaceted and that interventions must consequently be aimed at a number of levels: the individual, organizational and governmental; and at settings such as the school, worksites, health care institutions and communities. Accordingly, the diversity of chapters contained in this volume provides entry points for understanding adolescent sexual and reproductive health at the policy, theoretical and ethical levels, at the community level, at the health services level and at the school level.

The authors aim to address some of the most salient issues to have emerged from recent research, including: the role of policy in planning adolescent sexual and reproductive health programs; the applicability of Western theories and models in the African context; the role of the media; the centrality of gender and its construction to sexual and reproductive health; the use of peer educators as change agents; the provision of youth-friendly health services; the current ethical challenges facing the field; and the need for rigorous evaluation of programs.

Superimposed on all of these issues, social change and the tension between the old and new ways of thinking and being, emerge as an overriding theme. Social, economic and political forces are rapidly altering the manner in which young people and adolescents grow up, having significant implications for their education, future employment and sexual and reproductive health. In sub-Saharan Africa, this is readily apparent in uneven, yet steady changes in terms of gender norms and expectations as evidenced in familial structures, the education and employment sectors, the media, and in policy. Similarly, our understandings of African sexuality have become more sophisticated and nuanced, which have prompted researchers to revisit critical issues related to how sexual and reproductive health interventions are conceived within certain frameworks; ultimately, how they are planned and implemented at all levels of analysis from policy to theory, ethics and practice.

Comprehensive overview

The volume is divided into four sections, with each section building on and reinforcing the others. The first section lays the groundwork by focusing primarily on the policy and theoretical underpinnings of sexual and reproductive health promotion. Having established the premises upon which interventions are built, the second section highlights a number of contextual issues surrounding adolescent sexual and reproductive health, and draws examples from studies conducted in a number of countries in East and Southern Africa through anthropological, sociological and psychological lenses. The third section of the book rounds out the first two sections by looking at the settings and arenas typically targeted by interventions, such as schools and health facilities. The fourth and final section of the volume consists of two chapters which appropriately sum up current findings in the literature by providing comprehensive reviews and evaluations of reproductive health interventions in Southern and East Africa.

In Chapter 1, public policy as a tool for promoting adolescent sexual and reproductive health is explored by looking at the processes involved in policy development and the inherent challenges it entails. This chapter highlights a theme recurrent throughout the volume, which is the centrality of adolescent participation in planning to maximize effectiveness and relevance of programming. In Chapter 2, a critical examination of the usage and applicability of social cognitive models designed in Western contexts, suggests that while these models may have relevance to African settings, sufficient attention must be paid to underlying cultural, structural and environmental factors which may compromise the efficacy of prevention or health promotion programs. In a similar vein, Chapter 3 questions the ability of interventions conceived in the West to be successfully transplanted to African contexts, given cultural, social and economic specificities. The authors introduce the Intervention Mapping (IM) approach as an alternative to developing and diffusing HIV prevention programs, which enables a more sophisticated and contextually aware understanding of the target population. Exploring the fundamental ethical dilemmas intrinsically involved in research in general and health promotion in particular, Chapter 4 raises important questions to be considered by researchers in the field and underscores the continuous need for reevaluating and revamping guidelines to keep pace with changing methodologies and practices. The recent emphasis on child participation is again raised in light of the new ethical dilemmas participation poses.

At the outset of Section II, Chapter 5 draws on the aforementioned theme of social change and attempts to make sense of the historical, sociocultural, political and economic contexts in which sex education has shifted from traditional initiation rituals to more explicit school-based learning. In this way, the chapter explores some of the more distal factors impinging on interventions that were detailed in the first section, in order to explain how and why sexual behavior is changing, and ultimately the implications of this for interventions. The dire implications of illegal abortion for the sexual and reproductive health of adolescent girls and the importance of addressing the lack of available youth-friendly health services is focused on in Chapter 6. The findings here demonstrate that lack of knowledge and access to services such as safe, legal abortion for adolescent girls is a pressing issue that needs to be addressed through policy and backed up by action and services. Developing these findings more broadly, Chapter 7 addresses the barriers adolescents face in negotiating safe and healthy sexual behavior by linking current sexual behavior in Tanzania to ongoing social and economic changes. Returning to the theme of social change, Chapter 8 takes a look at how vulnerability and the onset of sexual behavior are shaped in the context of HIV in Tanzania.

Section III begins with Chapter 9, which provides an in-depth look at the increasing use of peer educators in the field of health promotion and sexual and reproductive health, with particular focus on interventions in sub-Saharan Africa. Health services geared towards adolescents in Uganda are detailed in Chapter 10. This chapter demonstrates how understandings of the needs of adolescents for health services tailored for their context has grown since the ICPD and provides a look at how this is being implemented on the ground. Similarly, in Chapter 11 the perceptions and attitudes of nurses and midwives who deal with adolescents in health service settings are explored in light of the impact this has on quality of care. These two chapters present important empirical data in an area where there is relatively little research documenting the effectiveness of youth-friendly health services in terms of their ability to attract young people, adequately meet their needs and ultimately, the outcome of their sexual health.

Finally, the last section of the book culminates in two chapters which are comprehensive reviews and evaluations of sexual and reproductive health and school-based interventions in sub-Saharan Africa, in order to highlight what has been done thus far and to identify the gaps in the literature which need to be addressed in future research.

The chapters in this volume aim to contribute new knowledge and evidence of the manner in which interventions through schools, the media, health services and community can contribute to the sustained sexual and reproductive health of adolescents. Identifying and scaling up successful interventions and implementing national strategies and policies backed by solid empirical data and financial commitment is critical to ensuring the present and future generation live long, healthy and productive lives. This volume represents an attempt from a research perspective to bridge the gap between policy, theory, rhetoric and action and in that way make a modest contribution to this ambitious agenda.

I

Policy and Theory Informing Practice

1. Public Policy: A Tool to Promote Adolescent Sexual and Reproductive Health

Yogan Pillay and Alan J. Flisher

Abstract

The term policy refers to an organised set of a vision and sets of values, principles, objectives and general strategies. Public adolescent sexual and reproductive health policy has the following purposes: to change behaviour at the individual and collective levels; to facilitate a higher priority being assigned to adolescent sexual and reproductive health; to establish a set of goals to be achieved, upon which future action can be based; to improve procedures for developing and prioritising adolescent sexual and reproductive services and activities; to identify the principal stakeholders in the field of adolescent sexual and reproductive health and to designate clear roles and responsibilities; and to achieve consensus of action among the different stakeholders. There are six key processes in developing policy: collect information; develop consensus; obtain political support; implement pilot projects; review; and solicit international support and input. In general, it is the responsibility of a task team or committee to carry out these activities. In developing policy, member states of the United Nations and regional multilateral organisations have an obligation to take into consideration treaties, conventions and instruments adopted by these bodies. There are several such agreements, including the Convention on the Rights of the Child, Programme of Action of the United Nations International Conference on Population and Development (ICPD), Programme of Action adopted at the United Nations Fourth World Conference on Women, African Charter on the Rights and Welfare of Children, and the Protocol on Health in the Southern African Development Community. Policies are more likely to be acceptable to adolescents if they are consulted and involved in the development of policies and their implementation. Governments need to commit resources to ensure that policies are effectively implemented and sustainable, which requires political and financial stability.

Policy is the thread of conviction that keeps a government from being the prisoner of events... (Ignatieff, 1992, quoted in Walt, 1994, p. 41.)

What is policy, and why do we need it?

The term policy refers to an organised set of a vision and sets of values, principles, objectives and general strategies. The development of policy occurs at many levels, for example the individual and public levels (Pillay, 1999). An example of a simple individual level policy is the decision to use a condom or to be monogamous, while an example of a public policy is the decision to permit termination of pregnancy in specified circumstances.

These examples provide a clue as to why we need policy. At the most basic level, policies are intended to influence behaviour at either the individual or collective level. Public adolescent sexual and reproductive health (ASRH) policy may also have the following additional purposes (World Health Organisation, 2001):

— to ensure that a higher priority is assigned to adolescent sexual and reproductive health;

— to establish a set of goals to be achieved, upon which future action can be based;

— to improve procedures for developing and prioritising adolescent sexual and reproductive services and activities;

— to identify the principal stakeholders in the field of adolescent sexual and reproductive health and to designate clear roles and responsibilities; and

— to achieve consensus of action among the different stakeholders.

Policies may also have unintended negative consequences. For example, whilst the legalisation on termination of pregnancy aims to give adolescents increased control over their reproductive health and to prevent the negative effects of 'back-street abortions', it may also result in teenagers using termination as their primary family planning method.

Policies differ from, but are related to, legislation. Institutions use policies as rules or guidelines to shape their behaviour. Legislation should be based on policy. It is related to policy in that they both set out to shape behaviour. However, legislation (unlike policies) also provides for sanctions and penalties. Once a policy is promulgated, it becomes an offence in terms of the law not to implement the policy. A further, related, difference between policies and legislation is that legislation provides more certainty than does the policy on which it is based. The vague and ambiguous aspects of a policy need to be clarified when translating a policy into legislation.

How do we develop policy?

There are six key processes in developing policy: (a) collect information; (b) develop consensus; (c) obtain political support; (d) implement pilot projects; (e) review; and (f) solicit international support and input (World Health Organization, 2001). In general, it is the responsibility of a task team or committee to implement these steps.

Collect information

Ideally, data in three domains inform the development of ASRH policy. First, one needs to have a *situation analysis* for each area that will be included in the policy. This is necessary to inform priorities and form a baseline to use in evaluating the effect of a policy. For example, if one is to develop policy to reduce the extent of unsafe sexual behaviour in a population of adolescents, one needs answers to basic questions, like:

– What is the prevalence rate of sexually transmitted diseases such as HIV infection among health facility users or community samples?

– What are the routes of HIV infection?

– What proportions of adolescents in each age and grade cohort engage in sexual intercourse and other forms of sexual behaviour?

– Are the sexual partners peers, as opposed to older adults?

– How well do the partners know each other?

– Are the partners in a committed relationship, or is their relationship driven mainly by spontaneous sexual desire?

– Are the sexual encounters characterised by violence, or threats of violence?

– What is the partner "turnover" rate?

– How many partners do adolescents have both serially and concurrently?

– What do they do to prevent pregnancy and sexually transmitted infections (such as AIDS)?

– What are the social norms around sexual behaviour in the peer, family and community domains?

- What is the influence of the following variables on sexual behaviour: self-efficacy for safer sexual practices, intent, knowledge about sexuality, and social and material barriers?
- Are there economic reasons for such behaviour?

In many cases, this information is not available. In this case, steps need to be taken to fill the gaps. Such steps can include embarking on new quantitative or qualitative studies, conducting rapid appraisals, convening expert panels and extrapolating from studies conducted in similar environments. Reviews may be useful in extrapolating from other contexts; for example, there are reviews of adolescent sexual behaviour in school populations in Sub-Saharan Africa (Kaaya et al., 2002b) and adolescent and youth sexual behaviour in South Africa (Eaton et al., 2003).

The second domain in which data are necessary to inform the development of ASRH policy is the *impact* of the scenario described in the situation analysis. If one stays with the example used above, one will need to understand the nature and extent of the consequences of unsafe sexual behaviour. Thus one would need to know the rates of unwanted pregnancy, terminations of pregnancy and sexually transmitted diseases such as HIV infection. Overall rates are necessary, especially for garnering support from key stakeholders and raising public awareness. However, for policy purposes it is also important to disaggregate such data according to key demographic variables such as age, gender and location. This will enable the policy to be fine-tuned to ensure that rates in high-prevalence groups are reduced while rates in low prevalence groups remain low.

The final domain in which data are necessary is around *interventions*. Policy decisions about interventions should be based on the best available scientific evidence about the efficacy and impact or effectiveness of potential interventions (Flisher et al., 2008). Again to pursue the above example, with regard to school-based sexual and reproductive health promotion efforts, a considerable body of evidence has emerged about the characteristics of effective programmes (Kirby et al., 1994; Mukoma and Flisher, 2008). New policy should take existing evidence into account. However, it is still necessary to develop programmes that are appropriate for each context. The chapter by Schaalma and Kaaya (2008) provides guidance on how to do this.

Develop consensus

The content of policies reflects the relative power of those influencing their content. According to Walt (1994), writing in the context of health policy specifically, health policy is about content, process and power: "It is concerned with who influences whom in the making of policy, and how that happens" (p.1). Partly for this reason, it is essential that the policy making process includes all key stakeholders. Prime among these are representatives of the group whose health the ASRH policy aims to address, namely adolescents themselves. Thus, it is important for policy makers to consult with adolescents and their representatives to ensure that their views influence the content of the policies, and that interventions take into consideration their objective and subjective realities. Failure to do so may result in inappropriate policies being adopted and difficulties in the implementation of these policies.

It is also crucial to include representatives of other sectors (besides the health sector) in the development of adolescent sexual and reproductive health, for two main reasons. First, there are a range of fundamental socio-economic conditions that are essential for adolescent health, such as peace, shelter, education, food, income, a stable ecosystem, sustainable resources, social justice, equity (Ottawa Charter, 1996). Second, these fundamental conditions can have an impact on the effectiveness of interventions. Adolescents, for example, are unlikely to be receptive to information about the importance of safer sex practices if they are homeless and dependent on income derived from commercial sex. In most cases, these conditions are not directly addressed in ASRH policies. However, it is necessary to ensure that policies, plans and programmes in other sectors support ASRH policy, by taking cognisance of the needs of adolescents. Thus, the involvement of other sectors is necessary to maximise the chances of this occurring. Box 1 lists the stakeholders that participated in the development of the National Adolescent and Youth Health Policy Guidelines in South Africa.

Obtain political support

Political support is necessary both during the development and implementation of policy. It facilitates a stable environment for implementation. Health workers and others responsible for policy implementation are more likely to be committed to a policy if it is not merely a short-term political priority. Related to this is that political support produces higher levels of accountability from those tasked with implementation. They are more likely to be called to account by politicians, and a failure to deliver may be more likely to have negative consequences. Finally, political support is necessary to secure sustained or increased funding.

In a recent editorial in *The Lancet*, its editor Horton highlights the negative consequences of political influence on public health policy using the current US government's attitude to abortions and the spill-over effect on such institutions as the US Centers for Disease Control and Prevention. He notes: "(this) culture of political censorship and fear, which now pervades many public-health institutions when reproductive health is at issue, is not only damaging the reputations of once highly regarded agencies…but also blunts the global contributions they can make" (Horton, 2006, p. 1549).

Implement pilot projects

Pilot projects can provide useful evidence from the beginning of a policy development process (Abeja-Apunyo, 1999). They can demonstrate that a programme is feasible in a subset of the sites for which it is being developed, which provides reassurance before rolling it out more broadly. They can indicate which aspects need to be improved, and contribute to estimates of the costs of implementing a policy.

An example of a pilot project is the Programme for Enhancing Adolescent Reproductive Life (PEARL), which was started in four pilot districts in Uganda in 1995. Its objective was to enhance adolescent reproductive health by providing adolescents with appropriate reproductive health counselling and services. A national steering committee was established to oversee the project and included: the Ministry of Gender, Labour and Social Development, the Ministry of Health and the Population Secretariat, two district level personnel, a sub-county officer and health unit service provider. The programme was implemented using peer mobilisers and parent/peer educators at parish or local level. In 1997 PEARL was expanded into four new districts and it was planned to expand into four additional districts every year until the entire country was covered. The expansion process will be guided by lessons learned as the project rolls out.

Review

A comprehensive review of a policy rests on two pillars. First, it is necessary to evaluate the policy itself, for which a framework is necessary. Such a framework can be used not only by people involved in developing policy but also by people who use the policy or are affected by it. Pillay (1999) has developed the following series of questions that can be used to evaluate and review policies:

- Who initiated the policy and why?
- What does the policy do?
- What is the desired impact?
- What are the benefits?
- Who are the beneficiaries and who will lose?
- Can the policy be implemented?
- Who will implement the policy?
- Are there systems in place to implement the policy and are the skills required available?
- What are the costs and who will bear them?
- Are the costs sustainable?

In a document released in 1999 entitled *Monitoring Reproductive Health: Selecting a short list of national and global indicators* the World Health Organization proposed a series of indicators which may be used to monitor ASRH. Included in the list are three policy related indicators: (a) existence of government policies, programmes or laws favourable to adolescent reproductive health; (b) age at first marriage by sex – does a legal minimum age exist, what is it and is it enforced? and (c) does policy or legislation that outlaws provision of family planning to persons who are unmarried or below a certain age exist? It may be argued that this is a very limited list but it should be noted that this was an attempt to include some aspects of policy monitoring in a short list of indicators.

The second pillar of a comprehensive policy review is to assess the implementation of the policy and its impact on the outcomes it was developed to affect. To achieve these goals, it is necessary to develop a set of indicators, which are quantitative estimates that reflect the situation at the time. If it emerges that there has not been any or sufficient change to an indicator or set of indicators, there are several possible reasons for this, such as: (a) the policy was not able to be implemented, for example because of inadequate fiscal resources or insufficient political or popular support; (b) there were problems in the implementation phase that were not anticipated; and (c) there were other problems with the policy, for example the interventions that were implemented were of dubious efficacy or the inappropriate subgroups of the population were targeted. If the indicators suggest that the policy was not successful, it is frequently necessary to conduct qualitative research to determine the reasons that this was the case.

Many countries have encountered challenges when attempting to develop a system to monitor policy implementation. This is often the result of a poor information "culture", a lack of information systems, and/or a lack of trained personnel to collate and report on the data. It is clearly preferable to use routinely collected data when possible, as this does not place additional burdens on health workers. Where this is not possible, special surveys may be necessary to complement routinely collected data. Reports that emanate from either routinely collected data or special surveys may be used to strengthen implementation, inform a review and adjustment of the policy; and account to both political representatives and communities. Examples of indicators used in policies in South Africa and Uganda are provided in Box 2 and Table 1 respectively.

Solicit international support and input

International experts, particularly those with experience in a range of countries, are potentially most helpful in the early stages of a policy development process. Their lack of detailed knowledge of the host country and the possibility of their solutions either being impractical or linked to international agendas that may not be in the interests of the country clearly have disadvantages and it is important to acknowledge this. However, international experts have some advantages. They are less likely to be indebted to or unduly influenced by local political factions, and less likely to be distracted by local particularities when formulating broad visions and values. The input of such experts can complement documents produced by the World Health Organization (for example, World Health Organization, 1999) and donor agencies (for example, Rehle et al., 2001). There are two further sources of international input: international policy instruments and policy documents from other countries. We will now review these two sources.

International policy instruments related to adolescents

In developing policy, member states of the United Nations and regional multi-lateral organisations have an obligation to take into consideration treaties, conventions and instruments adopted by these bodies. There are several such agreements, which will receive attention below.

Convention on the Rights of the Child

The United Nations adopted this convention in November 1989 (United Nations Children's Fund, 1990). The Convention requires parties to the Convention to make the principles and provisions of the Convention widely known by active means to adults and children alike. Signatories are also required to submit reports to a Committee established under the Convention on measures adopted which give effect to the rights recognised in the Convention and on the progress made on the enjoyment of those rights. The Convention contains 54 articles and aims at protecting the rights of children (defined as those aged younger than 18 years of age). The Convention contains several articles that impact on policy-making regarding the reproductive health of adolescents, which are listed in Box 3.

Countries in Sub-Saharan Africa and elsewhere have developed their own plans to fulfil their obligations in terms of the Convention. In South Africa, for example, the National Programme of Action for Children in South Africa (NPA) is the instrument by which South Africa's commitments to children in terms of the Convention is expressed. It is a mechanism for identifying all plans for children developed by government departments, NGO's and other child-related structures, and for ensuring that all these plans converge in the framework provided by the Convention, the goals of the 1990 World Summit on Children and the Reconstruction and Development Programme (National Programme of Action Steering Committee, 1996).

Programme of Action of the United Nations International Conference on Population and Development (ICPD)

This programme was adopted in Cairo in 1994. It recognised that reproductive health needs of adolescents have been largely ignored. As its basis of action the Programme of Action proposed that information and services should be made available to adolescents to help them understand their sexuality and protect them from unwanted pregnancies and sexually transmitted diseases. In addition, the Programme of Action acknowledged that programmes targeting adolescents are most effective when they are involved in needs analysis and in designing intervention programmes.

The ICPD proposed four actions that governments should implement. First, countries must ensure that the programmes and attitudes of health workers do not restrict the access of adolescents to reproductive health information and services and that health services must safeguard the rights of adolescents to, amongst others, privacy, confidentiality, respect and informed consent. Second, governments should promote the rights of adolescents to reproductive health education and reduce the incidence of adolescent pregnancies. Third, countries, with the assistance of non-governmental agencies, should meet the special needs of adolescents in the areas of gender relations, violence against adolescents, responsible sexual behaviour, family planning, sexually transmitted diseases and AIDS prevention. Fourth, programmes should also target those responsible for providing guidance to adolescents, viz., parents, guardians, communities, religious institutions, the educational system, the media and peers.

Programme of Action adopted at the United Nations Fourth World Conference on Women

This conference was held in Beijing in October 1995. The Conference reiterated many of the issues found in the Convention on the Rights of the Child and the ICPD. For example, it recognised:

- the need to remove barriers to access to education for women, in particular pregnant adolescents and young mothers;
- that adolescents have limited access to information and health services in many countries;
- that countries should commit themselves to the promotion of respectful and equitable gender relations;
- that the transmission of sexually transmitted diseases, including HIV, is sometimes the consequence of sexual violence;
- that adolescent reproductive health programmes should take into account both the rights of the child and the responsibilities, rights and duties of parents; and
- that access to comprehensive sexual and reproductive health services for adolescent mothers should be a priority.

African Charter on the Rights and Welfare of Children

Article XIV of this Charter provides that every child shall have the right to enjoy the best attainable state of physical, mental and spiritual health. The Article further provides that parties shall take measures to ensure the provision of necessary medical assistance and health care to all children.

Protocol on Health in the Southern African Development Community

Article 17 of this Protocol specifically deals with child and adolescent health and states that in order to provide for appropriate child and adolescent health services essential for the growth and development of children, parties shall develop policies with regard to child and adolescent health and co-operate in improving the health status of children and adolescents.

Policy examples from selected African countries

The accounts of specific adolescent sexual and reproductive health policies in this section exemplify some important general points. First, in most cases the policies have been developed with the explicit aim of implementing the international instruments that were introduced above. Second, such policies can be located in either sexual and reproductive policies, or adolescent health policies, or both. Clearly, if they are located in both it is essential that, at the least, there are no incompatibilities between the policies. Ideally, they have been developed in concert and there is a seamless integration between the two. Third, in most cases, most of the processes that should occur when developing policy have been followed. In cases where this is not explicit, it may be that limitations of space precluded addressing all aspects of the processes used to develop the policy.

The selection of these specific policies in these particular countries is to an extent arbitrary and informed by the information that we had to hand, as opposed to any more systematic data collection procedure. Thus, the omission of a specific policy and/or a specific country should not be taken to imply that they do not exist. Use of selected country examples should therefore be considered illustrative.

Namibia

The Namibian government has, with the support of the United Nations Population Fund (UNFPA) and the United National Children's Fund (UNICEF), taken a number of steps to implement the Convention on the Rights of the Child. Many of these steps focus on helping to protect adolescents from HIV infection. One example is the Youth Health Development Programme, which is a joint government-non-governmental initiative (UNAIDS, 1996b). The following government departments and organisations are partners in this initiative: Ministry of Basic Education and Culture, Ministry of Youth and Sport, Ministry of Health and Social

Services, Polytechnic Institute, Ministry of Information and Broadcasting, Juvenile Justice Programme, University of Maryland, UNICEF and a range of local non-governmental organisations. After talking with the youth, teachers, nurses and others three projects were designed:

- "My future…MY CHOICE!" – a life skills programme which aimed to reach 80% of the youth in the 10–18 year age group by 2001;
- an information and communication project to mobilise the youth and community members to create an environment which promotes healthy living – the project aims to create places for the youth to meet and participate in healthy activities like sports; and
- strengthening services and policies for youth by involving the youth and developing youth networks – key features of this project are to develop youth leaders and analyse existing policies and services.

UNFPA has also supported the Namibian Youth Health Programme by providing reproductive health counselling and services to the youth at the Katutura Multi-Purpose Youth Resource Centre and the Youth Centre in Opuwo. In addition, drama groups are sponsored to build awareness about HIV/AIDS (UNAIDS, 1996a).

South Africa

In a recent report from South Africa (Republic of South Africa, 2000) in which progress towards fulfilling the commitments in the Convention on the Rights of the Child were documented, several milestones were cited:

- the introduction of life skills training in schools;
- strategies to decrease maternal mortality, which should ensure that pregnant adolescents become healthy mothers;
- access to safe termination of pregnancy, since the passage of the Choice on Termination of Pregnancy Act of 1996 allows adolescents the right of access to health facilities that offer terminations;
- the drafting of a South African AIDS Youth Programme, which aimed to reduce the spread of the HIV virus and other sexually transmitted diseases;
- a series of activities in which both the public sector and non-governmental organisations are involved to ensure that clinics are youth friendly; and

– the drafting of national policy guidelines for adolescent and youth health.

The national policy guidelines for adolescent and youth health aim to prevent and respond to specific health problems in adolescents and youth, such as unsafe sexual behaviour, and facilitate the development of capacities, attributes and opportunities that promote the health of young people. The outline of the policy guidelines is provided in Box 4 (Department of Health, Republic of South Africa, 2001). Key features of the policy guidelines are a series of six *guiding concepts*, five *general intervention strategies* and seven *settings*. Each of the general intervention strategies can be applied in each setting. A matrix can be developed and used to assess the extent to which a comprehensive approach has been achieved in the way that each intervention strategy is implemented in each setting.

Tanzania

Tanzania does not have a comprehensive policy on adolescent sexual and reproductive health (A. Badru, personal communication, 2000). However, the Reproductive and Child Health Unit within the Ministry of Health and other partners are currently advocating for such a policy. The proposed mechanism is to lobby the Planning Commission, which is responsible for policy formulation in Tanzania, to accept the need for such a policy. It is anticipated that once the Planning Commission accepts the proposal it will take about a year before the policy drafting process is complete and the policy adopted.

Tanzania does have a general Youth Policy in which issues pertaining to adolescent reproductive health are mentioned. The Policy requires that the Ministry of Health conduct a range of activities pertaining to youth health (see Box 5).

The Tanzanian experience is also instructive with regards to the integration of policies and programmes. Berer (2003, p. 8) provides some examples of the lack of integration between policies: "The policy on health service user charges did not exempt adolescents from charges, whilst another called for services for adolescents to be free…Sexual health education in schools was proposed in one, but out-of-school youth were not mentioned".

Uganda

Uganda has a comprehensive policy for adolescent health. This has several components involving sexual and reproductive health such as adolescent sexuality, fertility concerns, contraception, unsafe abortion, care of the pregnant adolescent, and sexually transmitted infections and HIV/AIDS. The strategies by which the goals and objectives will be met include: advocacy; information, education, and communication; training; service provision; resource mobilization; research; and coordination. A specific strength of the Ugandan National Adolescent Health Policy is the explication of the specific roles of a number of government ministries, committees, inter-governmental agencies, non-governmental organisations and research institutions in implementing the policy. Uganda also has a national action plan for women and a minimum package for sexual and reproductive health, both of which have sections devoted to adolescents.

Zambia

In December 1997, the Zambian Ministry of Health issued a set of strategies and guidelines in reproductive health (Ministry of Health, Zambia, 1997). According to this publication the concept of reproductive health was introduced in 1996 after Zambia's adoption of the International Conference on Population and Development programme of action. The document spells out the process used in developing the strategies and guidelines: "The formulation process of the Reproductive Health Policy has been participatory, involving representatives of related institutions and organisations. An initial workshop was organised to prepare the outline of the Reproductive Health Policy, with the help of a national team and consultants from UNFPA Country Support Teams (Harare) and the Programme of Research on Human Reproduction, WHO (Geneva). A core team was established to develop the draft national Reproductive Health Policy, under the leadership of a national consultant, while a larger group of representatives were available for review and comments…Lastly, district board teams provided their constructive inputs to ensure feasibility of implementation" (p. xiv). Unfortunately a list of organisations and institutions was not attached to the document to ascertain if youth organisations were consulted. While the role of consultants from international agencies appears to be large, the fact that district teams were consulted with respect to implementation issues does suggest that the policy drafters were concerned with its feasibility.

One of the six priority interventions listed in the Zambian Reproductive Health Strategies and Guidelines booklet is adolescent sexual and reproductive health. One of the twelve objectives is "To identify and address the Reproductive Health needs of adolescents and youth and to enhance their total development" (p. 39). Strategies to reach this objective include: identification of the reproductive health needs of youth and adolescents; the provision of appropriate reproductive health information and services to this sector depending on their needs; sensitisation and education of communities on reproductive health needs, including the effects of early marriage; increasing the role of other government ministries, non-governmental organisations, religious institutions and the private sector; improving communication and the provision of services through training; and strengthening participation in the provision of Family Life Education for those in and out of school.

Conclusions

Policy making and implementation are not easy processes. However they are key to any successful programme of action. There are many international and national programmes of action that target adolescent reproductive health – clearly we are not short of knowledge on what needs to be done! What is often lacking, however, is effective implementation of these policies and plans.

These instruments and a review of the literature suggest that policies are more likely to be acceptable to the youth if they are consulted and involved in the implementation process. This requires a certain level of organisation on the part of adolescents and youth at national and sub-national levels and an attitude, on the part of policy makers and implementers, that is youth-friendly.

Governments need to commit resources to ensure that policies are effectively implemented and sustainable. This requires political and financial stability that is not often present in Sub-Saharan Africa. Armed conflict, ineffective macro-economic policies, corrupt and inefficient bureaucracies, and a disorganised civil society all contribute to instability and result in ineffectual policy implementation. To ensure that adolescent reproductive health policies are implemented governments have to accept the need for political and economic stability and democratic practices. As has been illustrated above, the international community, through the United Nations and other bi-lateral and multi-national agencies, has a role to play in assisting countries in the region to draft and implement policies that impact positively on youth and adolescents.

Table 1. Strategic objective, actions and indicators for adolescent reproductive health, Uganda
(Ministry of Gender, Labour and Social Development, Government of Uganda, 1999)

Strategic Objective	Strategic Actions	Indicators
To promote responsible behaviour amongst adolescents in the area of reproductive health	Provide gender sensitisation to parents, teachers and community leaders on family life education for adolescents	Number of parents, teachers and leaders sensitised amongst adolescents
	Continue programmes that help young people to clarify and formulate their attitudes towards responsible behaviour	Change in attitude and practices amongst adolescents Number of 'life clubs'
	Provide sex education targeting adolescents, parents and guardians	Programmes in place Number of joint AIDS awareness programmes
	Encourage behaviour change amongst the youth to prevent HIV/AIDS and other STDs	Number of awareness and support programmes Number of new cases of HIV/AIDS amongst the youth Proportion of sexually active teenagers using condoms Number of teen pregnancies Prevalence of STD rates amongst teenagers

Box 1

Stakeholders who participated in the development of national adolescent and youth health policy guidelines in South Africa
(Department of Health, Republic of South Africa, 2001)

Task team

Chief Director, Cluster: Maternal, Child & Women's Health, Department of Health, Republic of South Africa (RSA)

Deputy Director, Sub-directorate: Adolescent and Youth Health, Department of Health, RSA (Chair)

Assistant Director, Sub-directorate: Adolescent and Youth Health, Department of Health, RSA

Representatives from the following directorates in the Department of Health, RSA:

– Chronic Diseases and Disabilities
– Environmental Health
– HIV/AIDS
– Mental Health and Substance Abuse
– Nutrition
– Oral Health
– Woman's Health and Genetics

Representatives from the following other national departments:

– Education
– Office of the President (National Youth Commission)
– Welfare

Representatives of the following non-governmental and community-based organisations and donor agencies:

– Aids Training, Information and Counselling Centres
– Medical Institute of Community Services
– Planned Parenthood Association of South Africa
– South African Association of Youth Clubs
– United Nations Population Fund
– Young Men's Christian Association (YMCA)

Additional organisations which attended one or more provincial or national workshops

Representatives of the following national and/or provincial government departments:

- Agriculture
- Correctional Services
- Education
- Health
- National Population Unit
- Office of the Status of Women
- Provincial Youth Commission
- Public Service Commission
- South African Police Services
- Sports and Recreation
- Welfare

Representatives of the following non-governmental and community-based organizations and donor agencies:

- National Progressive Primary Health Care Network
- Youth Development Trust
- Youth Council
- Border Institute of Primary Health Care
- Winterveldt Aids Trust
- Youth Academy
- Health Academy
- Health Care Trust
- Family and Marriage Society of South Africa
- Tanzanian Youth Organisation
- Women's Health Project

Representatives of the following tertiary educational units:

- Department of Psychiatry and Mental Health, University of Cape Town
- Health Systems Development Unit, University of the Wiwtatersrand
- Reproductive Health Research Unit, University of the Witwatersrand

Faith-based Organisations:

- Apostolic Faith Mission Worship Centre
- South African Council of Churches
- Religious AIDS Programme

Box 2
Examples of indicators for adolescent and youth sexual and reproductive health in the National Policy Guidelines for Adolescent and Youth Health in South Africa (Department of Health, Republic of South Africa, 2001)

Age at first pregnancy

Age of coital debut

Characteristics of male progenitors (age, educational level, type of employment)

Existing standards for reproductive health care

Fertility rates

Levels of satisfaction of adolescents and youth with reproductive health services

Maternal mortality ratio (<17 years)

Number and percentage of young people sexually active

Number and percentage of young people who use each type of contraception

Number and percentage of pregnant young people according to educational level

Number and percentage of young people who receive some formal type of sexual education

Organisations, associations or services providing each type of contraception

Percentage of births attended by fathers

Percentage of pregnancies among young women < 20 years ending in abortion

Percentage of pregnant young people initiating antenatal care by each trimester of pregnancy

Percentage of women with first birth < 20 years

Percentage of young people living with HIV/AIDS

Percentage of young people with STD's (excluding HIV infection)

Source of sex education

Violence incidence and prevalence against young people, including sexual abuse

Young people's knowledge about sexuality, contraception, STD's

Box 3
Provisions of the Convention on the Rights of the Child relating to health
(United Nations Children's Fund, 1990a)

Article 3
Parties to the Convention shall ensure that institutions, services and facilities responsible for the care or protection of children conform to standards established by competent authorities, particularly in the areas of safety and health.

Article 12
Parties shall assure to the child who is capable of forming his or her own views the right to express those views freely on all matters affecting the child, the views of the child being given due weight in accordance with the age and maturity of the child

Article 19
Parties to the Convention shall take all appropriate legislative, administrative, social and educational measures to protect the child from all forms of physical or mental violence, injury or abuse, neglect or negligent treatment, maltreatment or exploitation, including sexual abuse, while in the care of parent (s), legal guardian(s) or any other person who has the care of the child.

Article 23
Parties to the Convention recognise that a mentally or physically disabled child should enjoy a full and decent life, in conditions which ensure dignity, promote self-reliance and facilitate the child's active participation in the community. Parties shall promote exchange of appropriate information in the field of preventive health care and of medical, psychological and functional treatment of disabled children.

Article 24
Parties recognise the right of the child to the enjoyment of the highest attainable standard of health and to facilities for the treatment of illness and rehabilitation of health. Parties shall ensure that no child is deprived of his or her right of access to such health care services. Measures shall be taken to develop preventive health care, guidance for parents and family planning education and services and the prevention of accidents. Parties shall take all effective and appropriate measures with a view to abolishing traditional practices prejudicial to the health of children.

Box 4

Outline of the South African policy guidelines for adolescent and youth health (Department of Health, Republic of South Africa, 2001)

1. **Preamble**
2. **Current legal, policy & treaty framework**
   2.1 The Constitution of the Republic of South Africa
   2.2 United Nations Convention of the Rights of the Child and the National Programme of Action for Children in South Africa
   2.3 African Charter on the Rights and Welfare of Children
   2.4 Protocol on Health in the Southern African Development Community
   2.5 White Paper for the Transformation of the Health System in South Africa
   2.6 Vision and mission of the Sub-directorate: Youth and Adolescent Health
   2.7 National Youth Policy
3. **Guiding concepts**
   3.1 Youth and adolescent development underlies the development of health problems
   3.2 Problems have common roots and are interrelated
   3.3 Youth and adolescence is a time of opportunity and risk
   3.4 The social environment influences youth and adolescent behaviour
   3.5 Not all youth and adolescents are equally vulnerable
   3.6 Gender considerations are fundamental
4. **General strategies**
   4.1 Promoting a safe and supportive environment
   4.2 Providing information
   4.3 Building skills
   4.4 Providing counselling
   4.5 Improving health services
5. **Intervention settings**
   5.1 Home
   5.2 School
   5.3 Health facility
   5.4 Workplace
   5.5 Street
   5.6 Community organisation
   5.7 Residential centre
6. **Health priorities**
   6.1 Sexual and reproductive health
   6.2 Mental health
   6.3 Substance abuse
   6.4 Violence
   6.5 Unintentional injuries
   6.6 Birth defects and inherited disorders
   6.7 Nutrition
   6.8 Oral health

Box 5

Key aspects of the Youth Health Policy, Tanzania

(Ministry of Labour and Youth Development, United Republic of Tanzania, 1990)

- Animate youths and the community in general to identify health problems which affect them especially STDs, AIDS and drug abuse.
- Ensure the availability of health services which will be accessible to youth without fear, intimidation or discrimination of any kind.
- Institute special programmes to combat the spread of STDs, HIV/AIDS and drug abuse
- Involve youths in preparing, planning and implementing health programmes geared to promote youth health
- Prepare a curriculum on youth health which will be used to train professionals and health workers at various levels Strengthen sexual health education to youth, both boys and girls

2. Social Cognition Models and Social Cognitive Theory

Predicting Sexual and Reproductive Behaviour among Adolescents in Sub-Saharan Africa

Leif E. Aarø, Herman Schaalma and Anne Nordrehaug Åstrøm

Abstract

Social cognition models and Social Cognitive Theory are widely used in research on health related behaviours. One of the main advantages of these theoretical frameworks is their usefulness when planning and conducting interventions, for instance educational approaches to the prevention of HIV/AIDS among adolescents. The present chapter provides a brief description of selected theories and models: the Health Belief Model, the Theory of Planned Behaviour, the Attitude-Social Influence-Efficacy Model, and selected aspects of Social Cognitive Theory. Strengths and weaknesses of social cognition models and Social Cognitive Theory are discussed. The few studies of sexual and reproductive behaviour based on social cognition models or Social Cognitive Theory which have been carried out in sub-Saharan Africa provide some evidence for the usefulness of such theoretical approaches under societal and cultural circumstances different from those of the Western countries. There is a need for research which can shed more light on the relevance of social cognition models and Social Cognitive Theory in cultures different from the Western ones they were designed in. In developing countries, however, it is particularly important to take into account factors beyond those covered by such models (the physical and organisational contexts as well as cultural and structural conditions).

Introduction

This chapter presents aspects of Social Cognitive Theory as well as a number of the most widely used social cognition models applied in health behaviour research. More basic learning processes such as classic and operant conditioning are not addressed, nor are theory and studies of more objective social influences, cultural factors, and societal and structural factors. Stages of behaviour change models and diffusion of innovation perspectives are also not dealt with in this chapter. Since Social Cognitive Theory as well as the social cognition models presented originate from Western cultures, we will discuss the usefulness and validity of these models when doing research on (health) behaviour in non-Western cultures, such as sub-Saharan Africa. For more exhaustive presentations of social cognition models we would like to refer to Gochman (1997), Abraham et al. (1998), Norman et al. (2000), Stroebe (2000), Rutter and Quine (2002), and Conner and Norman (1996; 2005).

The first research-based social cognition models relevant to the study of health behaviour were proposed in the 1950s, and a number of new models have been developed over the years. Before presenting a number of these models, we shall take a brief look at a simple common sense-based model that has been around since the beginning of health education (Hamilton et al., 1980; Tones & Tilford, 1994). The model is sometimes explicitly spelled out; at other times it is just implicit in the "naïve" approach of practitioners.

The "KAP model"

The KAP model postulates that health education is carried out in order to increase *knowledge* regarding the health consequences of certain behaviours. Increased knowledge is expected to lead to a change in *attitudes* towards health compromising behaviours as well as health enhancing or risk-reducing behaviours. Attitude change is assumed to lead to a change in *practice* (behaviour). Behaviour change (in the direction advocated) is assumed to lead to an improvement in health or a reduction in risk of disease, injuries or death. Almost three decades ago, however, Silversin (1979) maintained that the evidence in favour of the KAP-model had not been convincing. Also, in more recent publications, such as Stroebe (2000), it is maintained that the KAP-model has serious shortcomings.

A number of studies have demonstrated that the association between knowledge about health consequences of a particular behaviour and the behaviour itself is usually low, and often even close to zero (Aarø et al., 1986; Osler & Kirchoff, 1995). Whichever are the proximal factors influencing such behaviour, epidemiological knowledge seems to be of limited importance. Providing information and increasing knowledge of health consequences of a specific behaviour will in the short term most likely lead only to marginal if any changes in this behaviour. The long-term behavioural effects within a culture of a high level of awareness and knowledge of the health consequences of the actual behaviour may still prove to be considerable. Such long-term processes at a group or population level are, however, not our present concern.

Within the KAP model the correlation between attitudes and behaviour is assumed to be substantial, and the model focuses uni-directionally on how attitudes are supposed to influence behaviour. Researchers have found, however, that the association between attitudes and behaviours as measured traditionally is weak. Wicker (1969), reviewing previous research, found that the mean correlation across a number of studies was as low as 0.15. Many studies found a correlation close to zero while few studies reported correlations as high as 0.30. Furthermore, such associations cannot be interpreted as reflecting a unidirectional causality only. On the contrary, a number of theoretical models point to alternative causal explanations (Festinger, 1957; Bandura, 1969; Bem, 1967, 1972).

More recent research on the relationship between attitudes and behaviour has revealed that rather substantial correlations between attitudes and behaviour may exist, provided that relevant attitudes are in focus and properly measured. A substantial body of research has also demonstrated the importance of attitudes in predicting behaviour (Fishbein & Ajzen, 1975; Ajzen, 1988, 1996, 2001). Furthermore, researchers have been able to identify a number of factors (moderators) which contribute to explaining variation in the association between attitudes and behaviour (Eagly & Chaiken, 1993). We are therefore in a better position to tell under which circumstances and conditions attitudes predict behaviour. The attitude concept, therefore, still deserves to be included in theories and conceptual models on health behaviour. In current theory, however, attitudes are not the only predictors of health behaviours, as was the case with the KAP model.

Although the KAP model has never had strong proponents in any of the behavioural sciences, and although the limitations of KAP studies on sexual behaviour are well documented (e.g. Huygens et al., 1996; Gilles, 1996; Schopper et al., 1993), it has been widely used to gain insight in sexuality, family planning and AIDS prevention in African contexts (e.g.

Ajayi et al., 1991; Konde-Lule et al., 1989; Schopper et al., 1993). Today, the KAP approach is still frequently used in developing countries to measure trends in knowledge, attitudes and behaviour, and for programme evaluation (MacNeil & Hogle, 1998).

The Health Belief Model

A model that has been used in a wide range of health related contexts is the Health Belief Model (Becker, 1974; Janz & Becker, 1984; Rosenstock, 1990; Rosenstock et al., 1994; Strecher et al., 1997; Abraham & Sheeran, 2005). The main components of the Health Belief Model (see Fig. 1) are based upon psychological expectancy-value theory. Within such theory it is assumed that human behaviour depends mainly upon the value placed by an individual on a particular goal, and upon his or her estimate of the likelihood that a given action will achieve that goal. With respect to health behaviour, the two main factors are: the desire to avoid illness or to get well, and the belief that a specific behaviour will prevent or reduce illness.

According to the Health Belief model, the likelihood that an individual engages in a given health enhancing behaviour is seen as a function of the following factors:

– *Perceived susceptibility:* One's subjective perception of the risk of contracting a particular disease, for instance the perceived risk of being infected with HIV.

– *Perceived severity:* Feelings concerning the seriousness of the consequences of getting the disease (medical, clinical and social consequences). Most people probably believe that being infected with HIV would mean reducing life expectancy substantially. Some people may believe that being HIV infected leads to social rejection and discrimination.

– *Perceived benefits:* The extent to which the individual believes that the various available actions are effective in reducing the threat. If use of condoms is regarded to be effective in reducing the risk of contracting HIV, the likelihood of taking such action is higher than if this is believed not to be the case. According to Strecher and colleagues (1997), non-health related benefits are also included.

– *Perceived barriers:* The potential negative aspects of a particular health action may function as impediments to undertaking the recommended behaviour. If a person believes that using a condom is going to reduce

pleasure during sexual intercourse, this is expected to reduce the likelihood that this person actually will use a condom.
– *Cues to action:* These may sometimes trigger appropriate health behaviour. This could be internal cues like bodily symptoms, or external cues
such as the death of a friend, social influences, or exposure to a mass
media campaign.

Susceptibility and severity jointly determine the *perceived threat* of the disease, sometimes referred to as vulnerability. Perceived benefits of a specific
action and perceived barriers to taking that action can be referred to as *outcome expectations* (Rosenstock, 1990). Rosenstock (1974:332) maintained
that "The combined levels of susceptibility and severity provided the energy
or force to act, and the perception of benefits (less barriers) provided a preferred path of action".

A number of adjustments and additional predictors of the Health Belief
Model have been proposed. In some versions of the model an individual's
general health motivation, defined as "readiness to be concerned about health
matters" has been included (Becker et al., 1977). Lau et al. (1986) have proposed that *the value that the individual places on health* should be included.
Wallston & Wallston (1981, 1982) have argued that *health locus of control
beliefs* (whether individuals consider their health to be under the control of
internal factors, powerful others, or chance) would add to the predictive
power of the model. Rosenstock and associates (1988) proposed *self-efficacy* (conviction about one's ability to carry out the recommended action)
as another candidate predictor. It was argued that this would improve the
explanatory power of the model. Becker and colleagues (1977) suggested
that *behavioural intentions* should be placed as a mediator between the predictors and behaviour.

According to Stroebe (2000) the formal relationships between the factors of the Health Belief Model have not been sufficiently spelled out. In
most studies based on this model, the six constructs described above have
been treated as separate groups of predictors. This has led some critics to
maintain that the Health Belief Model should not be regarded as a systematic theory, but rather as a collection of variables (Conner, 1993; Schwarzer,
1992). Some researchers have, however, proposed more specific models.

Figure 1. The health belief model

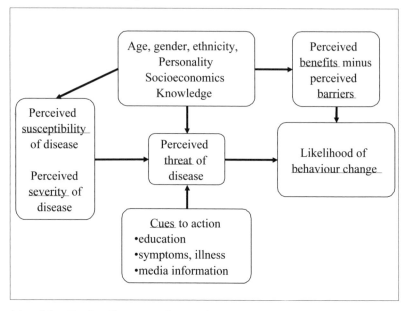

Adapted from Strecher, Champion & Rosenstock, 1997.

Benefits and barriers are sometimes combined into one single index (see for instance Gianetti et al., 1985), and this has also been the case with susceptibility and severity (Sheeran & Abraham, 1996). Strecher and colleagues (1997) have argued that the model should not be regarded as a list of promising predictors which can be thrown into a multiple regression analysis in order to identify which variables are "the best swimmers". They have provided advice regarding measurement of variables and guidelines for statistical analysis including a number of interaction effect hypotheses.

Rosenstock (1990) claimed that the Health Belief Model has received considerable empirical support. In their review of studies based on the model, however, Harrison and associates (1992) concluded that the four predictors that have most frequently been studied (susceptibility, severity, benefits, and barriers) on average have shown only modest associations with health behaviours. "Cues to action" and "general health motivation" have more or less been neglected in empirical tests of the Health Belief Model (Sheeran & Abraham, 1996).

In two reviews it is concluded that "perceived barriers" was the single most powerful predictor of health behaviours across all studies reviewed

(Janz & Becker, 1984; Harrison et al., 1992). This may seem surprising since perceived barriers is the only factor among those originally included in the Health Belief Model which clearly goes beyond the sphere of health concerns. This may actually point to one of the weaknesses of the model. The Health Belief Model seems to be based on an assumption that health concerns are the most important kind of predictors of health behaviours. This is not necessarily the case. Other concerns, such as the social consequences of a specific behaviour or the immediate pleasure associated with some health compromising behaviours, may be at least as important predictors of health behaviour as worries about health consequences. The Health Belief Model focuses mainly on health-related cognitive factors. The social and contextual factors which may influence behaviour, and emotions and effect are not sufficiently explicated and taken into account.

The Health Belief Model has also been criticised for lack of clarity regarding its key concepts and how they should be operationalized. Two of the predictors included in the model (perceived barriers and cues to action) are defined too broadly to make sense from a more theoretical perspective. Its lack of operational homogeneity and conceptual clarity has weakened the position of the model among scientists (Harrison et al., 1992).

The Theory of Reasoned Action and The Theory of Planned Behaviour

During the seventies Fishbein and Ajzen developed their Theory of Reasoned Action (TRA) (Fishbein & Ajzen, 1975; Ajzen & Fishbein, 1977). In the eighties Ajzen expanded the theory by adding a new predictor, and the new model was called the Theory of Planned Behaviour (TPB) (Ajzen, 1988). Since TRA can be regarded as a special case of TPB, both will be presented under the same heading.

As illustrated in Figure 2, both theories are based on the assumption that *intentions* lead to behaviour. Obviously this is not always the case. Factors such as situational constraints and lack of skills may contribute to reducing the association between intentions and behaviour. Furthermore, behaviours often tend to develop into habits which are conducted repeatedly and automatically. If this is the case, conscious elaboration on outcomes of behavioural options is less important in predicting behaviour. As indicated by its name, however, the theory is restricted to behaviour which is under at least some volitional control (Ajzen, 1996).

Figure 2. The theory of planned behaviour

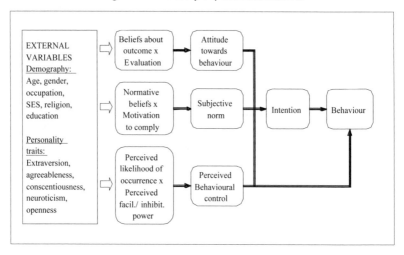

Adapted from Conner & Sparks, 1996.

According to Ajzen (1996) intentions are influenced by three factors: (1) *personal attitudes towards the behaviour,* (2) *subjective norms,* and (3) *perceived behavioural control.* While the Theory of Reasoned Action includes the two first factors only, the Theory of Planned Behaviour also includes the third one. Attitude refers to the overall feelings of favourableness or unfavourableness towards performing the behaviour. Subjective norms refer to perceptions of what others think one should do. Perceived behavioural control refers to one's beliefs that one can perform the behaviour even under various difficult circumstances. According to Fishbein (2000:275) ".... it is important to recognise that the relative importance of these three psychosocial variables as determinants of intentions will depend upon both the behaviour and the population being considered." Whereas one kind of behaviour may be primarily determined by attitudes, another may be primarily determined by perceived social norms or perceived behavioural control. Thus, while a specific behaviour may be primarily determined by attitudes in one population, it may be normatively driven in another. This implies that, before being able to design adequate interventions to change intentions to a specific behaviour in a specific population, one should know the relative importance of each of these psychosocial determinants (Fishbein, 2000).

In order for attitudes to predict a particular behaviour, one has to measure attitudes towards the specific behaviour in question. General attitudes are not strong predictors of a specific behaviour. In order to be able to predict the use of condoms, one should measure the specific attitudes towards use of condoms rather than attitudes towards safe sex in general. Moreover, attitudes and behaviours have to be measured at the same level of specificity. This means that there must not only be an exact specification of what kind of *behaviour* is focused, but also the *target*, the *time*, and the *context* must correspond. As such, every behaviour is unique. For instance, using a condom to prevent unwanted pregnancy is very different from using a condom to prevent HIV infection, and using a condom when having sex with one's main partner may be very different from using a condom when having casual or commercial sex.

In statistical analyses of data based on the Theory of Planned Behaviour, attitudes are assumed to be predicted by two sets of variables: (1) measures of the perceived probability that the behaviour in question will lead to particular outcomes *(behavioural expectations, also referred to as behavioural beliefs)* and (2) measures of how this outcome is evaluated *(evaluation of expectations or beliefs)*. After multiplying (1) and (2) for each possible outcome, all products must be added. According to the theory, the resultant variable is a good predictor of attitudes.

Subjective social norms refer to subjective beliefs about social norms and expectations (Fishbein & Ajzen, 1975; Cialdini et al., 1990). Subjective norms are measured by asking an individual what kind of behaviour significant others expect from this person *(normative beliefs)*, and how much one cares about the views of the significant others *(motivation to comply)*. An index for subjective norm is created by multiplying normative beliefs and motivation to comply for each significant other (e.g. partner, parents, friends), and by adding these products. The subjective norm variable represents a substantial expansion of the scope when compared with the previous models. While the other models have focused mainly on personal factors, the Theory of Planned Behaviour (as well as the Theory of Reasoned Action) takes into account interpersonal processes, or at least the subjective aspect of such processes.

Perceived behavioural control refers to the subjective expectation regarding to what extent the behaviour is under personal control. Perceptions of behavioural control are affected by beliefs concerning factors that are likely to facilitate or inhibit the performance of behaviour, and by judgements about the power of these factors (Ajzen, 1988; 1991). Perceived behavioural control can be assessed by multiplying the perceived frequency or likelihood of occurrence of facilitating and inhibiting factors by the subjective perception of the power of each factor to facilitate or inhibit the performance of the behaviour (Ajzen, 1991). The sum of these products (with relevant signs) results in an index for perceived behavioural control. The concept of perceived behavioural control is similar, but not identical to Bandura's self-efficacy concept (1986).

Intentions play a key role in the Theory of Planned Behaviour. In a meta-analysis Sheeran (2001) found that in prospective panel studies, intentions account for about 28 per cent of the variance in behaviour. Although it can be argued that this figure probably is an underestimation of the actual strength of prediction, a lot of variance remains unexplained. Gollwitzer (1999) has suggested that the induction of an implementation intention may improve the prediction of actual behaviour. Implementation intentions specify when, where, and how the intended behaviour should be performed. Empirical studies have shown that induction of implementation intentions does increase prediction of behaviour (Sheeran, 2001).

Social Cognitive Theory

Bandura's Social Cognitive Theory was originally called Social Learning Theory. There were at least three social learning theories. The most influential one and the one which has been most widely applied in health behaviour research is Bandura's version (Bandura, 1977). Bandura has made *outcome expectancies* (the expected outcome of a specific behaviour) and *self-efficacy* (perceived ability to perform the behaviour) two of the most central concepts of his theory on how to understand the causal processes behind behaviour. Examples of his influence on other theories relevant to the analysis of health-related behaviours have already been mentioned.

An important tenet of Bandura's theory is his principle of "reciprocal determinism". He distinguishes between three important sets of factors: behavioural, personal, and environmental. These can all be cause and effect. Inducing a change in one of the factors may lead to changes in the other factors. Compared to the theories described above, which are mainly focusing on causal paths from various psychosocial factors to behaviour, Social Cognitive Theory with its more complex systems of causal processes involved, represents an important improvement.

In 1986 Bandura published an elaborated version of his theory and simultaneously called it *Social Cognitive Theory*. In a couple of recent publications, Bandura (1998, 2004) described how his theory can be applied to the study of health behaviours. A list of Bandura's main behavioural predictors includes:

– Self efficacy
– Outcome expectancies (physical, social, self-evaluative)
– Goals (proximal, distal)
– Socio-structural factors (facilitators, impediments)

Based on his theory, Bandura (1998, 2004) has developed a more specific model for prediction of behaviour (Figure 3). This model has some elements in common with the Theory of Planned Behaviour. Instead of intentions, Bandura uses the concept "goals". Instead of "attitudes" and "subjective norms" (which are predicted by expectations and evaluation of expectations) he uses "outcome expectancies" (which can be physical, social and self-evaluative) as predictors. Instead of "perceived behavioural control" he uses the concept "self efficacy". Furthermore Bandura includes "socio-cultural factors" (facilitators and impediments) in his model. The causal paths in Bandura's model are not identical to the paths in the Theory of Planned Behaviour.

Figure 3. Social Cognitive Theory: Model for prediction of behaviour

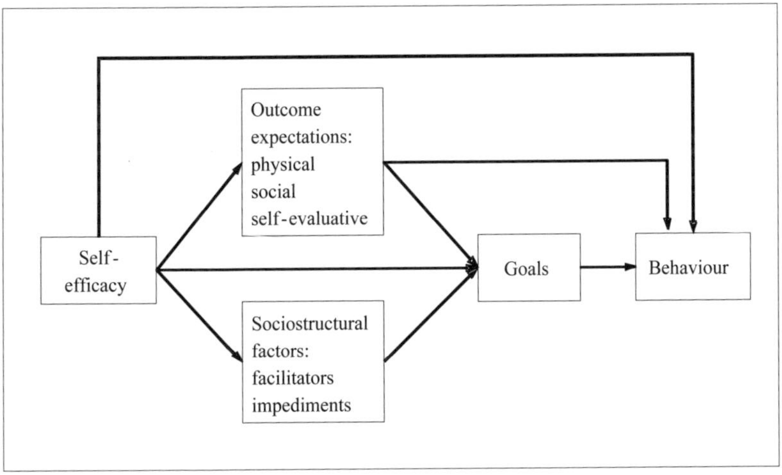

Adapted from Bandura, 2004.

The "Maastricht" ASE-model

A group of researchers in the Netherlands (at Maastricht University) has presented a revised version of the Theory of Planned Behaviour: the Attitude-Social Influence-Efficacy Model, also refereed to as the ASE-model (De Vries, Dijkstra & Kuhlman, 1988; Kok et al., 1991; see Figure 4). Basically, the ASE-model combines the Theory of Reasoned Action and Bandura's ideas about social influences and self-efficacy. Also the ASE-model assumes that intentions predict behaviour. However, the influence of intentions on health behaviours depends on two factors: *skills* and *barriers*. If a person intends to use condoms during the next intercourse with his or her partner, but simply lacks the skills to use the condom properly, positive intentions are unlikely to lead to adequate use of the condom. Furthermore, unavailability of condoms could represent another hindering factor, in their model labelled a barrier. The model could have been improved even more if 'barriers' had been supplemented with enhancing factors. Even if the intention to use a condom is not particularly strong, easy access to condoms could greatly increase the likelihood that a condom was actually used. The importance of situational factors in influencing and 'triggering' behaviours is well documented (Ross & Nisbett, 1991).

Figure 4. The Maastricht model for behavioural determinants

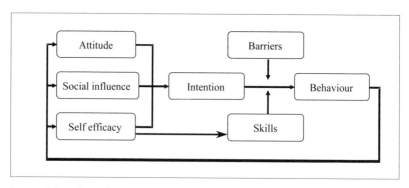

Source: Kok et al., 1996.

In the ASE-model, intentions are influenced by attitudes, social influences, and by self efficacy. The model also assumes that actual behaviours can influence the three predictors of behaviours. Although the ASE-model is generally quite similar to Ajzen's Theory of Planned Behaviour, it moves beyond the "subjective norms" notion of social influences in the Ajzen & Fishbein models towards an inclusion of more objective social influences. Examples of such more objective social influences are the observed behaviours of others (descriptive norms), social pressure, and social support (Kok et al., 1996).

A few years after the ASE-model was launched, Fishbein (2000) suggested a new "integrative" social cognition model, a sort of revised Theory of Planned Behaviour, which is strikingly similar to the ASE-model, but without any reference to the publications of the Dutch group.

Critical remarks on social cognition models

Bandura (2004) maintains that there is considerable overlap between the various psychosocial models of health behaviour. They include almost identical determinants, but under different names. Higher order constructs are often split into seemingly different determinants, but under different labels. One example is that different forms of anticipated outcomes of behavioural change are included as different constructs under the name of attitudes, normative influences, and outcome expectations. Researchers who do not sufficiently well recognize the similarity of constructs sometimes overload their studies with factors that contribute only marginally to prediction of health behaviours because of redundancy.

Some researchers have claimed that social cognition models are most useful when planning interventions to influence health behaviours. Sutton (2002) has summarized the steps involved in designing such interventions. Changes in behavioural intentions (and thereby also in behaviour) are assumed to be produced by changing existing salient beliefs, making existing non-salient beliefs salient, or creating new salient beliefs. Beliefs are regarded as the highway to influencing behaviour. Bandura (2004), however, maintains that social cognition models cannot be used in the process of designing effective behaviour change interventions. Drawing on insight from Social Cognitive Theory he describes a more comprehensive set of tools to behaviour change.

Social cognition models and Social Cognitive Theory have been used in thousands of health behaviour studies in over 50 countries in both the developed and the developing world. A comprehensive body of knowledge has accumulated, and the complexity and theoretical elaboration of such research is impressive. As already emphasized, the social cognition models have much in common, and there are also important communalities with Social Cognitive Theory. This is not only a problem. It also has the advantage of leading to considerable cross-fertilisation across models.

During the almost 50 years of theory-based research on health behaviour some patterns of change can be seen. There has been a development towards:

1. Taking into account a broader range of perceived consequences of behaviour than those which are related to risk of disease, injuries or death.

2. Expanding the range of cognitive factors included in the models and postulating more complex interactions among such factors.

3. At present we may be witnessing a move beyond purely personal and cognitive predictors towards including more "realistic" social influence processes (Bajos & Marquet, 2000).

Critics of social cognitive models have emphasized the importance of also moving beyond the immediate social and physical context and taking into account a wider range of societal and cultural factors and processes (Airhihenbuwa & Obregon, 2000; Eaton, Flisher and Aarø, 2004).

The more recent emphasis on "realistic" social influence processes is paralleled in research on interventions among adolescents where more person-centred frameworks have been replaced by a social influence approach (U.S. Department of Health and Human Services, 1994). Comprehensive interventions based on the so-called social influence model as well as community-wide interventions have proven more effective than interventions based on more traditional (individualistic and person-centred) models.

Health behaviour researchers have, however, been much more eager to include new social cognition factors in their models than to explore the domain of "realistic" social influences. When social influence factors are measured, the preferred strategy has been to focus on the subjective side only (as with subjective norms), and the way social influences are conceptualised is rather simplistic. It is important to keep in mind that in some instances the social cognition models only account for a small variance in health behaviour (Norman & Conner, 1996). Exploring the ability of more objective social factors to add to the prediction of health behaviours, such as suggested by the group behind the ASE-model, seems worthwhile.

The strong focus on social cognition factors and the perceived side of social influences may even have hampered the research on "realistic" social influence processes. According to Gochman (1997), in spite of a rich litera-ture on school-based health education programmes, there is little research linking schools as social and physical environments with health behaviours. He also pointed to the scarcity of studies linking community character-istics to health behaviour. Eakin (1997) maintained that in the field of workplace health promotion and occupational health and safety, studies of health behaviour emphasize personal determinants rather than the nature of the work environment. Baranowski (1997) summarising research on family influence on diet concluded that only a few such studies exist. Dressler & Oths (1997) criticised health behaviour research for neglecting cultural fac-tors and processes and for examining health behaviours narrowly in terms of individual motives and attributions.

Although social cognition models have been widely used to predict and understand a variety of health behaviours (e.g. Conner & Sparks, 1996; Godin & Kok, 1996), these models have been subject to substantial cri-tique, especially regarding their applicability in studying theoretical aspects of AIDS risk reducing behaviours in developing countries.

Studies of sexual and reproductive behaviour

The various theoretical models presented above have been used in a large number of empirical studies of sexual and reproductive behaviour, al-though little research has been done outside of North America and Europe (MacNeil & Hogle, 1998). Sheeran and Abraham (1996) described several studies that have used the Health Belief Model to explore HIV risk behav-iour. They concluded that the main Health Belief Model measures (sus-ceptibility, severity, health beliefs) are not useful predictors of adolescent condom use, and not effective in predicting HIV risk-reducing behaviour among homosexual men. According to Sheeran and Abraham (1996:52) the Health Belief Model "portrays individuals as asocial economic decision-makers and consequently fails to account for behaviour under social and affective control", such as sexual behaviour.

The Theory of Reasoned Action and the Theory of Planned Behaviour have also been extensively applied in studies exploring the use of contra-ceptives and AIDS related condom use (for a meta-analysis see Sheeran & Taylor, 1999). Sheeran and Taylor concluded that attitudes and subjec-tive norms demonstrated medium to strong effect sizes, and that perceived behavioural control was a reliable predictor of intentions to use condoms explaining variance over and above the effects of attitudes and subjective norms.

Many studies which included measures of self-efficacy have shown that especially belief in one's capability to negotiate safer sex practices, such as condom use, were strong predictors of such behaviours (e.g. Abraham et al., 1995; Basen-Engquist & Parcel, 1992; Kasen et al., 1992; Schaalma et al., 1993; Sheeran et al., 1999).

When comparing predictors of sexual practices such as for instance condom use across studies, systematic differences between Western countries and cultures in the developing world (such as sub-Saharan Africa) are likely to be revealed. In a study by Lugoe and Rise (1999) carried out in Tanzania, subjective norms turned out to be a markedly more powerful predictor of intentions to use condom use than attitudes. In a similar study among adolescents in Holland, attitudes towards the behaviour turned out to be a much stronger predictor of intentions to use condoms consistently than subjective norms (Schaalma et al., 1993). This is consistent with the assumption that North-Western European cultures are regarded as rather individualistic whereas collectivism is assumed to be common among African cultures (Brislin, 1993). Personal attitudes are expected to be more important in predicting behaviour in individualistic cultures, while subjective norms are expected to be more important in collectivist cultures. In both studies the prediction of behavioural intentions is substantial. This supports the notion that, when used in an appropriate way, value-expectancy theories are relevant even in cultures different from the Western ones in which they were designed. The usefulness of social cognition models and the importance of subjective norms as predictors of behavioural intentions have also been confirmed also in other studies from sub-Saharan Africa (Bosompra, 2001; Giles, Liddell and Bydawell, 2005).

It is most important to note that even though the value-expectancy models may be applied in different contexts and cultures, their operationalization depends strongly on the local circumstances. The selection of outcome expectancies may, for instance, vary considerably across cultures. So may also the selection of significant others when measuring subjective norms. The assessment of self-efficacy or impeding situations or mood states may furthermore vary considerably across cultures. Both Ajzen (1988) and Fishbein (2000) do in fact strongly recommend that in new contexts, interviews and focus groups be used in order to identify salient beliefs to be employed in subsequent quantitative studies. Moreover, one should be very careful with translating English or American theoretical concepts into other languages since words that may seem to be straight translations may still have different interpretations, meanings and connotations.

The study carried out by Lugoe and Rise (1999) is one of very few studies of sexual behaviour in sub-Saharan Africa in which a social cognition model has been applied. Another example of sub-Saharan research based on one of the social cognition models is a study of intention to be sexually active among primary school children in northern Tanzania (Klepp et al., 1994). The study, which was based on a slightly extended version of the Theory of Reasoned Action, confirmed that attitudes, subjective norms and self-efficacy were all significant predictors of intention to have sexual intercourse within the next three months. Prior behaviour, however, was the strongest predictor of intention. A study among adults in Bulawayo, Zimbabwe, which was based on the Health Belief Model revealed that perceived social support for behaviour change was the major predictor of HIV-related behavioural risk reduction (Wilson et al., 1991).

A review of such research (Kaaya et al., 2002) among school students covering the period 1987–1999 has identified only eight studies which were guided by a systematic theoretical framework. Kaaya and associates point to the need for not only more research on sexual and reproductive behaviour among adolescents in sub-Saharan Africa, but also for research which is planned on sound and relevant theory. The theoretical perspectives should, however, not be limited to the kind of factors covered by social cognition models, but also take the wider cultural and socio-economic context into account.

Eaton and associates (2004) have reviewed studies on unsafe sexual behaviour in South African youth covering the period 1990–2000. Again there are only a few studies applying social cognition models. Evidence indicates that high perceived vulnerability and anxiety about personal risk are linked to greater intended and actual (positive) sexual behaviour change (Strebel and Perkel, 1991; Van Aswegen, 1995; Van Wijck, 1994). Two studies with young adults suggest that self-efficacy for condom use is linked to higher self-reported condom use (Peltzer, 1999; Reddy et al., 2000).

The few studies of sexual and reproductive behaviour based on social cognition models that have been carried out in sub-Saharan Africa do after all provide some evidence for the usefulness of this theoretical approach under societal and cultural circumstances different from those of the Western countries. Eaton and associates are, however, hesitant about the idea of leaning too much on social cognition models when studying sexual behaviour in a developing country context. Although social cognition models do recognise the relevance of factors beyond the individual, they tend to emphasise personal (mainly cognitive) processes and the subjective aspects of social influences. Objective aspects of social influences, the physical and organisational context, as well as the more distal societal and cultural factors are to a large extent neglected. Eaton and associates point to several relevant factors beyond those covered in social cognition models. Such factors have proven important as predictors of unsafe sexual practices in South African youth, for instance lack of access to condoms, low access to media, poverty, male domination in sexual relationships, and the cultural construction of masculinity in the South African culture. They maintain that in a developing country like South Africa, the physical and organisational contexts as well as cultural and structural conditions take on particular significance. Campbell (2003), drawing on experiences from an HIV/AIDS intervention programme which took place in a community in South Africa, has delivered a rather strong critique of the use of social cognition models in that particular context.

Conclusion

As shown in this chapter, there is considerable overlap between the various models and theories in the field of social cognition. There are examples of cross-fertilisation among the models, and one could hope for a development towards consensus regarding which are the main psychosocial predictors of health behaviours. An attempt to create such consensus was made by the Aids Program of the National Institute for Mental Health (Washington D.C.) in October 1991. Leading researchers participated, including Bandura (Social Cognitive Theory), Becker (Health Belief Model), and Fishbein (Theory of Reasoned Action). They actually succeeded in reaching consensus on which factors they regarded as particularly important in predicting health behaviours (Fishbein et al., 1991). The eight factors were:

- Intention
- Environmental constraints
- Ability (skills)
- Anticipated outcome (or attitudes)
- Norms
- Self-standards
- Emotion
- Self-efficacy

Most of these are factors already dealt with in the theories and models presented above. The researchers did not, however, reach consensus regarding the underlying causal model.

As described above, health behaviour theory has changed over time. Yet there is a need for a further expansion and inclusion of additional perspectives. Albert Bandura expressed similar views when he stated:

> The newest generation of intervention requires an expanded social perspective to human adaptation and change. Because of individualistic bias, our knowledge base and models for effecting social change leave much to be desired. Psychological programs that increase success rates by creating social structural support for personal change are rarely adopted despite their success. They are troublesome to create and their management requires attention to the mundane hassle of everyday life. ... If we are to contribute significantly to the betterment of human health, we must broaden our perspective on health promotion and disease prevention beyond the individualistic level. (Bandura, 1998:642, 647)

It is equally true that our perspectives should be enriched by research in new cultural contexts, such as in sub-Saharan Africa.

The purpose of research on sexual behaviour and behaviour related to risk of HIV/AIDS is first of all to develop knowledge and insights relevant to the planning and implementation of preventive measures. Research-based programmes are more likely to be successful than action based on common sense and good intentions only. Knowledge developed through research in Western countries and cultures may, however, be of limited relevance when planning health education and public health interventions in sub-Saharan Africa. Adequate preventive approaches and effective practices can only be developed if based on research among and with the populations concerned. In such a context, provided that they are sufficiently modified and adapted to local circumstances and cultures, social cognition models may prove to be relevant and important.

3. Health Education and the Promotion of Reproductive Health

Theory and Evidence-Based Development and Diffusion of Intervention Programmes

Herman Schaalma and Sylvia F. Kaaya

Abstract

Various reviews and meta-analyses of Western HIV prevention programmes have shown that programme effectiveness is dependent on the degree to which programmes are based on 1) needs assessments among target populations and communities, and 2) analyses of theory-based options for corrective action. In addition, many have indicated that the impact of programmes depends on widespread and accurate diffusion, and that Western programmes cannot be exported to other cultural, social and economic contexts. This leads to the question: how should health education planners develop interventions that are likely to be effective and widely implemented?

This chapter presents *Intervention Mapping* (IM), an approach for designing theory and evidence-based health promotion programmes. IM provides guidelines and tools for the empirical and theoretical foundations of health promotion programmes, for the application of theory, for the translation of theory into actual programmes and materials, and the management of programme adoption and implementation. In this chapter IM is illustrated in relation to HIV prevention amongst African youth populations.

Introduction

It is widely acknowledged that the reproductive health of youth is one of the most important individual, social and economic challenges that are facing sub-Saharan African countries. The risks related to sexual activity and early childbearing jeopardise not only young people's physical and emotional health, but also their economic and social well-being. The major reproductive health risks that young people face include sexually transmitted diseases (STDs and HIV), sexual violence and coercion, and early (unintended) pregnancy and childbearing. This leads us to consider the question of how we can promote young people's sexual health.

In this chapter we will present a general approach for the theory and evidence-based design of health education and health promotion programmes, *Intervention Mapping* (Bartholomew et al., 2001; 2006). We will discuss the process of intervention development: needs assessment, programme design, programme diffusion, and programme evaluation. We will present some results of illustrative studies that have been conducted in African contexts with a focus on HIV prevention. First, however, we would like to clarify the concepts of health education and health promotion.

Health education and health promotion

Health education is a planned activity stimulating learning through communication to promote healthy behaviour (Green & Kreuter, 2005). The concept of health education needs to be distinguished from the concept of health promotion. Health promotion refers to 'any planned combination of educational, political, regulatory, and organizational supports for actions and conditions of living conducive to health of individuals, groups, and communities' (Green & Kreuter, 2005: G-4). Health promotion objectives are: 1) primary prevention, e.g. the prevention of HIV infection by the promotion of condom use; 2) early detection and treatment, e.g. the screening of pregnant women for HIV infection to prevent mother-child transmission; and 3) patient care and support, e.g. the care and support for people with AIDS. Health education refers to 'any planned combination of learning experiences designed to predispose, enable, and reinforce voluntary behaviour conducive to health in individuals, groups, or communities' (Green & Kreuter, 2005:G4). As such, health education is one of the instruments of achieving health promotion goals. Other health promotion instruments are making resources available (e.g. health care services) and rules and regulations (e.g. compulsory school-based HIV/AIDS education).

Generally, health promotion is most effective when it involves several mutually reinforcing strategies, and when it affects different levels of society. Condom use promoting campaigns will only be successful when condoms are easily available. School-based prevention programmes may only work when they are linked to in-service teacher training and a favourable school policy to support them. Screening programmes only make sense when treatment facilities are made available.

Theory and evidence-based health education

When developing health education programmes, health education planners often tend to reach conclusions before going through a systematic planning process that supports these conclusions. It is a common observation that health education planners immediately jump from a health problem to suggestions for health education campaigns and programmes. 'Let us do a peer-education programme', 'Let us design a social marketing campaign' or 'Let us make strong fear arousing posters or brochures' are common responses when health education planners are confronted with health problems and are looking for hasty solutions. This, however, is not the way it should be. Various reviews and meta-analyses of health education programmes (Bartholomew et al., 2006) and HIV-prevention programmes (e.g. UNAIDS, 1997a; Kaaya et al., 2002a; Schaalma et al., 2002) have shown that programme effectiveness is largely dependent on the degree to which programmes 1) are based on a careful analysis of the health problem, problem-causing behavioural and environmental factors, and the options for corrective action, and 2) have a formal theoretical ground. In addition, many have emphasised that the impact of interventions also depends on widespread adoption and accurate implementation (Oldenburg & Parcel, 2002). How then should health education planners develop theory- and evidence-based interventions that are likely to be effective and widely implemented?

Intervention planning depends upon needs assessments that are sensitive to the experiences of, and risks faced by, target populations and communities. Such assessments should include analyses of health problems and related quality-of-life concerns, of behavioural and environmental causes of health problems, of the determinants of proximal behavioural and environmental causes of health problems of interest, and of the resources of the community (Green & Kreuter, 2005; Bartholomew et al., 2006). This implies that different target populations may require different combinations of interventions to change their health behaviour. Consequently, simple forms of technology transfer, such as exporting effective Western programmes to developing countries, may fail because of cultural, social and economic differences. Health promotion recommends local, collaborative development of health education programmes that are responsive to the particular needs of a population in a specified geographical, economic and cultural context. Figure 1 depicts a planning and evaluation model for the theory- and evidence-based development of health education programmes (Kok, 1992; Green & Kreuter, 2005). Table 1 provides a summary of the main issues that have to be addressed in each of the phases of the model.

Table 1. Theory- and evidence-based development of health education programmes

Diagnosis of the health problem
- What are the individual and social consequences of the health problem?
- Is the health problem related to other health and social problems?
- What are the community's health promotion resources and capacities?
- Who has the health problem, and why?

Diagnosis of behavioural and environmental factors
- What are the behavioural risk factors that are related to the health problem?
- What environmental changes are needed to reduce the health problem?
- Who are the decision-makers that are responsible for environmental change?

Analyses of determinants
- What are the determinants of the behavioural and environmental factors that are linked to the health problem?
- What factors must be changed to initiate and sustain the process of behavioural and environmental change?

Programme development
- What do people have to do to reduce their risk?
- What has to change in the environment?
- What theoretical methods and practical intervention strategies seem useful in accomplishing risk-reduction or environmental change?
- How can we combine intervention strategies to a programme, anticipating barriers to widespread programme diffusion?

Programme diffusion
- How can we facilitate and support widespread dissemination of the programme, high quality programme implementation, and maintenance of programme use?

Programme Evaluation
- Has the programme reached the target population?
- Has the programme been implemented as planned?
- What are the intermediate programme effects on behavioural determinants?
- What are the programme effects on behaviour, health and quality of life concerns?

Figure 1. Planning and evaluation of health intervention

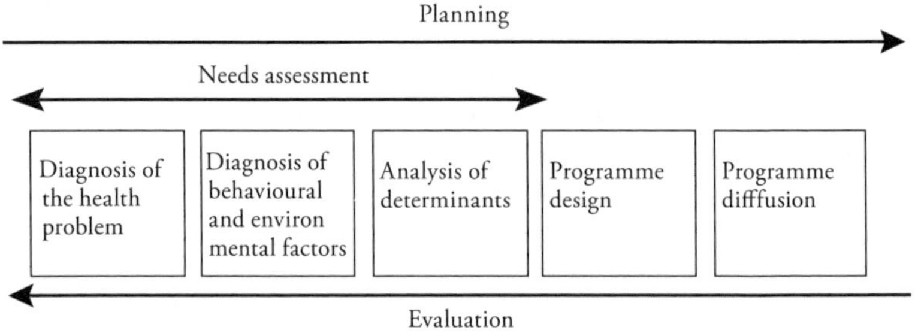

Cf. Kok, 1991.

Needs assessment

The objective of the first phase in the planning process is to get a clear understanding of the health problem, its individual and social consequences, and its relationship to other health and social problems (Green & Kreuter, 2005). Epidemiological studies are needed to determine the magnitude of the problem, and who has the problem. Social assessments explore in greater depth individual and social consequences of the problem and its relationship to other health and social problems. Information to address these concerns can be based upon key informant interviews, community forums, focus groups, nominal group processes, and surveys (Gillmore & Campbell, 1996).

When health problems have been identified, health education planners should identify the factors that contributed to them: the determinants in the aetiology of the causes of death and disease (Green & Kreuter, 2005). So the next step refers to the systematic analysis of the behavioural, environmental, genetic and biological causes of the health problems that were identified in the social and epidemiological assessments. Epidemiological studies should reveal whether the health problem is linked to specific behaviours, and if it is, to whose behaviours. Based on insight into the associations between risk factors and the health problem, health education planners should be able to rate the importance of risk factors. Based on an assessment of the changeability of risk factors, planners should be able to select the focus of programmes or interventions.

When these analyses have identified relevant behavioural causes of the health problem, health education planners need a clear understanding of why people behave as they do: determinants, antecedents or correlates of behaviour (Green & Kreuter, 2005). According to Green and Kreuter any given behaviour can be explained as a function of three categories of factors.

Predisposing factors are those cognitive antecedents that provide a rationale or motivation for behaviour (e.g. knowledge, risk perceptions, attitudes, self-esteem, health locus of control, identity concerns, values, social and cultural norms, and goal priorities). *Enabling factors* are the antecedents that enable the enactment of behavioural intentions (e.g. availability and accessibility of health resources, government laws, as well as individual competencies). *Reinforcing factors* are the factors that, following a behaviour, determine its persistence or repetition (e.g. social support, physical consequences, feedback provided by health-care providers). Consideration of these factors can highlight differences between risk-taking and risk-reducing behaviour.

Many social-cognition models or theories relate to these factors, especially to predisposing factors. See Aarø et al. 2008) for a description of such models.

HIV and African youth

It is estimated that more than 60% of all people living with HIV live in sub-Saharan Africa – almost 26 million (UNAIDS, 2006). At the end of 2005 about 65% of new infections occurred in Africa, and 77% of the people that died of AIDS were Africans. Approximately 5% of African women aged 15–24 and 2% of African men aged 15–24 are living with HIV. Wide variations in HIV prevalence rates occur across sub-Saharan African countries and regions, with the lowest prevalence rates in West Africa, and the highest in southern Africa (UNAIDS, 2006). In southern African countries HIV-prevalence rates for the adult population aged 15–49 years vary between 16 in Mozambique to 33 in Swaziland. Since the start of the epidemic AIDS has created some 12 million orphans, and up to two-thirds of new HIV infections in the developing countries may occur in young people aged between 15 and 24 years (UNAIDS, 2004).

In sub-Saharan Africa the main mode of transmission for those living with HIV/AIDS is unprotected heterosexual intercourse (UNAIDS, 2004). It is generally recognised that African youth is sexually active and suffers from the consequences of routine unsafe sexual practices such as teenage parenthood (Koawo, 1999), illegal abortions (Silberschmidt & Rasch, 2001) and sexually transmitted diseases (STDs) including HIV/AIDS (Tengia-Kessy et al., 1998). A review of school-based studies of adolescent sexual behaviour in sub-Saharan Africa supports observations that significant proportions of youth are sexually active by the time they are in their mid-teens, many have had sexual intercourse with two or more partners and that condoms are rarely used routinely (Kaaya et al., 2002b). Although few school-based studies explored other high-risk sexual practices, it is not unlikely that a substantial number of youth has experience with unprotected anal intercourse (Flisher et al., 1993; Feldman et al., 1997; Matasha et al., 1998).

Only the prevention of HIV transmission can significantly slow down the spread of HIV/AIDS. To reduce their risk for HIV infection, both sexually active adults and youth will have to change their sexual behaviour through, for instance, delay of the onset of sexual activity amongst youths, long-term fidelity and a reduction in numbers of sex partners, and uptake of consistent safer sexual practices such as condom use. While some data on young people's HIV-related sexual risk behaviours and knowledge are available from school-based populations in sub-Saharan African countries (e.g. Pattullo et al., 1994; Buga et al., 1996; Kasule et al., 1997), there is a clear lack of theory-based research on the social and cognitive antecedents of HIV-risk reducing sexual behaviour amongst African youth. Some studies suggest that intentions to have sex and/or to use condoms are significantly related to such individual level antecedents as perceived susceptibility, attitudes, perceived outcome-efficacy, perceived social support and self-efficacy regarding coping with embarrassment and social anxieties related to using condoms and refusing high-risk sexual activity (e.g. Bandawe & Foster, 1996; Klepp et al., 1996; Venier et al., 1998; Adih & Alexander, 1999; Stanton et al., 1999; Meekers & Klein, 2002). Some other factors that seem to be related to sexual risk-taking include partner refusal to use condoms (Pattullo et al., 1994; Maswanya et al., 1999), unexpected sex opportunities (Abdool Karim et al., 1992), substance (ab)use (Lugoe et al., 1995), peer pressure and passion (Buga et al., 1996). Much less is known about how wider contextual factors may facilitate or be a barrier to safe sexual practices. Low accessibility of condoms has been reported in some studies to be associated with sexual risk taking (Pattullo et al., 1994). Environmental factors operating at the level of the school and home environment as well as institutional levels as enhancers or barriers to individual level efforts for safer sex and HIV/AIDS prevention need to be understood in the sub-Saharan African context for effective and sustainable intervention strategies to be more widely implemented.

The lack of theory-based studies on sexual-risk-reducing behaviour among African youth populations underlines the strong need for future research to extend our knowledge of sexual behaviour of African youth populations, and to explore further how core concepts that underlie social cognition models can be contextualised to African settings. Without a clear understanding why people act as they do, attempts to change their behaviour are unlikely to be effective.

Figure 2. Model of behaviour change by education

Communication variables

Behaviour change by education	Message	Audience	Media	Messenger
1. Attention				
2. Comprehension				
3. Attitude change				
4. Social influence change				
5. Self-efficacy enhancement				
6. Behaviour change				
7. Maintenance				

Cf. Kok, 1991.

Programme development

The phase following the needs assessment addresses the development of a health education programme. In this stage insights from theory and research have to be translated into educational methods and strategies. A shift must be made from *explaining* behaviour to *changing* behaviour. There is no such thing as a magic bullet: no intervention method is universally effective. Health education programmes have to be tailored carefully to the target behaviour, behavioural determinants, and target population (Bartholomew et al., 2006).

Intervention Mapping (IM) is a protocol for the development of theory- and evidence-based health promotion interventions (Bartholomew et al., 2001; 2006; see Figure 3). IM incorporates a needs assessment as defined by Green and Kreuter (2005), and it describes the process of programme development in five steps: 1) specifying programme objectives, 2) selecting theory-based intervention methods and strategies, 3) designing, organizing and pre-testing the programme, 4) specifying adoption and implementation plans, and 5) generating an evaluation plan. The protocol guides programme developers through each of these steps by means of specific tasks, which generate a product that in turn, provides the basis for subsequent steps. For example, a question regarding determinants might be 'Why do adolescents fail to delay sexual activity?' A question regarding methods might be 'How can we promote positive attitudes towards condoms?' A question regarding programme implementation might be 'How can teachers' self-efficacy regarding using the programme be increased?' IM empowers programme developers to answer these questions by a) searching and using empirical

Figure 3. Intervention Mapping

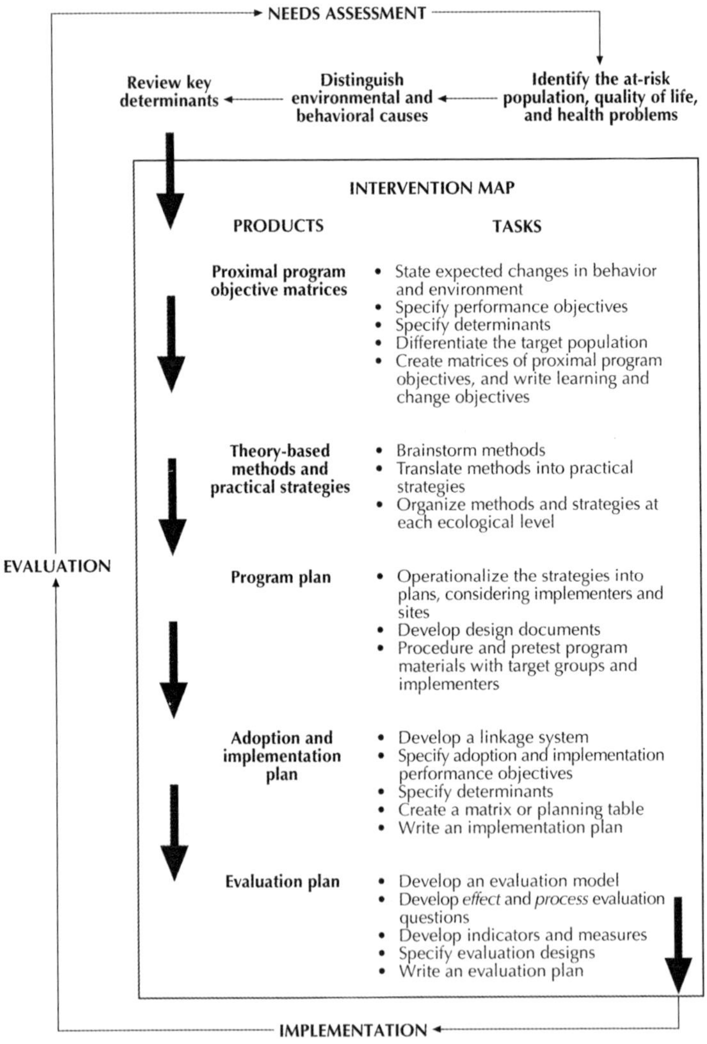

NEEDS ASSESSMENT

| Review key determinants | ← | Distinguish environmental and behavioral causes | ← | Identify the at-risk population, quality of life, and health problems |

INTERVENTION MAP

PRODUCTS	TASKS
Proximal program objective matrices	• State expected changes in behavior and environment • Specify performance objectives • Specify determinants • Differentiate the target population • Create matrices of proximal program objectives, and write learning and change objectives
Theory-based methods and practical strategies	• Brainstorm methods • Translate methods into practical strategies • Organize methods and strategies at each ecological level
Program plan	• Operationalize the strategies into plans, considering implementers and sites • Develop design documents • Procedure and pretest program materials with target groups and implementers
Adoption and implementation plan	• Develop a linkage system • Specify adoption and implementation performance objectives • Specify determinants • Create a matrix or planning table • Write an implementation plan
Evaluation plan	• Develop an evaluation model • Develop *effect* and *process* evaluation questions • Develop indicators and measures • Specify evaluation designs • Write an evaluation plan

EVALUATION

IMPLEMENTATION

Source: Bartholomey et al., 2001

findings from the literature, b) by accessing and using theory, and by c) collecting and using new data.

Specifying programme objectives: Based on an assessments of needs and assets IM continues with the specification of general health promoting programme objectives into specific objectives that explicate who and what will change as a result of the intervention programme: proximal programme or change objectives. Programme change objectives specify what individuals need to learn or what must be changed in the interpersonal, organizational, community or societal environment. They may refer to individual level change (e.g., 'adolescents will express confidence regarding negotiating condom use with a sexual partner'), organizational level change (e.g., 'school administrators will acknowledge the advantages of condom distribution in school'), community level change (e.g., 'community leaders will approve of the sale of inexpensive condoms in schools and meeting places'), or national change level (e.g. 'politicians will promote youth friendly health services').

Selecting theory-based intervention methods and practical intervention strategies: The next step in programme development is the selection of theoretically based intervention methods that may be effective in accomplishing specified change objectives and deciding upon practical strategies to operationalize these methods. For instance, a theoretically based method for enhancing self-efficacy is modelling. A practical intervention strategy for this method could be role-playing, peer-model stories in written material, and/or watching competent models on video. Theory-based intervention methods can be derived from the scientific literature. Information about the feasibility and effectiveness of practical intervention strategies can be derived from needs assessments, contacts with other health educators, collaboration with programme implementers and users, and from small-scale pilots. An important task at this step is to consider the conditions that may limit the effectiveness of intervention methods and strategies. A method or strategy that has proven to be effective among a particular target group in a particular context is not necessarily effective among other populations or in other contexts.

Designing and organizing the programme: When methods and strategies have been identified, programme developers design a plan for the production and delivery of the programme. This involves organisation of the strategies into a deliverable programme with components that are comprehensible and acceptable to programme implementers and participants. IM can help developers specify the scope and sequence of programme components, the channels of delivery of intervention strategies, and how each programme component will reach programme participants (e.g., public service announcements on radio, magazines or lessons delivered by classroom teachers). This step also involves transfer of a programme specification to production (e.g., health educators, graphic designers, text writers), and testing of pilot materials. A close collaboration between the people who develop an intervention (e.g. a research team or health education authority), the users who are expected to adopt and implement the programme (e.g. youth organizations, schools), and recipients or clients (e.g. young people attending school) is important at this stage. At best, this phase in programme design incorporates small scale pilot testing of the programme and its components.

Planning programme adoption and implementation: The production of the programme must be closely linked to adoption and implementation planning, and reliable diffusion procedures are essential to programme impact. IM describes how programme developers can anticipate programme diffusion by setting objectives for programme adoption, implementation and maintenance and by linking these objectives to theoretical methods and practical strategies for promoting adoption and implementation. Thus interventions are required, not only to change individual behaviour, but also to facilitate adoption and implementation of health education programmes.

Generating an evaluation plan: Finally, IM in the planning of process and effect evaluation. The products of the previous steps provide the basis for developing evaluation tools. Programme developers need to develop instruments capable of evaluating the impact of the intervention on behavioural determinants, environmental conditions, health and quality of life outcomes. They must also specify the time frame appropriate for expected outcomes. These tasks generate an evaluation map. Assumptions related to theoretical methods, practical strategies, and the implementation plan can be assessed in formative and process evaluation through both qualitative and quantitative methods to study the rate of programme dissemination, adoption and implementation, participant exposure, and programme users' and participants' reactions to the programme.

Systematically going through these 'intervention mapping' steps more or less guarantees an explicit link between programme objectives, theoretical methods and final intervention activities and materials. It makes it more likely that all intended learning outcomes are covered by educational activities and materials, and that all activities and materials have a theoretical foundation. It also reduces the chance that the final programme includes activities and materials that are not linked to objectives and theory. As such, going through these steps makes it more likely that the programme will be effective. IM is an iterative process where programme planners are expected to return to previous planning steps as insights are gained, and one has a clear insight into the consequences of early decisions on subsequent steps.

Current social psychological theoretical frameworks that distinguish phases or stages of behaviour change are especially relevant for behaviour change through communication. The Persuasion-Communication model describes the various stages that people go through, from the initial response to an educational message to, hopefully, a maintained change of behaviour (McGuire, 1985). This framework was simplified and extended into seven phases: 1) *attention* to the health recommendations, 2) *comprehension* of the health recommendations, 3) changes in the *attitude* towards the health recommendations (changes in e.g. knowledge, values, risk perceptions, health concerns, outcome expectations), 4) changes in *social influences* regarding the health recommendations (e.g. changes in perceived norms and social support), 5) changes in *self-efficacy beliefs* regarding the enactment of health recommendations, and subsequently 6) *change of behaviour*, and 7) *maintenance of behaviour change* (Bartholomew et al., 2006). These phases can be linked to four categories of so-called communication variables: audience variables (e.g. age, educational level), messenger variables (e.g. attractiveness, reliability, expertise), media (e.g. written material, face-to-face communication, mass media), and message variables (e.g. one-sided messages, discrepancy, time horizon). The essence of this framework is that programme components or intervention strategies may be different for each of these phases. For instance, a strategy that is useful for attracting the attention of a target group may be unsuitable for changing self-belief in skills. Or, a messenger that is useful for the transfer of facts about health risks (e.g. a medical doctor), may be useless for the accomplishment of attitude change among youth. For the latter, a peer educator may be more useful.

Another framework for behaviour change that has become very popular in the field of health education is the Transtheoretical Model (TTM) (Prochaska et al., 2002). TTM describes behaviour change as a process that takes time to develop: people go through a series of stages before they internalise a new behaviour: pre-contemplative (not recognizing the problem or a need to change); contemplative (seriously considering the problem and the possibility of change); preparation (making a commitment to change; making decisions as to that); action (successful initial behaviour change); and maintenance (continuation of behaviour change for a long period). An important implication of TTM is that people in different stages of change may need different educational interventions. Educational interventions tailored at different stage transitions may be different with respect to educational methods and strategies. For example, consciousness raising strategies are needed to move people from pre-contemplation to contemplation, whereas strategies at the maintenance stage should, among other things, encourage refinement of skills to avoid relapse and to allow productive coping with set-backs.

Within these general frameworks, various specific theories can be applied to guide the development of specific components of health education programmes (see for an overview: Bartholomew et al., 2006). For example, theories about fear-appeals (Ruiter et al., 2001) and persuasive communication (Petty and Wegener, 1997) can guide the design of educational strategies to improve people's attitudes towards health behaviours. Other theories, such as Goal Setting (Locke & Latham, 1990) and Relapse Prevention (Marlatt & Gordon, 1985) can be helpful in developing interventions that focus on the maintenance of behaviour change. Although these theories often cover only specific phases in the process of behaviour change, they can be helpful in the design of specific intervention components.

Examples: Ngao and core values

Although many programme developers claim that their intervention is theoretically and empirically based, descriptions of the way in which data and theories were actually applied in health education programmes are rare. Consequently, we have little knowledge yet about the efficacy of specific intervention methods and strategies to promote healthy behaviours (Bartholomew et al., 2001; 2006). More and more programme developers, however, recognise the value of a sound theoretical basis for prevention programmes, and promising attempts and suggestions have been made.

Ndeki et al. (1995) describe a school-based programme for Tanzanian youth (the *Ngao* programme) that was based upon the Theory of Reasoned Action (Fishbein & Middlestadt, 1989) and Social Learning Theory (Bandura, 1986). The *Ngao* programme was focussed on increasing young people's awareness of AIDS, its magnitude and severity, at increasing their knowledge about HIV and AIDS, transmission and prevention, at fostering attitudes and social norms reducing their intentions to engage in unsafe sexual behaviour, and at enhancing social skills that may increase the ability to avoid high-risk situations. The programme included, among other things, traditional didactic methods to transfer information, interactive techniques (e.g. peer-led small group discussions) focussed at the formation of attitudes favouring sexual-risk reduction, and role-playing activities to enhance and practise refusal skills relating to sexual behaviour.

Obasi et al. (2006) describe a community-based programme (the *Mema kwa Vijana* programme) that involved primary schools and government health centres in Mwanza region, Tanzania. This programme was focussed on (i) providing basic knowledge of reproductive and sexual health; (ii) improving students' risk perceptions; (iii) encouraging students to adopt safer sexual behaviour by targeting perceived benefits of, and barriers to, sexual risk reduction; (iv) improving students' self-efficacy regarding negotiating safer sex; and (v) discussing current gender stereotypes. It included a teacher-led, peer-assisted primary school programme that was based upon the principles of Social Learning Theory (Bandura, 1986). The school programme included, among other things, traditional didactic instructions by teachers, interactive techniques as drama, stories, role-play, and games and exercises aimed at the personalisation and internalisation of the information provided.

Programme diffusion

The diffusion of a health education programme is an essential part of the health promotion planning process. Underestimating diffusion barriers is one of the major causes of ineffectiveness in health promotion. While the need for information about the determinants of individual behaviour is commonly accepted, the need for information about the antecedents of institutional 'behaviour' (such as the adoption and implementation of a programme by organisations) is not widely recognised. Consequently, many programmes are never adequately applied in the contexts where they are most likely to be effective.

The diffusion of a health promotion programme can be described as a process consisting of four phases: dissemination, adoption, implementation and continuation (Oldenburg & Parcel, 2002). Dissemination concerns the transfer of information about the programme to potential users. For instance, school principals and teachers have to be aware of the existence of HIV prevention programmes. This phase involves the selection of communication channels and systems that facilitate the diffusion of the programme to a target population. Adoption refers to potential users' intention to use the programme. This phase includes a diagnosis of the target population with regard to their needs, values and attitudes, and their perception of programme attributes and adoption barriers. This phase also includes the diagnosis of the ways in which target adopters can be motivated to adopt the programme, and the ways to overcome barriers. For instance, a study among Dutch teachers revealed that their decision to adopt an HIV prevention programme was affected by their perceptions of what important others, such as colleagues, would like them to do (subjective norms), and by the behaviour of their colleagues (descriptive norms). In addition, adoption was affected by their perceptions of whether the curriculum includes clear instructions, is easy to teach, does not require much preparation time, and is enjoyed by students (Paulussen et al., 1994).

Implementation refers to the actual use of the programme. The major focus in this phase is on the enhancement of adopters' self-efficacy and skills (e.g. by means of teacher training), and on encouraging trial programme implementation. Maintenance or continuation succeeds initial implementation. This phase refers to the stage in which the programme has become current practice and in which the allocation of resources is routinely made. At this stage, for instance, HIV education would be explicitly incorporated in school policy.

According to Orlandi et al. (1990) many health promotion innovations have failed because of the gap between programme development and diffusion planning. To bridge this gap, they stressed the need for a *linkage system* between the resource system that develops and promotes the programme (e.g. the Health Education Authority), and the user system that is supposed to adopt the programme (e.g. youth organisations, schools). Such a liaison group should be formed before programme design starts, and should include representatives of the user system, representatives of the resource system, and a change agent facilitating the collaboration. Diffusion of the programme may be carried out by any of the members of this liaison group. The essential point is that the programme development process and the programme diffusion process have been developed through co-operation to improve the fit between the programme and user, to attune innovative programmes to practical possibilities and constraints, and to facilitate widespread programme implementation and maintenance.

The development of a diffusion strategy can be based on a planning process that is similar to the planning of a health education programme. A diffusion strategy should be based on insights in the determinants of potential users' decisions regarding the adoption, implementation and continuation of a health education programme. These determinants can be measured with the same kind of protocol as is used in the determinants of behaviour analyses, using the same kind of theories (Kok et al., 1996). A diffusion strategy should further be based on useful theoretical methods and theory-based strategies. Because programme diffusion often involves organisations and community groups making decisions and changing practices, the application of organisational change and community development models is critical to identify the factors that facilitate or hinder programme adoption and implementation.

Diffusion of school-based HIV prevention programmes in Tanzania and Uganda

To date few successful school-based HIV prevention programmes seem to have been implemented effectively on a wide scale (UNAIDS, 1997b; Schaalma et al., 2004) and the scientific literature hardly provides examples of theory-based strategies that have been designed to enhance the widespread diffusion of HIV prevention programmes. At best, programme designers have collaborated closely with teachers and other representatives of the school system to anticipate barriers to widespread diffusion of prevention programmes (Kaaya et al., 2002a). For instance, Ndeki et al. (1995) anticipated programme implementation by consulting with local teachers and health workers *before* writing the *Ngao* programme. To facilitate programme implementation, they also included a one-week training workshop for teachers. Shuey et al. (1999) reported on an intervention in Uganda aimed at, among other things, the improvement of existing educational systems at a district level in order to facilitate the implementation of a national school health curriculum, and in order to improve the quality of individual student counselling. They also dealt with implementation and diffusion issues by means of a close collaboration between researchers and representatives from the school system (health and education staff, local teachers, and students), as well as by means of community involvement in the development and implementation of the intervention.

Both Ndeki et al. (1995) and Shuey et al. (1999) provide examples of attempts to facilitate the diffusion of HIV prevention programmes, taking into consideration local contexts. These studies and similar examples of successes and barriers encountered provide important insights on approaches that may be successful in other African settings. However, ongoing research is required on how widespread implementation and maintenance of programmes can be achieved and how institutional, political, religious and cultural barriers to implementing effective sex education can be overcome.

Programme evaluation

The final task of health education planners is the evaluation of their acts and products. Because a detailed discussion of evaluation issues is beyond the scope of this chapter, we will limit ourselves to some general remarks about the importance of evaluation and evaluation practice. For a detailed discussion of the scientific, technical and practical issues of evaluation we would like to refer to Windsor et al. (1994).

Although evaluation is the final task, programme planners should anticipate evaluation right from the start of programme planning. Only then will programme planners be realistic in defining their programme goals, and in specifying what changes should occur within a specific time frame. Programme planners should also reach agreement about goals with their funding agencies, and they should avoid objectives that are too ambitious, too vague to measure, and/or that cannot be reasonably assessed within the time frame of the programme. Regarding the latter, we would like to emphasize that 'hard' outcome indicators, such as behaviour change or a decrease in prevalence or incidence statistics, are usually beyond the time-frame of a programme. This, for instance, would be the case with HIV-risk reducing programmes for young adolescents.

Programme evaluation is just as important as programme planning. Without evaluation we will never know what works. Regardless of the role of an individual in programme design or programme evaluation (a politician, a member of a funding agency, a programme manager, or a scientist), without evaluation we will never be able to continue to support programmes that work, and we will never stop spending money on programmes that do not make a difference. This may seem like common sense, but in health education or health promotion practice, evaluation is often neglected. This may be partly due to the fact that evaluation can be threatening. Politicians may not be interested in the effects of their decisions, since their decisions may have been based on pleasing their voters. Programme managers, or other people that are involved in a programme, may also not be interested in the effects of their programme since negative outcomes may stop their programme, and may ruin their career. Nobody likes to be the brain behind a programme that does not make any difference.

Generally, all evaluation refers to two basic questions: 'Does the programme make a difference (*effect evaluation*)?' and 'Was the programme delivered the way it was planned (*process evaluation*)?' Effect evaluation and process evaluation need to go together. Without insight in the delivery process, we will not be able to interpret the results of effect evaluation.

Effect evaluation requires a comparison between those who participated in the programme (intervention group), and those who did not (comparison group). Outcome indicators of effect evaluation may be quality of life, health, behaviours, environmental conditions, and/or proximal programme objectives. With effect evaluation we can make a distinction between: 1) *efficacy*, which refers to programme evaluation under optimal conditions, e.g. an experimental field setting, and 2) *effectiveness*, which refers to programme evaluation under 'real life' conditions.

Process evaluation identifies the quality of programme delivery and programme design. 'Was the programme delivered as planned?' 'Why was it delivered as it was?' Process evaluation may also include an evaluation of the quality of programme design. As such, process evaluation assesses the quality of the decision processes underlying programme development and diffusion. With process evaluation, outcome indicators depend on the interest of stakeholders, evaluation resources and evaluation purposes. It may be clear that process evaluation only needs an intervention group.

Both effect and process evaluation requires a good understanding of the theory of the programme, i.e. the logic behind the programme for effecting desirable outcomes. Without clear programme theory evaluators do not know what to evaluate, and consequently what to measure. As such, any evaluation needs a kind of intervention map, a detailed description of the programme and programme delivery.

In recent decades many programmes have been developed to educate African youth about HIV/AIDS. Only few of these initiatives, however, have been subjected to rigorous evaluation. In their worldwide review of the impact of sex and HIV education programmes on sexual behaviours of youth Kirby et al. (2006) identified nine African studies that could match evaluation standards, among which were *Ngao* and *Mema kwa vijana*. Despite this low number of African studies, the results of the review suggest that sex and HIV programmes can be effective 'in different countries and cultures throughout the world' (p.19), especially programmes that were based upon assessments of young people's needs and assets, that focused on clear HIV/AIDS prevention goals and on specific behaviours leading to these goals, that targeted the psychosocial factors of these specific behaviours by means of multiple educational activities that incorporated active involvement of youth, and that employed activities and messages that were geared to young people's culture, values and experience. Other factors that determined the impact of programmes were a sound implementation, pilot-testing and community and political support.

Conclusions

From a public health perspective the promotion of reproductive health of sub-Saharan African youth has many benefits. Unprotected sex is directly related to sexually transmitted diseases including HIV, early pregnancy and childbearing, unsafe abortions, single parents and so on. As such, unprotected sex jeopardises not only people's physical and emotional health, but also their economic and social well-being.

Young people's sexual health can be promoted through prevention programmes, provided that these programmes are theory and evidence-based. Sexual health promotion programmes should be based on a design approach combining empirical findings, theoretical insights and practical considerations taking into account target groups and local contexts.

Many researchers have addressed sexual risk-taking behaviours of sub-Saharan African youth. Fewer have addressed the psychosocial determinants that are related to sexual risk-taking and risk-reducing behaviour. Hardly any have addressed the systematic use of empirical data and theoretical insights in designing reproductive health promoting interventions, or the effectiveness of attempts to facilitate large-scale diffusion of such interventions. To fill these gaps there is a strong need for future research on reproductive health in sub-Saharan Africa. In our view this research should be action-driven: studies on sexual risk taking behaviours should be linked to the development of prevention programmes. There is also a strong need for detailed systematic descriptions of the design process of HIV interventions, and high-quality evaluation. Many intervention reports do not provide enough information to allow precise replication. Many intervention programmes lack a thorough evaluation. Both the lack of programme descriptions and evaluations encourage reinvention of previously evaluated "wheels" and so retards knowledge development. Using the Intervention Mapping protocol will stimulate programme developers and evaluators to be explicit about their planning and evaluation decisions (Bartholomew et al., 2006).

Last, but not least, we need to know how to effectively market programmes to decision-makers and programme users if they are to affect the sexual risk behaviour of young people. Research into implementation barriers could have a powerful impact on the extent to which research into effectiveness has an impact on HIV spread. Local research is required to clarify attitudes towards the reality of teenage sexual behaviour and the delivery of preventive programmes. Where barriers are identified, research should seek to explain why, for example, decision-makers may believe that sex education increases sexual activity among teenagers, and should seek to provide insights into how such views can be changed. Only then may health education significantly contribute to promoting the reproductive health of African youth.

4. Ethical Dilemmas in Adolescent Reproductive Health Promotion

Gro Th. Lie

Abstract

The HIV epidemic has challenged dominant conceptions of how sexuality in general and adolescent sexual behaviour in particular should be addressed, but these issues are still sensitive and controversial. Ethical guidelines may be useful and necessary. The question raised in this chapter is whether the available and dominant ethical guidelines are useful and sufficient for the challenges and dilemmas encountered in the process of promoting adolescent reproductive health. This chapter describes some important pre-existing systems for regulating ethics in health-related work and research, and discusses the inherent limitations in current ethical standards and guidelines. Ethical challenges may also arise from the fact that research and health promotion actors in sub-Saharan Africa often come from many different countries, from the South as well as the North. This fact may pose cross-cultural challenges. Guidelines are also affected by the historical dominance of western research traditions, and by the fact that money for health-related work addressing adolescents' reproductive health and research on it is often donated from the rich part of the world. In this way, research funding and development policies are related, and development issues pose ethical challenges that go beyond what is traditionally thought of as research ethics or ethics of health work. This chapter identifies some of these complex dilemmas and suggests collaborative research and the use of participatory approaches as a potential way of overcoming some of the existing dilemmas. Involving the adolescents themselves in identifying their needs, concerns, worries, and hopes, is essential when using participatory approaches. But such approaches also raise new ethical dilemmas. Voices and experiences of adolescent Africans in the era of AIDS are used to illustrate factors of importance, dilemmas encountered and potential future problems. The chapter argues that we constantly need to be sensitive to potential ethical dilemmas. We constantly need to develop our ethical standards and guidelines.

Introduction

The HIV epidemic has dramatically affected sub-Saharan African societies and has challenged dominant conceptions of how sexuality in general and adolescent sexual behaviour in particular should be addressed by local communities and political authorities. A growing number of African adolescents have lost their parents due to AIDS. Many more young people have witnessed their communities change because of the epidemic. After two decades with the AIDS epidemic, young Africans are increasingly aware that they are vulnerable to the deadly virus and to other health hazards. Are their needs and concerns taken seriously?

Adolescent reproductive health-related work may be considered to be within the tradition of health promotion and health promotion research. "Health promotion is the process of enabling people to increase control over the determinants of health and hereby improve their health" (Ottawa Charter, 1986:1). Participation is considered essential to develop and sustain health promotion action (Bangkok Charter on Health Promotion, 2005). Such a definition and understanding of health promotion clearly involves ethical principles. Inherent in this and other definitions of health promotion are respect for human integrity and the right for people to influence their own life-situation. Participation at all levels in health promotion action and health promotion research opens ways for new experiences and different research findings than those hitherto gathered through top-down research on "the other". But such work may also give rise to new dilemmas and new conflicts.

I didn't tell my children that we were sick when we tested positive .... How can you tell a child that you are infected? The child will think how did my father get that infection? ... You can't talk sex affairs with the children. It is obvious here in our culture, those affairs I would call them internal. Those are internal affairs which should not be known even to neighbours. It is very confidential. ... But it is stupid to tell children such affairs.
(From an interview with a Ugandan HIV-positive widower who lost his wife to AIDS and who is now living with 8 children, several of them adolescents. Apila, 2001)

We have a right to know what our parents suffered from and why they died. We have a right to know how AIDS is transmitted and how we can protect our lives!
(From a focus group discussion among adolescent AIDS orphans in Tanzania. None of these orphans had been informed about AIDS or their parents' HIV-positive status, either by their parents or other close relatives. The adolescents understood that their parents died from AIDS because they had some knowl-

edge about AIDS from public HIV prevention campaigns and because neighbours, extended family members and others rejected them. Mrumbi, 2006)

Research on issues related to adolescent sexual behaviour and reproductive
health is sensitive because it is so closely linked to people's conceptions of
morality. Conceptions of morality may vary within a community, as well as
between communities. When doing research and working with sensitive issues, ethical guidelines may be useful and necessary. So, what ethical guidelines exist, and are they sufficient to prepare us for the many challenges we
face in the promotion of adolescent reproductive health?

Ethics can be defined as explicit, philosophical reflections on moral beliefs and practices. Ethics are an act of consciously stepping back and reflecting on morality (Hinman, 2001). Since there might be many different
conceptions of morality, reflecting on morality may not be an easy venture.
Such reflection may point to contradictions and dilemmas. How should we
prioritise when one moral view seems to contradict another moral view?
How should we act when ethics developed in one area do not fit with the
needs identified in another area?

Sexuality and ethics

Sexuality is a sensitive issue in any culture, even if norms regulating sexual
behaviour may vary from one geographical area to another, from one subculture to another, and even from one age-group to another. Approaching
issues of sexuality and reproductive health involves careful consideration
of how to address people, for instance how to ensure that an individual's
integrity is protected, and how to show respect for existing societal values
and sub-cultural values. When approaching adolescent reproductive health,
diverging normative views may become even more evident: How old should
young people be before we (researchers, health promoters) may ask them
questions related to their own sexual activities? When may we introduce
issues on how and what kind of precautions to take to avoid sexually transmitted diseases, HIV, unwanted pregnancies etc.? We know that most parents, teachers, and religious societies have strong opinions on these topics.
Such opinions are also reflected in policies, rules and regulations - for instance in national laws, school ministries, and regulations for ethical clearance of research protocols.

Concerns related to adolescent reproductive health may also be raised
from a different point of view, not from the point of view of the researchers, health promoters, parents or teachers, but from the point of view of the

adolescents themselves. A number of issues and questions arise, such as: At what age can young people ask questions on sexual issues and on AIDS? To whom can they put their questions and why? What kinds of questions are they entitled to ask according to cultural and moral codes? What kinds of questions do they really want to ask and why? How are their questions and worries interpreted and met within their own local contexts? Do adolescents find meaningful answers to their worries? Based on the Ottawa Charter's (1986) definition of health promotion, the adolescents themselves have an important role to play in the protection and promotion of their own health, and their voices should be heard.

Ethical standards and guidelines for health workers

Most professional health workers, regardless of whether they work in Africa or Europe, are guided by some professional code of ethics. These codes of ethics are meant to guide health workers in their everyday professional work so as to keep a high moral standard in their work. The guidelines should also help health workers to prioritise when facing ethical dilemmas. Such guidelines are never comprehensive, but do reflect certain important moral principles regarded as central within a professional union in a given country at a given time in history. Such codes of ethics usually state that *the patient/client (who is perceived to be the weaker party in the relationship) should be respected and protected.* Human rights and respect for human integrity are key aspects of health workers' codes of ethics.

Codes of ethics are not always adhered to and they may not always seem relevant. In preventive work and in health promotion there is not always a patient, and it may not always be obvious who the weaker party is. Often several people are affected or may be affected by a problem (e.g. family members, groups of people) and if they have conflicting needs, who do we respect and protect, and who do we consider to be the weaker party? Preventive work may not necessarily address individuals; often it is group-oriented (e.g. school classes) or even policy-oriented. But even if the professional codes of ethics do not seem to be relevant, sufficient, or valid in many of the contexts that health workers and researchers addressing adolescent reproductive health find themselves in, ethical challenges do exist, and we need to sensitise ourselves to identify them and to be able to deal constructively with the many challenges.

International and national ethical guidelines for research and research publications

Just as in health work, there are codes of ethics for researchers. Since research is important for the development of efficient health promoting programmes, some of the key documents regulating research ethics will be presented here and some limitations of these documents with regard to health promotion and health promotion research will be discussed.

The Helsinki Declaration

The most important existing document on research ethics in medical research is the Helsinki Declaration (1964). The declaration was based on the experiences that led to the Nuremberg Code of 1946. During the Nuremberg Process it was verified that the Nazis had performed medical experiments on prisoners of war during World War II. Such experiments had caused suffering, pain and in some cases death to individuals experimented upon. Needless to say, there was no informed consent involved. The Helsinki Declaration, building upon the Nuremberg Code, states as a basic principle, the respect for individual integrity. Historically, the Helsinki Declaration is very important in a human rights perspective and forms the foundation for international agreements on basic ethical principles in research.

The Helsinki Declaration was, however, first and foremost developed to give guidelines for biomedical experimental research. Its section I, point 1 reads:

> 1. Biomedical research involving human subjects must conform to generally accepted scientific principles and should be based on adequately performed laboratory and animal experimentation and on a thorough knowledge of the scientific literature.

Health promotion does not usually involve biomedical experimental research. Often it concerns cultural conceptions of risk, surveys on risk behaviour, knowledge and belief systems, or on health policy issues. Yet, there are principles in the Helsinki Declaration that are equally important in other research designs, e.g. section I, point 6 and point 9:

> 6. The right of the research subject to safeguard his or her integrity must always be respected. Every precaution should be taken to respect the privacy of the subject and to minimise the impact of the study on the subject's physical and mental integrity and on the personality of the subject.

9. In any research on human beings, each potential subject must be adequately informed of the aims, methods, anticipated benefits and potential hazards of the study and the discomfort it may entail. He or she should be informed that he or she is at liberty to abstain from participating in the study and that he or she is free to withdraw his or her consent to participation at any time. The physician should then obtain the subject's freely-given informed consent, preferably in writing.

The key role of physicians in this document is obvious, but in health promotion there are often other professions involved. The issue of "informed consent, preferably in writing", cannot apply if people cannot read and write. The issue of age (e.g. the age of children and adolescents) is also a critical one. Who decides if adolescents are free to participate?

The Helsinki Declaration is the most important document on health related research ethics for several reasons:

1. Internationally, it is the document on research ethics that has the widest acceptance worldwide. It was adopted by the 18th World Medical Assembly, Helsinki, Finland in June 1964 and amended in Tokyo 1975, in Venice 1983, in Hong Kong 1989 and in South Africa in 1996.

2. The Helsinki Declaration constitutes the basic document for most countries' committees in charge of authorising Ethical Clearance of research protocols. This is also the case for African countries.

3. It is a model document on research ethics not only for medical research (for which it is written), but also for related research areas such as health promotion research.

The fact that the Helsinki Declaration is a model document also represents a dilemma, because it takes as its point of departure the experimental design. The experimental design has in many contexts been regarded as a gold standard for research. This perspective illustrates the dominant role in research of experimental medical trials and the dominant role of positivistic research paradigms.

The experimental design as a gold standard for research in health promotion has been criticised by several health promotion researchers world-wide (Bracht, 1999). It is important to be aware that the experimental design is but one of several possible designs in health promotion research.

If we look at the definitions of health promotion, we see that the research issues in health promotion are of a different kind, include different approaches, are often multidisciplinary oriented and are put in a more holistic and multifaceted context than what is usual in an experimental medical trial. In addition, health promotion research is not limited to research at the individual level. It includes group level, community level, and policy level. However, even if the research approaches and the research paradigms do not fit with the experimental design and the positivistic traditions, we still need standards for good research. It is unethical to conclude and generalise on the basis of poorly performed research. Thus, ethical guidelines do not only deal with respect for human integrity, but also with the quality of the research. The ethical guidelines should assist us in answering the question: Are the research approaches scientifically sound enough for us to generate new knowledge?

The Helsinki Declaration is an important document designed to protect the integrity of the individual in the research context and to ensure quality of research. The declaration is also often used internationally to assess whether or not we can get ethical clearance for our projects. Thus, everyone in health related research ought to be familiar with it. This does not, however, mean that the Helsinki Declaration is always suitable or sufficient to guide us in ethical issues related to health promotion research.

Ethical standards in research publications

The Vancouver Convention (1997) also plays an important role in the international research scene, and is a model document for ethical issues related to research publications. Its history started with a group of editors of general medical journals who met in Vancouver, British Columbia, in 1987 to establish guidelines for the format of manuscripts submitted to their journals. The group became known as the Vancouver Group. This group has evolved into the International Committee of Medical Journal Editors. The committee has produced five editions of the "Uniform Requirements for Manuscripts Submitted to Biomedical Journals" and the contents are regularly updated.

The convention deals in detail with topics of relevance for publishing research findings. Among these are issues to consider before submitting a manuscript: acceptable secondary publications, protection of patients' rights to privacy, requirements for the submission of manuscripts, preparation of the manuscript, authorship, abstract and key words, what should be covered in an introduction, how to present methods, the importance of ethics (with special reference to the Helsinki Declaration), requirements for presenting statistics, and results, discussion, acknowledgement, and how to make a list of references.

The "rules" presented in the Vancouver Convention are strict, such as the rules on experimental design, and the format for writing requested of contributors presupposes that the contributors are familiar with the details of the format and the rationale behind the strict rules. The Vancouver Convention plays a key role in ensuring the quality of research presented. Everything cannot be published in the name of "research". By defining certain criteria for how research should be done and presented, the Vancouver Convention aims at providing quality criteria for good research. Ensuring that research has been done in an appropriate way and that this is clearly reflected in the publication is also concerned with ethical standards. For instance, presenting poor research or generalisations made from research designs that do not permit such generalisations is considered to be unethical.

Like the Helsinki Declaration, the Vancouver Convention plays a dominant role in health related research and constitutes a kind of gold standard for research publications. It does not have the same widespread acceptance in certain countries of the world as the Helsinki Declaration has, but this might be due to its shorter history.

The Vancouver Convention is oriented towards publications on the kind of research that is central in the Helsinki Declaration, and it is thus most suitable for experimental biomedical trials (as indicated in the title's use of the expression: biomedical journals). But the convention is also essential for health promotion researchers exactly because of its role as model for publication of other kinds of health-related research. With regard to relevance for health promotion research, the Vancouver Convention suffers from the same kinds of limitations that characterise the Helsinki Declaration. We may therefore conclude that The Vancouver Convention is important, but not sufficient for the ethical challenges we encounter and have to take into consideration when publishing and disseminating research of relevance to the promotion of adolescent reproductive health.

Ethics in research dissemination

The existence of The Vancouver Convention raises another ethical dilemma: How do we disseminate and share research findings if people do not read international research journals? Ethical challenges include not only respect for individual integrity and ensuring quality of research, but also include questions like: For whom are we doing research, who may benefit from research findings, are research findings accessible for those who may be empowered by the findings, how can we make research findings accessible to the wider public and still ensure quality and relevance of the findings?

Internet facilities open new avenues of accessing important information. In recent years health-related research journals have increasingly been made available on the internet. This may make access to relevant research findings easier in the African context as well, but even today few Africans have access to computers and to internet facilities. Also in this context we find an increasing unbalance in terms of access to important information between the "haves" and the "have-nots".

With access to the internet, we can find the Helsinki Declaration, The Vancouver Convention and several articles on ethics. But typically the available articles on ethics are addressing biomedical issues, vaccine and drug trials. Rarely are the articles on ethics addressing adolescent reproductive health within disease prevention or health promotion perspectives.

Cross-cultural diversity and ethics in choice of research questions and paradigms

Sub-Saharan Africa is an enormous region fragmented into more than 40 states with more than 1,000 ethnic groups differing markedly in terms of language and other important cultural traits. African researchers warn that making generalisations about such a huge geopolitical area is certainly fraught with dangers (Nsamenang, 1993). However, it seems expedient to examine the subject matter with the foreknowledge that several of these countries have common historical experiences. Pertaining to the social sciences, what readily comes to mind are colonial subjugation and economic exploitation, academic domination and denigration of the indigenous systems of knowledge, and their replacement with western systems of learning, and science. African knowledge systems have for a long time been excluded from the corpus of social science and psychological knowledge (Nsamenang, 1993). The most remarkable breakthrough in African psychology was the discovery that research framed entirely on Eurocentric terms failed "to connect appropriately with the ways in which people whose behaviour is described think about that behaviour themselves" (Nsamenang, 1993, p. 178). A great deal of African knowledge is locked in maxims, proverbs, and folklore, not easily translatable into 'scientific jargon' except at the cost of impairment to its essence, or distortion of its full meaning (Nsamenang, 1993).

Does this mean that western researchers with their cultural heritage and their scientific training based on theory and research from a western perspective will not be able to grasp the essential phenomena of adolescent sexual behaviour in the African context? "Many researchers find their well-laid research plans must be modified after arrival in another culture", says Brislin (1986, p.137). This is because all too often they realise, to their dismay, that "most of the concepts, taxonomic labels, and conceptual systems they are familiar with become inapplicable, ...even impossible to employ" (Nsamenang, 1993, p. 181).

However, we should also keep in mind that societies are rapidly changing. The effects of western "modernisation" and globalisation are certainly visible in African societies and among African youth. Radio and television programmes, and the pop music industry may have had impact on African adolescents' own cultural norms, their self-perceptions and their sexual behaviour. Global challenges, like the HIV epidemic need to be studied from many perspectives. The understanding of adolescent sexual behaviour will depend on both the understanding of cross-cultural similarities and the acceptance of the diversity that characterises humanity. The development of science is dependent on cross-cultural studies. This is also recognised by African researchers. Researchers "should know that compulsive confinement in one cultural niche does not advance 'their science'. We ought to intensify and evolve new insights from cross-cultural collaborative research" (Nsamenang, 1993:182).

Ethical challenges related to South–North collaborative research

Adolescent reproductive health research is often a cross-cultural collaborative venture consisting of researchers and health workers from diverse African countries as well as northern/western countries. The collaborative efforts of the researchers in such projects are characterised by a wish to overcome some of the inherent imbalances of the dominant research traditions. But in spite of the cross-cultural collaborative efforts there is imbalance. Researchers from the North, generally speaking, have easier access to the international research society, are more familiar with international research journals and have better working conditions (including internet facilities) as compared to their African colleagues. Usually funding for the ongoing research and intervention programmes comes from the economically rich part of the world. Such inherent imbalance of power in a research co-operation between our colleagues from the South and colleagues from the North is in itself an ethical challenge. This imbalance in power structure is not limited to the financial aspects and funding for research and health promotion, but is also reflected in the fact that most research and academic theory building has historically been done in the West by white male researchers. We may therefore state that researchers on adolescent reproductive health issues are working within the historical context of western academic and economic male dominance, addressing sensitive adolescent issues in the era of AIDS, issues among which the sexuality of young African girls has proven to be the most vulnerable. This very fact should make us particularly alert to issues of ethics and to the question posed by Robert Chambers (1994): "Whose reality counts?"

"Whose reality counts?" Ethical links between research and development issues

Even researchers involved in biomedical research have recently questioned the existing international guidelines for ethical conduct of research. "Some of the debate surrounding the ethical regulation of international research indicates that while issues of study design, ethical review, and standards of care have been highlighted, the underlying socio-economic deprivation and inequities are largely ignored" (Bhutta, 2002:115). Western dominance and challenges in cross-cultural research are closely linked to issues of development policies. Anti-poverty rhetoric is widespread. Current conditions are, however, often appalling, trends in many places negative, and future prospects bleak for hundreds of millions of people. The current status of the HIV epidemic "mocks development and makes fantasy of current debate about development. With AIDS, as in other ways, the South is more exposed and vulnerable, will suffer more, and will be far more devastated than the North" (Chambers, 1994:5).

Global data from population-based HIV-screening surveys and surveillance of the epidemic confirm that poor countries are more affected by the epidemic than richer countries are. Poor people within poor countries (as well as within richer countries) are more vulnerable, and young people are at high risk of HIV-transmission. Among young people, the adolescent girls are more vulnerable and at risk of being exposed to sexual health hazards than adolescent boys (UNAIDS, 2000–2001).

The modern economic paradigm continues to predominate in the realm of development discourse. In assessing conditions and deciding what must be done, the realities of development professionals are universal, reductionist, standardized and stable. This type of understanding is expressed in poverty thinking, for instance concerning income-poverty, and employment thinking which may be concerned with jobs. Professional biases have been challenged, but they remain deep, secure and distorting (Chambers, 1994). Development progress is usually described in an 'input – output' terminology. As opposed to the realities of "development expert" professionals:

> The realities of poor people are local, complex, diverse and dynamic. Income poverty, though important, is only one aspect of deprivation. Participatory appraisal confirms many dimensions and criteria of disadvantage, ill-being and well-being as people experience them. In addition to poverty, these include social inferiority, isolation, physical weakness, vulnerability, seasonal deprivation, powerlessness and humiliation. (Chambers, 1994:1)

The local, complex, diverse and dynamic realities of the AIDS epidemic can be illustrated by quoting Roland Msiska, a former National AIDS Programme Manager in Zambia:

> So, none of these deaths are the same. Each death raises different questions, different challenges. Each time you change, you become less dogmatic, more one who asks questions … Each death gives a different dimension to the epidemic. Yet we may have been dealing with the epidemic as if it is a single epidemic. There are different epidemics, moving around; they are constantly dynamic. (Parnell et al., 1996:48)

Chambers (1994), as well as other critics of the dominant trend in international development aid, addresses the need for other paradigms.

> A paradigm of reversals and altruism demands a new professionalism. The paradigm and the new professionalism put people before things, and poor people and their priorities first of all. The challenges presented are institutional, professional, and personal. The policy and practical means to promote and sustain wellbeing, livelihoods and equity include two complementary agendas, one conventional and one new. Underlying the new agenda is basic human right of poor people to conduct their own analysis. (Chambers, 1994:1)

Such a statement addresses the ethical importance of involving those concerned to take part in analysing their own situation. Here we see that ethics in development policies and ethics in research can be combined.

In search for alternative paradigms

Let us now return to the WHO's definition of health promotion (Ottawa Charter, 1986). Participation is seen as essential both in the tradition of health promotion and among critics of the dominant development paradigm. In dominant research traditions, as well as in traditional development aid, strategies for change are often referred to as "intervention" and "intervention strategies". Intervention implies that someone does something to someone else (the other is the object of the intervention). There are ethical and scientific limitations inherent in the use of such concepts. Such concepts are also not compatible with the definition of and the ideology of health promotion. Some alternative concepts have been raised by researchers and practitioners involved in participatory research and in the development of a new paradigm for research, action and change processes. Key concepts in the alternative paradigm are "people's participation" and "communicative action" (Fals Borda, 1998).

The movement advocating for participatory research has a relatively short history, but is truly international in its scope. Within the movement of participatory research the following are considered the pioneers of participatory approaches: Paolo Freire (Recife / Sao Paulo, Brazil, 1921–1997), G.V.S. De Silva (Colombo, Sri Lanka, 1928–1980), Andrew Pearse (Crewkerne/ Oxford, England, 1916–1980), D. Myles Horton (Savannah / New Market, Tennessee, 1905–1990), Anton De Shutter (Holland and Mexico, died in 1985), and Joao Bosco Pinto (Brazil and Colombia, died in 1996). All these individuals are also known for their ethical reflections and their concern for poor people and global challenges. A lot of inspiration for ethical reflection can be gained from studying the work of these pioneers in participatory research (Fals Borda, 1998).

The movement of participatory research is an exception to the often western dominated schools of thought. What I find very interesting, especially since I am concerned with cross-cultural studies and global health challenges, is the fact that those who are considered to be the pioneers in participatory research are from five different continents, and that knowledge generated through participatory action for change has been based in countries on all the continents of the world. Another striking feature is that they come from diverse academic disciplines. Thus, the movement of participatory research is truly cross-continental and multi-disciplinary (Fals Borda, 1998).

Participatory research may be said to combine at least two observable elements that distinguish it from other forms of scientific or investigative work: 1) an evaluative or ideological structure, with critical attitudes to knowledge and its use, social context, and cultural patterns undergoing or in need of improvement and change; and 2) an array of combinable multidisciplinary survey techniques derived from a holistic perspective (Fals Borda, 1998).

At the "World Congress of Participatory Convergence in Knowledge, Space and Time" in Cartagena, Colombia, 1997, theoretical foundations of participatory approaches were summed up and methodological guidelines for participatory research were made (Fals Borda, 1998). According to the World Congress: "participatory research may be defined as a method of study and action that goes hand in hand with an altruistic philosophy of life to obtain useful, reliable results for improving collective situations, particularly for the popular classes" (p. 168). It is inter- or multi-disciplinary and applicable in continua ranging from micro- to macro-universes studied (from groups to communities and larger societies), but never losing its existential commitment to the life-philosophy of change that characterises it (Fals Borda, 1998).

According to the principles of participatory research, as defined at the Cartagena World Congress (1997), we could reformulate our concerns by stating: If we really care about the reproductive health of African adolescents, our research approach must involve them, and our joint research findings must be translated into actions that empower adolescents to promote their own sexual health and into actions that make the environment more health promoting.

Voices and concerns of some African adolescents in the era of AIDS

Multidisciplinary groups of researchers using a wide range of approaches are involved in promoting adolescent reproductive health. I have argued for the reasons why we have an ethical responsibility to include young people as partners in the research process. The adolescents themselves are both partners and stakeholders in this venture of promoting reproductive health. But the voices of these adolescents are not always heard by parents, teachers, community leaders, policymakers, or international development agencies. Their voices are also not always heard by researchers. Yet, the promotion of reproductive health concerns young people's health and future.

Adults often have preconceived ideas about what risks young people face and what precautions should be taken. Let us illustrate this point with some examples from projects in the EU-funded Adolescent Reproductive Health Network (ARHNe). In the first ARHNe workshop (Arusha, Tanzania, 1997) activities on community work to promote adolescent reproductive health were presented. In one community in particular, leaders had decided that the discos should be closed because such places represented risk arenas for unwanted sexual behaviour. When the young girls in that community were invited by ARHNe colleagues to voice their concerns and to identify risk situations, it became obvious, however, that these girls did not attend discos, yet still they perceived themselves to be at high risk. They identified the way to and from school (particularly to school in the morning) as the most risky contexts for unwanted sexual encounters and risk for HIV-transmission. This certainly demonstrates the need for different kinds of approaches for risk prevention and for empowerment of young girls other than through the closing of local discos.

Adolescent AIDS orphans, what do they tell and teach us?

Many AIDS orphans are not aware that their parents have died of AIDS (UNAIDS, 2000; Apila, 2001; Ngaina, 2002). Others may be aware or suspect that their parents died of AIDS, but they are afraid to talk about it because of the shame and stigma associated with the disease. Many of these adolescents have dropped out of school and may therefore not benefit from school-based HIV-prevention and health promotion.

In a study in northern Tanzania among orphans getting assistance from an NGO, the following statements were given in a focus group discussion with eight orphaned boys between 12 and 17 years of age:

> (Male youth:) *Other organisations should come and educate us about youth and HIV.*
> (Researcher:) *Do you know how HIV is transmitted?*
> (Male youth:) *By sharing bath towels and spoons.*
> (Researcher:) *Any other means?*
> (Silence in the group.)
> (Ngaina, 2002)

In the particular geographical area where these orphaned boys lived, several school-based HIV/AIDS prevention programs have been conducted. But these young boys had dropped out of school. In this area, AIDS is still very stigmatised in spite of the many AIDS-related programs, so caregivers and neighbours avoid the issue of AIDS when addressing these young boys.

From the research it became evident that these young boys had less knowledge about HIV/AIDS than the general public in the area, less knowledge than their peers and even less knowledge than orphaned girls.

The organization helping orphans in need in this particular area was run by women. Women in sub-Saharan Africa are often the most active ones at grassroots level in both care and prevention. Women seem to be more alert and pay more attention to the vulnerability of young girls. However, such alertness may also create a bias in the sense that the needs of young girls get more attention than the needs of young boys. Among orphaned adolescent girls (focus group discussion) from the same study, the opinions were expressed differently as compared to the boys (Ngaina, 2002):

> (Researcher:) *What kind of assistance is the organization offering you:*
> (One female youth:) *Training on how to make batik, – and advice about the moral conduct, especially about women's problems – girls' disturbances.*
> (Another:) *They provide uniforms and pay school fees for orphans. They fight the HIV/AIDS epidemic by conducting various seminars, even the World AIDS Day, the first of December, they educated people about the problem. They also teach us to have good manners and that we should not be trapped to involve ourselves in sex.*

To these girls the connection between HIV/AIDS and sex is evident – not so for the young boys.

Young people are not always in a position to voice their own opinions, worries and concerns. Orphaned adolescents may be in an even more difficult situation to voice their opinions, criticism or worries, out of fear of being chased from their current guardians/caregivers (Apila, 2001; Ngaina, 2002). Such fears also prevent vulnerable adolescents from raising questions and worries concerning their own sexual health.

> (Researcher:) *Do you think you get enough support from xx (name of organisation)?*
> (Female youth:)*We get proper support from xx (name of organisation), but it is not enough. For instance, they should visit us and know where we stay, talk to us, just the way you are doing now, and we will be very happy. ….*
> (Researcher:) *Is there any advice you think you would give to xx* (name of organisation) *in order to improve the support offered to you?*
> (Female youth:) *… to make follow-up to know their* (the orphans') *progress and their needs* (including reproductive health needs and how to protect themselves) *. ….. I also pray that they continue to fight HIV/AIDS and to support the orphans.*

From this study it also became evident that caregivers/guardians avoided the orphan support-centre and that, according to the AIDS orphans, this was due to AIDS-related stigma:

> *.... Xx* (name of the organisation*) should advise the guardians. This is because when we are told to come with our guardians they refuse. They say if they come to the centre people may think/say that their relatives* (the parents of the adolescents) *had died from AIDS. They also think that the people who visit the centre may be HIV-positive, or have AIDS.*
> (Researcher:) *Do you think that by doing so the guardians are helping you* (the orphans)?
> (Female youth:) *No!*
> (Researcher:) *What advice would you give to the guardians?*
> (Female youth:) *They should listen to what the children tell them. Xx* (name of the organisation) *should also educate them, since if a child tries to explain to them (the guardians) they will not understand, they will understand when xx educates them.*

Here the adolescents themselves raised the issues of who has the right (legitimacy) to ask questions, raise worries and to explain, and who has credibility when addressing sensitive issues. Obviously the orphaned adolescents themselves felt that they were not listened to by their guardians, and when they were asked how the support organisation could improve their situation, they wanted the organisation's members to visit and talk to their guardians.

It was obviously easier for these adolescents to talk to and give advice to other young orphans:

> (Female youth:) *I advise them* (the other orphans) *not to engage in prostitution, or smoking bang* (marihuana). *They should feel that it will reach a time when God will help them and they also get support from different people. They should be very careful because this hardship of life can force them to engage in prostitution, which will put them into risk of contracting "Ugonjwa wa Kisasa"* (HIV). *....*
> *I advise my fellow orphans not to engage themselves in luxury things "Anasa" which can put them into temptation ....*

They also had opinions on what kinds of information could be important to them and on the form such information could be given in:

> (Female youth:) *I advise them that they have to be attentive and listen to different sources of information which they receive as it will help them, for example role plays with HIV/AIDS messages, effect of drug use, early pregnancy and abortion. There was a time when a certain organisation, I do not remember the name, taught*

us about AIDS using role play whereby they were playing with a glass throwing it to each other until the glass broke! And the message behind that was: do not allow anyone to play with your life as it may break easily like how the glass broke. Do not give a chance to anyone to destroy your future life.
- Others taught us through "Vikargosi" (puppetry).
(Researcher:) *Do you think such education / information is important to you?*
(Female youth:) *Yes, of course, because through getting those informations from different organisations, we can be able to get a variety of information other than AIDS, such as the menstrual cycle, what we are supposed to do when we are bleeding, as well as problems related to early pregnancy and drug abuse.*

In another study among 12 to 17 years old AIDS orphans, conducted in Dar es Salaam (Mrumbi 2006), it became evident that no one had talked to the orphans about what their parents had suffered from and why they died. It was through rumours from neighbours and based on how people avoided them, they understood that their parents had died from AIDS. These adolescents said that the interviewer (a Tanzanian male psychologist) was the first person ever to talk directly to them about their parents' deaths and about AIDS. No one had addressed them on these essential issues and no one had talked to them on issues concerning their own health. They expressed relief when they could finally express their feelings and raise their concerns. They also raised issues of the legal and moral rights of children and youth:

We have a right *to know what our parents suffered from and why they died. We have a* right *to know how AIDS is transmitted and how we can protect our own lives!*

Based on these and similar statements from other studies (Bjørgo, 2001) we may realise that probably we – as adults, parents, teachers, health educators, and researchers - have a lot to learn from the adolescents themselves about their needs and how we can help to promote their reproductive health. Through working with the adolescents we often discover phenomena of importance – phenomena that deviate from the more generalised picture. Such deviations and exceptions are of central importance when working with change processes.

Ethical dilemmas involved in participatory approaches

New research paradigms raise new ethical dilemmas – dilemmas of a different kind. The relationship between the researcher (the outsider) and the participants themselves (the insiders), in our case the adolescents, is not based on equality. Information given to us may be very sensitive within the given cultural context and within the given historical point of time. How we handle the information is of the utmost importance and may have significant consequences for the adolescents themselves. The power imbalance in the relationship between adolescents and adults, whether these adults are parents, other guardians, teachers or other important people in the community, is obvious. The vulnerability of young people concerns not only the risks directly related to their reproductive health, but even risks in terms of exposing their "morally inappropriate" worries, exposing questions they ask that "are not supposed to be asked" and in terms of voicing opinions on issues where youth are not supposed to have opinions. The vulnerability becomes particularly evident in the case of orphans who feel that they may even risk losing the little support and security that they have.

Some participatory researchers (Elden & Levin, 1991) have remarked about the participatory research approach:

> Oddly enough, for a communication process aimed at empowerment, power equality, and democracy, inequality is a hallmark of the dialogical relationship. Insiders and outsiders have different power and knowledge bases. The outside expert has much more powerful and explicit "sense making" models. Indeed the researcher could be said to be in the business of being professional sense-makers. (Elden & Levin, 1991:135)

The awareness of the power imbalance is thus still an ethical challenge to the researcher and to those who use participatory approaches. It is essential to understand the diverse life circumstances of adolescents in order to be able to promote environments conducive to empowering young people to avoid sexual risks, and to protect and promote their reproductive health. The needs of adolescents are varied. Such variations may be important for how we develop and manage good health promotion programmes. By co-operating with adolescents on these important and sensitive issues we also risk exposing them to new kinds of difficulties in their relations to more powerful adults that they may be dependant upon. Through cross-cultural research collaborations and participation with adolescents themselves, we may identify existing cultural norms and practices that may be oppressive and endanger the reproductive health of young people. Norms and practices are also shifting in changing societies. These factors should remind us all that in our work to promote adolescent reproductive health, we must continue to raise questions related to ethics and we must always look for unintended side-effects of our own research approaches and health promotion programmes. The answers to the resolution of ethical dilemmas cannot always be found in international or national ethical guidelines and regulations. We need to continuously sensitise our ethical awareness in order to be able to identify relevant ethical dilemmas and to work jointly to find ways of resolving such dilemmas.

II

Contextual Aspects of
Adolescent Sexual and Reproductive Health

5. From Initiation Rituals to AIDS Education

Entering Adulthood at the Turn of the Millennium

Graziella Van den Bergh[1]

Abstract

In this chapter, I discuss some historical, socio-cultural, and politico-economic processes framing sexual initiation in urbanising sub-Saharan Africa. Departing from the fact that appropriate guidance is vital for young people in the era of AIDS, I first describe past practices regulating children's transition to adulthood in various settings. Initiation rituals marked, and in some places still mark, the inception of sexual relations. In earlier times, sexual initiation seemed to be strictly controlled by the older generation, and transfer of knowledge on sexuality was their responsibility. There was a great diversity of rules and norms according to the socio-cultural context. In today's increasingly urbanising and multi-ethnic communities, the inception of sexual relations seems more and more to be regulated by the youth themselves. A case study from Tanzania shows that the uncertain post-colonial context, new education systems and the impact of the AIDS pandemic seem to go along with an intergenerational crisis of authority. A characteristic of the negotiation of sexual relations is its commodification, something making the youngest more vulnerable in a poor socio-economic context. A comparative analysis points to how these relations can be understood as increasingly individualised gift exchanges, where gender, age and class hierarchies play an important role. I point to how institutions such as the school and the clinic interfere with the negotiation of sexual and power relations, while adults operate between hesitance and coercion when controlling knowledge, thus poorly responding to young people's needs. The ideological underpinning of the regulation of sexual onset points to the importance of situating local institutions in a global setting of opportunities and constraints. Finally, I point to the value of a holistic, multi-sectoral approach when measures are to be chosen to increase life-skills among girls and boys, and to promote intergenerational communication on the issue of sexuality and HIV prevention.

---

1. Grateful thanks are due to Prof. Gunnar Kvaale, Centre for International Health, University of Bergen, for suggesting my participation during the last Adolescent Reproductive Health Network conference in Nairobi. Thanks are also due to the Faculty of Health and Social Sciences, Bergen University College, for facilitating the completion of my two chapters in this book. Collegial thanks are due to Dr. Haldis Haukanes and Dr. Gaudencia Mutema, Centre for Women's and Gender Research and Dr. Marguerite Lorraine Daniel, Hemil Centre, University of Bergen, as well as to the Editors and the NAI reviewers for critical comments and proof-reading.

Youth in changing sub-Saharan contexts

Since the advent of the HIV epidemic, research has increasingly demonstrated how sexual health and sexual relations cannot be understood separately from the broader social context where they evolve (Bond et al., 1997; Kalipeni et al., 2005). This is not less true in the case of youth, and historical and political events, social cultural organisation and economic resources must be considered in order to situate adolescents' lives.

One may ask what position youth hold in sub-Saharan settings at the turn of the millennium. Economic crisis, political instability and the marginalisation of Africa on the international scene are recurrent characteristics of the general situation in many countries (Chabal, 1996; UN, 2000). Structural adjustment programmes such as those imposed in the 1980's and 1990's seemed to go hand in hand with a weakening of the state in the provision of social and health services, the latter especially affecting vulnerable groups (Ekwempu et al., 1990; Mbelle, 1996; Meghji, 1996; Stromquist, 1999). In spite of the Millennium Development Goals (MDGs) and a post-adjustment focus on poverty reduction strategies, opportunities for education and employment for youths continue to decline (UN, 2006), and young people may still be characterised as "a lost generation" (Cruise O' Brien, 1996) in a number of contexts where poverty, civil unrest, migration and demographic expansion still prevail (Honwana & De Boeck, 2005). Societal stress is reflected by the increasing use of substances as well as by the prevalence of suicide by youths (Kilonzo & Kaaya, 1994). Moreover, as the present anthology suggests, countries in sub-Saharan Africa are often leading when it comes to adolescent morbidity, unsafe abortion or deaths from reproductive health problems (Barnett & Schueller, 2000), and they account for the largest numbers of youths between 15 and 24 living with HIV, where most of them are girls[1] (UNAIDS, 2004; WHO et al., 2007). This suggests the even more important role of the adult generation in guiding young people into adulthood and sexual life (Harcourt, 1997). In the economic recession that spans the continent, understanding intergenerational dynamics is more important than ever.

---

1. Sub-Saharan Africa has just 10% of the world's population, but it is home to about 60% of all those living with HIV. Among young people between 15–24 years, about 6.9% of the girls and 2.2% of the boys were living with HIV at the end of 2004 (UNAIDS, 2004)

The regulation of the youth's sexuality, from past to present

When defining the "body-politics" of sexuality, Foucault refers to the regulation, surveillance, and control of bodies (individual and collective) in sexuality, reproduction and sickness. As he puts it:

> Sexuality must not be described as a stubborn drive ... It appears rather as an especially dense transfer point for relations of power: between men and women, young people and old people, parents and off-spring, teachers and students, priests and laity, an administration and a population. (Foucault 1998: 103)

The purpose of this chapter is to provide a historical and politico-economic interpretation of some of the radical changes which have occurred in regard to children's socialisation into adulthood in a globalising context. In the field of health promotion, such an anthropological contribution may help explain empirical findings and broaden their application beyond specific locations in time and space (Bledsoe & Pison, 1994). In the era of AIDS, it may help explain the social production of disease (Schoepf, 2001).

Historically, sexual initiation was part of initiation rituals performed in most sub-Saharan countries (Mair, 1969; Paulme, 1963; La Fontaine, 1985). In many rural contexts, these are still practised, though to a lesser extent or in changed forms. These rituals were the necessary social preliminary to the entry into adulthood and to the inception of sexual relations. Thus, sexual initiation was controlled by the parents[1] and by other elders in the community, and transfer of knowledge on sexuality was the responsibility of the adult generation. These rituals also formalised the social control of female sexuality and fertility within lineages and between males, something which was further confirmed by marriage and bride-wealth exchanges (Rubin, 1975).

Such as will be discussed below, many youth living in urbanising settings apparently enter into sexual life more independently, and the commodification of sexuality seems to be an expanding phenomenon which increases young people's vulnerability. I will trace processes framing the making of female and male identities in an impoverished environment, because this has important implications for the youth's life-chances.

---

1   In several African contexts, a number persons may be defined as "the parents". For instance, in Tanzania, a mother may be "mama mzazi", being the biological mother, and "mama mdogo" or "mama mkubwa", the younger or older sister of the mother. The sisters and brothers of the father have also specific and different parental functions.

Sexual initiation and the socio-cultural context: A historical perspective

Pre-independence societies and cultural variety

An important feature to be noted at the outset in regard to initiation rituals and the regulation of youths' sexual onset world-wide, is the enormous variation in norms to be inculcated and followed. According to anthropological narratives covering pre-colonial and colonial sub-Saharan Africa, pre-marital sex could be permitted, expected or sanctioned within different ethnic groups and societies (Mair, 1969). Formal instruction was usually given at puberty rites, which laid much emphasis on moral norms, sex and marital duties. Sexual abstinence was not always regarded as a virtue in itself, and for the unmarried youth, sexual activity could be permitted when it did not lead to conception, and when confined within prescribed limits of time and space (Mair, 1969).

Among many of the peoples in East Africa for instance, pre-marital sex was permitted in defined circumstances. Sometimes pre-marital sex was organised, such as among the Kikuyu of Kenya (Ahlberg, 1991), or through age-grade institutions as among the pastoral Masaai of Kenya and Tanzania. For the latter, sex was allowed with uninitiated girls as young as 11 years, and as long as it did not lead to pregnancy. This seems still to be practised today, with the mothers of the girls facilitating the event (Mair, 1969; Talle, 1994). Among the Kipsigis of Kenya, a hut was built by the boys with their fathers' help for the purpose of sleeping with their sweethearts. However, pregnancy before initiation, (not before marriage), was considered particularly shocking, and could end with either infanticide or suicide by the pregnant girl. On the other hand, with the Luhya of Kenya, it was the girls who slept in a common hut and had their lovers there. Sometimes pre-marital relationships were regarded as an element of courtship, as with the Nuer of Sudan, where the girl could allow full intercourse to a youth who intended to marry her. In contrast to this, as with the Luhya, a man who intended to marry a girl should not make sexual advances to her, but behaved in a formal and distant manner (Mair, 1969). In some cases, girl's virginity was valued as well, such as among the Ha, the Chagga or the Sukuma of Tanzania. To ascertain this, physical examination could be performed before marriage (Van Sambeek, 1949; Dundas, 1968; Mair, 1969).

In the case of Southern Africa, Mair describes that initiation schools practising circumcision were held for boys by the Xhosa, Tembu and Fingo peoples. This simultaneous initiation seemed to create a corporate sense among all the boys in one locality. After migration took off and after the increase of inter-ethnic marriage, it seems as if circumcision lost its former ritual value when taken out of its tribal context (Mair, 1969: 34). For girls, pre-marital chastity and virginity were often the ideal in pre-colonial times, and social censure was directed against the unmarried girl who became pregnant. For instance, traditionally, among the Zulu, there was only a choice between two alternatives: marriage, or the payment of a fine by the boy, which closed the matter (Krige, 1930: in Mair, 1969).

In the ethnic groups of Central Africa, living in what is today called the Democratic Republic of Congo, Angola, Zambia or Malawi, rules of marriage and family life differed in many ways from those of the southern Bantu, according to Mair (1969). Typical, though not universal, is the system of matrilineal descent, which is characterized by a stronger relationship of the child to her/his mother's kin. In the north-eastern part of the region, special emphasis was laid on the initiation of girls. These were betrothed before puberty, and the initiation rites, which followed as closely as possible on the first menstruation, were the immediate preliminary of marriage. A girl should therefore not become pregnant before initiation, as the ceremony gave the appropriate magical preparation for adult sexual life. For an uninitiated girl to bear a child was regarded with real horror by the Bemba, and to the Yao, it was so important to prevent this that by the 1950's they had advanced the initiation age so that the girls went through the ceremonies at 9 or 10 years old. For the boys among the Ila, Luba, Yao and Wiko, initiation rituals are described as a combination of trials of endurance, fertility magic, and sexual and moral endurance (Mair, 1969).

Similar variety in the preparation, codification and practice of initial sexual relations amongst youths is described for West Africa. The extremes of severity and tolerance are represented by the Nupe, who prohibit pre-marital sex all together, and the Korongo and Mesakin of the Nuba Hills in Sudan with whom "premarital licence is complete, and chastity and virginity play no part" (Nadel, 1942 in: Mair, 1969:118).

Thus, initiation rituals varied highly in practice and in meaning across ethnic and geographic settings, although they shared some common features. The rituals represented moral schools where instruction was provided at puberty (Richards, 1982). The ceremonies also marked a division of the sexes, which produced the justification for male domination, even in matrilineal societies (La Fontaine, 1985). It can be assumed that the hierarchic and gendered norms and rules regulating sexual onset were occasionally contested but most often followed by the young, and that they were effectively imposed by the parent generation.

The colonial impact

However, colonial regimes of cash cropping, mining and labour migration in Central and Southern Africa brought about a break-up of the family and traditional household patterns, in the sense of not only a weakening of parental control, but of the actual separation of husbands from wives and children from parents and the extended family (Mair, 1969). In the meantime, children were often left in the charge of an elder child or a neighbour, who may not have had the same compelling sense of responsibility towards them as a relative. The development of the cash economy had effects in the substitution of individual wage earning for the joint work of kinsmen, and in the economic independence of the younger generation. Already by the 1930's, this had resulted in increased bride-wealth payments, which again led to an increase in the interval between betrothal and marriage. In many places, this resulted in pre-marital pregnancies, which were sanctioned to a decreasing degree. Locally, these changes were (and still are) popularly attributed to the curtailment of traditional instruction at puberty and the increased individual freedom of girls and boys from parental and adult authority (Mair, 1969; Van den Bergh, forthcoming). The organisation outside the family for inculcating norms and rules in the next generation was weakened, and it was difficult for parents to meet these needs when they had to earn money. The ease with which a seducer could avoid sanction and disappear in some distant place, as well as the decline in the belief in supernatural punishment were also given as reasons (Mair, 1969). According to older Pondo informants of Southern Africa in the 1930's, the refusal of courts to recognise the claim of a father for a gift from a young man for the privilege of "sweet-hearting" with his daughter had done much to increase irresponsibility among boys (Hunter, 1933: in Mair, 1969).

Many of the pre-colonial rituals relied on ideologies of inequality between men and women and between the old and the young, and belief in supernatural punishment and social sanctions was indispensable to maintain these principles.[1] It is documented that whenever coercive elements started weakening, and when youth perceived the rites as oppressive, they tried to

---

1. In the hierarchy of beings within African cosmology, older people had greater proximity to the spirit world. Youth who disobeyed their elders risked falling out of favour with the spirits (personal communication by Gaudencia Mutema, October 2002).

escape. As Geisler (2000) points to a critique of the politics of "tradition" in South Africa[1], young women have not always been keen to participate in such rituals. As early as the 1940's, a Tonga girls' rebellion was reported against puberty ceremonies (Geisler, 2000). Thus, these often gerontocratic institutions rapidly changed in meaning and content. In the following section, I will discuss how the introduction of a cash economy and of primary education may have influenced gender and intergenerational relations.

Post-independence and the introduction of modern education

Following independence and the organisation of universal primary education (UPE), the passage to adulthood was radically prolonged in many sub-Saharan settings, thus calling for new social roles for youth. Education was considered by many to be a good thing within a positive ideology of "development", and it is plausible that for the privileged adolescent generation of that time, codes of abstinence or/and avoidance of pregnancy until one was close to achieving higher education or marriage was pursued. According to some of my Tanzanian well-educated informants in their late thirties or forties (both males and females), it was not unusual that they had passed 20 years of age before engaging in sexual relations (Van den Bergh, forthcoming). At least, so they claimed. This has been documented for highly educated groups in other countries as well, such as in Nigeria (Orobaton, 2000).

However, this may be a trait only characterising a small minority of adults in colonial and independent Africa. Indeed, by the late sixties, premarital sex relations were said to be extremely common in Southern Africa (Mair, 1969). At the same time, opportunities for sex seemed to increase. For instance, the practice of secluding girls at their first menstruation and the warning against continuing the sexual play with boys which was usual between children seemed to be abandoned altogether in urban locations. By then, going to school could be used as a pretext for evading the parental eye, and slipping out unnoticed into the bush or onto the street. Girls would for instance attend the cinema with young men, and the latter were said to regard the girl's acceptance of their escort as implying a promise of sexual

---

1. After reviewing the practice of girls' initiations in Southern Africa today, she concludes that these ceremonies perpetuate male dominance and that in all cases they are informed by the wishes and needs of men. She mentions a recent revival of virginity checks. In the context of AIDS, this means that girls are made responsible for their chastity, and ultimately for stopping AIDS, even though they are daily at risk of being raped (Geisler, 2000).

intercourse (Mair, 1969).[1] At the same time, personal economic transactions seemed to increasingly accompany the negotiation of sexual relations.

Anthropological literature has extensively illustrated the role of symbolic and material transactions in transferring legal rights in a woman's labour and in her sexual and reproductive potential through the institution of marriage and bride-wealth (Levi-Strauss, 1969; Scherer, 1965; Goody & Tambiah, 1973; Kuper, 1982). However, according to Mair (1969), after the colonial introduction of cash, a mercenary element that was not present in the old days was introduced, thus replacing the symbolic gifts and services traditionally included in the marriage formalities. This commoditising trend seems to have been influencing an increasing number of social relations.

The commodification of sexuality

Indeed, in several African countries of the 70s and 80s, such as Zambia, Liberia, Uganda, Ghana, Nigeria and Kenya, women's increasing reliance on relationships with men to improve their own social and economic status has been described (Gage & Bledsoe, 1994; Bond et al., 1997; Nelson, 1987). In 1992, when discussing sexuality and the problems of AIDS in Africa from an African feminist standpoint, McFadden stated that AIDS was confronting societies with the unravelling of myths surrounding female/male sexuality and adult/adolescent sexuality (McFadden, 1992). She defined three reasons why sex was essentially performed in still patriarchal, post-colonial societies, though with individual and gendered variations: she named reproduction, pleasure and money, with the lines between these three parameters remaining fluid (McFadden, 1992: 167). She suggested that sex may have become one more consumer item, and this may have led to women being viewed as consumer items as well (ibid.). The perspective of young female sexuality promoted and exploited as a consumer item is important in the present globalising context.

However, women's economic survival strategies can also be interpreted within a framework of "reciprocal transaction", rather than exploitation. For instance, Adomako Ampofo (1997) explains that for Ghanaian women, engaging in profitable, sexual relationships with men is a compelling reality in

---

1. The young men were reported to go to considerable lengths of physical violence to secure it (Mair, 1969).

Ghana's present economic situation.[1] In Botswana, men's labour migration to neighbouring countries has triggered the development of female-headed households where economic and sexual exchanges between men and women are related in more ways than merely marriage (Gulbrandsen, 1986). In Tanzania, female migration to towns has been described in some cases to entail sexual relations as part of an economic strategy allowing women to send money back to their home villages (see Mascarenhas & Mbilinyi, 1983; Swantz, 1985). Such gendered survival strategies seem to have been reproduced from one generation to the next, in spite of, or along with, the girls' increasing access to education.

Education and the commoditized regulation of young female sexuality

In Sierra Leone for instance, several historical and legal aspects have changed the regulation of sexual relations, and new forms of sexual unions are emerging. Among the youth, the most important trends are the unions of older schoolgirls (Bledsoe, 1980: in Bledsoe & Pison, 1994). Declining economic conditions are said to have put pressure on parents to let their daughters accept school-fees from sponsors or "supporters", who are usually men of wealth and influence. These school-fees imply an investment of either a marital or sexual nature. "Sponsors" may include school-teachers, a phenomenon already observed in 1976 in Ghana by Bleek (1976), or older wealthy bureaucrats in the urban area, called "sugar daddies". Although such support often excludes marriage, girls use such relationships to further their education or job career (Gage & Bledsoe, 1994).

Similar phenomena involving school-youth more specifically have been described in several countries of East, West, Central and Southern Africa (Tumbo-Masabo & Liljeström, 1994; Øye, 1995; Haram, 1995; Schoepf, 1998; Anarfi & Fayorsey, 2000; Kalipeni et al., 2005 etc.). In urban Tanzania, where a secondary school based study was performed, four out of five girls interviewed admitted that they received money from their boy-friends, and in Dar es Salaam, a saying has come about: *Hapendi mtu bali pochi*, literally meaning: "No money, no love" (Komba-Malekela & Liljeström, 1994: 140). According to Tanzanian primary school pupils, this seems to be true for an increasing number of youngsters today (Van den Bergh, forthcoming).

---

1. The scholar refers to both Burns' exchange theory and Mauss' anthropological theory of gift-giving to explain the phenomenon.

The making of sexual relations: A contemporary case

During a one-year fieldwork performed in 1998-1999 in Kigoma Rural and Urban Districts, I examined primary school children's journey to adulthood. Cognitive, socio-cultural, politico-economic and other factors influencing their sexual debut in a poor and refugee-impacted region of western Tanzania were assessed, as well as their coping with problems such as unwanted pregnancy (Van den Bergh, forthcoming). Participant observation in daily life was a necessary method to situate gender, generational, class and kinship relations, though insufficient to provide enough insight into youths' sexual behaviour. Therefore, various qualitative methods were combined, such as in-depth interviews, focus-group discussions, role-plays, etc., and the study also included a quantitative survey. Research was multi-sited, and was conducted in 27 urban and rural primary and secondary schools in two lake-shore districts. I visited clinics, attended seminars and public events as well as setting up small intervention projects. This resulted in multiple accounts about pupils' sexual debut and about the ways they coped with the various consequences of unequal relations and of unprotected sex (Van den Bergh, forthcoming).[1]

The pupils reported about "unruly" behaviour (*uhuni*) many among them adopted, and which only a few of their parents seemed to be aware of. As I elaborate elsewhere (Van den Bergh, same volume), alleged sexual debut often occurred before 14 years of age for the girls, and the number and type of short relationships was alarming. Yet, neither girls nor boys felt susceptible to AIDS, which was seen as the predicament of "street-youths" and adults.

Relations were induced by boys and men offering small gifts to the girls. The acceptance of these material and symbolic gifts by girls seemed to justify sexual access for those they had received presents from (Van den Bergh,

---

1. The fieldwork was part of my doctoral research project, and material was collected over a period of about 13 months. The study was facilitated by fluent knowledge of Swahili, acquired during six years of living and working in the region, the first time in 1983. Yet, enquiring about children's and youths' sexual relations, as well as on institutions dealing with "disciplining" sexuality, reproduction, health and death implied several ethical and methodological dilemmas. One attempt to cope with these dilemmas was to pursue a participatory research design employing a "dialogic epistemology" (Schoepf, 1995), where the aim was to engage young people in the issue of prevention. Other dilemmas cannot be discussed here, given limitations of space and their being of less relevance; see Van den Bergh (forthcoming) for fuller discussion.

1996; 2008)[1]. Then, it seemed almost impossible for the girls to refuse sex, and if they did so, force was resorted to. These gift exchanges could, over the short term, develop into more lasting relations of support with older partners. When problematic situations arose, such as cases of unwanted pregnancy or forced sex, reciprocity seemed to foster antagonism between males and females, and between the young and the old.

Sexual initiation and knowledge transfer in times of AIDS

According to the pupils of Kigoma, the adult generation fell short in guiding young people about sexual matters, and it was repeatedly confirmed that parents, teachers and health-workers were not conveying useful preventive skills.

Youths' worlds, parents' worlds: Gaps in awareness

A first feeling the youths expressed was that many parents felt that school-expenses were a burden they could not always afford. Indeed, in Kigoma by 1999, drop-out from primary school was high, and only about 5 per cent would proceed with secondary education (Regional Education Officer (REO), 2001). In the poorest neighbourhoods and lake-shore villages, meagre educational and vocational prospects seemed to result in girls wanting to get married early. This also could elicit transactional patterns in sexual relations, where some girls would get older partners. Sometimes, it seemed to promote the same trend as in urban slums, where parents may comply or even suggest to their daughters to offer their sexual services, such as in the slums of Nairobi (Zulu et al., 2005).

Besides the weakened position of deprived families, the gap between pupils' norms and practices and their parents' expectations was said to be irreducible. As put by a group of pupils: *"Some parents do know about their children's sexual activity, others don't. If they get to know, they will take action. They may follow them up closely, they may tell them about AIDS, but the youths will not care, because they do not believe that they may get AIDS."* Thus, by and large, parents were kept oblivious to their children's early steps into the sexual arena. Pupils explained that: *"Times are changing, you know, we are soon entering a new century..."* Consumer goods such as snacks, shoes

---

1. Mauss' theory of gift giving (1990) can be applied as an analytical perspective for understanding the reciprocal relations between the sexes. Yet, when situations become precarious, "negative" reciprocity is not to be excluded (Van den Bergh, 1996; Van den Bergh, forthcoming; Narotzky & Moreno, 2002).

or clothes seemed to be symbols of a global youth culture which attracted many youths. The youths defined this search for new symbols of identity as the result of their "greediness" (*tamaa*) making them opt for immoral behaviour. Yet, in spite of this, they rejected their parents' attitudes as old-fashioned.

Notwithstanding, if pregnancy occurred, some of the parents would pay for an abortion so as to hide the shameful event and allow their daughter to go on with schooling. Others would try to force the girl to say who made her pregnant, but many times, the girl was afraid of revealing it, because the boy or man might not be able or willing to care for her. The parents' reactions would vary according to their ambitions on behalf of their daughters, or how much they trusted her morals. Trust was, in fact, not always present, as evidenced when rape occurred. Some parents were said to react in the following way when told by their children that they had been raped: "...*labda na wewe unavijua...*" (...Perhaps you knew what you were to get?). Therefore, many girls would keep it secret.

Finally, much false and little correct information was almost exclusively transferred by peers, sisters, brothers, or friends. In the case of the girls, the mothers were sometimes talking with them, while fathers were nearly absent from the picture. In Kigoma by 1999, pupils never named initiation rites as providing "useful" knowledge on sexual issues.[1] This seems to be true in many places in Tanzania as well as in other countries, and most often, initiation rituals, if still existing, seem to have no preventive effect in the era of AIDS (Klepp et al., 1995; Leshabari et al., 1997; Geisler, 2000; Rivers & Aggleton, 2004; Van den Bergh, forthcoming).

If sexual initiation once was clearly controlled by the parents, today, sexual knowledge transfer has been increasingly relegated to the modern education sector.

Sexual education and the role of the school

However, in Kigoma, with an education sector having serious shortages of facilities and of teachers (REO, 2001), sexual education was not yet a real concern. Among pupils, there seemed to be extremely poor knowledge about bodily maturation, sexuality or reproductive health issues, also at the secondary school level. For instance, among all the participants in the thirty groups, very few really understood what the menstrual cycle implied. At the

1   The secrecy of the rituals might be one reason (McCurdy, 2000). Yet, the fact that the rites were postponed until the girl was older, and that many families could not afford to pay for the ceremony is another likely reason.

same time, awareness about power inequalities and self-assertive skills was not stimulated.

In Tanzania, the topic was on the teacher's curriculum and on the pupils' schedule as part of Family Life Education and in Biology during the last year of primary school, and as "AIDS education" which had been campaigned for some years earlier. In practice, most schools in this marginal region did not provide it. "Family life education" and sexuality related topics seemed to be considered taboo. The interest on the part of the pupils was very clear though, as the questions during the research sessions confirmed.

The potential effectiveness of well-taught "AIDS education" turned out to be more than evident in one of the schools in rural Kigoma. This school could be characterised as more resourceful, as most of the pupils were children of military personnel employed at the National Service Camp located nearby. The pupils there knew about an officer who had died of AIDS, and they were well-informed about how to avoid getting infected. They seemed to distinguish themselves from pupils from neighbouring villages, whom they described as ignorant and careless about the possible consequences of engaging in sex. They seemed to have acquired, at school, the awareness and skills necessary to envision AIDS as a problem which could affect them, but which they also could avoid. This was true both for girls and for boys.

However, they were quite unique when it came to risk perception and reflectivity about being young and having sexual relations. So their committed female teacher was responsible for teaching about AIDS.[1] In nearly every other school out of the 27 we visited, pupils viewed the teachers' shyness as one of the reasons why the subject was not taught. Shame and lack of communication skills in addressing youths on the subject of sexuality seemed to characterise teachers and parents alike. If knowledge was transferred at all, it was said to be superficial and inefficient. And, accordingly, own risk perception was very poor among pupils. Because people known to have died of AIDS usually are older than pupils, many adolescents seemed to consider that HIV infection did not concern them.

In addition, the school applied some new control mechanisms of the youth's sexual activity, and these may be interpreted as rudiments of former disciplining techniques. For example, after suggestion by educational authorities, school-girls could be called to the local health centre to be checked for pregnancy. Further, in spite of national guidelines suggesting that pregnant girls should return to school after delivery, the reality was that most of

---

1. She was said by the pupils to be a very committed teacher and was talked about with respect.

them were expelled from school for ever, thus hampering their educational and economic independence. Such prevailing control and sanction methods to prevent pregnancy among pupils would be unlikely to function, in the long run, in promoting HIV prevention among girls.

Another problem which may affect intergenerational communication is the local and economic strategies of those expected to educate, guide and treat today's children and youths. Both health and education institutions and personnel are increasingly involved in an informal economy and commercialisation of their services, the latter often transgressing ethical and professional codes and basic human rights. One example is the expanding institution of private, paid tuition at the primary school level, creating layers of pupils who can afford and those who cannot afford a better education. Another example is the commercialisation of health care services, such as abortion for instance, which though illegal, is widely practised (Van den Bergh, forthcoming; Rasch & Silberschmidt, 2008). There is a clear trend where state responsibility for basic needs is still weakened, in spite of the millennium goals. Where poverty still prevails, the tendency towards privatising sectors such as health, social welfare and education makes these services unequally – or even less – accessible.

Adolescent sexual health services: "Hot topic" or only rhetoric?

The third important arena where young people today might acquire life-skills to help them safely into sexual adulthood is the health sector. Yet, as indicated above, the silence around and illegitimacy of young unmarried sexuality does not facilitate this function.

Indeed, as primary school-girls suggested, to avoid unwanted pregnancy was almost impossible. Many standard V and VI pupils got pregnant, it was said: *"But what to do? They do not manage to find ways of avoiding pregnancy. They do not know how to do ... So, they decide to do it just like that, without caring about whether they will get pregnant or not. You know, they do not dare to go to the clinic* [for family planning]. *To get contraceptives is not proper for a school-girl…"* In spite of guidelines suggesting the provision of contraception to whoever needs it, unmarried girls most often relied on informal channels, such as drugstores or private health entrepreneurs. Indeed, in many places, contraception is only provided after giving birth, and the Mother-and-Child Health (MCH) clinic becomes for girls a belated site for receiving information. An option for them was to lie about their own age and marital status at the clinic, to obtain contraception, yet, HIV prevention was seldom addressed.[1] The same was true for girls admitted for abortion. When unwanted pregnancy occurred, girls often attempted to have an abortion, either by their own means, or by paying for a safe intervention in a health facility.[2] Reproductive health workers at all levels could then be a potential channel for information and guidance. Yet, the illegality of abortion made it happen in secrecy, with no time for good post-abortion counselling. For those admitted with complications, overworked nurses with little or no training on the issue of youths' specific needs were another obstacle. Moreover, paternalistic and authoritarian attitudes towards girls most often resulted in frightening them away.[3] Considering that integration of prevention and cure, as well as of sexual and reproductive health services was lacking even for adults entitled to receive these, youths who were perceived to have behaved improperly would get even less care.

Entering adulthood in the 21st century

In this chapter, I have reviewed how sexual initiation of the youth has been organised in different sub-Saharan contexts, from pre-colonial and colonial times and up to the present. The resulting picture is one of African youths who wish to have more say in their lives, and who embrace the new opportunities brought after independence. But these new models of the "good life" are difficult to navigate through. Under the cloak of progress in which the youth believe, there are many pitfalls, and new sub-groups and hierarchies are created, which in turn produce and/or reproduce oppression and exploitation.

I have pointed to how the regulation of young sexuality and fertility, and the transfer of potentially life-saving skills to school-aged children are in crisis. Adult institutions are characterised by insecurity about which values ought to be pursued. This generates multiple crises of authority, where the construction of gender and increasingly commoditized social relations play an important role. Parents and relatives, the community at large, to-

---

1. Among older girls using contraception, the most popular and allegedly most adopted method was hormonal contraception, while the condom was almost never used.
2. Fieldwork in the health sector implied a collaborative research approach with participant observation during clinics, training courses and AIDS sensitization seminars, and group and in-depth interviews with health-workers and service-seekers. A youth-friendly clinic was also run.
3. For boys, a likely arena where they could receive sexual health information was when seeking treatment for sexually transmitted infections. Yet, also among them, self-medication and overburdened services were important barriers.

gether with rural elites such as teachers and health-workers grapple with the contradictions of changing cultural norms in a social-economic context where adult self-confidence is difficult to boost. Various institutions seem to react with discourses of silence on young people's lives and risks. As was formerly the case of elders, their authority seems to rest on withholding knowledge, and it is this which supports and justifies their control of the youths (Meillassoux, 1981).

The problem of the unsettled and disturbed status of youth in societies in transition is certainly not a new one, nor is it peculiar to the African setting. Margaret Mead, in 1929, described the American civilisation as an example triggering the restlessness of youth, with many immigrant strains, dozens of conflicting standards of conduct, hundreds of religious sects and shifting economic conditions (Mead, 1949). This picture seems to describe the situation in several countries today. Increasingly impoverished economies, the frail social institutions where children are growing as well as the new and fictive images of youth, development, freedom and sexuality brought by global media all contribute to the youth's aspirations for something else. Such processes seem to strengthen youths' resistance to traditional forms of authority and to forms of sexuality that they consider as out-dated.

A popular lay explanation for the problems that youths are facing in times of AIDS is the breakdown of traditional institutions previously guiding them into adulthood. I suggest that it is questionable whether knowledge distribution and power hierarchies as they applied in the past would have curbed an epidemic today. Indeed, a scrutiny of these practices illustrates that, although traditional mores enhanced the social order, many of the practices inculcated during initiation rites would be unsafe in the context of an epidemic.

Another important feature is that the previous variation in forms of control by the adult generation differs in a contrasting way from today's youth's apparently uniform, self-regulated and unprotected entry into the sexual arena. Yet, these new strategies which the youth adopt seem in fact to replicate former age, gender and class identities and power constellations. Indeed, through the commoditization of sexuality, the young and female remain dominated by patriarchal structures, which are locally strengthened by increasing poverty and class differences, and exacerbated by global neo-liberal economic structures. These economic underpinnings, in a context of AIDS, significantly increase children's and the youth's vulnerability because they then remain easily manipulated by elders. The issue of adolescent sexual health and life-chances thus calls for holistic interventions at different levels: the transnational, national, community and individual level.

Concluding remarks

In times of AIDS, adult guidance into adulthood should make young people aware of gender, generational and class hierarchies, as well as of their sexual vulnerability. An important measure might be to radically increase educational and vocational opportunities promoting young people's self-worth and economic independence. At a transnational level, the MDGs are a step in the right direction, yet, as presented in the 2006 Report, gendered and geographical gaps persist in education and the labour market (UN, 2006). Moreover, in the era of globalisation of the market and of the media, the promotion of subordinating consumption patterns and gender roles (such as the spread of pornographic material), and gendered violence need to be focused upon (Van den Bergh, forthcoming). At national levels, young people need to be put at the centre of attention, through multi-sectoral commitment, systematic involvement of the local communities, and intensive training of professionals, such as teachers, health workers, religious and political leaders and other brokers (Ng'weshemi et al., 1997). In addition, the methodical implementation of young people's sexual rights has proved to be fruitful (Sundby, 2006). At the local level, in addition to promoting economic development, there seems to be a tremendous need to work with the adult generation – both women and men – as transmitters of knowledge, with the aim of coping with declining parental authority and unequal gender relations. Some elements from the past might be adapted, as in the case of rituals celebrating and reinforcing shared female identity and the collective strength of women (Arnfred in Geisler, 2000; McCurdy, 2000; Boddy, 1989).[1]

However, the questioning and contestation of systems which are perpetuating young people's subordination should be stimulated. For instance, in Kenya, girls' increasing self-assertiveness has made them oppose female

---

1. Among the Tonga of Zambia, young girls look forward to initiation rituals, as these involve weeks of celebrations, where the girls are the centre of attention, freed from daily work duties, and receiving presents (personal communication by Peggy Chilembo, Centre for Women's and Gender Research, University of Bergen, October 18, 2002).

circumcision rituals. In order to assert their individual right to refuse genital cutting, they took their own parents to court (NRK, 2002).[1]

In times of AIDS, there is a need for constantly and critically assessing appropriate sexual and reproductive health education, services and rights for the youths. Awareness-raising among children on issues of gender relations and human rights might be most effective through involving the adult female and male generation and by empowering whole communities towards social development.

---

1. The documentary film made by Kim Longinotto: "The day I will never forget", was discussed during a Norwegian television programme on October 21, 2002 (Safari).

6. Illegal Abortion among Adolescents in Dar es Salaam

Vibeke Rasch and Margrethe Silberschmidt[1]

Abstract

The objective was to identify adolescent girls who had undergone illegally induced abortions, and describe the girls' sexual activity, their relations with their partners, their contraceptive use, and the circumstances which characterised the induction. A hospital-based study was conducted among adolescent girls who were admitted to a district hospital during the period July to September 1997. In total, 51 girls who had obtained an illegal abortion were identified and participated in an in-depth interview. Adolescent girls with illegal abortions were found to be sexually active at an early age. They had sex regularly with different sexual partners. Sometimes they dated more than one partner at a time. They did not attend the family planning clinics, because 1) they were unaware that they could get pregnant, 2) they were unaware that they had the right to contraception, 3) they feared moral judgement from the staff. Instead, many of the girls interviewed relied on access to illegally induced abortion. The few girls who had used contraception in the past had often used the method incorrectly. The majority of the girls had a safe illegal abortion performed at the district hospital at high cost. Those girls who were not able to raise the money involved in having a safe abortion performed had resorted to unsafe procedures. They were subsequently admitted to the hospital because of complications. In conclusion, adolescents with illegally induced abortions are unaware that they are running a great risk of both having an unwanted pregnancy and acquiring STDs/HIV. In order to avoid repeating the process of unprotected intercourse, unwanted pregnancy and subsequently illegal abortion it is essential to link abortion care and family planning together. In addition, the alarming figures on illegal abortions and maternal mortality should be addressed by guaranteeing all women access to safe legal abortion.

---

1. Parts of the results have previously been published in V. Rasch, M. Silberschmidt, Y. Mchumvu, V. Mmary, "Adolescent Girls with Illegally Induced Abortion in Dar es Salaam: The Discrepancy between Sexual Behaviour and Lack of Access to Contraception", *Reproductive Health Matters*, 2000, 8:52–62. The funding of the reserach has come from the Clinical Institute of the University of Southern Denmark.

Introduction

At the Population Conference in Cairo in 1994, the provision of sexuality education and contraceptive services to adolescents not to mention induced abortions was one of the most controversial and also one of the most discussed issues. The issue still continues to stir up controversy in many countries – including Tanzania.

Until 1992, family planning in Tanzania was mainly used for child spacing. Family planning advice and services were therefore given primarily to married clients with at least one child. The consequence of this policy is reflected in a study from 1992 in which it was found that 61 per cent of secondary school pupils were sexually active but only 15 per cent had ever used a contraceptive method (Kapiga et al., 1992). The family planning policy was changed in 1994. According to the new policy guidelines, all males and females of reproductive age, including adolescents, shall have the right of access to family planning information, education and services (Ministry of Health, 1994a). In spite of these changes in the family planning policy, most adolescents are still reluctant to attend the family planning clinics. Consequently they are at substantial risk of experiencing an unwanted pregnancy. Some of these unwanted pregnancies are carried to term, others end in a spontaneous abortion – yet others are terminated by an induced abortion.

In Tanzania, like in many other sub-Saharan African countries, induced abortion is highly restricted and permitted only if the pregnancy is threatening the woman's life. Consequently, women who want to have an unwanted pregnancy terminated have to resort to clandestine and unsafe interventions. According to the conditions in which the abortions are performed and the methods used, a variety of complications may occur. Complications such as sepsis, haemorrhage, genital and abdominal trauma, perforated uterus or poisoning may be fatal. An estimated 5,000,000 unsafe abortions are performed annually in Africa and 34,000 women die from an induced abortion, a number that is equivalent to 13 per cent of all maternal deaths (WHO, 2004b). These deaths could have been avoided if the women/girls had had access to contraception and/or safe legal abortion.

Several studies have been performed among women who had undergone illegally induced abortion. According to these studies the general picture of a woman seeking care for abortion complications is a single woman, without children, less than 20 years old, in school or unemployed. Hospital-based studies not only from Tanzania (Justesen et al., 1992; Rasch et al., 2000a) but also from Ethiopia (Madebo & Tsadic, 1993; Abdella, 1996),

Kenya (Sjöstrand et al., 1995; Lema et al., 1996; Ankomah et al., 1997), and Nigeria (Megafu & Ozumba, 1991; Konje & Obisesan, 1991; Anate et al., 1995) have reported findings which match the above description of women with induced abortion. However, only a few studies have focused on adolescents with illegally induced abortion (Rasch et al., 2000b).

The problem of the unmet contraceptive need and the occurrence of illegal abortion among adolescents is illustrated in a hospital-based study from Dar es Salaam. The study found that more than half of the women admitted with abortion complications were adolescents who had never used contraception (Rasch et al., 1999). It also underlined the discrepancy between adolescent girls' sexual activity and their access to contraception. Based on this, the aim of this present study was to elucidate the reason why the girls in our study did not use any contraception in relation to the intercourse during which they conceived. Related to this, another aim was to acquire more in-depth knowledge of the girls' sexual activity, their relationship with their partners and the circumstances characterising the induction.

Subjects and methods

Dar es Salaam, which is the main commercial city in Tanzania, is divided into three districts. The city has one referral hospital and each district has one district hospital. The study was carried out at one of the district hospitals.

From July to September 1997 all girls aged 15–19 years who were admitted to the hospital with a diagnosis of incomplete abortion were asked for an interview. Only those admitting to an induced abortion were included in the study group. A total of 51 girls were interviewed in-depth in a separate room on the gynaecological ward. A nurse-midwife in the ward with extensive experience in interviewing women with induced abortions conducted the interviews. She worked from guideline questions concerning relationship with partners, sexual activity, access to and use of contraception as well as the circumstances around the induction. She used these questions to focus the discussion but was not limited to asking only those questions. The interviewer was encouraged to have an open discussion, to probe respondents for explanations and further details, and to create a close interaction between the respondent and the interviewer.

Individual interviews were repeatedly discussed in detail between the researchers and the interviewer during data collection. This made it possible to incorporate experience gained during the interviews and to add new guideline questions, in order to deepen understanding. The interviews were conducted in Kiswahili and the interviewer transcribed them in English. Each interview lasted 2–2½ hours. At the end of the data collection all the interviews were computerised and grouped thematically in the following categories: baseline data, partner and relationship with him, sexual activity, contraceptive access and circumstances characterising the induction.

All patients were informed that participation in the study was voluntary and that there would be no negative consequences for further treatment whether they participated or not. Informed consent was obtained orally, since most of the girls feared a lack of anonymity if they signed a consent form. None of the girls who were invited to take part in the study refused to participate.

Results

Socio-economic characteristics

The girls interviewed were aged 15–19. 28 of them were still in school. The remaining girls were employed either as house girls, barmaids, skilled workers (hairdressers, tailors) or engaged in petty trade. Regarding educational level, 7 girls were educated below standard 7 level, 24 had finished standard 7 and the remaining 20 girls were educated above standard 7 level (Table 1).

Relationship with the partner

The girls' relationships with their partner are summarised in Table 1. About half of the girls stated that their partner was already married. 83% were involved in a sexual relationship with men who were aged above 30 years.

A predominant finding was that the girls interviewed had an instrumental approach to their partner. Extracting money or gifts in exchange for sexual services was of major importance for many of the girls' relationships with their partner, whereas sheer love or the expectations of marriage were of secondary importance or none at all. An interview with Joyce, who was a 19 year old form IV student, illustrates this:

> Joyce and her partner, who was 40 years old and married, met each other at a party, which was held for one of Joyce's friends. The man approached Joyce and asked her to come outside. He told her that he had fallen in love with her and wanted to be her friend. That evening they made an appointment for a meeting. Joyce said that the man gave her 5,000 Tsh the first time they met and had intercourse. Other days he gave her 3,000–4,000 Tsh, but not always.

Although, according to Joyce, they were in love with each other she would not continue the relationship if she did not receive money from her partner. As she said, there is no use of a partner who has no money.

This connection between money or presents and sexual relationships was a recurrent finding. It existed to some extent also among girls who had boyfriends of the same age.

Anastasia, a 17 year old form II student who was dating a 22 year old form VI student, told that her boyfriend had given her 2,000 Tsh on their first date. Later on when they met he sometimes gave her money but not always. She knew other girls who were given nothing by their boyfriends, and as she said: Something is better than nothing. Anastasia was now looking for a man who could afford to give her more money. She also told that she had other sexual encounters at the time she got pregnant.

Those girls who had a sexual relationship with an unmarried partner were often promised marriage and considered themselves fiancées. The pregnancies among these girls were in some cases intended, the girl hoping that her partner would marry her if she became pregnant.

Tuli was a 16 year old house girl who considered herself engaged to her boyfriend. He was 30 years old and earned his money by selling oranges near the house where Tuli was working. They had started dating eight months ago when he had told her he was in love with her and wanted to marry her. Tuli told that they were discussing the issue of marriage each time they met. They were both aware of the possibility of Tuli becoming pregnant, but neither of them minded, since Tuli's boyfriend had told her he needed to have a baby with her. Moreover, Tuli thought of a pregnancy as a way to hold on to her boyfriend. When Tuli told her boyfriend about her pregnancy, he denied the possibility that it was he who had impregnated her and accused her of cheating him.

Sexual behaviour

Among the 51 girls interviewed, seven (14%) stated that they had previously had an STD. As described in the literature, gaining trustworthy answers on sexual activity has proven to be difficult due to the sensitive character of the issue (Huygens et al., 1996; Rosenthal et al., 1996). After evaluating the first 35 interviews, it was found that the majority of the girls said that they had had two or three sexual partners (on average three) since their sexual debut. The interviewer was then urged to probe if this really corresponded to the reality. As a result, the average number of sexual partners rose from three to six with the number of sexual partners varying from one to eight in the remaining 16 interviews, and with many of the girls reporting that they had several partners simultaneously. One out of four in the total sample admitted having had more than one sexual partner at the time she got pregnant. These girls did not know who was responsible for their pregnancy.

Forced sex

Many of the girls had experienced forced sex, especially in relation to their first intercourse. The following stories illustrate this finding:

> At her first intercourse, Mariana went to collect water with another girl at a Koran school. That day, the school-teacher called Mariana to a separate room telling her that he wanted to give her the Koran, so that she could study it alone at home. In the room the teacher removed Mariana's underwear by force and raped her. He penetrated both her vagina and her anus. She said she bled a lot.

> Christina, a 16 year old standard 6 student was 15 years old at her first intercourse. It took place early in the morning when she was collecting water together with another girl and a boy. Nearby, there was a half built house. The boy, who was 20 years old, called Christina to the half built house and forced her to have sex with him. Christina shouted and some people heard her. The boy got afraid and ran away.

> Anastasia was 14 years old at her first intercourse. Her parents had a houseboy and one day, when only Anastasia and the houseboy were at home, he called her to his room. Here he forced her to have sex with him. She did not inform her parents when they came home. It was her secret, she said.

All 51 girls interviewed thought that only women who had children were allowed at the family planning (FP) clinics. They were afraid of being considered a prostitute if they attended the FP clinics. A few girls had instead bought contraception from health personnel working at the FP clinic. Apart from one illiterate girl, all the girls interviewed knew about condoms and the vast majority had heard of oral contraceptives and injections (Depo-Provera). However, their knowledge was very superficial, and they were often seriously misinformed about how to use the method properly (e.g. using oral contraceptives and taking the pill only the day they were having intercourse).

The vast majority of the girls had heard about different side effects caused by modern contraception. They had obtained this information from their friends or relatives. Some had also heard that modern contraception might lead to infertility if taken by a girl/woman who had not given birth before. In two cases the girl's mother had advised her not to use contraception, using the argument that modern contraception could cause cancer of the uterus. Other side effects mentioned were irregular bleeding, abdominal pain, hypertension, obesity, and heart palpitations.

The girls' contraceptive use is summarised in Table 2. Here it is revealed that the majority (55%) had never used a contraceptive method. Oral contraceptives had been used by ten girls. The reason they stopped varied. Some had stopped because of experienced side effects (e.g. bleeding twice per month), some because they intended to become pregnant, expecting their partner to marry them, and others had become pregnant while using the method. Condoms had been used by 11 girls and Depo-Provera by three. Among those girls who had used contraception, the method was often used incorrectly or just occasionally. For instance, all the girls who had used Depo-Provera, which is a highly effective contraceptive, had become pregnant while using this contraceptive. This, however, may be explained by the well-known fact that they did not show up for a new injection after expiration of the previous one. A striking finding was that 28 per cent of the girls relied on induced abortion, and had therefore not used any contraception. These girls had often been told by their partner not to worry, as he would help solve the problem if she got pregnant. In 23 cases the partner actually did take responsibility and arranged and paid for the induction.

A common feature for many of the girls interviewed was that their partner refused to use a condom. Different excuses were used such as skin reactions around the penis or telling the girl there was no reason for fearing HIV as he only slept with her. In other cases, the explanation was lack of time, since the intercourse took place in a hurry and under very secret circumstances, and both the girl and her partner were afraid of being discovered. However, the most common reason for not using a condom was that the partner said he did not get full pleasure out of the intercourse if he used a condom, a viewpoint which some of the girls shared.

The following stories illustrate the different reasons for not using contraception:

> Anastasia was a 17 year old form II student. She was aware of the possibility of becoming pregnant. Anastasia had not intended to become pregnant but had not used any contraception. She had heard that birth-control pills might cause cancer of the uterus or lead to infertility if taken by a woman who had not previously given birth. Anastasia and her boyfriend had instead used a condom at

the beginning of their relationship. They stopped using the condom since they found it disturbing both to wear and to remove. Besides, they enjoyed sex more without using it. Furthermore, her boyfriend had told her that sperms entering the vagina were good for her and should not be wasted. Anastasia was aware of the possibility of becoming pregnant when having unprotected sex. In the back of her mind, though, she thought that if she got pregnant, she could get an induced abortion.

Stella was a 16 year old standard 6 student, she had been dating her boyfriend for four months. He was 27 years old and earned his money by selling oranges. Stella and her partner had never used any type of contraception. Stella thought only girls above 18 years were the ones who were able to become pregnant. This was confirmed by her partner who had once told her that she should not worry about becoming pregnant since she was too young to conceive.

Subila, an 18 year old house girl, had intended to become pregnant. She was well informed about contraception, and had used oral contraceptives until she met her present partner. She bought them from a woman who got them for free from a family planning clinic where she worked. Subila had stopped using contraception because her present partner had promised to marry her. She thought that if she became pregnant there was no way her partner could leave her. Later on, when Subila told her partner about her pregnancy, he denied that he was responsible for the pregnancy. He also told Subila that he was married, had two children and still loved his wife. He did not want to see Subila anymore.

Summing up, the main reasons for becoming pregnant can be divided in four groups:

1. Not being aware of the possibility of becoming pregnant: The girls thought that they were either too young to conceive, that the time they spent having sex was too short for them to conceive, or they simply did not think about the possibility of becoming pregnant.

2. Barriers to contraceptive use: The girls did not use contraception as they either thought they were too young to attend FP clinics, feared or had experienced side effects or found it too expensive. Instead, these girls chose to have an induced abortion.

3. The pregnancy was intended and initially wanted: The girls expected their partners to marry them, and then changed their minds because of their partners' reactions.

4. Contraceptive failure: Mainly because the method was used incorrectly.

Circumstances characterising the induction

The results are summarised in Table 3. The majority (75%) of the girls had their abortion performed at the district hospital by an assistant medical officer who was often assisted by a nurse. All these girls had had their induction performed by using manual vacuum aspiration. The girls had been asked to buy the analgesic needed and bring it with them to the hospital. Consequently, many of them were semiconscious during the procedure and had not felt pain.

Six girls had the induction performed at a private clinic, where dilatation and curettage was used to induce the abortion. They were advised to attend the district hospital two days after the induction, in order have a manual vacuum aspiration performed. The remaining seven girls had the induction performed at a private house by an unskilled person who had used herbs or cassava roots. These girls were admitted to the hospital because of complications such as abdominal pain and sepsis.

Regarding the cost of the induction, 23 of the girls were not aware of the cost as their partner had arranged and paid for the induction. Among the remaining 28 girls, two had not paid for the induction as they themselves or their partner knew the person who had induced the abortion. Among the 26 girls who were aware of the cost, 20 girls had paid 25,000–35,000 Tsh (equivalent to the government minimum salary per month for unskilled workers). The cost of the induction was associated with where and how it was performed. The girls who attended the district hospital or a private clinic had on average paid 30,000 Tsh, whereas the girls who had the induction performed by an unskilled person had paid 15,000 Tsh. Those girls who had the induction performed at the private clinic or by an unskilled person and afterwards attended the district hospital for an evacuation, were charged an additional 10,000 Tsh at the hospital for the evacuation.

The following stories illustrate different circumstances under which the induction was performed:

> Mary was a 17 year old form II student, who had a relationship with a 20 year old form IV student. When she discovered she was pregnant she told a friend about her situation. The friend advised her to go to a certain traditional healer. The healer induced the abortion by using three different sizes of cassava roots. The roots were inserted in the uterus one after the other. The last root was short, and Mary was told to leave it in the vagina for 12 hours. Then the pregnancy would come out with the root. Mary paid the traditional healer 15.000 Tsh for the induction. Four days later Mary got ill with fever and vaginal dis-

charge. Her mother took her to the district hospital where they paid an additional 10,000 Tsh for having an evacuation performed.

Anna was an 18 year old student (form III), involved with a 40 year old married, businessman. She had not used any contraception during intercourse as she found contraception too expensive, and she needed the money for daily use. Instead, she had relied on having an induced abortion. She had discussed the issue with her partner, who had promised to assist her if she became pregnant. When Anna discovered she was pregnant she told her partner who then arranged the abortion. An assistant medical officer performed the induction at the district hospital. He was assisted by a nurse. Anna was given analgesic before the induction which was performed by the use of manual vacuum aspiration. She did not feel much pain. Anna did not know the price of the induction since her partner had arranged and paid for it.

Discussion

Induced abortions are prevailing among adolescents, and particularly in urban areas, an increasing percentage of those having abortions are unmarried adolescents; in some urban centres, they represent the majority of all abortion seekers (WHO, 2004b). In order to better address the problem of induced abortion among adolescents, this qualitative study focused on the girls' relationships with their partners, their sexual activity, the barriers they faced in regards to contraception and the circumstances characterising the induction.

In a study on illegal abortion, the main problem lies in the selection of patients to be investigated. Since the intervention is illegal, women might be reluctant to admit having had an induced abortion. This study used a hospital-based approach in order to identify adolescents who had had an illegal abortion performed. Obviously, it does not comprise adolescents who died outside the hospital because of complications due to an unsafe induced abortion. Neither does it comprise adolescents who had a perfectly safe illegal abortion performed at a private clinic or hospital. Further, a similar study conducted in a rural part of Tanzania would most likely produce quite diverse results, as adolescents in rural areas often have other attitudes regarding sexual behaviour, marriage and desired number of children than adolescents in urban areas.

Studies in sub-Saharan Africa have shown that women who have undergone illegal abortion are reluctant or unwilling to discuss their experiences for fear of negative personal, social, legal and even medical consequences (Bleek, 1988; Royston & Armstrong, 1989). In order to better assess the magnitude of the problem of illegally induced abortion, the WHO Task Force on Sequelae of Abortion developed a set of criteria based on both clinical examination and information from the patient (Figa et al., 1986). However, it was discovered that the use of these criteria might lead to a substantial misclassification (Jewkes et al., 1997). A recent study conducted among women with illegally induced abortion in Dar es Salaam revealed that the use of an empathetic dialogue was much more efficient in classifying women with a truly induced abortion (Rasch et al., 2000c). Consequently, the previously published empathy-oriented approach was utilised in this study.

There is no doubt that the girls in our sample represent a privileged group of young women. More than half of them were students. In terms of their educational level, 86 per cent had completed primary school (standard 7) and 39% were educated above primary school level (secondary school). In comparison, the Tanzania Demographic and Health Survey 1999 reported that among girls aged 15–19, 38.9% had completed primary school and only 5.4% were educated above primary school level (National Bureau of Statistics, 2000). The girls in this study were also privileged because many of them had partners/relatives who paid for the induced abortion or they raised the money themselves. Consequently, they cannot be compared with the young girls living on the streets of Dar es Salaam who in order to survive are sexually exploited by poor men who cannot afford to pay for an induction (Silberschmidt & Rasch, 2001).

Regarding the girls' relationships with their partner, it was found that 83% of the girls interviewed were involved in sexual relationships with men who were above 30 years of age. Moreover, about half of the girls stated that their partner was already married. These findings are in accordance with a previous study conducted among teenage girls in Dar es Salaam which showed that 30% of the girls' partners were at least ten years older than the girls and a quarter of them were married and had family responsibilities (Komba-Malekela & Liljestrom, 1994). Another study from Dar es Salaam conducted among women with induced abortions in 1990 reported that almost a third of the adolescent girls had male partners aged 45 or above (Mpangile et al., 1993). The girls had regular intercourse; one to three times a week and the majority had unprotected sex, despite knowledge of contraception and the possibility of getting pregnant.

The girls interviewed in our study were also found to have an instrumental approach towards their partner. Studies from other sub-Saharan

African countries have shown the same trend of men's sexual appetites and women's instrumental approach in extracting money or gifts in exchange for sexual services (Obbo, 1982; Bledsoe & Cohen, 1993; and many more). This trend might be explained by the fact that teenage girls' status within the peer group is often dependent on having nice clothes and other material possessions. Such things are achieved most easily by entering a sexual relationship with a man. This sugar-daddy phenomenon is widespread in African cities (Mpangile et al., 1993; Komba-Malekela & Liljeström, 1994; Fuglesang, 1997; Silberschmidt & Rasch, 2001). With the increase in HIV/ AIDS awareness, older men are shunning prostitutes and luring younger, safer girls, who are hopefully not infected by HIV, into sexual relations by promising them some degree of protection and financial security (Mpangile et al., 1996; Fuglesang, 1997). Although many of the girls were involved in this exchange of sexual services and gifts, prostitution as an occupation was thought of with disgust. This was also found in another Tanzanian study (Komba-Malekela & Liljestrom, 1994).

As mentioned above, obtaining reliable information about sexual activity is often difficult (Huygens et al., 1996; Rosenthal et al., 1996). In the first 35 interviews, only two of the girls reported having had more than three sexual partners. This number seemed low, so the interviewer was encouraged to probe the remaining respondents further. In the following 16 interviews, the number of sexual partners reported rose, and ranged from one to eight. This discrepancy in reported number of sexual partners shows how essential it is to first of all gain the respondents' confidence and trust. In addition, when collecting data on sexual behaviour it is necessary to probe certain issues in order to obtain more trustworthy information.

Experiences of sexual harassment and rape at first intercourse were a predominant finding. Sexual abuse and rape are increasingly becoming a public concern and a frequent mass media issue in Tanzania. The phenomenon has been described in different Tanzanian studies, although not very systematically (Tumbo-Masabo & Liljestrom, 1994; Fuglesang, 1997).

All of the girls interviewed believed that they were not allowed to attend the family clinic, and many had become pregnant because of lack of family planning information. Many girls thought they were not able to conceive. Others believed that modern contraceptives had serious side-effects and some girls were misinformed about how to use modern contraception. They had only superficial knowledge of modern contraception and they were often seriously misinformed about how to use the method and about side effects. Their lack of knowledge combined with difficult access to contraception makes adolescent girls very vulnerable. However, at the same time they often take many risks. To some extent they were aware that they could get pregnant – but without access to preventive contraceptive measures – many counted on access to induced abortion. The same positive attitude towards induced abortion combined with a lack of access to contraception has been reported in a qualitative study conducted among adolescents in Kenya and Nigeria (Barker & Rich, 1992).

Focusing on the circumstances that characterized the induction, the vast majority of the inductions were performed at a district hospital. An assistant medical office had performed the procedure by the use of manual vacuum aspiration. These abortions can be considered safe – in contrast to the unsafe abortions performed by unskilled persons using herbs and cassava roots. The procedure used in our study was reflected in the cost of the abortion. A safe abortion performed at the district hospital was more than twice as expensive as an unsafe abortion performed by an unskilled person. As can be expected, it is more expensive to have a safe than an unsafe abortion, a trend also reported in a Mozambican study (Machungo et al., 1997). Those girls who were not able to raise the money involved in having a safe abortion had to resort to unsafe procedures, and they were subsequently admitted to the hospital because of complications. Findings from this study demonstrate adolescents' unmet need for access to information and contraceptive services. They also underline that it is of great importance that all women, regardless of their socio-economic situation, have access to safe legal abortion services in the event of contraceptive failure or contraceptive misuse, thereby guaranteeing equal rights for women to decide whether or not to have children.

At the Population Conference in Cairo in 1994, the provision of sexuality education and contraceptive services to adolescents not to mention induced abortions was one of the most controversial and also one of the most discussed issues. Since ICPD in 1994 a lot of efforts have been made in Tanzania to improve reproductive health and promote family planning. As part of these efforts a Reproductive and Child Health Service Section was established in 1995 (Oliff et al., 2003). Further, a National Package of Essential Reproductive and Child Health Interventions in Tanzania was formulated with the purpose of promoting the provision of reproductive and child health services to men, women and children (Reproductive and Child Health Section, 2000). The issue of family planning and adolescents' reproductive health has also been addressed in the National Reproductive and Child Health communication strategy for 2001–2005 (Ministry of

Health, 2000). These initiatives may be part of the explanation for the increase in the contraceptive prevalence rate which Tanzania has experienced during recent decades. According to the Tanzania Demographic and Health Survey 2004–05, 20% of married women and 36% of sexually active single women use modern contraceptives. In 1991–92, the corresponding figures were 7 and 12% (National Bureau of Statistics, 2005).

However, in spite of efforts at improving sexual and reproductive health among adolescents, they still comprise a vulnerable group who are at increased risk of being trapped in a vicious cycle of unwanted pregnancies and subsequently induced abortions, which are often performed in an unsafe manner. Linking abortion care together with family planning could end this cycle. The importance of post-abortion family planning in protecting women's health was highlighted at the 1994 International Conference on Population and Development (ICPD). Operations research in various countries has explored service delivery models for improving the organisation and quality of care (Solo et al., 1999; Johnson, 2002, Rasch et al., 2004). When developing efficient service models for post-abortion family planning it is of importance to be aware that post-abortion patients have different needs. Women who have experienced spontaneous miscarriage of a wanted pregnancy may not be interested in discussing contraception. Furthermore, the need for post-abortion family planning among adolescents might differ from the rest of the group, as they are often involved in unstable sexual relationships with men who are considerably older than they are. Since adolescents run a great risk of both becoming pregnant and infected with a STD/HIV, it is of importance to emphasise the need of using a condom in combination with a modern contraception when providing post-abortion family planning to this specific group of young and vulnerable women.

Conclusion

Adolescent girls who have had an illegal abortion in the setting studied are not only sexually active at an early age, they are also having sex regularly with different sexual partners at the same time. This sexual behaviour combined with a low or incorrect use of contraception means that adolescent girls are running a great risk of both having an unwanted pregnancy and acquiring STD/HIV. In order to avoid repeating the process of unprotected intercourse, unwanted pregnancy and subsequently induced abortion, it is essential to link abortion care with access to family planning. Most importantly, a halt in the alarming figures on the link between illegal abortions and maternal mortality can only occur if all women are guaranteed access to safe legal abortion.

Appendix

Table 1. Occupation, educational level, partners age and partners marital situation among adolescent girls who have had an illegal abortion.

	Number (n=51)	%
Occupation		
Student	28	55
House girl	7	14
Petty trade	8	16
Barmaid	5	10
Skilled worker	3	6
Educational level		
Std 3–6	7	14
Std 7	24	47
Form I-IV	20	39
Partner's Age		
< 19	1	2
20–29	13	26
30–39	23	45
40+	14	28
Partner's marital situation		
Married	23	45
Not married	17	33
Didn't know	11	22

Table 2. Sexual activity and contraceptive use among adolescent girls who have had an illegal abortion.

	Number (n=51)	%
Age at first intercourse	N=51	
13	1	2
14	20	39
15	23	45
16	7	14
Previously affected by an STD		
Yes	7	14
No	44	86
Number of sexual partners (interviews 1–35)	N=35	
1–3	33	94
4–5	2	6
6+	0	0
Number of sexual partners (interviews 36-51)	N=16	
1–3	2	13
4–5	14	25
Contraceptive use*		
Never used contraception	28	55
Condom	11	20
Oral contraception	10	22
Depo-provera	3	6
Attitudes toward induced abortion		
Relied on induced abortion	14	28
Did not rely on induced abortion	37	73

* Does not add up to 51 as one girl had used both a condom and oral contraception.

Table 3. Circumstances characterising the induction

	Number (n=51)	%
Place of induction		
District hospital	38	75
Private clinic	6	12
Private house	7	14
Person who performed the induction		
Assistant Medical Officer	44	86
Unskilled person	7	14
Method used		
Manual vacuum aspiration	38	75
Uterine sound	6	12
Casava roots and herbs	7	14
Price of the induction		
< 25,000	6	6
25,000–35,000 Tsh	20	18
No charge	2	4
Did not know	23	45

7. Adolescent Sexuality and the AIDS Epidemic in Tanzania

What Has Gone Wrong?

Melkizedeck T. Leshabari, Sylvia F. Kaaya and Anna Tengia-Kessy

Abstract

Despite efforts taken to address reproductive health issues amongst youth, available data show unprotected sex and related consequences are still a major problem in Tanzania. It is estimated that 60 per cent of all new HIV infections occur in the age group 15 to 24 years. This implies that sexual and related risk behaviours that expose youth to transmission of HIV are still fairly common despite efforts to raise the level of awareness about AIDS using various forms of communication. Efforts to address this problem in the last two decades were directed towards youth and little attention was paid to factors in their environment that reinforce or minimize observed problem behaviours. There is an urgent need to address barriers to healthy and safe sexual practices and access to reproductive health information and services among adolescents in order to reduce consequences of unprotected sex including HIV infection in this population sub-group. The purpose of this chapter is to review existing knowledge on proximal antecedents of adolescent sexual behaviours in Tanzania in the light of the existing socio-cultural and political-economic context.

Introduction

AIDS was first reported in 1983 in north western Tanzania, and by 1986 cases of the disease were reported from all of the 20 regions of the country. A total of 18,929 AIDS cases were reported to the Tanzania National AIDS Control Programme (NACP) in 2003; the main mode of transmission remains heterosexual, accounting for 76.8% of all cases (NACP, 2004). Simulation models estimate that only 1 out of 14 AIDS cases are reported, bringing the estimated cumulative AIDS cases to 176,102 from 1983 to 2003.

Data from the Tanzania HIV indicator survey (TACAIDS, 2005) estimates the national HIV seroprevalence at 7%, rates being higher amongst females (8%) compared to males (6%). Wide variations in rates occur across regions of the country with the highest rates being reported in Mbeya (14%), Iringa (13%) and Dar es Salaam (11%). Amongst more than 2,500 15–19 year-olds and 20–24 years olds that participated in the HIV/AIDS indicator survey, acceptance of HIV testing was high with 79% and 80% respectively tested. The age-specific HIV seroprevalence in these two groups of youth was 2.1% for both males and females in the younger age group; 6% amongst females and 4.2% amongst males in the older age group.

The trend of higher HIV prevalence rates amongst females compared to males persists to the 40–49 years age group where this trend is reversed and rates are higher in men, suggesting a higher vulnerability to HIV transmission risks amongst young females. While there are some indications that HIV seroprevalence rates may be declining, comparison of sentinel surveillance data amongst pregnant youth aged 15–24 years old in 2001/2 and 2003/4 indicates HIV seroprevalence rates did not differ much (7.6% and 7.4% respectively) when compared to the slight decrease in rates observed amongst women aged 25–34 years who attended for antenatal care (13% to 11.2% respectively) (NACP, 2005). This suggests either a lack of effects of HIV transmission risk preventive interventions in the younger age cohort, or a peaking of the epidemic in this age group or methodological problems such as selection bias due to avoidance of booking for care at clinics conducting anonymous HIV testing by high risk pregnant females.

Studies that attempt to increase our understanding of sexual behaviour amongst youth in Tanzania have often been descriptive, focusing on a narrow range of risky and protective sexual behaviours and possible socio-demographic correlates. Such focus on the personal level often results in recommendations for interventions at the level of the adolescent. These include interventions that delay onset of sexual behaviour and encouraging safer sexual practices amongst youth, through provision of information, with less emphasis on services and social-skills building. The potential environmental barriers and enhancers of safer sexual behaviours in this population given the wider socio-economic, political and cultural environment within which children and youth are socialized are often also ignored.

In order to develop effective interventions to reduce risky sexual behaviours amongst youth, the recognition of the existence of such behaviours is only a preliminary step. Eaton et al. (2003) note the importance of an understanding of factors at various levels that may impact on sexual behaviours including personal factors, proximal and more distal antecedents. Flisher et al. (this volume) note the utility of organizing information on antecedents of sexual behaviours into explicit theoretical frameworks in the development of programmes targeting adolescents aimed at sexual behaviour change. The authors note that basing programme development in theory helps increase understanding of pre-existing bodies of knowledge that support behaviour change theories; including understanding if findings from previous successful theory led interventions can be generalized. Social cognitive theories have been found to be valid and useful in attempting to understand proximal antecedents of adolescent sexual behaviours in the contexts within which they have been developed. Several major theories have been applied in understanding and attempting to change HIV-risk behaviour.

The Health Belief Model (Becker, 1974, 1988) holds that health behaviour is a function of an individual's socio-demographic characteristics, perception of personal susceptibility, perceived severity of the consequences of getting the disease and a perception that action yields benefits that outweigh the barriers to action. Perceived susceptibility and severity determine the perceived threat of the disease, while perceived benefits weighed against barriers determine belief in the effectiveness of health behaviour.

The Theory of Reasoned Action advanced in the mid-1960's, adds to this concept the construct of behavioural intention as a determinant of health behaviour (Azjen & Fishbein, 1980). Other models and theories have extended and developed new conceptual approaches to understanding sexual behaviour during the HIV/AIDS era that have been reviewed by other authors (UNAIDS, 1999; Kalichman, 1988). These theories, collectively known as "social cognitive" within the health psychology literature mainly focus on attempting to understand the relationships between health behaviours, personal and interpersonal factors and processes (Eaton et al., 2003).

The key cognitions and assessments addressed by these theories include: vulnerability to a health risk; perceived severity of the health outcome; likelihood that changed behaviour will protect against the risk; confidence in changing one's behaviour effectively; the costs versus benefits associated with risky behaviour; perceived emotional and social consequences of heath-related behaviours; and perceptions about social norms (what other people think and feel, and whether the individual is motivated to comply with these perceived pressures) (Eaton et al., 2003; UNAIDS, 1999). These variables may influence behaviour itself or the intention to behave in a certain manner (Ajzen & Fishbein, 1980).

However, in cultural contexts outside those in which models and theories are developed, careful adaptation of constructs to local realities and meanings and an understanding of wider factors that pose significant barriers and enhancers of personal health behaviours are important. Airhihenbuwa et al. (2000) in the debate on relevant theories and models for behaviour change, note that while social learning /cognitive theories and the hierarchy of effects are based on individual psychology, in some non-Western contexts, such as in Africa, many decisions originate from group norms and processes. The authors further argue the need for recognizing culture as central to planning, implementing and evaluating health communication and promotion programmes in HIV/AIDS prevention and care. Addressing issues outside the individual adolescent allows for the inclusion where possible of methods that give consideration to wider structural issues when attempting to understand sexual behaviour, develop interventions and evaluate outcomes.

An understanding of the distal antecedents of adolescent sexual behaviour in the Tanzanian context includes a consideration of objective socioeconomic, political and cultural factors. These factors may influence not only the determinants and hence the most important indicators for sexual behaviour and behaviour change amongst adolescents, but also decisions regarding the most appropriate approaches and levels of intervention strategies (Eaton et al., 2003). The purpose of this chapter is to review existing knowledge on the proximal antecedents of sexual behaviours in Tanzanian youth, and provide some insights into the socio-cultural and political-economic context of Tanzania that might impact on such behaviour. The findings from published studies that have explored adolescent sexual health from 1992–2000 will be used to inform the discussion, utilizing the structure provided by Eaton et al. (2003) to organize the presented material. The chapter will conclude with implications for future intervention programmes and research on sexual health amongst adolescents in Tanzania.

Sexual health amongst contemporary adolescents and youth in Tanzania

Over the past ten years, there has been an encouraging steady increase in published research that has focused on the sexual health of youth in the country. This review will focus on literature published in peer-reviewed journals between 1992 and 2004 that provides information on the sexual behaviour of youth, aged 12–24 years. A database search of MEDLINE, PUBMED, PSYCH-INFO, HEALTHSTAR, and OVID as well as a hand search of the Tanzania Medical Journal and the Dar es Salaam Medical Journal retrieved 13 articles. The findings retrieved from these articles are summarized in Table 1. Our major focus in this section will be on evidence from the findings of these studies of any interplay between personal, interpersonal and more structural factors that may impact on the decision to engage in sexual intercourse and use of protection against the consequences of sexual intercourse.

Personal factors

Knowledge as a prerequisite of healthy sexual behaviour

While knowledge alone is not a major determinant of health related behaviours it is an important pre-requisite. Available survey data indicate that large proportions of the Tanzanian population including adolescents are aware of HIV/AIDS (Ndeki et al., 1994; Ngallaba et al., 1993). A recent survey, assessing whether youth aged 15–24 years agreed HIV transmission can be prevented by having sex with only one uninfected partner and by using condoms consistently and whether they know that a healthy looking person can have the AIDS virus and that HIV cannot be transmitted by mosquito bites or sharing food with a person who has AIDS, indicated lower levels of comprehensive knowledge in 15–19 years olds (38.5% females, 42.6% males) and in 20–24 year olds (50.4% females, 56.5% males) than in older age groups. (TACAIDS, 2005). Small scale studies that have comprehensively explored levels of sexual health, HIV/AIDS transmission and prevention knowledge have also reported low levels of knowledge amongst particularly younger adolescents (Kapiga et al., 1992; Ndeki et al., 1994; Klepp et al., 1996; Matasha et al., 1998; Maswanya et al., 1999).

Several misconceptions among youth have been documented. For example, about half of adolescents of mean age 14 years believed HIV infection could be acquired through hugging an infected person, and a larger proportion did not know that an HIV-infected person could be symptom free (Ndeki et al., 1994). Furthermore, over 20% of adolescents below the age of 18 years were not aware of the link between menarche and the ability to conceive and only 16% knew when during the menstrual cycle conception would be most likely (Kapiga et al., 1992). Todd et al. (2004), note persistence of misconceptions about HIV transmission risks as well as measures to prevent pregnancy in a primary school population in Mwanza, and of concern was the significantly higher proportions holding such misconceptions amongst learners that reported they had been exposed to any school based sexual and reproductive health sessions.

Kapiga et al. (1992) in a sample of older adolescents did not demonstrate any association between level of contraception knowledge and reported contraceptive use behaviour. Maswanya et al. (1999) also note amongst older adolescents a lack of significant associations between HIV/AIDS knowledge and consistency of condom use and/or the reported number of sexual partners. In younger populations though, Matasha et al. (1998) noted no association between knowledge of STD prevention and sexual activity and that there was a better knowledge of HIV amongst sexually experienced students and those that used condoms. The low performance on the test for the majority of students, particularly at the primary school level in this study, suggests that being sexually active might have resulted in a search for accurate information, while seeking protection against or after exposure to consequences related to sexual activity.

Low risk perception

Despite evidence of large proportions of sexually active youth, many do not necessarily perceive themselves to be at risk of HIV transmission. Only two of the retrieved studies provide information on risk perception for HIV infection (Ndeki et al., 1994; Maswanya et al., 1999). Ndeki et al. (1994) in a sample of senior primary school students of mean age 14.7 years noted high perception of personal risk of acquiring HIV in a high compared to a lower risk HIV-transmission area. However, only two Likert items – "extent students perceived AIDS to be a threat for primary school students" and "fear they might become infected with AIDS" were used to assess risk perception, and the authors caution on their ability to discriminate high and low risk perception. Maswanya et al. (1999) note amongst senior secondary and junior college students (mean age 18.3 years for females and 19.8 years for males) very low perception of personal risk of acquiring HIV/AIDS (25%), a large proportion (41%) reporting that their peers were at higher risk than themselves. However, there was an increased likelihood of inconsistent condom use and/or multiple sexual partners in the previous year amongst students who perceived themselves to be at low risk of HIV infection, compared to those that perceived themselves to be at higher risk.

Though risk perception was not quantitatively explored in an exploration of sexual practices of a sample of adolescent girls just after an illegal abortion, findings indicated a lack of awareness of self-vulnerability in a context where transactional factors played a larger role (at least on the part of the girls) in their relationships with sexual partners (Silberschmidt & Rasch, 2001). There is clearly need for further studies that explore risk perception amongst adolescents, the wider structural factors that influence risk perception and the associations between such perception and protective sexual behaviours.

Attitudes and subjective norms towards sexual intercourse and intention to engage in sexual or protective behaviours

Few of the reviewed studies have systematically explored intentions, attitudes and subjective norms as these relate to sexual behaviours in the Tanzanian context. Seha et al. (1994) demonstrated that the socio-cognitive concepts of intentions to have sex and use condoms were valid amongst young Tanzanian adolescents, this variable correlating significantly with attitudes, social norms and the frequency of sex.

Intention to engage in sexual intercourse in the next three months was also noted by Klepp et al. (1996) to be positively associated with less restrictive attitudes and subjective norms towards sexual intercourse. While in general young adolescents tend to have restrictive attitudes and subjective norms in relation to sexual intercourse, less restrictive attitudes and subjective norms towards sexual intercourse were reported amongst boys and rural young adolescents compared to girls and those in urban settings respectively. These associations are further confirmed following a school-based intervention that revealed significant and sustained changes in the intention to become sexually active in intervention schools; the intervention was also noted to influence development of more restrictive subjective norms regarding sexual intercourse (seven Likert items – alpha 0.66) amongst young adolescents in the short and long term (Klepp et al., 1994, 1997).

Amongst older adolescents and youth, Maswanya et al. (1999) noted a high endorsement (19.3% to 66.3%) on various negative attitudes towards condoms. An opinion that condoms reduced the sensation of romantic sex received the highest endorsement. Negative attitudes towards condoms were independently associated with inconsistent condom use and/or reported multiple sexual partners in the previous year. Kapiga et al. (1992) also noted a direct relationship between positive attitudes towards contraception use and use behaviours in a sample of school-based adolescents.

Low perceived self-efficacy to abstain from unsafe sexual practices

Perceived self-efficacy (perception that one can successfully complete behaviour) to abstain from sexual intercourse or to practise protective sexual behaviours is postulated to be an important predictor of whether one attempts the behaviour (Bandura, 1989). Only one study systematically explores this variable; Klepp et al. (1996), using a seven-item Likert scale (alpha 0.64) note average mean scores on perceived self-efficacy to abstain from sexual intercourse (defined as confidence that he/she could resist pressure from others to engage in sexual intercourse) for young adolescent males and females. Urban adolescents were more confident in this regard than their rural counterparts.

Interpersonal factors

Low interactions with responsible adults on matters of sexual health

Norms governing sexual partnership and intimacy, and how these are transmitted to younger generations are largely influenced by culture. As explored by Bledsoe and Cohen (1993), access to sex in many traditional African societies while embedded in a wider socio-political system was not necessarily synonymous with reproductive entitlement that was earned through a succession of ritualized steps that ordered and paced life sequence from birth, through puberty, training, marriage, parenthood, entry into work and death. While youth were allowed to engage in limited forms of sexual expression, reproduction was sanctioned before entitlement to reproduce was earned. External forces such as Christianity, Islam, colonization and modernity have influenced cultural systems and structures in Tanzania, as in the rest of the African continent. Several socio-cultural contexts that are in transition serve to provide a background for understanding sexual health communication with responsible adults amongst contemporary Tanzanian adolescents. These include changes in the nature of sexual socialization of youth.

Sexuality in many communities in Tanzania is shaped by the patterns of social, economic and political lives (Mbunda, 1988). Traditional socialization structures for youth including instruction within the extended family and rites of passage provided a formal setting for communication on matters of sexual health, which emphasized and gave meaning to existing patterns of sexuality and sexual lives. Before the advent of the HIV/AIDS epidemic, rapid socio-cultural changes had challenged many traditional deployments of alliance, resulting in a rupture of the ordered sequence of maturational events that underlay successful reproduction and the loss of the control of elders over youthful reproductive life and practices (Ntukula, 1994; Shuma, 1998).

Traditional rites of passage that were the forum for communication on sexuality related issues and community living skills between selected adults and younger generations, are currently reported to lack relevance where they continue to be practised or are on the decline (Ntukula, 1994; Shuma, 1998). Rites of passage to a large extent have not been replaced in many societies where initiation into adulthood is no longer practised. Cultural barriers exist in many communities to direct communication between parents and children/adolescents on matters of sexual health and behaviour that persist even where the formalized traditional guidance structures for adolescents during puberty have declined (Schapink et al., 1997). The adult–child/adolescent communication barriers on matters of sexual health are perhaps reproduced in settings such as the schools, health services and in religious institutions where the potential for meaningful communication between responsible adults and children/youth exists. The implications of the loss of this body of knowledge, before structures to replace it have developed, includes less awareness amongst adults of the challenges to sexual health faced by contemporary adolescents and low knowledge on issues of sexual and reproductive health amongst adolescents, both of which may facilitate the use of sex for recreational and material benefits amongst males and females.

The lack of adult to child communication on matters of sexual health is supported by survey data. Evidence from existing literature indicates that while basic sexual health information is reported by adolescents to be primarily acquired from peers, information on STDs including HIV/AIDS and pregnancy prevention is acquired from the mass media (Kapiga et al., 1992; Ndeki et al., 1994; Matasha et al., 1998). Across these studies less than 10% of students reported parents as primary sources of information on issues of sexual health. However, there are indications that adolescents prefer to receive sexual health information from health workers, teachers and parents (Matasha et al., 1998) whom they also consider credible sources of such information (Masatu et al., 2003). Focus group discussion narratives amongst rural school-based adolescents indicated a perception that significant adults such as teachers and parents were reluctant to discuss with particularly younger adolescents, issues related to sexual health even when included in the teaching of an integrated family life education course in the school system (Kaaya et al., 2005).

The need to improve parent/adult-adolescent communication on sexual health issues is supported by some evidence of the benefits of such interactions. Maswanya et al. (1999) demonstrates a positive association between parental communication on sexual health issues amongst older adolescents with more consistent condom use and fewer sexual partners (in the previous year). Getting information from friends was positively associated with inconsistent condom use. It is promising that recent evidence from a national representative sample indicates that 60.7% and 68.8% of females and males respectively had a positive attitude towards children aged 12–14 years being provided with education about condom use (TACAIDS, 2005). Studies that focus on how the skills of parents and other responsible adults can be improved to allow for implementation of acceptable and sustainable HIV preventive interventions for young adolescents are required.

Coercive, male dominated sexual relationships

A wider understanding of gender dynamics in intimate sexual relationships is important to make sense of the vulnerabilities of adolescent girls and boys to the consequences of unprotected sexual acts. The extension of the period between pubescence and marriage creates an increasing need for skills in negotiating healthy and safe relationships with the opposite sex. This is particularly the case for adolescent girls, given the lower status of women in many communities, their subservient roles, and contradictions in traditional expectations of chastity while sexual exploits amongst boys are tacitly condoned.

Census data indicate a steady decline in the proportion of youth (15–24 years) that are married over the past forty years suggesting an increasing age at which marriage occurs in Tanzania (Figure 1). The relatively lower proportions of young married males compared to females in all the census years, suggest that females tend to marry partners who are much older than themselves. Some authors have reported similar age differentials between sexually active single adolescent girls and their partners. Mwakagile et al. (2001) reported wide age differentials between adolescent girls with STDs and their sexual partners in a study in Dar es Salaam. Similar age differentials are also reported in an ethnographic study of a clinical population of single adolescent females following induced abortions (Rasch et al., 2000) A recent survey of 2,564 youth aged 15–24 years resident in urban and rural localities indicates 22–28% and 17–25% respectively of sexually active females aged 15–19 years reported a sexual partner in the previous year who was 10 years or older than themselves (NACP, 2004). These observations suggest the tradition of men courting younger partners, often to become second or third wives, continues in the absence of controls to ensure relationships culminate in marriage. Within a context of increasing poverty, sex becomes a strong hand to play in negotiating satisfaction of sexual desire amongst males and material gain amongst females. The biological risks of vulnerability to STDs and HIV transmission due to a less mature genital tract in adolescent girls, are magnified by relationships with older, hence more sexually experienced and exposed, men.

There are indications that female adolescents in particular are vulnerable to coercive sexual acts. Nnko & Pool (1997) in a discourse analysis of data derived from role-plays developed and conducted by adolescents note that adolescent girls in particular may feel pressured or forced into a sexual relationship. They also note difficulties however, in making a distinction between coercion and courting rituals amongst adolescents in their data set. The presence of coercive sex from the perspective of adolescents is supported by findings of between 23% of primary school girls (Todd et al., 2004) and 28% and 45% of primary and secondary school girls respectively (Matasha et al., 1998) reporting ever being exposed to coercive or forced sex. An area less explored in the adolescent sexual health literature is coercive sex amongst secondary and primary school boys that is reported by Matasha et al. (1998) with lower rates of 13% and 14% respectively.

Various unpublished reports (Leshabari et al., 1996; Muhondwa, 2000; van den Bergh, 1996) suggest that gender variations in interpreting the processes involved in sexual relationships amongst youth are indicative of dissonance in communication on sexual matters. Such communication is rarely explicit, and in some cases boys may assume that once a girl accepts friendship or is very friendly, she has tacitly agreed to or wants to engage in sexual intercourse particularly where friendship also involves being offered and accepting a gift. In the context of such dissonance, refusal on the part of the girl may lead to coercion or even rape. More information is clearly warranted on communication on matters related to intimate relationships amongst adolescents to inform interventions that might reduce the high rates of coercive sex reported.

Finally there is evidence of an association between intimate partner violence and HIV/AIDS transmission risk that provides some urgency for the development of a body of knowledge that will allow for an understanding of the complex interaction between violence and HIV transmission risk. A study in Dar es Salaam, Tanzania at a stand alone voluntary counselling and testing facility found that HIV positive women reported more lifetime experiences with violence (OR 1.65; 95% CI 1.02–2.67), and more physical and sexual violence with the current partner (OR 2.42; 95% CI 1.20–4.87 and OR 2.39; 95% CI 1.21–4.37). In this study it was striking that in women younger than 30 years of age the adjusted odds of reporting current partner violence were ten times higher in HIV-positive compared to negative women (Maman et al., 2002). Similar associations between HIV-positive serostatus and violence have been reported amongst men (as perpetrators of partner violence) and women (as recipients of partner violence) in Kigali, Rwanda (Van der Straten et al., 1998). Likewise in female respondents in Soweto, South Africa, an association was observed between HIV sero-positive status and both intimate partner violence and high levels of male control in a woman's current relationship (Dunkle et al., 2004).

The physical and organisational environment

The political-economic context

The performance of the Tanzanian economy post-independence in 1961 to the early 1970s was generally good, with a Gross Domestic Product (GDP) growth rate of around 6% per annum, and a population growth rate of about 3% (Mbele, 1996; World Bank, 1998). During the early post-independence era, several successes of social policy implementation were documented. A focus on the health status of children under the age of five years resulted in the development of one of the best immunization programme in the developing world (de Quadros, 1985), which ensured that more children reached adolescence. There was a three-fold increase in rural dispensaries and rural health centres increased ten-fold (Heggenhougen, 1984). By the late 1980s, 93% of the population lived within 10 km of a health facility and 72% were within 5 km (MoH, 1994b). The country reported a literacy rate of over 90% (88% for adult females and 93% for adult males) by 1986 compared to literacy rates of 12 % amongst females and 45% amongst men in 1969 (BEST, 1991). An accelerated programme of universal primary education (UPE) that was part of the Second Five Year Development Plan (1969–74) resulted in an increase from 49% to 93% in the proportion of school-aged children enrolled between 1974 and 1980. The Education Act of 1978 legislated compulsory primary education for all children aged 7-14 years of age, and equity in enrolment to primary school was achieved all over the country by the early 1980s (ibid).

Several factors described elsewhere (Bigsten & Danielson, 2001), inter-acted to precipitate economic upheavals in the country between the early 70s to the early 80s. The micro-level welfare implications of the crises and subsequent reforms were a reduction in per capita income growth from an average of 1.95% in 1961 to 1967 to minus 5.6% at the peak of the economic crisis in 1983. In 1989, the GDP growth rate stood at 2.6% and the proportion of allocation of public funds for the health sector had declined from 9.4% in the early 1970s to 5% by 1990/91. Within the education sector, 6.3% of the total budget was education expenditure in 1991; this proportion dropped to 2.5% by 1997 (ibid). Gross primary school enrol-ment dropped to 67%, while secondary school enrolment was 6% in 1995 (BEST, 1997).

In 1989, a second phase of reforms resulted in improvements in macro-economic indicators and restored donor confidence. Sustained per capita income growth has only been evident since 1995 and a steady increase from 0.6% per annum to an estimated 2.5% by 1999 is documented (Bigsten & Danielson, 2001). Per capita expenditure on health was estimated at $8 in 1998, constituting 14.9% of the government budget, with little change in the education sector indicators at this time (UNAIDS, 2000). However, the downsizing of the public sector and closure and selling of loss making public enterprises was bound to have adverse impacts at community level. In the beginning of the 1990s the parastatal section contributed nearly 25% of non-agricultural wage employment and generated about 13% of total GDP; hence vested interests of citizens were confronted directly through loss of jobs and privileges both in the government and parastatal sections (Bagachwa, 1992). There are indications that income distribution has worsened over the years and income has declined in absolute terms in the face of currency devaluation. It is estimated that 50% of the population live in poverty, most of them in rural areas (Mutalemwa, Noni & Wangwe, 1998). While there has been a slow but steady increase in life expectancy at birth from 41.7 years in 1962 to a peak of 52 years by 1992, the AIDS epidemic is partly responsible for a decline to 44.4 years by 2004 (CIA, 2005).

The economic changes noted above have had adverse implications for the education sector as a major institution for the formal socialization of youth, access to employment opportunities, as well as informal structures of socialization within families. The effect on the development of adolescents and young adults contributes towards observed sexual behaviour.

Organizational and capacity issues in the socialization role of the education sector

In order to understand the relevance of the education sector in preventive health education programmes in Tanzania, it is important to review historical developments in this sector and impacts of economic factors on its capacity.

The Education for Self-Reliance Policy of 1967 intended the school system to produce graduates with the knowledge, attitudes and skills required for improving living conditions in the community; each school cycle (either primary or secondary education) was intended to be an end-stage and not a means for progressing to the next stage. This was one step in reforming an inherited racially segregated education system (Nyerere, 1968; Maliamkono & Msekwa, 1979).

The lack of sufficient operationalisation of the Education for Self-Reliance Policy did not allow for the meaningful communication of its objectives to communities served by schools. Despite the introduction of agricultural and other vocational training activities in primary schools, assessment of pupils' competence remained academic with a focus on passing examinations and gaining admission to the few places available for secondary education. The criteria for success in primary education remained the number of pupils who passed school-leaving examinations and proceeded to public secondary education. Outcomes in terms of proficiency in agricultural and other vocational activities were not officially or unofficially recognized, and pupils graduating from primary schools did not often have readily available job markets in rural areas (Kamm, 1977). To date, parents continue to perceive self-reliance activities as "stealing" time from the "normal" teaching curricula and not benefiting children, contrary to their expectations (Lugalla, 1993, Cooksey et al., 1993). Partly as a result of the premises of the Education for Self-Reliance Policy, investment in expanding public secondary school education was low (Hazlewood, 1989).

An accelerated programme for UPE was set for implementation in 1977, 13 years earlier than planned mainly for political reasons (Ligate, 1982). The new time frame for implementation of UPE coincided with the beginning of an economic recession. The existing primary school education infrastructure was overwhelmed by an increase in school enrolment, making it difficult for teachers to provide adequate attention to individual children. Consequent declining enrolments, increasing drop out rates, growth in private education, shortages of suitably qualified teachers particularly in rural areas and subsequent decline in standards of education have been reported as major challenges to UPE (Omari, 1995; Malangalila, 1998). In some districts, less than 6% of primary school graduates score an average of 50% in primary school leaving examinations (Komba, 1995). The disproportionate expansion in primary compared to secondary education is reflected in a reduced proportion of primary school graduates who joined secondary schools from 29.2% in 1963 to 3.4% by 1984 when the first UPE cohort completed primary education and a current rate of about 29.5% (BEST, 1997 & 2005).

Encouraging measures have been put in place to increase the numbers of secondary schools through community efforts. Some efforts have also been made to address the needs of the large proportion of children who are not in school. The Complementary Basic Education Programme in Tanzania (COBET) was initiated in the late 1990s with the objectives of meeting basic education needs of 2.5 million school aged Tanzanian children who were out of school (45% school age population). The programme aimed to provide basic education to children, especially girls who have either dropped out of or had not had the chance to enter primary education, and documented some preliminary success in its implementation (Helgesson, 2001). The pressure to build more secondary schools has, however, paid less attention to the need for important inputs such as sufficiently qualified teachers and teaching and learning materials that are essential for provision of good quality education. Problems related to quality of education observed in primary education hence risk being reproduced in secondary education settings. The number of students sitting for their final O-level examinations after completing secondary education increased from 24,068 in 1989 to 35,025 in 1993. However the proportion graduating with a distinction (Division one passes) declined progressively from 7.1% in 1989 to 4.8% in 2005 (BEST, 1994 & 2005).

Despite the many shortcomings noted above, the education sector provides a captive audience of youth, at an important stage of sexuality development when healthy behaviours can be influenced. The possibility for schools to mount effective interventions for sexual behaviour change exists. It has proved feasible to train teachers and local health workers to provide HIV/AIDS education in primary schools, guided by theoretical frameworks derived from social cognitive theories, peer education and with community involvement (Klepp et al., 1997; Schapink et al., 1997; Klepp & Lugoe, 1999). Despite these findings, strategies to sustain pilot interventions or to diffuse developed curricula to other districts have been slow in developing. Several wider problems related to the curriculum at primary and secondary school levels, the capacity of the education sector, and organization of the school health programme may account for this delay.

The Education and Training policy document of 1995, was an attempt to maximize finite resources and improve the quality of education in Tanzania. Resulting strategies that have been in implementation since 2000, include the Basic Education Master Plan and the Education Sector Development Programme (1996). A consensus in many policy documents that the education sector was too centralized resulted in devolution of some responsibilities to local district authorities and schools. It is envisaged that local governments (district level) would become the main locus of local decision making; a decision that was enhanced by the provision of a block grant to local authorities instead of recurrent expenditure for primary education that allowed greater ability for local authorities to make decisions on their areas of priority. Teachers' employment previously managed by the central Teachers' Service Commission also became the responsibility of local councils. A greater role for parents within the school system was also envisaged.

As a result of implementation of these strategies, parent-teachers committees are appearing in primary schools, and though larger contributions from parents for education have not been maintained for primary education, user fees are increasingly evident at higher levels of the education system. Infrastructure changes aimed at reducing class size are also evident as a result of the implementation of some of these strategies. However, much needs to be done in the decentralization process and in improving the actual quality of teaching in primary schools (Therkildsen, 2000).

Within local school settings, four major problem areas are notable that may impact on health promoting programmes. Firstly, teaching and learning methods in the education system in Tanzania given the large teacher-student ratios have of necessity remained predominantly didactic, an approach that encourages rote learning which does not facilitate an interactive learning and skills development approach that has proven effective in school-based sexual health interventions (UNAIDS, 1999). Secondly, anecdotal information suggests in some areas, the need to strengthen working linkages between the schools' management and parents in the communities they serve. Such links will increase possibilities for supportive structural elements for interaction between schools, parents, students and the community in school-based programmes (Peersman & Levy, 1998; Kalichman, 1988). The few interventions that have documented a decrease in intention to be sexually active or to engage in safer sexual practices in the short-term, indicate the possibilities to involve parents in a participatory approach to teaching and learning issues related to sexuality (Klepp et al., 1997, Schapink et al., 1997). These are important considerations that have to be addressed when interventions in the school setting are planned.

Thirdly, delayed enrolment in school to ages above 10 years results in a wide variation in the ages of children in a single class. Age may range as widely as from 12 to 19 years in a senior primary school class, making it difficult to provide sexuality related knowledge and skills that would be appropriate for all pupils. Finally, teachers are demoralized due to lack of resources for basic teaching/learning let al.one extra curricula activities and low salaries (Schapink et al., 1997). Motivation to teach new courses in the school system requires innovative approaches that will change the teaching and learning environment to make it more conducive and sustainable compared to what currently exists. Should these measures not be considered it would be over-ambitious to expect significant changes in health-related behaviours based on proposed new intervention packages aimed at health education and promotion that are introduced at various levels.

At the national level, there are inherent structural and organizational problems in the existing School Health Programme that might deter its implementation. While the programme was developed by a unit in the Ministry of Health, implementation tools such as the syllabus and training of teachers is the responsibility of the Ministry of Education and monitoring of implementation of activities at the level of the school is the responsibility of the Ministry of Regional Administration and Local Government. This organization compounds difficulties in coordination leading to few if any health-related activities occurring at the school level. Efforts are required to re-think the organization of school health-related programmes to ensure ease in coordination and sharing of resources in order to increase their effectiveness in meeting the health needs of children and youth.

Changes in the family and community as agents of socialization

Changes in the socialization process of children and youth and impacts on sexuality and sexual behaviour are perhaps a difficult area to investigate, and very little empirical data exists in Tanzania. While in the past, communities were relatively homogenous and adults were actively involved in setting boundaries and providing discipline amongst children regardless of whether they were the biological parents or not, reports indicate that parents and adults sense a decreasing "hold" over the thinking, experiences and decision making processes of the young (Omari, 1977; Leshabari et al., 1996).

The perceived loss of traditional parental roles and authority over youth is illustrated in narratives from ethnographic studies in northern Tanzania that associate engagement in less traditional and hence less respectful (particularly for male youth), though more lucrative, petty trade activities and concepts of "(bad) moral character" (*tabia)* and "desire" (*tamaa)* (Setel, 1999). Affluence amongst youth is perceived from these analyses to be associated with high mobility, excessive alcohol use and indiscriminate relationships with the opposite sex. The birth of "desire", an emotion with negative connotations, contains within it a layered set of implicit statements about personal disposition and changes brought about by population dynamics and modernity (Setel, 1999). This perception of youth perhaps represents a process of acculturation with decreasing homogeneity in norms and values, including those related to sexual behaviours. The lack of homogeneity in norms and values within communities may challenge existing parenting practices and create dissonance in patterns of parenting and the realities that face youth.

In urban settings where traditional support from the extended family for socialization of children and adolescents is limited, challenges to parenting practices may be more pronounced than in rural settings. One or both parents in urban localities often work outside the home and child-care is contracted out, often to low income earning child minders known as "house-girls". Most house-girls are themselves adolescents who have completed or dropped out of primary school and left rural communities in search of employment in urban settings. Many different house-girls may be hired before a child reaches adolescence, this having implications for consistency in care and stability for the child. These changes in wider structural factors and their impact on the sexual health of youth have not been systematically explored and more studies are required to inform interventions that can strengthen the psychosexual socialization of youth in the home.

Variations exist in the magnitude of HIV/AIDS and responses to the epidemic in various regions of the country that may influence awareness of HIV/AIDS, knowledge, attitudes or risk behaviours in relation to transmission amongst adolescents. Different socio-economic and cultural contexts across rural and urban localities in the country might also influence differently personal predictors of sexual behaviour. Only five of the reviewed studies explore sexual behaviours across different localities of adolescents simultaneously and two distinguished findings by locality (Klepp et al., 1996; Ndeki et al., 1994). Ndeki et al. (1994), document higher exposure to information and better knowledge on HIV/AIDS in an adolescent population from a high HIV transmission compared to a low transmission locality. In this study, locality was an important determinant of the variance noted in reported sexual intercourse in the sample. Furthermore, Klepp et al. (1996) noted amongst young school-based adolescents that restrictive subjective norms were a stronger predictor of the intention to be sexually active in rural and semi-urban localities than in urban localities. Self-efficacy on the other hand was a stronger predictor in urban compared to the other localities.

Youth and employment and the implications of poverty

The growth of the Tanzanian population has exceeded growth in the service and industrial sectors of the economy, with implications on employment opportunities. Each year the primary school system produces over 400,000 graduates that join an unemployment pool in which the youth already constitute the majority (BEST, 1994). Among the few who join secondary education, an increasing number of both those that fail and pass their O-level examinations and graduate from universities and colleges add to this pool of unemployed youth. The government's reduction in its work force by 24% compounds this situation as youth and young adults, that were the most recently employed and the least experienced in their jobs were the most vulnerable to redundancy (PSRP, 1999). The proportion of economically active youth is reported to be higher in rural areas at 62% compared to only 45.4% in urban areas (Bureau of Statistics, 1992). These figures may conversely be a result of the rural to urban migration of youth.

The migration of youth to urban areas can be linked to both unstable economic conditions in rural areas, as well as an attitudinal mind set that is encouraged by a lack of social and economic incentives that make work in a rural setting attractive for primary school graduates (Chacha, 1994). Lugalla (1995) notes, as elsewhere in the world, there is a direct association in Tanzania between the educational level attained, employment opportunity, income and socio-economic status. With current geographic differentials between rural and urban areas in access to post-primary education, rural youth migrants are unlikely to find jobs with ease in urban areas. They consequently risk transforming a state of rural poverty to that of urban poverty where the unfamiliarity of such settings increases their vulnerability. Many rural migrants to urban areas experience difficulties in securing both employment and accommodation and are forced to live in make-shift houses in squatter settlements that lack basic social service facilities (Lugalla, 1997).

A lifestyle characterized by poor access to social support resources, and low base skills for adaptation to the urban environment might also increase the vulnerability of many adolescents and youth to health risk behaviours including sexual risk behaviours. The HIV indicator survey indicated that a smaller proportion of 15–24 year-olds in the lowest according to wealth quintiles had comprehensive knowledge on HIV/AIDS prevention; knew where to access condoms; and used condoms. Furthermore a larger proportion in the lower wealth quintiles reported sexual activity before the age of 15 years (TACAIDS, 2005). These findings support earlier qualitative studies that suggested association between poverty and consequences of unprotected sex. Discourse analysis of narrative data derived from role-plays developed by adolescents, indicated girls from poor families were more likely to get pregnant than girls from more affluent families (Nnko & Pool, 1997). Adult informants provided similar information noting that the exchange of money in negotiations for sex was a greater incentive for girls from poorer families (Schapink et al., 1997).

Concluding remarks

While there is evidence that factors in the social environment play an important role on the development of health behaviour programmes for adolescents, this is the least area explored in research on adolescent sexual behaviour in Tanzania. Perry (1999) provides a broad framework within which adolescent behaviour is viewed as being strongly influenced by parents, siblings and close friends. Furthermore, the community at large including teachers, religious leaders, neighbours and other relatives also has a role to play. It is the interaction of these and personal factors, together with community policies, media and advertising as well as forces in the wider society that influence adolescent behaviours including sexual health and related problems.

The AIDS epidemic in Tanzania erupted and has persisted at a time of great changes in many socialization institutions for children and adolescents. Within families, decline in purchasing power and socio-cultural changes might influence child-rearing practices. Within a young education sector, there is a struggle for maturity against many odds to meet its primary mandate, amidst serious problems in delivery of its official curricula. When advocating for the school system as an entry point for knowledge and skills building on health-related issues to effect changes in attitudes and behaviours of youth, serious consideration needs to be given to its capacity. Questions of appropriateness of this setting need to be addressed, as well as mechanisms through which effective interventions can be put in place.

There is hence a need to develop further conceptual models for a more holistic understanding of adolescent sexual behaviour and behaviour changes that take into account the interaction of all these factors. At the moment for example little is known about what parents know about sexual health, and the extent to which they are willing to share such knowledge with their children. The same applies to teachers, religious leaders and other significant adults who in one way or another have the potential to influence adolescent health related behaviours. Furthermore, little is known about the type of medium that is most effective for communicating different types of sexual health messages and who in the social environment of adolescents should be responsible. Yet specific information on these factors is of paramount importance in interventions focusing on sex related problems of the adolescent population.

Table 1. Summary of studies on sexual behaviour conducted amongst adolescent/youth populations in Tanzania 1992–2004.

Authors	Population	N	Design	Self-reported sexual intercourse (%)/ Intentions (I) to be sexually active		>/= two sexual partners or mean number of sexual partners		Condom use (%)/ Intentions (I) to use condoms		Key determinants of sexual behaviour/ behaviour change/ HIV risk
				Boys	Girls	Boys	Girls	Boys	Girls	
Kapiga et al., 1992	Random sample of 14–22 year olds (mean age 17.9 yrs) secondary school pupils from urban localities.	481	Cross-sectional	80.3	24.1			7.2		Most (82.7%) had a positive attitude towards using contraceptives. Those with a positive attitude towards use were significantly more likely to have used a contraceptive method.
Klepp et al., 1994	Random sample of sixth to seventh graders stratified by urban/rural location of mean age 13.6 years in control (C) group and 13.5 years in the intervention (I) group.	B: 2,026 F: 1,785	Quasi-experimental nested case control intervention design	I: B/F; 1.48/1.28 C: B/F; (I. scale range 1-4)	1.4/1.4	–	–	–	–	Six months post a health education intervention, intervention pupils reported significantly higher access to AIDS information, communication regarding AIDS, AIDS knowledge, positive attitudes towards persons with AIDS, restrictive subjective norms and lower intentions to become sexually active. No programme effects were noted for attitudes towards sexual intercourse.
Klepp et al., 1996	Primary school pupils of age range 10–17 years, mean age 14, stratified by urban/rural location.	2,026	Cross-sectional	63.3	24.4	–	–	–	–	Restrictive attitudes (overall, strongest theoretical construct) and subjective norms, previous sexual behaviour and self-efficacy were all predictors of the intention to be sexually ative. The amount of variance in intention to engage in sexual activity accounted for by these variables is low to modest. Most of the effect of prior behaviour upon intention was not mediated by attitudes and subjective norms or self-efficacy. Restrictive subjective norms were a stronger predictor in rural and semi-urban than urban schools, while self-efficacy was a stronger predictor in urban and semi-urban compared to rural schools in Arusha.

Authors	Population	N	Design	Self-reported sexual intercourse (%)/ Intentions (I) to be sexually active		>/= two sexual partners or mean number of sexual partners		Condom use (%)/ Intentions (I) to use condoms		Key determinants of sexual behaviour/ behaviour change/ HIV risk
				Boys	Girls	Boys	Girls	Boys	Girls	
Klepp et al., 1997	As for Klepp et al., 1994; 12 month follow-up.	F: 814	As for Klepp et al., 1994	I: 50.8	10.4					Sustained and statistically significant changes noted in intervention sites compared to control sites in the intention to engage in sexual intercourse, and other cognitive predictors noted in Klepp et al., 1994, except for restrictive attitudes towards engaging in sexual intercourse so that though higher, differences were not statistically significant.
Lugoe et al., 1996	Secondary school students stratified by urban/rural location; gender and school grade level of mean age 18.6 years amongst males and 17.7 years in females.	825	Cross sectional	82	33.3			Ever: 26.8 Recent: 21.5		Age and higher school grade level and less religiosity were associated with non-virginity. Higher level of education, delayed sexual debut, prolonged duration of dating before intercourse and having only one sexual partner were all factors associated with condom use in the last sexual encounter.
Lugoe et al., 1995	15–19 years old secondary school students.	655	Cross-sectional.	77.9	34.3					Sexual experience correlated positively with other problem behaviours studied, including smoking, alcohol use and attending discotheques. Sexual experience correlated negatively with measures of religiosity. Findings supported the conventionality–unconventionality polarity suggested by problem behaviour theory.

Authors	N	Population	Design	Self-reported sexual intercourse (%)/ Intentions (I) to be sexually active		>/= two sexual partners or mean number of sexual partners		Condom use (%)/ Intentions (I) to use condoms		Key determinants of sexual behaviour/ behaviour change/ HIV risk
				Boys	Girls	Boys	Girls	Boys	Girls	
Maswanya et al. 1999	1,041	All urban senior secondary and junior college students from accepting institutions (66.7% and 50% acceptance rates respectively) with mean age of 19.8 years amongst males and 18.3 years in females.	Cross-sectional, comparative analysis	75.0 † 56.0	40.0 27.0	††19.0	8.0	‡53.0	36.0	Overall 25% perceived themselves to be at personal risk of acquiring HIV/AIDS; 41% felt their peers were at higher risk than themselves. Males had a lower perception risk than girls. Self-reports of ever being sexually active and current regular sexual activity increased with age and school grade level. Inconsistent condom use was associated with male gender, rural residential locality; peers as sources of HIV/AIDS information and negative attitudes towards condoms. Inconsistent condom use and multiple sexual partners were associated with lower grade level in school; higher risk perception; alcohol use; negative attitudes towards condom use and perception that one can take care of a patient with HIV/AIDS.
Matasha et al., 1998	892	Randomly selected semi-urban primary (PS) and secondary school (SS) students of mean age 15 years.	Cross-sectional	PS: 80.0 SS: 89	68.0 48.0			PS: 31.0 SS: 62.0	25.0 53.0	There was relatively good knowledge on the effects of early sexual activity amongst PS and SS students, though 71% and 76% of PS boys and girls respectively had no knowledge on STDs and their transmission. Rates for SS counterparts in this regard were 26% and 69% respectively. Similar high proportions of PS boys and girls were classified as having no knowledge on HIV/AIDS prevention (42% and 54% respectively). Of the sexually active, 47% of primary and 37% of secondary school girls reported the first sexual act was forced compared to 14% and 13% of their male counter-parts. Of those that were not sexually active, 29% of primary school boys and 14% of secondary school boys were abstinent due to the fear of contracting HIV or STDs, rates for females being 51% and 24% respectively.

Authors	Population	N	Design	Self-reported sexual intercourse (%)/ Intentions (I) to be sexually active		>/= two sexual partners or mean number of sexual partners		Condom use (%)/ Intentions (I) to use condoms		Key determinants of sexual behaviour/ behaviour change/ HIV risk
				Boys	Girls	Boys	Girls	Boys	Girls	
Ndeki et al., 1994	Randomly selected rural and urban primary school students in grades 5, 6, and 7 of mean age 14.7 years, from a low HIV transmission locality (LH) and a high HIV transmission locality (HH).	1,119	Cross-sectional comparative	38.4 LH45.9 HH25.8	14.5 16.9 10.3					HIV/AIDS awareness increased with grade level and locality being higher in the HH locality. Generally girls had more restrictive attitudes towards sex than boys. Perceived risk of HIV/AIDS was high in both LH and HH localities, this being slightly more amongst boys compared to girls. Male gender, LH locality, exposure to AIDS education and attitudes towards sexual behaviour contributed to 12% of the variance in reported sexual behaviour. Knowledge was not significantly associated with sexual behaviour.
Nnko and Pool, 1997	Primary 6 and 7 students of age range 13–18 years.	31	Discourse analysis using role play	-	-	-	-	-	-	Love and sex emerged as ambiguous terms for adolescents; relationships develop to sex rapidly, are short-lived and multiple partners are not unusual While desire motivates males to sexual encounters, girls are motivated by a combination of transactional issues and attraction – poverty increases the transactional nature of sexual relationships. Girls prefer older more experienced partners that provide more material rewards and are more able to be discreet. Pressured or coerced sexual relationships are an issue for particularly girls.
Seha et al., 1994	Pupils of grades 5 and 6 in four purposefully selected rural and urban primary schools. Males: mean age 14.1 years; Females 13.5 years.	464	Cross-sectional formative study – instrument piloting	48.6	12.7	1.6	1.1	2.6 (I. scale range 1–4)	1.9	There was relatively high internal consistency and reliability with alphas ranging from 0.46 to 0.75 for scales measuring social efficacy, social norms, attitudes, knowledge and information exposure. Knowledge, attitudes, social norms, and self-efficacy scales all measured different constructs. AIDS information and communication were positively associated with knowledge; AIDS knowledge was positively associated with restrictive attitudes and social norms toward sexual intercourse and negatively correlated was not associated with sexual behaviour or intention to engage in sex.

Authors	Population	N	Design	Self-reported sexual intercourse (%)/ Intentions (I) to be sexually active		>/= two sexual partners or mean number of sexual partners		Condom use (%)/ Intentions (I) to use condoms		Key determinants of sexual behaviour/ behaviour change/ HIV risk
				Boys	Girls	Boys	Girls	Boys	Girls	
Tengia-Kessy et al., 1998	Multi-stage cluster community based sample of rural youth 15–24 years.	1,104	Cross-sectional survey	46.4	53.6	62.0	52.0	-	-	Males were more likely than females to report an earlier age at sexual debut. Behavioural risk factors for HIV infection amongst both females and males included increasing age. In females they also included blood transfusion in the past 10 years, four or more sexual partners and self-report of oral sex, while in males risk factors were marihuana or nicotine use and self-report of a past STD.
Todd et al., 2004	Children registered in years 4-6 of 121 primary schools in 20 rural communities of Mwanza region, Tanzania.	9,970	Cross-sectional baseline survey	51.2	20.9	72.4 29.6††	46.2 24.1††	2.6‡‡	4.8‡‡	Amongst learners that reported previous exposure to school-based sexual and reproductive health (SRH), both males and females were significantly more likely to know that a healthy looking person could have HIV/AIDS; they were also more likely to know that taking contraception daily will prevent pregnancy; and females were more likely to know consistent condom use prevented pregnancy. However, they were also more likely to have misconceptions about HIV transmission and measures to prevent pregnancy, despite exposure to the existing SRH programmes in the schools. Males were more likely to report an earlier age at sexual debut than females, 33% and 7% respectively reporting onset of sexual acts before their 14th birthday. Reported sexual activity was significantly associated with presence of Chlamydia and N. Gonorrhoea infection in females but not males. Only 39% (n=114) of females and 44% (n=27) of males with biological markers of sexual activity reported ever having sex.

Key: † proportion reporting regular sexual activity at the time of the study; †† proportion reporting multiple sexual partners (not defined in manuscript);
‡ Proportion reporting consistent condom use; ‡‡ Condom use at last sexual act; †† Two or more sexual partners in past 12 months as opposed to in one's life time reported above.

Figure 1. Percentage of married youth (15–24 years)
extracted from 1967, 1978 and 1988 census data.

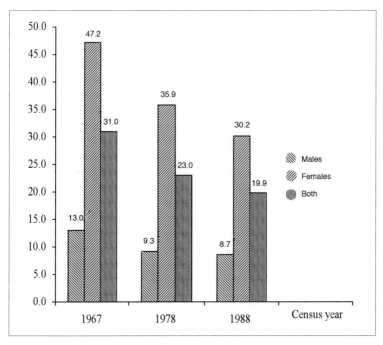

Source: Leshabari and Kaaya, 1997.

8. To Risk or not to Risk? Is It a Question? Sexual Debut, Poverty and Vulnerability in Times of HIV

A Case from Kigoma Region, Tanzania

Graziella Van den Bergh[1]

Abstract

The aim of this chapter is to focus upon the vulnerability of the younger adolescents in some contexts aggravated by the AIDS epidemic. This discussion of the micro-dynamics of the epidemic is based on empirical findings resulting from year-long fieldwork in a historically and economically underdeveloped region of Tanzania experiencing a substantial influx of refugees. The age-group between 5 and 14 years have been called the "window of hope" because they usually attend school and have been less affected by HIV infection. In my discussion based on primary school pupils' narratives of their entering the sexual arena, I argue that in poverty-stricken contexts, part of this group may represent a "porthole of concern". According to the pupils' accounts, and in spite of some general awareness about the epidemic, a number of preadolescents and adolescents appear to start having unsafe sex much earlier than generally recognised. The youth reported behaviours implying sexual intercourse even before they had attained sexual maturity, and the trend of having several, short-lasting sexual relationships was repeatedly described, by girls and boys. Awareness of their own susceptibility to infection was very poor, and this was combined with a substantial communication gap between generations. My argument is based on material collected through focus group discussions, and I thoroughly inspect possible methodological biases. Further, although the phenomenon I discuss relates to specific districts in Tanzania, I argue that this trend may be emerging in a number of underprivileged settings. I finally point to the urgency of addressing the issue openly, and to the implications for preventive strategies for this extremely vulnerable group. This is particularly vital considering the increasing number of orphans, the weakening caring capacity of communities, and the consequences of sexual abuse and violence against the youngest in times of AIDS.

1. Thanks are due to all who assisted me during my fieldwork in Kigoma, not least young people, and to the Tanzania Commission for Science and Technology for granting ethical clearance for my PhD research on the topic of adolescent reproductive health. I gratefully thank Dr. Akosua Adomako Ampofo, Institute of African Studies, University of Ghana; Dr. Haldis Haukanes, Centre for Women's and Gender Research and Dr. Marguerite Lorraine Daniel, Hemil Centre, University of Bergen, as well as the editors, NAI reviewers and Sheri Bastien for critical comments and proofreading.

In the face of the grave threat posed by HIV/AIDS, we have to rise above our differences and combine our efforts to save our people... History will judge us harshly if we fail to do so.
(Nelson Mandela, addressing the delegates at the AIDS Conference in Durban, July 2000.)

Vulnerable children, sexual debut and HIV: Breaking the smothering silence

It is recognised that young age, in addition to gender, disability, poverty, migration and periods of social-cultural and/or political and economic transition are all factors making individuals vulnerable to HIV. At the turn of the millennium, nearly half of all HIV infections world-wide occurred among people under age 25 (Barnett & Schueller, 2000). Every day, an estimated 6,000 youth are infected with the virus, and of the 15–24 year old youths living with HIV, 63% live in sub-Saharan Africa[1] (UNFPA, 2005; WHO et al., 2006).

In Botswana, South Africa, and Malawi, HIV prevalence among antenatal clinic attendees less than 20 years of age varied between 15 % and 30% in the late 1990s, and rates continue to rise (UNAIDS, 2004a,b,d). In Zimbabwe, since 1995, an average of 30% of pregnant clinic attendees less than 20 years of age have tested positive for HIV, which in Harare included 28% of girls 15 to 17 years of age.[2] (UNAIDS, 2000). By 2004, it was estimated that incidence has stayed roughly steady since 1996–1997 (UNAIDS, 2004a). In East Africa, the situation may be more heartening. In 1997 in Tanzania, HIV prevalence among the 15–24 years group ranged from 4% to 44% prevalence, and age details from 1995–1996 showed that 7% of those less than 20 years of age tested HIV positive. However, intense prevention efforts in one region made HIV prevalence among 15–24 year-old women fall from 20.5% in 1994–95 to 14.6% in 2000, while in another region where only sporadic efforts were mounted, prevalence in the same age group rose from 22.5% in 1994 to 30.2% in 1999 (UNAIDS, 2000a,b,c,d,e; 2004a, b, c). By and large, in sub-Saharan Africa, girls aged 15–24 years are about three times more likely to get infected with HIV/AIDS as compared to young men of the same age, and in South Africa, Zambia and Zimbabwe, even up to six times more likely (UNAIDS, 2004a; 2006).

---

1. 21% live in Asia-Pacific (UNFPA, 2005).
2. Peak infection rates of 49% were among women 20 to 24 years of age (UNAIDS, 2000).

Thus, statistics show the vital importance of focusing on adolescent girls. However, numerical measures do not explain the micro-dynamics fuelling of the epidemic, and medical categorisations are biased when it comes to issues pertaining to sexuality. For instance, demographic and reproductive health statistics usually operate from 15 years and onwards. Further, there is a tendency to see HIV/AIDS as being an issue that should be dealt with by the health sector only. Yet, factors exposing a 13 year old school-girl to sex will be quite different from those influencing a marriageable 16 year old girl, not to speak of a 24 year old woman. Age, gender-roles, location, class and young people's life-world are crucial and interrelated determinants of health (Pedersen et al., 2003; Allen, 2004).

During the African Development Forum 2000 Conference, AIDS was defined as the greatest leadership challenge, and specific factors were recognised as negatively affecting national responses (United Nations, 2000). I suggest that some of these factors apply to the case of children, such as the absence of an adequate sense of urgency, and the smothering silence about their sexual exposure to HIV/AIDS, in spite of the increasing awareness about young people's early and unprotected sexual involvement, and of their being abused (Munthali et al., 2006; Leach, 2004). One reason may be that children's and adolescents' sexuality is something which in many societies of the world tends to be kept secret, and this is also the case for sexual abuse. It is time, however, to lift this cloak of silence.

The Window of Hope, and the porthole of concern?

In this chapter, the focus is on the age group between 5 and 14 years, or those defined as representing the "Window of Hope" (UN, 2000). The group is associated with lower prevalence of HIV infection than older age groups, and these children represent hope because they are likely to be either in primary education or in the lower classes of secondary school. Being at school is expected to provide life skills and protection from HIV infection. However, the increasing number of orphans and the socio-economic impact of the epidemic have resulted in lower school attendance (World Bank, 2002; UN, 2006). Further, in many contexts, school participation is not entirely risk free.

In this chapter, I will discuss findings collected in 1998–1999 in a deprived and marginal region of Western Tanzania, when I studied young girls' coming of age and their coping with the negative consequences of being sexually active. The phenomenon discussed here relates to the time of onset and type of sexual relations among a number of children and youth, and my argument is that a noteworthy group of the pre-pubescent and adolescent generation are exposed to unsafe sex much earlier than generally recognised. The behaviours young people reported implied unprotected sexual intercourse, most often combined with very poor awareness about their own susceptibility to HIV infection, something which seems to be furthered by an increasing communication gap between generations.[1] Though my material relates to specific districts in Tanzania, I argue that cognitive aspects particular for this young age group, their peer-culture, combined with socio-cultural and politico-economic factors together may explain this age group's emerging liability in a number of disadvantaged settings. This implies that social and educational pre-sexual exposure measures should be emphasised. Moreover, additional qualitative research on children's and youths' living conditions and sexual vulnerability is needed (Scheper-Hughes & Sargent, 1999; Van den Bergh, forthcoming).

Research setting, methodology and constraints

The case of Kigoma Region, Tanzania

During the mid-19th century, the Tanganyika Lake shore districts of Kigoma Region were reached by the Arab slave and ivory route. Ujiji was colonized by Swahili merchants, and became a slave market (Brown, 1971). Later on, colonial policies of cash cropping carved out the region deliberately as a 'labour-reservoir' bringing about a massive male work migration out of the region (Iliffe, 1979). These invasions significantly altered life-patterns in increasingly multi-ethnic communities, and brought about disruption of household structures and abrupt changes in the socialisation of children. After independence, social development programmes and universal primary education (UPE) were implemented. However, in spite of being part of Nyerere's African Socialism project, Kigoma region is still described as one of those with the lowest social economic status[2] (Van den Bergh, 1995; forthcoming; Mbelle & Katabaro, 2003). The region had a population of over one million inhabitants according to 1996 population projections, of whom more than 50% were under 19 years. The actual population size in-

---

1. See Van den Bergh (2008) for a discussion of intergenerational relations.
2. The maternal mortality rate for Kigoma Urban district was of 349/100,000 by 1996, something which suggests a poor reproductive health status in general. 50 per cent of the region's population is living below the poverty line and the GDP per capita in the region ranks next to last among the 20 mainland regions of Tanzania (United Republic of Tanzania, 1997b).

creased enormously in late 1993, following the refugee flow from Burundi and Congo, and as of September 2000, 350,693 refugees were registered (Landau, 2000).

To understand contemporary social differentiation and life-chances for young people in these post-colonized and impoverished contexts in the era of AIDS, I addressed children in one of the principal arenas where they move about, the school.

Enquiring about children's and youths' sexual relations

The empirical material on which my argument is based was collected during a 13 month period of fieldwork stretching from April 1998 up to December 1999 (Van den Bergh, forthcoming). A variety of research techniques were used throughout the fieldwork, such as the recording of young people's life-stories, interviews, small interventions such as peer-health education courses and a youth-friendly sexual health clinic. In the discussion below, narratives collected during group interviews are the main source, and the excerpts were chosen because they resulted in being representative of the life-realities of many youths.

In fact, participant observation in urban daily life was a necessary method, though insufficient to provide adequate insight into youths' interpersonal and group behaviour in the field of sexual relations. I lived in a middle-class neighbourhood surrounded by households having adolescents either as family members or as employees. Girls employed as house-workers were taking care of children, cooking, cleaning and working in the garden, while boys usually became part of the household for farming work, and for running petty-trade invested in by their patron-household to supplement the latter's low official salaries. This allowed me to experience how young people are socialised, and to observe their relations with adults. It also allowed me to see what events and relations meant for them in a day-to-day perspective, and what life-prospects individuals saw for themselves. However, their sexual relations remained secret. This made it imperative to use active interviewing methods.[1]

Thus, 31 focus group discussions were conducted in 27 primary schools in Kigoma Urban and Rural Districts during the autumn of 1998 and

---

1. Throughout the fieldwork, small, collaborative projects were organised. The goal was to enable youths to reason about their risk of HIV and pregnancy. Moreover, interactive methods were expected to generate rich material, informed by a dialogic epistemology (see Schoepf, 1998). This was facilitated by several years of health-work and research experience in the region, as well as by fluent knowledge of Swahili.

spring of 1999. I travelled by boat to isolated fishing villages along the lakeshore and to inland road-settlements and distant villages on the way to Burundi by car. In the schools, groups were composed of pupils from standard V, VI and VII classes. The participants were aged between 12 and 20 years, and girls-only, boys-only and mixed groups were interviewed, while teachers were systematically kept out of the group discussions. These were usually conducted in a classroom or a place under a tree, and participants were picked out casually. It cannot be ruled out that some times, subconsciously, those who looked most assertive were selected, and that the more shy ones, and perhaps less sexually active ones, were less represented. Further, participation was based on children's consent, after selection had taken place.

We were usually two researchers who alternated in the function of facilitating and recording the discussions. The pupils used to discuss their amorous life quite openly and pragmatically, while romantic feelings seemed not to fit in the forum of these discussions. A reason may be the problem-oriented focus of the probing questions, which took up unwanted pregnancy, abortion, AIDS and the need for sexual education and services, thus justifying the intimate topics which were discussed. The pupils were eager to debate these problems, which clearly seemed to concern their daily life realities. They seemed at ease talking with adults willing to address these subjects, and they had innumerable questions to ask at the end of the sessions. However, because the focus was upon sexual activity and its consequences, the behaviours and motivations of those who chose not to be sexually active were not addressed.

The research assistants were mainly nurses and midwives from the governmental health services. They felt comfortable in answering children's questions about sexual and reproductive health issues, even though these could be extremely surprising to them, as to me. From an ethical point of view, the focus group discussions were experienced as a fair exchange of knowledge. After the discussions, in each school, we left educational material such as videos and booklets with the pupils' representatives, so as to enable them to distribute some of the knowledge acquired.[1]

---

1. It was noted by several teachers that, in fact, the whole school would have benefited from this type of participatory research session.

Primary school or the key to a "good life"?

Life is hard, you know...

What were children's perceptions about attending the institution where many spend large parts of their childhood? To what extent did it correspond with the idealised postage stamp pictures of well-clothed girls and boys with bright white blouses and socks? A 16 year old school boy in Kigoma town had the following to say:

> Well, pupils' life is good you know, except when economic problems arise... Many parents do not afford to help their children... This is because many have a poor income... It is true, if they earn something, they use it for covering the needs of the family, for food... If they have a field such as for instance in the river-delta, they may save some money, and get some surplus, but many do not have... They have no money to rent such a field, and certainly not to buy it...

In the primary schools of many of the lake-shore villages, poverty was very often said to influence children's daily life. For instance, the fact that some pupils got neither uniform nor shoes from their parents, and therefore felt ashamed to meet at school, was one of the repeated reasons given for absenteeism. The poor economic and social background of the pupils gave further grounds for what children themselves interpreted as problematic behaviour. A boy in a mixed group said: *Many youths have problems: they lack money, they smoke cannabis, they drink alcohol.... To get this money, they resort either to theft or to sex for money (umalaya).* Yet, disciplinary punishment was another cause given for not thriving or not coping well as a pupil: *Some are afraid of being beaten, especially if... they misbehaved, or did not attend school without justification...* Corporal castigation was practised on a daily basis in most schools, and was perceived as a recurring motive for truancy, both for boys and girls. Another reason for not attending was having to care for sick family members at home.

Statistics from the Regional Education Office on truancy rates confirm that poverty at a household level is significant. For instance, during 1997, an average of 10% to 20% of primary school children in the region dropped out at each level from Standard IV to VII, culminating in 25% truancy at Standard VII level. Figures for 1998 seemed to become even higher. Reasons given for truancy are labour, as house-helps for girls, and on tobacco plantations, in mines or in petty-trade for boys (REO, 1998).[1]

---

1. Poverty and the effect it has on girls is reflected by the fact that several of those very few who were chosen to go on with secondary school could not do so because

The Case of Tabu

Something of the life history of Tabu, an 11 or 12 year old schoolgirl, may be illustrative of how prevailing contexts easily divert children from continuing school. When I met her, Tabu was enrolled in Standard II in the primary school where one of my acquaintances was teaching, but soon after, she ended as one of the many school "dropouts".

Due to inadequate governmental salaries, most employees find alternative economic niches to combine with their work. For teachers, private tuition of primary school children at home, after school, is one of these. Another is the sale of various foods, sweets and other items in the school setting, where the pupils themselves in fact become the largest client group. Often, pupils are assigned to "help" their teachers with these kinds of private commercial tasks, before or during school time. When Tabu moved into her teacher's house, my acquaintance told me that her pupil was not motivated for schoolwork, and that she had poor attendance and performance. Therefore, her teacher suggested to her that she became one of her house-girls, to stay at her place and help her produce and sell cakes and ice-bits. Thus, Tabu moved into the teacher's house, where she shared a room together with another house-girl and a younger relative of the teacher.

She soon learned how to mix water with sugar and colorants, how to put it in small plastic bags and how to cauterise these. She carried these in a picnic box to crossroads or near schools for sale. One day, at most two months after having left school for work, she was surprised by her employer while chatting with boys on the street. She was accused of being negligent and untrustworthy, and money was said to be lacking. She was fired, and was replaced by an older boy from a village. I met Tabu some months later, hanging around the market. She had abandoned school forever, and was only "helping her mother" with petty-trade. She was a charming, pretty, and light-hearted girl-child, and, as I will show, a potentially very easy prey for boys and men bargaining with promises and small rewards for her sexual favours. She represents very well the increasing number of girls with poor support from home, little motivation for schooling and who are extremely vulnerable to premature sexual exposure. However, although school dropouts are unquestionably more at risk in the present epidemic context, the in-school youths should also be considered. Indeed, even if pupils are privileged, and even if they can be expected to be less prone to sexual involvement because of educational aspirations, peer-cultures at school appeared not to be harmless.

of inability to pay for further education (REO, 1998).

From "playing" to "making love": The imperceptible onset of sexual intercourse

According to the narratives of the primary school children in both districts, starting to have sexual intercourse with pupils and youth of the opposite sex is something which may begin pretty early. This seemed to be especially true for girls, but also for boys, and the latter's expressed wish for a love affair with a girl may evolve very fast to "real things". As views and perceptions were repeated, in one group after another, it became clear that the pupils seemed to conceptualise sexual relations differently, often according to the age of those practising sex, and according to the gendered construction of these relations (Van den Bergh, forthcoming).

In a girls-only group in a fishing village along the lakeshore, it was said that half of the pupils at school had started having sex with each other: *They start when 10 to 13 years old and onwards... It is the boys who start first...,* the girls claimed. In another girls only group, the prediction of sexual onset was said to be around 12–13 years, while sexual activity among pupils by the end of primary school was suggested to be approximately 90 per cent. The same female group asserted that those who kept with the same lover for a long time were *...very, very seldom*. In a boys-only group, one said: *Girls may start when they are about 8 and up to 15... it depends where they are living, in which neighbourhoods... They start also before they get their first menstruation. To have sex helps them to mature faster.*[1] When asked about estimating how many among last year pupils had started their sexual career, another boy in the same group said*: About 75 per cent of the boys and 100 per cent of the girls have already started having sex... Very few girls finish primary school without having been involved in sex...* In a mixed group, a boy stated: *For boys, they usually start when 14 years old, and some may also frequent "wavuta bangi" (cannabis smokers) by then...*

There seemed to be two recurrent interpretations for the very early sexual experiences according to the pupils. One was that children were "starting playing sex" together (*wanaanza kucheza*) or "experimenting, as children usually do". "Playing sex" seemed first and foremost to imply the ingenuousness and very young age of those involved, and the lack of more elaborate courtship rituals, which seemed to be associated with more adult-like, gendered exchange relations. Even if in practice, erotic manipulation of the

---

1. The idea of sperm as promoting female sexual maturity is common in a number of African settings (see Talle, 1994). The lowest age cited for sexual debut was 7 years. This was stated in a lakeshore village close to Burundi.

genitals and penetration could be both attempted and practised by girls and boys, this seemed to be considered as innocent behaviour.

Another and less inoffensive explanation given for very early sex was that the children lived in families where ...*they saw such behaviour happening in the house, so they learned from it.* The opinion that children tend to imitate what they observe from adults or on pornographic videos was often voiced, also by adults, who emphasised today's overcrowded housing as an important reason for what was happening with "today's children's behaviour"[1]. The pupils also repeatedly pointed out that younger children could be approached by older people wanting to involve them in a sexual event.

To sum up, female sexual debut around 12 years of age was said to be current among a number of pupils, in town as well as in the villages. Schoolgirls were not really seen as more protected from the temptation of getting involved than out-of-school girls. As expressed by a mixed group of 15 year old pupils:

> *Some girls start "kufanya uhuni"* (to behave immorally) *even before they have started menstruating. They just decide to start... The girls who involve in sex when 10 years old, they do it often with older pupils or adult men... As a school-girl, you get more easily addressed by delinquents. A man may suggest to you to escort you on your way to school, and he brings you to his place. At school, the teacher will think you stayed at home that day...*

I will now attempt to explain how and why sexual initiation is occurring, as alleged by the Kigoma youngsters. Considering that primary education has created a long non-marital period of adolescence which did not exist in pre-colonial and colonial times, and considering the biological and social vulnerability of the youngest, it is more important than ever to put the rationales of early sexual debut into focus.

Love, lust and gift exchange: The gendered initiation of sexual intercourse

A common discourse among youngsters explaining why many of the 12–13 years old and onwards engaged in sex was *"tamaa"*, which meant desire, but which easily could become "greed". Yet, younger girls were believed to be purposely lured into a sexual relationship, either by other girls or by men. In contrast to innocent childish sex-play, adult-like sexual relations between

---

1. All of the interviewers, the Tanzanian women assisting me and myself, were disturbed when group after group detailed the age of sexual debut for some youngsters.

pupils or with older partners were induced by seduction rituals implying various promises. A mixed group in town depicted the following scenario between a schoolboy or young man encountering a female pupil:

Hello, sister, can you do me a favour?" If the girl offers him attention, the boy will soon tell her that he likes her very much. When asked whether girls would agree to listen, most pupils affirmed yes indeed, and added that most girls will answer that they too like the guy. "They will very soon start talking about sex, and planning for it, and many girls will go for it, without thinking about AIDS… Finally, when he has made love to her, he may just drop her, because he got what he wanted and that was just to see how she was shaped…

In addition to verbal advances, sometimes boys send a letter to the girl, and, also then, it will only take a short time before they have sex. Yet, in Kigoma, the writing of love-letters was not popular.[1] These were said to represent a threat, because these could either be discovered by the adults or could be shown to teachers by the girls who did not want sex.

The issue of girls being cheated was not only a self-apologizing female claim. A boys-only group confirmed this, as well as the boys adding other male and female rationales:

A girl, you can get her by cheating her, or by money, or she may like you herself, so you agree both of you, without giving her money… But many girls do it because of their greed for money (tamaa ya pesa)…Boys, they just have lust (tamaa ya mapenzi). School-girls do these things because they are following a trend (kufuata mwenendo). Most of their lovers are boys from outside, and some are pupils… Older lovers may be bus-conductors, or employees, or petty-traders, or those running small affairs….

Thus, the prompt acceptance of "many" girls to get involved in these relations was asserted, and explained in the following manner by 12 to 13 year old girls and boys:

Temptations (for girls) are numerous you know, especially if you decide to frequent out-of-school girls, the result will be that you too involve in "uhuni" … These friends will bring you in contact with men, and instruct you on how to start talking with them, and finally how to have sex with them (kufanya mapenzi). The reward will be 500 shillings[2]… Or small things to eat, such as biscuits, sweets etc. Many girls will agree. Those who are forced are only few of them. If you tell the boy about HIV/AIDS, he will not bother; he will press you to have sex… That's why many

---

1. This finding contrasted with the situation in Kilimanjaro, where the writing of love-letters was very common (Van den Bergh, 1996).
2. 100 Tanzania Shilling in 1999 was equivalent to 0.14 Euro.

times, girls get involved in sex (tendo la kujamiiana), after being cheated by peers. Therefore, some girls may have 3 to 5 or even more boy-friends.

Some additional ways to seduce a girl were also revealed. One was the use of traditional medicines, to make the girl agree, or to get her to fall in love with you; another was to give the girl "sleeping drugs". Regarding the timing that was chosen for having sex, it was said that either they would do it during school-time, or it could happen when parents sent their children to do an errand for them. The youths would then cheat their parents, and tell them for instance that they visited somebody. Instead they would go and hide where nobody might see them, or go to the guesthouse.[1]

Thus, for pupils, having sexual relations was perceived as morally wrong. However, the social rewards of engaging in sex made some overcome these objections, and pressure from both peers and from assertive boys or men seemed to be persuasive.

The negotiation of desires: Gifts of scarcity and gendered pragmatics

To involve in "*uhuni*", or improper, wrong behaviour, was thus considered as something that "...*many girls do these days... This is because they need things for school, such as fees, or a uniform... Then, once she has begun, she gets used to this way of helping herself, and she will even forget to follow well at school....*" The most widespread gift, money, could amount to as little as 10 shilling, while the highest was 5,000 and 10,000 shillings. These were rare extremes, and the receivers were respectively the youngest and the oldest girls. Common amounts were 200, 500 and 1,000 shillings. Besides these gifts of scarcity, gendered pragmatics could develop into specific types of relations: "*Some girls at school have started having sex because they got a regular "mshikaji" (a boy-friend), or a "mshefa" (a protector-lover)... They are not afraid of AIDS... They are happy to get their wants fulfilled, such as shoes to go to school, or other goods*". However, this attitude to sex was not the only one. For instance, in a girls-only group in a lakeshore village, the pupils asserted that some girls were waiting to have sex until they finished primary school, because they understood the "...*importance of education...*".

Notwithstanding, in one of the most talkative mixed groups in town, it was affirmed that boys and girls by and large preferred furtive and temporary relationships, thus allowing them to have several partners, though

---

1. Guesthouses are small hotels where rooms can be rented for short periods.

trying to keep these unaware of each other. Indeed, if a boy discovered his girlfriend had another boyfriend, this would create conflict, and the girl would be beaten up or left, while a fight between the boys involved was also an alternative. Therefore, a girl would take care to have her boyfriends located in different places: "*...maybe one at school, one in the neighbourhood, one among the petty-traders on the street...*" According to girls, having more than one boyfriend was a way of coping with the fact that they were easily given false promises, offended and taken advantage of.

Boys seemed to follow different norms when they pursued multiple relationships. It was a question of competing to be the greatest seducer in the eyes of other boys, and having many lovers at the same time was expected behaviour for males. By girls, boys were perceived as always looking for new partners because they soon got tired of the same girl.

Thus, having multiple relationships could be true for both sexes, although the groups seemed to perceive boys' and girls' motivations and practices as different. In a primary school in an isolated mountain village, the pupils suggested that boys could have an average of 4 lovers, while girls only 2, and that boys changed partner more often. Further, the same mixed group of 12 to 18 year old pupils suggested that one quarter had "real love" relationships (*upendo wa kweli*), while the rest had as many lovers as possible. Maybe, in small villages, simultaneous multiple relationships were less common than in town. However, having secret affairs in other villages was said to be an alternative.

To sum up, sexual initiation and relations between schoolgirls and boys or men were reported to be usual for many pupils attending the three or four last years of primary school. Girl-only groups were by no means less affirmative about this picture. Sex was considered as something many pupils felt easy to get involved with in their early teens, and in spite of the fact that they knew it was illicit in the eyes of the adult community. The girls' and boys' motivations seemed to be different. For girls, sexual relations were almost always accompanied by symbolic and material gifts or services. The promise of a lasting relationship involving support of one kind or another was not least motivating for girls living in communities where prospects of future economic independence were poor. For boys, the pleasure of seducing and of boasting about female conquests was rewarding, though limited by one's ability to persuade girls or to offer them presents. Yet, it was regularly argued that boys cheated girls with false promises (*kudanganya*).

As I suggest elsewhere, the gift-for-sex exchanges characterising these relations may be understood as a childish copying and transformation by the youngest of cultural forms of exchange since erstwhile regulating gender and generational relations. The negotiation of female sexuality and fertility through marriage for example, was often enacted through the exchange of socially embedded gifts, such the bride-wealth. This situated the control of female reproduction within lineages and between males (see Rubin, 1975). In present time, such gendered and generational hierachies seemed to persist during coming of age, yet in changed forms. Weakened parental authority had freed more space for both girls and boys to choose when to enter the sexual arena, yet at the same time exposing them more to new forms of unequal power relations, depending on class or economic positioning. Many groups claimed that at least half of the pupils had started having sex before leaving primary school, while others could not believe that there were any virgins left by then. Even so, resilient love relationships maybe lasting until marriage were reported to exist, but to occur very rarely in town, and a bit more frequently in rural settings.

I will now elaborate on cognitive, social and cultural factors possibly influencing the gendered play and the premature sexual relations of the younger adolescents.

Pre-adolescent and adolescent peer cultures

During pre-adolescence and adolescence,[1] children are struggling to gain stable identities, and their peer cultures provide a sense of autonomy from adults and an arena for dealing with uncertainties. At the same time, it is a period when they recognize how they are affected by the adult world (Corsaro, 1997). Gender identity and relations develop significantly then, including the children's perception of who they are as females and males, and of their place in the social structure (Whiting, 1990).

Anthropological and sociological studies of childhood show that friendship, social differentiation and gender are related phenomena in the peer cultures of pre-adolescents (Thorne, 1993; Corsaro, 1997; Scheper-Hughes & Sargent, 1999). According to studies focusing primarily on societies in the northern hemisphere, girls concerns centre around the valuing of compliance and conformity, romantic love, and an ideology of domesticity, while boys' concerns revolve around a cult of masculinity, around physical

---

1. Pre-adolescence is the period from 7 to 12 or 13 years of age, according to Bledsoe, Lerner & Guyer, 2000 and Corsaro, 1997, respectively. WHO's definition of adolescence is between 10 and 19 years of age.

contests, autonomy and self-reliance (Corsaro, 1997).[1] Studies of pre-adolescent children's lore, such as verbal dispute routines and cross-gender play and rituals in school and daily life illustrate how children in the process of engaging in these activities address issues related to self, identity and autonomy from adult control. Conflict and co-operation are often overlapping processes that are embedded in the larger ethos of gendered playfulness (Thorne, 1993). The gendered sexual courtship as described by the Tanzanian pupils brings to mind these informal cross-gender rituals observed in other contexts. For example, the gendered verbal disputes and sex-for-gift exchanges of the Kigoma pupils resemble the type of conflict and co-operation processes between children in Californian schools (Thorne, 1993), only differing in form and content. The giving and the accepting of gifts by Tanzanian boys and girls is related to the search for an adult identity in a context where material and symbolic gift exchange characterizes adult gender and sexual relations.

Moreover, as suggested in studies in Norway, the exchange or sale of sexual services by younger teenagers cannot be sufficiently explained by economic need or despair. Emotional needs and the youths' interpretation of these sexual favours as acts of friendship or love are important factors to consider (Hegna & Pedersen, 2002).

Yet, in a context of AIDS, and when peer pressure together with unequal power relations often results in unprotected sexual intercourse, these relations lose their innocence. "Gendered plays" are indeed conditioned by and entail consequential structures of power. As Thorne reminds us: "…The metaphor of play goes a long way in helping one grasp the social construction of gender, but at a certain point, like all metaphors, it falls short…" (Thorne 1993:6). Thus, the play of gift exchanges may be the core of young girls' vulnerability. In sub-Saharan settings where only a small minority of girls may expect to attend secondary school (World Bank, 2002), getting married remains their main goal. This may lead them to get involved in relations, which they know can result in pregnancy, but also in an independent household.

From "playing" to abuse

As demonstrated thus far, there was little awareness among children of imbalances in negotiating power between girls and boys and between children and adults.

---

1. However, a separate gender culture view of peer relations has been challenged by studies documenting a greater complexity in gender relations (Corsaro, 1997).

For instance, once the girls responded to the boys' or older men's approaches, their sexual career could evolve very fast and far before any notion of "safe" sex might develop. As it was told, boys could tell the girl how beautiful she was, and praise her, or they could offer her a free bus-trip, or let her see the video for free, or any other gift. ...After that, "...*you can "want her", because you have already done so much good for her, and she can't refuse anymore..."* Thus, receiving gifts implied that the girl had to reciprocate. If she refused, she would be forced, and broken deals always fostered gender-antagonism.[1]

A lack of solidarity also appeared when unwanted pregnancy occurred. Many of the teenagers who chose to have an abortion, and whose age ranged from 13 years and onwards, had got pregnant with older boys or wealthier men, who had disappeared when pregnancy was a fact (Van den Bergh, forthcoming). Yet, some times, when the men were well-established and married, and the girl's pregnancy could be a threat to their reputation, they would pay for the abortion.

In several groups, hardship and sheer poverty (*umaskini*) were seen as the main incentives for premature sexual relations. In the most distant community visited to the south, where the large ships docked, girls explained that, in their search for subsistence, some would have sex for free, because they [unknowingly] accepted out-of-date money from Zaire, which had no value anymore... Or they did it for just 200 shillings...The girls clarified: "*There are people from many tribes here..., the girls do not choose, the issue is to get money..."*

Poverty and social misery, combined with children's generally low ranking position easily make them susceptible to more extreme sexual abuse, as the following example found in a populous division in Kigoma town illustrates.

As members of Ndela, a newly established youth project emphasising HIV prevention, we decided to start classes for children of primary school age who were out of school. A teacher voluntarily surveyed her neighbourhood for those children interested in afternoon classes, and she assembled a class of 18 children. After teaching them for a while, she noticed that two sisters who were 9 and 11 years respectively were repeatedly tired during the classes, and that they were not attending regularly. After some enquiries in the locality, it appeared that the family had a bad reputation. The mother had two adult sons living at home, while her husband was said to be in jail.

---

1. Teachers or other authoritative figures in the youths' daily life were not excluded from these relations.

She was producing alcohol for sale, and her neighbours told the teacher that the daughters were used sexually by the customers and other acquaintances of the mother and brothers. The girls themselves told the teacher that the men who visited them also practised anal sex on them.[1]

When discussing the case with health workers, with intervention in mind, they all defined the situation as hopeless, and totally out of their reach. These girls living in delinquent households may represent those children who, according to the narratives of pupils, engage in sex because of "...*their family background*". They probably represent only a small minority of those school-aged children living in miserable conditions. However, this minority may be increasing together with the number of orphans and destitute created by the AIDS epidemic. Orphans and street-children are more vulnerable to violence and to sexual ill-being, because what matters is the immediate problem: to survive (Rajani & Kudrati, 1996). The breaking down of traditional forms of communal control over the welfare of children and the increasing burden of disease on the caring capacity of communities may promote victimisation of this very young age group in general, and girls in particular.

Local phenomenon or social trend?

At this point, I will discuss the phenomenon of early sexual socialisation described above critically. A first compelling question may be of methodological character. In fact, although early sexual debut was reported time and again by a large majority of the groups, misconceptions amongst the pupils and overestimation of the sexual behaviour of their peers cannot be ruled out. Indeed, deviant norms and behaviours may be attributed to a majority when this in fact is not justified; something called the "majority fallacy" (Pedersen, 1993). In a survey on Norwegian adolescents' alcohol use, the 5 per cent of the students in 7th, 8th and 9th grade, who themselves reported weekly alcohol use, overestimated the number of fellow students using alcohol every week seven-fold! (Aas & Klepp, 1992). This phenomenon may be explained by "false consensus", which implies that one's own experiences are regarded as more common in the reference groups than is warranted. On the other hand, the fact that certain individuals with more deviant

---

1. A neighbour of the family had explained to the teacher that her 7 year old son had had a urinary tract infection for a long time. After attending the hospital, the infection turned out to be a sexually transmitted disease, and the neighbour mother claimed that the child had admitted to having played sex with one of the girls in question.

norms are to be found in many people's reference groups, may also explain alleged excessive behaviour (Pedersen, 1993). Thus, the most talkative pupils may have projected their own or a few others' "*uhuni*" behaviour onto the majority of fellow pupils. As pointed to earlier, the pupils ranged from 12 to 20 years, and the opinion of the older ones may have overshadowed the narratives.[1]

However, when the early age for being involved in sex was stated the first times during the interviews, we were sceptical about what was being told. But when female groups were as affirmative as male ones, and when the phenomenon was repeatedly described both in urban and rural settings, we as researchers moved towards believing the accounts. Focus group discussion being a qualitative research technique, it makes little sense to guess approximate percentages of those actually engaging in early sexual intercourse in our case. In any case, even if unsafe sexual relations were the norm only in a minority, awareness raising both about misconceived and actual risky behaviours remains of prime importance.[2]

A second critical question may be whether the local context of Kigoma Districts reflects very particular historical, social and economic realities, which are difficult to imagine in other geographic sites. There were huge contextual differences between the multi-ethnic and multi-religious urban contexts of Kigoma and Ujiji, and that of rural areas, and between a boat-linked location along Lake Tanganyika, or along the road. In Kigoma town and in the road villages, images from the outside world were perhaps more penetrating, with several personnel from the UN High Commission for Refugees (UNHCR) and other NGO's engaged in refugee-related activities being part of the landscape, displaying goods, well-being and money on their way to the refugee camps. These attractive windows on the world's affluence certainly create different dreams and desires amongst youth, and

---

1. It might also be argued that what the pupils told about were manifestations of inflated identity contrasting the "bad" others with the "good" respondents (NAI reviewer, 2006). Probably, the youngsters in the 31 groups did not identify with the most extreme examples they gave, but time and again, they repeated the very same trends as occurring among pupils in general, without suggesting having totally different life-styles themselves.
2. When answering questions at the end of each session, we insisted upon the biological vulnerability of the youngest ones in regards to HIV transmission. Further, the "majority fallacy" points to the importance of correcting misconceptions about how much sex fellow pupils really have. Indeed, a fictitious norm pressure may develop, and in particular young people in loosely integrated groups are thought to be at risk, although friends too may be promoting deviant behaviour, such as was proven in the case of drug-use (Pedersen, 1993).

in geographically or culturally isolated settings such an impact may be less obvious. However, despite these differences, it seemed to be the social and economic insecurity affecting children's lives and expectations in general which was the common issue for them. These uncertainties are present in several contexts, in Africa and elsewhere, and to an increasing degree today because of the HIV epidemic (UN, 2000; Honwana & De Boeck, 2005).

Moreover, similar trends of early intercourse debut and exchange have been described in other contexts. According to research conducted in Tanzania, it has been concluded that about half of the youths have initiated having sexual relations before the age of 15 years. A study run in 1992 among primary school pupils found a mean age of 14 years for sexual debut (Klepp et al., 1995). Research carried out in the regions of Lindi, Tanga and Iringa indicates that most adolescents there start having sexual relations by an average of 13-14 years and are experienced by 17–20 years (Mwateba et al., 1999; Pfander, 2000). According to a survey in Mwanza region, about half of the girls interviewed in the highest three classes of 62 primary schools had had sex, and a large proportion of them had had sex before their first menstruation (Mgalla et al., 1997).

Thus, pre-adolescents and adolescents engaging, to different degrees, in sexual relations may be a social trend characterising today's children's and peer cultures. Qualitative research has illustrated that this may be the case in other sub-Saharan countries. According to peer health educators in Ethiopia, information should be given as early as age 10 to12 because they experience that children are practising sex at an early age (Barnett & Schueller, 2000). Similar trends were observed in communities along Lake Victoria in Uganda (Arube-Wani, personal communication).[1] Further, a survey from 1995 in Botswana combined with qualitative data suggests that adolescents become sexually active at an early age, and that many of them, males and females alike, have multiple sex partners. There, the authors conclude that adolescent reproductive health programmes should target youth aged 13 years or younger (Meekers & Ahmed, 2000).

In most of these studies, early sexual debut is seldom directly associated with the commoditization of children's and adolescents' sexuality. However, the transformation of female sexuality and fertility into commodities is increasingly acknowledged as jeopardising women and girls in HIV affected countries. In industrialized countries such as Norway, the phenomenon of sexual exchange, love and abuse can be observed among younger people liv-

---

1. This was communicated during the last ARHNe Workshop, in Nairobi, October 2000.

ing at the margins of society (Larsen & Pedersen, 2005). There is an urgent need to focus on this aspect of the dynamics of sexual relations in the case of the youngest generation.

Responding to children's needs: Addressing the challenges

As indicated thus far, a number of children and youth seem to escape control and protection by the older generation when negotiating their social and sexual lives, and they may get too little authoritative support from parents, the community or the state. At the same time, parents' own knowledge and skills in bringing up children in an AIDS context is insufficient and wanting. This powerlessness at an intergenerational and institutional level is in fact allowing for more child-abuse and sexual violence and maybe also resulting in an unconscious adoption of the "weapons of the weak" by the pubescent generation. Where economic and social conditions are difficult, increasing numbers may have adopted the idea of sexual relations as a commoditised good to be consumed ever earlier. The economic, social and emotional factors conditioning these relations must be given serious attention, because the youngsters' strategies in the end are weakening their life chances. As common sense and research are showing, it is those who have least access to making choices, to information, to education and to health services, who are the easiest victims of the AIDS epidemic. Where poverty prevails, it seems that responding to short-term survival or satisfaction needs assumes greater importance than protecting very uncertain long-term benefits. This appears to socialise a part of the pre-pubescent and pubescent youth into "risky" sexual relations, where the human drive for recognition becomes a race with death. There seems to be little social preparedness to address the youngest group. In schools, if taught at all, Family Life Education, or AIDS education is seldom adapted to children's and youths' life-realities.

Here, the role of research and of combining qualitative and quantitative methods in uncovering the needs and promoting viable interventions is critical. For instance, most surveys covering sexual and reproductive health issues, such as contraceptive use, abortion or STD prevalence, have ignored children below 15 years. In addition, when the age at first sexual intercourse is estimated in demographic health surveys, older age groups are addressed. In Tanzania, according to the 1996 Demographic and Health Survey, the median age for first sexual intercourse was assessed among groups older than 20 years, and for the group 20–24, and both women and men had a median age of 17 years at first sexual experience (United Republic of

Tanzania, 1997a). Yet, as has been shown, biological age and sexual maturation are not the only factors influencing sexual debut.

Moreover, most children are not aware and do not care about their risk of infection, probably helped by a feeling of invincibility, and by the fact that infection may lie dormant for several years. In addition, risk perceptions are gendered, leaving girls most concerned with avoiding pregnancy, rather than HIV infection. Thus, when research indicates that half of the people who acquire HIV become infected before 24 [1], when a large number of children between 5 and 15 years are enrolled in school, and when half of the pupils become sexually active before 15 years of age, the issue of investing in children's living conditions, the issues of pre-exposure education in life skills and on AIDS as well as the issue of postponing sexual debut are extremely urgent ones. According to what was concluded in the report on HIV/AIDS and Education in East and Southern Africa (UN, 2000), there is a clear need for education programmes to take serious account of the youth culture, the construction of sexuality in gender and intergenerational relations, and the seemingly increasing tendencies of sexual abuse and violence against young people, by fellow youths and by the older male generation. Indeed, research from both Kenya (Omale, 2000) and Southern Africa (Human Rights Watch, 2001; UNAIDS, 2004a) shows how this is a subtly institutionalised problem. This has to be reacted upon, because the situation may easily be exacerbated by economic depression and by the increasing number of orphans (Human Rights Watch, 2001).

As suggested by the African Development Forum 2000, the 5–14 year old age group may increasingly be a "Window of Concern", even for those attending school. Therefore, to quote former president Mandela's words, *"The problem should be dealt with now, and right now!"*

---

1. It has been suggested that because there are many more AIDS and AIDS-related cases among those aged 15–19 than among those aged 5–14, HIV infection might have occurred long before the individual reached age 15. This presupposes a period of progression of 5–10 years from HIV to AIDS (UN, 2000). However, the progression of the disease is also considered highly variable (NAI reviewer, 2006).

III

Addressing the Needs of Adolescents:
Arenas for Action

9. Peer Education for Adolescent Reproductive Health

An Effective Method for Program Delivery, a Powerful Empowerment Strategy, or Neither?

Sheri Bastien, Alan J. Flisher, Catherine Mathews and Knut-Inge Klepp

Abstract

Peer education has been widely utilized in sub-Saharan Africa and worldwide as an educational strategy for the past 15 years in health promotion strategies including HIV and AIDS prevention programs. Yet, despite the widespread use of peer educators, there is a distinct lack of conceptual clarity, and great diversity in the stated aims, methods and strategies, implementation, evaluation and findings of peer education programs. This chapter aims to address a number of salient issues challenging the use of peer education by: revisiting the historical origins of peer education, discussing the concept in relation to other related concepts such as peer leaders and opinion leaders, exploring the theoretical underpinnings and rationale for using peer educators; reviewing the extent to which programs in SSA are making use of peer educators with some concrete examples; discussing the opportunities and limitations both theoretically and practically when employing peer education, and finally; identifying the existing gaps in the literature and providing suggestions for future research.

Introduction

The past decade has seen a burgeoning interest in the use of peer educators in health education and promotion, particularly in the area of adolescent sexual and reproductive health. Young people in sub-Saharan Africa are at high risk for a number of sexual health concerns including sexual transmitted infections (STIs), HIV infection, unwanted pregnancies and abortion. Increasingly, it has been recognized that interventions are more likely to be effective if they are contextually and culturally sensitive and are developed in collaboration with members of the target population. Peer education has the potential to efficiently tailor prevention messages to suit the context and needs of the intended audience in a language they can relate to, and generate community support and mobilization.

The rise in the use of peer education in adolescent sexual and reproductive health interventions necessitates a review of the concept, including its historical origins, conceptual and theoretical basis, and rationale for its use. However, this chapter aims not only to recapitulate and synthesize the vast and growing literature on peer education, but also to contribute to the conceptual clarity and broader understandings of peer education in the African context, by reviewing existing studies and by suggesting the way forward for research and interventions.

Origins of peer education

Harnessing peer influence for educational purposes is not a novel or recent approach. The origins of peer education from a Western perspective have been traced back to Aristotle by some authors (Wagner, 1982; Sax, 2002) who reference his use of "archons" or student helpers when he taught larger groups, and indeed, it is possible that peer education was one of the first forms of pedagogy and has taken place since human existence, for instance older siblings passing on knowledge to their younger counterparts on edible berries and roots (Jenkins & Jenkins, 1987). Certainly in regards to sex education, it is widely acknowledged that peers tend to share information and consult each other on their sexual lives and relationships. In an example from the African context, Setel (1996) has described how as a result of rapid societal changes in the 1960s and 70s in Kilimanjaro, peers have increasingly become a source of information about sex and sexuality for young people, and have supplemented more traditional forms such as the aunts' role in educating their nieces.

One of its earliest uses documented in Europe was a "monitorial system" established in London by Joseph Lancaster in the early 1800s whereby teachers taught "monitors", who in turn conveyed their knowledge to other children (Svenson, 1998; Mellanby et al., 2000). It was also used in the United States in 1957 at the University of Nebraska in a student influenza immunization initiative (Turner & Shepherd, 1999), and has been used extensively in peer support groups such as Alcoholics Anonymous.

Recent attempts to harness the power of the peer group in behavior change campaigns include interventions to address smoking cessation (Perry et al., 1986), drug and alcohol abuse (Perry et al., 1989; Klepp et al., 1986; Ward, Hunter & Power, 1997), nutrition education (Story et al., 2002; Buller et al., 1999), violence prevention and date rape (Holmcomb & Seehafer, 1995), and reproductive and sexual health (Hayes et al., 2005). Activities and strategies used by peer educators also vary widely according to context and target group, from facilitating discussion and brain storming, engaging in drama, music or sport presentations, to counseling, lecturing, operating hot-lines, distributing materials, referrals to services and providing support. Peer education can also be dovetailed with other complementary initiatives in HIV prevention, such as condom marketing and the utilization of social networks and outreach services (Hope, 2003).

Despite its long history, there is a distinct lack of conceptual clarity in the literature on the nature of peer education. It may be regarded as an approach, a technique, a communication channel, a methodology, a philosophy, or an intervention strategy (Kerrigan, 1999). According to Kelly (2004), it is an ill-defined, generic concept, while Shiner (1999) refers to it as an "umbrella term". There has for instance, been no widely used strict delineation of similar terms circulating in the literature such as peer leaders, peer facilitators, peer tutors, partner learning, peer helpers, peer counselors, peer mediators and popular opinion leaders. Careful consideration of the terms suggests that many perceive peer education primarily as a mode of delivery, with the terms being differentiated by the role that is to be played by the peer educator (Shiner, 1999). Yet given that it is highly probable that in reality, these roles co-exist and, indeed, overlap the need for unpacking the semantics surrounding the concept is readily apparent.

As a consequence of a lack of common language, explicitly stated goals and defined standards of practice, Deutsch et al. (2003) contend that programs will continue to evolve haphazardly, operate independently and inconsistently, and ultimately impede evaluation and efforts to scale up. Thus, the following section will attempt to explore and disentangle some of the concepts intrinsically connected to peer education.

Conceptual considerations

The concept of peer tutoring, which is predicated on the belief that peer interactions form the basis for cognitive and intellectual development, was popularized in the United States in the 1960s. It has since been used widely in education for many purposes, such as increasing literacy and second language skills, mathematics, science and aiding students with disabilities. Similar, though vague variations on the term are peer helping, which may be used in more general contexts, and partner or peer to peer learning. The peer counselor approach on the other hand, emerged out of peer tutoring and is one method used in helping young people deal with personal and social issues such as addictions, or in coping with traumatic events such as sexual abuse and death of a loved one. This approach largely draws on social learning theory and social inoculation theory (Svenson, 1998).

Peer leaders and, most recently, popular opinion leaders, are often differentiated from more traditional peer educators mainly by how they are selected. In the latter case, they are selected by teachers or they volunteer. In the former case, they are selected by identifying those who display leadership qualities and therefore have potential to influence group norms (Klepp et al., 1986; Kelly, 2004; Flisher et al., 2005). Peer educators are those members of a social network that are visible, popular, respected and influential, and who are trained to influence social norms through informal networking. The popular opinion leader approach is grounded in the diffusion of innovations theory which posits that peer educators, who are seen as innovators, use communication to influence their social networks towards a critical mass and stimulating widespread change (Flisher et al., 2005). This approach has been experimented with in the South African school setting by Mathews et al. (2001) who have probed the viability of identifying opinion leaders in high schools and their willingness to participate in an HIV prevention program, with positive results, suggesting that this may prove to be a fruitful area for future research. In the interests of contributing to conceptual clarity, a matrix comparing the characteristics of peer educators and opinion leaders in Table 1 highlights the manner in which the approaches differ.

Table 1. Comparison of peer educators and popular opinion leaders

Characteristiccs	Peer educators	Popular opinion leaders
Recruitment approach	Volunteers or selected by teachers or others in authority	Identified through socio-metric and/or qualitative methods
Personal characteristics	Pro-social Highly regarded by those in authority	Pro-social or anti-social Not necessarily highly regarded by those in authority (the opposite may be the case)
Whether the peer educators or opinion leaders are in fact opinion leaders	Not necessarily	Definitely (by definition)
Theoretical backdrop	Mainstream pedagogical theory	Diffusion of Innovations Theory
Principle mechanism of change	Individual influence	Changing social norms
Main setting for interventions	Formal settings, such as classrooms	Informal opportunities, exploiting natural social ecology
Extent of planning of situations where education or influence will take place	Planned beforehand	Spontaneous and unpredictable

It is likewise important to define what is meant by the term "peer". The term is historically British and was used to indicate membership in one of the five ranks of nobility. However, contemporary uses and dictionaries typically define a peer as one of equal standing with another (Svenson, 1998). While many authors demarcate peers as those being of the same age, others differentiate between the use of cross-age and same-age peers, or take a more flexible view to encompass "near-peers". Some prefer to adopt a more nuanced view that a peer group may be defined according to other criteria such as sexual orientation, occupation, ethnicity, religion, style of dress, gender, and social class or status. However, little mention is made in the literature of the importance of defining peer from the vantage point of the target group, and the importance of basing peer educator selection on the criteria deemed most desirable by those whom the intervention is aiming to target, though the use of popular opinion leaders addresses this issue to some extent.

Although many peer education programs may adopt a definition of the concept that is tailored to reflect the focus and aim of the program, the underlying premise is typically shared and comprises training and supporting members of a given group to effect changes in terms of knowledge, attitudes, beliefs, behavior and norms among members of that same group. For instance, Stakic et al. (2003:4) define peer education as the:

> ...process whereby well trained and motivated young people undertake informal or organized educational activities with their peers (as defined by age, background or interests) over a period of time, aimed at developing their knowledge, attitudes, beliefs and skills and enabling them to protect and be responsible for their own health.

In this way, peer educators may be regarded as "change agents" and "experts" relative to their peers and may serve as facilitators, guides and motivators (Pearlman et al., 2002; Hope, 2003; Onyango-Ouma et al., 2005). This diversity evident in the roles often taken on by peer educators is similarly reflected in the diversity of theories peer education is drawn from, as highlighted below.

Theoretical background of peer education

In their review of the literature, Turner and Shepherd (1999) found that there are generally few references made to theory, and when there are, the analysis tends to be superficial with little empirical evidence to support claims of effectiveness. Ultimately, the authors concluded that peer education may be more accurately seen as a method in search of a theory than the application of theory to practice, in recognition of the fact that multiple, often evasive processes underpin success of peer-led approaches.

Though no single theory per se has been articulated for the purposes of explaining the effectiveness of peer education, its theoretical foundation derives primarily from a wide cross-section of social psychology and cognitive-based behavior change theories[1] such as Social Cognitive Theory (Bandura, 1986), Theory of Reasoned Action (Fishbein & Ajzen, 1975), Diffusion of Innovation (Rogers, 1983), and cognitive development theories (Piaget, 1977; Vygotsky, 1978; Sutherland, 1947), which are coupled with empowerment, collective action and education theories, namely Freire's (1970) Theory of Participatory Education. Given the usage of peer education in crime prevention and other "risk" behaviors such as substance abuse, it has also been loosely connected to other theories such as Social Inoculation Theory (McGuire, 1964), Role Theory (Sarbin & Allen, 1968),

---

1. Detailed descriptions of these theories have already been provided in previous chapters and therefore, will not be dealt with in greater depth here. See for instance Chapters 2 and 3.

Differential Association Theory (Sutherland, 1947), and Subculture Theory (Cohen, 1955).

Recently, Campbell and MacPhail (2002) have advocated that utilizing multiple interlocking concepts, namely social identity, empowerment, critical consciousness and social capital may shed new light on peer education processes. Based on their extensive work in the South African context, this approach may be particularly useful for highlighting how gender norms and relations may be renegotiated, reinforced or contested through the peer process, and for identifying the various constraints individuals face. For instance, the peer education program sought to build social capital in two ways: by fostering the development of homogeneous groups (such as school students) characterized by trusting and supportive relationships and a collective positive social identity. This was to set the stage for empowerment and collective critical consciousness, which in turn would stimulate the contestation and renegotiation of harmful gender norms and raise awareness of the role of poverty as barriers to behavior change (Campbell, 2003).

Such attempts to infuse fresh insight into the study of peer education are crucial to advancing understandings of the peer education process so that successes may be built upon and learned from. Their loose framework is also further demonstrative of the broad and expanding range of theoretical underpinnings of peer education, which provide fertile ground for a number of assertions and arguments to be made advocating for its use.

Rationale and justification for peer education

The literature on peer education is primarily descriptive and anecdotal in nature, and various authors have detailed benefits of this approach. In their review of the peer education literature, Turner and Shepherd (1999) found that among the many advantages extolled by advocates of peer education, the following 10 are the most cited:

1. It is more cost-effective than other methods;
2. Peers are a credible source of information;
3. Peer education is empowering for those involved;
4. It utilizes an already established means of sharing information and advice;
5. Peers are more successful than professionals in passing on information because people identify with their peers;
6. Peer educators act as positive role models;

7. Peer education is beneficial to those involved in providing it;

8. Education presented by peers may be acceptable when other education is not;

9. Peer education may be used to educate those who are hard to reach through conventional methods, and;

10. Peers can reinforce learning through ongoing contact

The discussion below will address each of these issues in succession, and identify studies which have supported the claims and those which have not substantiated them.

Cost effectiveness

Particularly in resource poor settings such as SSA, considerable attention must be focused on the allocation of funding in the interests of identifying what works and scaling up. Yet, assessing the cost-effectiveness of an intervention is not straightforward. In his recent review of the evidence base of cost-effectiveness of HIV prevention strategies in developing countries, Walker (2003) emphasizes that evidence is decidedly thin. He also suggests that methods applied and results reported raise a number of questions related to reliability, validity and transparency of the data, which may compromise comparability. There is currently no comparative large-scale review available in the published literature that assesses the cost-effectiveness of interventions and specifically which looks at peer education in SSA against other intervention strategies.

Assuming that the intervention is effective, the logic of the multiplier effect[1] dictates that with adult supervision of teams of peer educators, a program's reach can be extended to more young people than traditional modes can and contribute to preventing teacher burn-out and frustration (Deutsch & Swartz, 2002). Yet despite claims that peer education is cost-effective in comparison to interventions requiring trained personnel, the logistics of training, implementing, and sustaining a quality program are often underestimated. There may be a high attrition rate of peer educators, requiring on-going training of new ones. In addition, the issue of payment to peer educators for their time and training is also an issue that must be contended with. It has been argued that compensation might best be provided in terms of fringe benefits such as bicycles and t-shirts, as opposed to monetary reimbursement for time and services rendered. However, the

---

1   This is elaborated on in Chapter 13 in this volume, which deals with evaluation.

potential for this to create a barrier between the educators and their peers must be carefully considered.

Credibility

Since one of the hallmarks of peer education rests on the ability of peers to convey information in a way that adults or those outside the social network are not able to, one of the practical issues that must be grappled with in the use and selection of peer educators centers on the notion of credibility. Peer educators must be deemed credible in the eyes of their peer group on three levels according to Shiner and Newburn (1999). Firstly, they must be credible in terms of their personal characteristics (which are often shared), such as their age, sex, religion, ethnicity, and other related factors to the target group. In addition, they must be perceived as having experience based credibility (which may be shared) in that they have undertaken study on the issue or had prior experience, for instance sexually or in drug or alcohol usage. In a different take on experience-based credibility however, Deutsch and Swartz (2002) point out that the "do as I say, not as I did" adage is simply not an adequate approach and that peer educators should focus more on stimulating critical thinking skills. Lastly, the audience should be convinced of the credibility of the message in terms of content and delivery being sent by the peer educator. However, it is plausible that the process of establishing credibility of the peer educator will also operate in reverse and be compromised if for instance, personal credibility is ascertained, but the message is not perceived as being credible in its content or form (Shiner & Newburn, 1999).

In their work on credibility in the school setting, Ozer et al. (1997) used the Peer Educator Rating Scale which was designed to measure two dimensions of participants' perceptions of peer educators: "positive regard" and "perceived similarity". The main findings ultimately concluded that positive regard for peer educators was more important than perceived similarity, suggesting that credibility may hinge less on shared characteristics than previously thought (see Bandura, 1986). Thus, credibility is clearly multidimensional and variable depending on the target audience and the type of intervention, suggesting that peers may not always be more credible than teachers or adults in all situations. Teachers and health educators may be regarded as more credible when conveying factual information for instance, while peers may be seen as more credible when addressing the social environment adolescents are part of (Klepp et al., 1986).

Empowerment

One of the potential advantages of peer education is that participation in the planning, implementation, and evaluation may foster a sense of ownership and subsequently empower those involved. In this manner, empowerment may be conceptualized as the process of equipping and enabling individuals and communities to take power and utilize it to transform their lives and environments. From a pedagogical standpoint the methodology used to train peer educators will also impact the potential and degree to which they are able to effectively utilize the participatory approaches central to peer education which aim to foster empowerment. In order to have a sound grasp not only of the concepts they will be delivering, peer educators need to be trained using the same methods and principles they will themselves be using in the classroom.

However, empowerment is a notoriously ambiguous concept that like peer education itself, has evaded precise operationalization and hence is not conducive to measurement. For instance, some researchers and authors focus on the psychological aspect of empowerment, while others argue this lacks sophistication and fails to account for the need for political and economic empowerment (Campbell, 2003).

In addition, participation may not in itself be as inherently empowering as many would claim. For instance, Crewe and Harrison (1998) query whether simply asking people's opinions constitutes participation, or whether something more fundamental is required. It is clear that the way in which meaningful participation can be accomplished is not easy or straightforward. Research on how to achieve true partnership is still in its infancy and moving beyond tokenistic participation remains a challenge. Indeed, the rhetoric of participation may disguise and perpetuate inequalities and power differentials, making it important to be vigilant that peer education programs do not exacerbate, rather than ameliorate, these issues. Ultimately, as Deutsch and Swartz (2002) reason, the opinions and perspectives of young people should be solicited and duly considered, but not romanticized or viewed uncritically.

Utilizing pre-existing networks

It is widely recognized that peer groups play a key role in defining and shaping identities and constitute an important influence on individual behavior, particularly during periods of significant transition such as in childhood and adolescence. Thus, the essence of peer education is that it attempts to utilize natural, everyday peer interactions and positively influence knowledge, attitudes, behaviors and norms (Turner & Shepherd, 1999).

However, as Shiner (1999) argues, social identity formation is complex and multifaceted, and shaped by innumerable factors such as roles and group categories an individual engages in or identifies with, and the experiences they have. These may be multiple and conflictual in nature, culminating in contradictory and fragmented identities. Thus, while peers do constitute an important group of social actors, age and other shared characteristics may not have the impact that is often anticipated and may vary from society to society, according to gender, age, religion, and social class. This underscores the fact that programs need to have an in-depth understanding of group processes and identity formation amongst their target population before recruiting and selecting the peer educators.

Effectiveness in comparison to adult-led programs

Peer education is not designed to supplant adult or teacher-led education, it is meant to complement it. However, one of the claims of proponents of peer education is that it is more effective than other conventional forms of education delivered by adults. This assertion is based on a number of assumptions, such as that peer educators have the multidimensional credibility discussed earlier, are adequately trained and have a sound grasp of the concepts taught, and that they have the pedagogic tools to deliver the message.

In their review of the literature, Mellanby et al. (2000) found indications that peer-led programs are at least as, or more, effective than adult-led programs, yet concede that methodological difficulties and analytical problems place limits on their findings. They ultimately concluded that both peers and adults have a role to play in effective school-based sex education, yet more work needs to be done to identify the areas or topics best suited to each group in delivering the program (Mellanby et al., 2001).

A quasi-experimental controlled trial in four inner city high schools in the United States found that opinion leaders were less effective than a classroom-based teacher-led intervention at one-year follow up. It was hypothesized that this effect was due to diminished social influence of the opinion leaders on their peers and possibly a result of the negative impact and impression that opinion leaders engaged in the very risk behaviors they were cautioning against (Fisher et al., 2002). A randomized controlled trial by Borgia et al. (2005) found that the only clear benefit in peer-led versus adult-led interventions is an increase in knowledge of HIV, while neither interventions produced changes in sexual behavior. Another recent study with Ghanaian youth demonstrated the benefits of peer-led versus adult-led programs, but concluded that a combination of the two has a greater effect than peers alone (Wolf & Pulerwitz, 2003). Therefore, the findings are contradictory, which as previously stated is partially attributable to the diversity of programs. With each study underscoring possible biases and methodological weaknesses, there is simply not sufficient evidence to conclusively state that peers learn best from their peers in all cases.

Role modeling

Through reciprocal peer interaction with those at a similar stage of development, young people learn important social skills such as empathy and critical thinking. In terms of health interventions, positive role modeling may consist of non-use (in smoking, drugs and alcohol) or advocating for abstinence or safe sex. The goal is to create a norm that fosters the desired behavior or outcome and provides alternatives to engaging in the undesired or "risk" behavior, typically through a life skills approach. Dispelling myths common amongst young people, such as widespread belief that everyone in their peer group is having sex is one strategy, since such perceptions may be influential in sexual behavior.

Yet, the process by which peer educators are recruited varies widely; therefore it cannot be assumed that all peer educators are capable "experts" who will always engage in positive role modeling. The extent to which they themselves engage in risk behaviors may be a source of concern and an area for further research in evaluations. Whether they are selected randomly, recruited as volunteers, selected via peer or teacher recommendation, must be carefully considered, as must their personal motivation (ie. religious affiliation, personal experience, altruism), in relation to how this may affect the outcomes of the program. In addition, the effect of the peer education training itself cannot be overlooked, as it may remove them from the peer group from which they were originally selected. Lastly, while recruitment and selection procedures may be specified in the planning documents, how this actually occurs during implementation is important to take into consideration in process evaluations. The use of social network analysis has been identified as one strategy which may be effective at identifying peer educators who may be both acceptable to the target group and capable of successfully applying their training in the intervention (Kerrigan, 1999). However, the manner in which peer educators are selected remains a challenging issue.

Mutual benefits

One of the benefits of employing peer educators cited by many are the dual benefits afforded to both the peer and the peer educator (Pearlman et al., 2002; Badura et al., 2000; Sawyer et al., 1997; Ebreo et al., 2002). Particularly crucial in building the future cadre of HIV/AIDS educators, peer education programs can foster the enthusiasm, knowledge and skills needed amongst young people (Deutsch & Swartz, 2002). Participating in peer education may promote the development of interpersonal and conflict resolution skills, result in cognitive gain, and foster respect for diversity and tolerance (Milburn, 1996).

In a study of school-based peer HIV prevention, Ebreo et al. (2002) investigated whether or not peer educators who were chosen because they themselves were at risk of engaging in the behaviors that the prevention program targeted, benefited from the experience. They compared self-reported knowledge, attitudes and behaviors in the two groups before and after a 16-session intervention. However, the findings largely did not indicate any significant results, save one behavioral impact on the peer educators in the negative direction (higher frequency of unwanted sex due to alcohol use), and the authors acknowledge that a number of logistical issues hindered their ability to generalize about the effectiveness of peer education programs.

The most significant findings in this area appear to come out of the peer counseling literature, where studies have shown that communication and social skills of peer educators are enhanced, and that self-esteem, ego development and other aspects of psychological and personal development also benefit from the experience (Ebreo et al., 2002). One study even found that while the opinion leaders themselves changed, the target population did not; a finding which the authors surmise is probably not unique (Ward et al., in press). Again however, there is simply not enough evidence to support this assertion unequivocally. Self-esteem for instance, develops over time and may not be easily amenable to measurement following an intervention. In addition, empowerment, as discussed above, is not a tangible outcome, making it difficult to garner evidence of support. In any case, as Main (2002) suggests, this type of comparison is inherently flawed since it does not allow for isolation of the effects of peer education. This is because peer educators and their target audience have different interventions and because peer educators are systematically different from their classmates at the onset.

Acceptability

It is believed that sensitive messages may be better received if they are dis-seminated by peers, or those of the same social group rather than those out-side the social network, such as teachers who may not be able to empathize and may employ authoritarian modes of interaction and pass moral judg-ments (Milburn, 1996). Given their influential status, intimate knowledge of the social context and nuanced language of their peers, it is thought that peer educators are more likely to have an impact as role models. Again how-ever, this assumes that peer educators are able to establish credibility and have the correct factual information. Deutsch and Swartz (2002) point out that the selection of peer educators in this way becomes particularly impor-tant, since if only model students are chosen, they may be perceived as mere mouth-pieces or messengers of teachers, thus discrediting them.

It must also be noted that, on the other hand, certain issues are unlikely to be discussed with peers such as sexual orientation and incest. It is doubt-ful that peers will have the skills to counsel or assist their peers in coping with certain issues or the required maturity to handle difficult situations, potentially even resulting in harm to both parties if they do not have suf-ficient coping mechanisms. Furthermore, how peers handle private, sensi-tive information they may receive as a result of serving as a peer educator raises a number of ethical issues as they are not bound by any professional code of conduct.

Reaching the hard to reach

Peer educators are commonly seen as a link between health professionals and the target group. Thus, peer education has been used in a wide variety of settings, and is a particularly popular component of school-based inter-ventions which seek to influence a large segment of the population at a time when there is an increased likelihood that they will engage or experiment with risky health-related behaviors. Other settings include youth centers, clubs, workplaces, community settings and informal networks, which rep-resent an invaluable way of accessing a large segment of the population including hard to reach groups such as military personnel, homosexuals, prostitutes, drug users, and other "at-risk" groups.

In Africa, peer education in HIV prevention has been used for a wide range of populations, including fishing village members in Tanzania (Balyagati et al., 1995); villagers in Burkina Faso (Tankoano, 1994); re-tail workers in South Africa (Sloan & Myers, 2004); traditional healers in

South Africa (UNAIDS, 1999); high school students in The Gambia (Mahe & Travers, 1997–98); female sex workers in Kenya and Zimbabwe (Ngugi et al., 1996), Senegal (Leonard et al., 2000) and South Africa (Campbell, 2003; Campbell & Mzaidume, 2001; Campbell et al., 2005); a mining settlement in Tanzania (Mollel et al., 1995); truck drivers in Tanzania (Laukamm-Josten et al., 2000); bar workers in Tanzania (Bergsjø et al., 1995); prisoners in Mozambique (Vaz et al., 1996) and recently young men in Tanzania to address violence and HIV (Lary et al., 2004). This tremendous diversity highlights the appeal of using peer educators as an intervention strategy, particularly amongst hard-to-reach groups and is an undeniable advantage of the approach.

Reinforcing and sustaining

Lastly, it is believed that since peers constitute a pre-existing social group, learning is continuous and therefore constantly being reinforced through day to day interaction and can therefore continue outside the school setting where the behavior being targeted is most likely to occur (Klepp et al., 1986). Yet, Milburn (1996) raises an important question about formal peer education and ponders whether or not it is possible to tap into a social process through artificial reconstruction or if something new is created which may not have the same function and outcomes. Indeed, it could be argued that the very process of peer education may alter the social process it seeks to tap into and have some unintended and occasionally adverse outcomes, such as creating inequities and distance between peers which did not previously exist.

Given the diverse spectrum of purported benefits associated with peer education, and its extensive use in various educational contexts, the next section will consider the evidence base which has emerged from African settings.

Peer education in sub-Saharan Africa

Despite its widespread use and popularity, there remains a dearth of empirical data backing up claims of efficacy of peer education programs. Indeed, few methodologically sound studies have evaluated and substantiated the merit of these claims, particularly in sub-Saharan Africa. A search of published work was carried out electronically in standard databases such as PubMed, Medline, Popline, AIDSLINE, Social Sciences Index, Eric, Science Direct, and HIV/AIDS Clearinghouse using the following key word searches: "peer education", "peer leader/s" and "peer training" in combination with "Africa". Only studies that were written in English, conducted in an African country and that focused on adolescents or young adults (10–24 years) were included. The purpose of this review was: i) to assess to what extent the widespread use of peer education in program implementation in SSA is reflected in the research literature; ii) to describe the varying approaches to peer education; iii) to assess whether evaluation results appear to support the widespread use of peer educators; and iv) based on available literature to identify gaps and areas for future research.

In this search, the precipitous rise of peer education in the literature was evident. For instance, the number of articles referring to peer education or similar terms in the search string rose from 38 between the years 1981–85, to 229 by the year 2000 and 306 by 2005. In the African context, a rise was also noted, from 0 articles by 1985, to 19 articles by 2000 and 31 articles by 2005. However, applying a broad definition of evaluation studies (including both process and outcome studies) only 15 papers based on 12 African studies published between 1990 and 2005 fulfilled the above criteria. These studies are summarized in Table 2 (pp. 209–213).

It is evident from this review that various peer education approaches are being used across a number of sub-Saharan African settings. For the most part, the authors report positive experiences and outcomes across studies employing different methodological approaches. At the same time, it is clear that the majority of the identified studies have a number of methodological limitations, including weak research designs. For instance, there are few randomized controlled trials or evaluations which produce robust data through the use of biological markers such as STI/HIV incidence or pregnancy rates as outcome measures. Rather, most studies focus on measures such as knowledge, attitudes, and beliefs, or outputs such as the number of peer educators trained and self-reported behavior change and use small sample sizes. Only one set of studies from Ghana (Wolf et al., 2000; Wolf & Bond, 2002; Wolf & Pulerwitz, 2003) documented a peer education program using both process and outcome measures, though in measuring the impact of peer versus adult communication on AIDS-protective behaviors, the authors acknowledge the limits placed on the study by the small sample size.

Furthermore, detailed information specifying the theoretical grounding of the intervention, the methods used for selecting peer educators and their training, including the length, who it was conducted by and what it was comprised of, are most often lacking from the reviewed literature. In addition, it was evident in the review of studies that peer education is also often used as one of multiple educational strategies, and it is therefore not possible to assess the effect due specifically to the peer education approach. Similarly, the review highlights the diversity of peer education activities used by the interventions which range from dissemination of information to engaging in drama and sport and even condom distribution. Thus, isolating intervention effects and attributing them to the use of peer education is problematic, since peer education encompasses so many different activities.

Flisher et al. (2005) contend that peer education programs should be subject to "methodologically seamless evaluations" which entail random allocation of schools to control and intervention groups with sufficient statistical power to detect effects. They also advise that evaluation should be comprehensive in nature and address three dimensions, namely: (i) input (the total amount of resources required for the intervention); (ii) process (the quality of the implementation of the intervention); and (iii) outcome (the effectiveness or efficacy of the intervention) (Flisher et al., 2005; Flisher et al., 2008). However, the authors also stress the importance of research aimed at understanding why an intervention is effective or not, with attention for instance to the social and cultural context. While much of the literature on peer educators tends to be of a quantitative nature (Backett-Milburn & Wilson, 2000), it is encouraging that a number of qualitative studies focusing on process evaluation were retrieved from our review.

In their review of adolescent reproductive health interventions in developing countries, Speizer et al. (2003) identified a number of barriers to undertaking rigorous evaluations, including: (a) cultural sensitivities surrounding sex among adolescents; (b) limited resources to include a control or comparison group; (c) ethical issues in withholding programs from youth in resource-poor settings; (d) the multiplicity of interventions in some settings; and (e) high mobility of the target group, which makes follow-up difficult. It has also been suggested that the lack of sound evaluations may be in part due to the nature of peer education: it has been described as a "moving target" for evaluators since programs typically involve a number of participants, utilize diverse settings, make use of social influences and diffusion to achieve the desired effect, and often entail the use of numerous activities (Svenson, 1998).

As a consequence of the lack of well-designed evaluation studies, new programs are continually developed which do not capitalize on the successes of others, and the scaling up of successful interventions is impeded. Since evaluation informs policy and practice, there is a great need for evidence of the efficacy of peer education programs in a variety of settings and a greater understanding of the processes which work alongside programs.

Examples of peer education initiatives in sub-Saharan Africa

While this chapter has taken a critical look at the limitations of available peer education research, it is also evident that promising initiatives supported by governments and NGOs in sub-Saharan Africa are attempting to fill the gap in the literature by rigorously designing and evaluating peer education programs. Two such interventions designed to reduce incidence and prevalence of HIV will be presented below to demonstrate how researchers are currently investigating the potential of peer education.

MEMA kwa Vijana

MEMA kwa Vijana ("Good Things for Young People" in Kiswahili) is a sexual health education program in Mwanza Region in rural Tanzania, initiated in 1998 by the Government of Tanzania and represents a collaboration between the African Medical and Research Foundation, the London School of Hygiene and Tropical Medicine and the National Institute for Medical Research of Tanzania, with implementation assistance from the Ministries of Health and Education and Culture. The project has multiple components and consists of a teacher-led, peer-assisted program for students in the last 3 years (aged 12–19) of primary school, training and supervision of health workers in the provision of youth-friendly health services, and peer condom promotion and distribution, in conjunction with other community-based initiatives (Hayes et al., 2005). By combining the use of teachers and students as educators, the program attempted to merge the strengths and overcome the weaknesses of using only one of the approaches.

The intervention utilized class peer educators (CPEs), who were selected by teachers and intervention staff from a shortlist selected by pupils, and received two days training by community-based trainers. In addition, three male and three female youths were elected by the advisory committee to act as Trainers of Peers (TOPs) who assist in the training of the (CPEs). In the first year of the intervention, TOPs trained 1,124 CPEs with the support of intervention staff, with an additional 372 trained each year. By the third year of the intervention, this role was relegated to the teachers in order to maximize sustainability (Obasi et al., 2006).

The project objectives aimed at delaying onset of sexual intercourse, reducing the number of sexual partners and encouraging the correct and consistent use of condoms among those already sexually active, and increasing use of health services. Primary outcome measures included HIV incidence and sero-prevalence of *Herpes simplex* virus type 2 (HSV2). Secondary biological markers included STI incidence and pregnancy rates. Also measured were sexual health-related knowledge and attitudes, self-reported sexual behavior such as age at sexual debut, number of sexual partners and use of condoms. In addition, rigorous process evaluation was undertaken to identify which components of the intervention contributed most to the outcomes through: (i) detailed monitoring of intervention activities; (ii) surveys of district officials, schools and health units to assess quality, coverage and additional activities in the communities; and, (iii) external evaluations of the intervention by national and international experts (Hayes et al., 2005).

The experimental program was implemented in 62 primary schools and 18 health facilities in targeted districts, with an equal number of schools and facilities serving as a control group. Participatory, in-class and informal methods were utilized to interact with students on sexual and reproductive health issues. The in-school component consisted of three *MEMA* teachers trained in participatory methods who taught students for one hour per week together with CPEs. This was complemented by CPEs who were given the task of performing carefully scripted drama which was designed to model appropriate and desired behaviors and convey selected key messages. One of the unique features of the intervention is that it secured equal status to other examinable subjects and was formally assessed in Standard 7 alongside other national examination subjects (Obasi et al., in 2006).

The intervention also trained 228 youth condom promoters and distributors (CPDs) who were elected by other community youth and given two days training to market condoms in the villages (four in each village). In the schools however, condom promotion was limited to discussion. Demonstrations of any kind in primary schools are not permitted by the Ministry of Education and Culture which requires that abstinence is the main focus. However, during the "youth health days", which took place at local health units, there were opportunities to see condom demonstrations. The program did however, experience problems in terms of the condom sales and distribution component, which although increased, resulted in the money earned being spent by peer educators to supplement their lack of a sufficient income. This in turn led to increased absenteeism and ultimately a drop in sales (World Bank, 2003).

Interviews and observations of the peer educators in pre-existing initiatives in other schools in the region indicated that a teacher-led approach would be more appropriate in rural Mwanza schools due to a number of reasons, including: i) rural pupils lacked the cognitive and social skills necessary to reliably pass on information and behavior change concepts to their peers, ii) training new pupils to be peer educators each year after the current ones graduate is less sustainable than investing in teacher training; iii) merging the training program into national or regional teacher training programs would enable large-scale intervention at low cost (Obasi et al., in press). Thus, one of the main findings of the program in relation to peer education is that while peer educators were able to positively contribute in some ways, such as in drama performances and in breaking the ice in sensitive discussions, it is difficult to train young people as peer educators and it is suggested that perhaps their role might best be served as facilitators (World Bank, 2003). These findings deserve attention, as they suggest that primary school students may not be capable of delivering a peer education program and that which activities they engage in must be carefully considered and matched with their abilities. The findings also indicate that peer-assisted programs may be most effective and sustainable, and more research should be conducted on this topic.

The authors report that there are limitations placed on the outcome of the trial, such as the fact that the evaluation did not assess individual components of the intervention but rather focused on the whole, and the statistical power of the sample size may be weaker than first anticipated. Nevertheless, this study represents the first randomized controlled trial of its kind in sub-Saharan Africa which utilizes a range of biological markers and it is the first to report on any outcome measures after a three year follow-up period (Hayes et al., 2005; Obasi et al., in press). In addition, the intervention is also seen as being feasibly replicable on a large scale. In the pilot phase which was resource and labor intensive, the costs were US$17 per student per year, but at present it has been reduced to about US$1.40 (Fox, 2000; World Bank, 2003). It therefore represents a step forward and a raising of the bar in terms of devising a contextually and culturally appropriate intervention and rigorous evaluation that must be strived towards.

Rutanang – peer education in South Africa

In December 2000, the South African Department of Health assembled 25 of the nation's health and education leaders who had some level of interest and expertise in peer education to discuss how it might be applied to HIV prevention. The result is a large-scale project [1] which represents one significant attempt to push the concept of peer education to another level and fill some of the gaps in the literature by synthesizing the existing body of evidence and defining a rigorous set of standards of practice and evaluation. Towards that end, it has been advocated that a new way of thinking about peer education is needed; a shift in thinking from peer education as an art to peer education as a technology or, as the authors explain, an application of science to art (Deutsch & Swartz, 2002). As a consequence, *Rutanang,* a Sotho term meaning "learning from one another" has evolved, which constitutes not only a rigorous set of documents and standards created over an 18 month period, but a sustainable process built on reflexivity, evaluation and programmatic improvement on a number of levels.

The *Rutanang* documents provide a shared vision of the potential of peer education. Central to this vision is the definition of the four fundamental roles of the peer educators: i) to educate their peers in a structured manner, regarded as the pivotal role; ii) to informally role-model healthy behavior; iii) to recognize youth in need of help and refer them for assistance; and iv) to advocate for resources and services for themselves and their peers. The documents also provide guidance about the requisite program structures and mechanisms for peer education programs. This guidance takes the form of S.T.E.P.Ps (Standards Towards Excellent Peer Programs) for each of the ten elements regarded as essential to peer education: i) planning; ii) mobilizing; iii) supervisor infrastructure; iv) linkages; v) learning program; vi) peer educator infrastructure; vii) management; viii) recognition and credentialing; ix) monitoring and evaluation and x) sustainability.

The *Rutanang* process involves the establishment of national reference groups to review, critique and support peer education programs. It also involves the provision of technical assistance to peer education programs, through the national Departments of Health and Education, the South African University Vice Chancellors Association, the Committee of Technikon Principals, and the Harvard School of Public Health. An Institute for Peer Education is in the process of being established in the Eastern Cape province, to formalize these functions, and to spearhead evaluation initiatives.

Rutanang has been the inspiration for a number of diverse peer education initiatives that have been established in South Africa, for youth in schools and in institutions of higher learning. For example, rising rates of infection

---

1. See the website: www.hsph.harvard.edu/peereducation for more details and downloads.

and the belief that peer education works have prompted the Provincial Government of the Western Cape to expand the existing school-based life skills program to include a peer education component called GOLD, which is informed by *Rutanang* principles and guidelines and will be rolled out in 100 schools during 2005 (Flisher et al., 2005). In the Eastern Cape province, *Rutanang* is the inspiration behind and support for several non-government organizations in their establishment of peer education programs in 1,000 schools.

Opportunities and limitations theoretically and practically

As has been discussed above, the distinct lack of conceptual clarity and empirical evidence in the use of peer education poses a challenge not only to researchers, but also to practitioners and educators contemplating designing and implementing a program. Without clear guidelines and standards on central issues such as what constitutes a peer educator, what their role is, and subsequently how to recruit peer educators and train them, there will continue to be a plethora of widely varied programs which preclude any basis for comparison of outcomes and identification and dissemination of best practices.

In a review of why peer education typically falls short of its objectives, Walker and Avis (1999) cite the following as reasons: (i) a distinct lack of clear aims and objectives; (ii) an inconsistency between the project design and the external environment/constraints which should play a role in the project's design; (iii) a lack of investment in peer education; (iv) a lack of appreciation that peer education is a complex process to manage and requires highly skilled facilitation; (v) inadequate training and support for peer educators; (vi) a lack of clarity around boundary issues; and (vii) a failure to secure multi-agency support. Some of these shortcomings resonate strongly with the reflexive critique of Catherine Campbell (2003) who was involved in a comprehensive, carefully-conceived project in a mining community in South Africa which utilized peer educators. In her evaluation she identified a number of factors which undermined the program, such as a school environment not conducive to the participatory, consciousness raising principles of peer education. Rather, the school was pervaded by authoritarian teaching methodologies and teacher-student relationships and gender inequalities. She concludes that attention to social and cultural context is imperative to the success of peer education programs, and identifies the ideal environment as being rich in social capital, and providing an 'enabling' community supportive for stimulating critical thinking and social change (Campbell, 2003).

Indeed, in the context of the school and HIV prevention, there are a number of mitigating factors which may work to hinder the ability of the school to serve as a health promoting, enabling environment. A recent study of three countries (Ghana, Malawi and Zimbabwe) suggests that the emphasis of the school as a vehicle for HIV prevention may be misguided for a number of reasons, including the limited amount of resources and time available, inadequate teacher training, and the attitudes of teachers themselves (Leach et al., 2003). Additionally, studies have probed the issue of sexual harassment and abuse in African schools, where teachers themselves may be the perpetrators (Human Rights Watch, 2001; Leach et al., 2003). Some studies have focused on the structural constraints limiting the success of HIV prevention programs such as restricted access of girls to education, power structures within the school, teacher discomfort and lack of knowledge of AIDS (Boler et al., 2003), and external barriers such as religious influences and parental disapproval, all of which may conspire to create an environment which is not conducive to facilitating discussion of sensitive and traditionally taboo topics.

If one of the aims of peer education is to move beyond provision and dissemination of factual information towards providing the impetus for sustained social change through the development of life skills and critical thinking capacities, the context it takes place in cannot be overlooked. The above discussion highlights the limitations of the school as an arena and underscores the importance of interventions built on an understanding of the social and cultural complexity of the school as a system. Clearly, the school's potential to serve as an arena or platform for change must be considered concurrently with the barriers which prevent it from doing so.

Peering into the future

Peer education has been promulgated as one of the most effective and innovative ways to influence behavior of young people and tailor prevention messages to suit a target population's needs, values and behaviors. Consequently, it has been increasingly used in the field of health promotion and in HIV and AIDS prevention in particular. Indeed, it is likely that the well designed and delivered peer education program is an invaluable strategy when embedded within and coupled with wider prevention strategies and initiatives and when it takes place in an environment conducive to and supportive of social change. However, the lack of unanimity in the current peer education literature in terms of semantics and terminology, the wide variation in strategies and methods, use (or lack thereof) of theory, and the levels of evaluation, make comparison of outcomes and identification and dissemination of best practices highly problematic. However, as the *MEMA kwa Vijana* and *Rutanang* initiatives demonstrate, there have recently been some strides made towards resolving some of the problems surrounding peer education such as conceptual clarity and lack of stringent evaluation. A stronger evidence-base than is currently available is critical in order for peer education to be prioritized by governments and organizations in charge of funding.

While the peer group may constitute one of the prime influences in the lives of adolescents and young people, it is not the only one and may be mediated or constrained by a number of socio-economic and cultural factors. Unraveling and unpacking the multitude of confounders in young people's lived realities which may be operating alongside peer education programs is not an uncomplicated task. Indeed, it is one that requires rethinking the theoretical foundations and rationale underpinning peer education and behavior change, processes which are increasingly being engaged with by some researchers.

Process, outcome and impact evaluations therefore need to be appropriately designed, multi-level and multidimensional, with careful attention paid to differential impact according to age, gender, intervention setting and social status, for instance. Comparisons of peer versus adult-led programs and mixed approaches should be undertaken and the need for long-term follow up studies of cohorts is also crucial. In addition, further research into the recruitment, selection and training of peer educators, and the activities they engage in is necessary to understand how these factors influence the outcome of a program. The yawning chasm that typically exists between research and practice needs to be narrowed as a more solid body of evidence emerges documenting what works in order to maximize and tap into the potential of peer education.

Table 2. Peer sexual health and HIV/AIDS education evaluation (process or outcome) studies from sub-Saharan Africa; 1990–2005

Authors	Country	Intervention	Objective	Population & design	Main findings
Agha 2002 & Agha, Van Rossem, 2004	Cameroon, Botswana, South Africa and Guinea	Selection of peer educators: not clear for all countries. Volunteers in South Africa, 28 trained in Cameroon, not reported in Botswana, 28 male and 28 female volunteers trained in Guinea Training: not clear in Cameroon and South Africa, in Botswana standardized training and refresher courses given, in Guinea trained on reproductive health and communication Responsibilities: facilitate discussion, condom sales & demonstrations, drama, leaflet distribution Theoretical basis: Health Belief Model	Evaluated impact of social marketing programs in 4 African countries in 1994–98. Peer education is one component of the intervention and varied in the extent of its use across countries. Indictors used related to perceptions and behaviors related to sexual health and risks.	Adolescents. Quasi-experimental design, used same statistical models, data from baseline and post-intervention surveys but length of intervention varied. Indicators were similar across countries but not always identical.	Interventions reached varying proportions of their target audiences, one of the reasons stated is that peer education programs were not closely monitored in some countries and most exposure to intervention came via other means. Improvements in health perceptions of females (benefits and barriers of protective behavior), positive effect on contraceptive use. Effects more limited on males, although in 2 countries evidence that it reduced multiple or casual partners. Multiple channels of communication most effective at changing attitudes and behavior.
	Zambia	Selection of peer educators: not clear Training: by a professional peer education trainer to use a variety of communication techniques Responsibilities: facilitate discussion, condom demonstrations, drama, leaflet distribution. Theoretical basis: not clear	Investigated changes in beliefs and knowledge on abstinence, condoms and risk perception following a 1 3/4 hour lesson taught by peer leaders.	Secondary school students (14–23 years). Quasi-experimental design: 3 schools randomly assigned to intervention and 2 to control condition.	Knowledge was higher; beliefs about abstinence significantly more positive and sustained for a 6-month period; normative beliefs about condoms took longer to develop; risk perception higher among students in intervention schools; and reductions in multiple regular partnerships.

	Country	Program	Aim	Sample / Methods	Findings
Brieger et al., 2001	Nigeria and Ghana	Selection of peer educators: indicates only that youth were involved. Training: sessions by youth services organization, focus on anatomy, physiology, sexual and reproductive health, communication, counseling and data collection forms. Responsibilities: information, education, drama, counseling, referral. Theoretical basis: not clear	To determine the feasibility and impact of a reproductive health peer education program on knowledge, attitudes and practices in different settings.	Secondary and post-secondary school students and out of school youth. Quasi-experimental: pre- and post-intervention cross-sectional surveys.	Significant intervention effects with respect to knowledge, use of contraceptives in the last 3 months, willingness to buy contraceptives and increased self-efficacy.
Campbell et al., 2005	South Africa	Selection of peer educators: not clear. Training: not clear. Responsibilities: not clear. Theoretical basis: not clear	Study of the impact of social context and environment on a participatory peer education program for youth using a six factor framework of analysis.	Diverse key informants: teachers, health workers, community leaders, school learners, peer educators, traditional healers, nurses, parents, PLWA, church ministers, govt. officials and more. Qualitative case study (incl. interviews, focus group discussions fieldworker diaries) in a peri-urban community.	Three dimensions of the social context which undermine prevention efforts: symbolic context, organizational/network context, material-political context. HIV prevention initiatives should work closely with social development programs to promote youth social and political participation, increase opportunities for economic empowerment, challenge negative portrayals of youth and protect their right to sexual health.
Campbell & MacPhail, 2002	South Africa	Selection of peer educators: twenty volunteers. Training: participatory methods course by clinical outreach coordinator of NGO. Responsibilities: role play, music, condom distribution. Theoretical basis: Freire's critical consciousness, social identity, empowerment and social capital	Study of factors that enable and constrain the potential success of school-based participatory peer education programs in a township context.	Young people (13–25 years). Qualitative case study incl. 8 focus group discussions with peer educators.	A number of factors hindering the success of peer education programs were identified: peer educators' preference for didactic methods, unequal gender dynamics, highly regulated and teacher-driven nature of school environment, and negative learner attitudes towards the program. Furthermore, limited opportunities for communication about sex outside of peer education setting, poor adult role models, poverty and unemployment, low levels of social capital and poor community facilities. Social and community development seen as a key to maximizing program success.

Hughes-d'Aeth, 2002	Zambia	Selection of peer educators: not clear Training: specialized training by NGO Responsibilities: drama, music, sports, anti-AIDS clubs, youth magazines, life skills booklets Theoretical basis: not clear	Assess peer education programs run by four non-governmental organizations.	Young people (14–25 years) in and out of school, PLWA, drug users, sex workers and other "at risk" groups. "Mini-case-study" approach incl. interviews with key informants and on-site observation of peer activities.	Projects were found to have raised community awareness of AIDS, basic knowledge was mostly accurate, anecdotal evidence of behavior change in terms of partner reduction, evidence that traditional practices were being modified, and that programs protected human rights and dignity.
Molassiotis et al., 2004	Zambia	Selection of peer educators: not clear Training: ongoing workshops and other peer educators Responsibilities: facilitate discussion, anti-AIDS clubs, sports, drama, condom distribution, outreach activities Theoretical basis: Empowerment	Evaluate the effects of a peer education program run by local people on behavior and the community, and dynamics of peer health promotion.	Participants and educators. Process evaluation incl. focus groups with both groups.	Reported impact on participants' attitudes to HIV, lifestyle and behavior in relation to sexual practices and cultural norms. The success is attributed to community mobilization and support, and the use of peer communication rather than professional teachers to disseminate information and serve as role models.
Okonofua et al., 2003	Nigeria	Selection of peer educators: 40 chosen via peer selection Training: trained on prevention and treatment over 4 weeks after school hours Responsibilities: awareness campaigns, counseling, referral, debates, drama, essay writing, films Theoretical basis: not clear	To evaluate the impact of an intervention designed to improve STD treatment-seeking behavior and prevent STDs among youth.	12 schools with youths aged 14–20. Randomized controlled trial, questionnaire used to evaluate intervention impact.	Statistically significant improvements in knowledge of STDs, condom use, partner awareness of STDs and STD treatment-seeking behavior. Prevalence of STDs significantly reduced in intervention schools compared to control schools.
Speizer et al., 2001	Cameroon	Selection of peer educators: 42 volunteers recruited and trained in 2 years from schools and youth associations Training: one week initial training by health professionals with refresher courses Responsibilities: facilitate discussion, one-on-one meetings, sports, referral, distribution of leaflets Theoretical basis: not clear	Assessing whether exposure to a peer educator led to increased knowledge and protective behavior.	In and out of school youth. Pre- and post-test quasi-experimental design. 353 discussion group sessions with 12,000 young people conducted.	Multivariate analyses indicated that contact with peer educator resulted in greater knowledge of contraception, symptoms of STI, and greater use of contraception such as condom.

Tankoano, 1994	Burkina Faso	Selection of peer educators: Villagers were asled to designate 3 young men and 3 young women from each village as peer educators. Training: By experienced 'field agents' of the same sex. Responsibilities: facilitate infomal and village discussion groups, organize special days with dance and skits Theoretical basis: not clear	Pilot project to test a peer education approach among young people.	Samples of youth and adults from 10 villages. Pre- and post-tests, interviews.	Reported condom use doubled from 9 % to 18%, and the project was scaled up to 105 villages with 1,495 village communicators (580 youth) trained.
Van Rossem & Meekers, 2000	Cameroon	Selection of peer educators: 28 peer educators, students and non-students "recruited" from target population Training: social marketing techniques and behavior change communications. Responsibilities: facilitate discussion, condom sales Theoretical basis: Health Belief Model	Examines the effectiveness of a youth-targeted social marketing program using peer education, youth clubs, mass media and behavior change communications.	Adolescents. Pre- and post-intervention survey, quasi-experimental design with intervention and comparison site.	Significant effect on sexual risk awareness, knowledge of contraception, and increased discussion of sexuality and contraceptives. Delayed sexual debut of females, and increased proportion of females reporting contraceptive use, but condom use is inconsistent. Proportion of males using condoms increased but is not attributed to intervention. No evidence of partner reduction.
Warwick & Aggleton, 2004	South Africa	Selection of peer educators: not clear Training: five-day participatory course, ongoing training Responsibilities: classroom lessons, drama, song, information provision, skills building, self-reflexive review of practice Theoretical basis: not clear	Aimed at: identifying if lessons improved sexual health and HIV/AIDS knowledge and practices; identifying if and how teachers valued the contributions of the peer educators; and considering the practical implications of the findings.	Five schools, grades 8–12 with data collected from learners and teachers. Participatory formative evaluation using a five-step evaluation plan beginning with observation, discussion, collaboration to develop evaluation instruments, data collection and finally, joint analysis of information.	– learners were not used to participatory approaches, having to reflect on values and developing life skills – changes in behavior less likely than changes in knowledge and attitudes – peer education successful in stimulating discussion and curiosity – teachers perceived content and structure of lessons by peer educators as valuable – addressing meso-level factors through a whole school approach will make an impact but may be constrained by lack of resources and local factors, a community-based approach is advocated – action-based evaluation could simultaneously build capacity at all levels, incl. teachers.

Wolf et al., 2000, Wolf & Bond 2002, Wolf & Pulerwitz, 2003	Ghana	Selection of peer educators: not stated Training: 5 one-day sessions on data collection procedures Responsibilities: administer questionnaire and conduct one-on-one interviews with peer contacts Theoretical basis: Social cognitive theory	Study aimed at examining peer education as an interpersonal communication process and its potential use for HIV prevention through looking at the similarities between peer educators and their contacts, and through comparing peer-led versus adult-led programs in terms of effectiveness.	In and out of school youth, 106 peer educators and 526 contacts or participants at 3 peri-urban and rural sites. Process and Outcome Evaluation – multiple semi-structured interviews, network analysis and surveys (N=490).	Insight gained into peer education in terms of: defining composition of peer contacts, identifying social norms playing a role in decision making and observing messages and services transmitted during peer education. Peer educators tend to reach people similar to themselves with respect to age, sex, ethnicity and school status. Having had contact with a peer educator significantly increased the likelihood of protective action against AIDS. Youth who talked to peers and adults were 2.08 times more likely (95% CI:1.23, 3.51) to report protective behavior than those who did not, while those who talked with peers only were 1.71 times more likely to protect themselves. – sexually active youth more than twice as likely to talk to peers than adults – specific AIDS protective behaviors reported varied depending on whether contact source was peers or adults.

10. Adolescent-Friendly Health Services in Uganda

John Arube-Wani, Jessica Jitta and Lillian Mpabulungi Ssengooba[1]

Abstract

A needs-assessment for adolescent-friendly health (AFHS) services in Uganda was conducted in five pilot districts, with specific objectives of: i) providing an inventory and assessment of existing adolescent health services; ii) identifying critical adolescent health and development unmet needs/ gaps; and iii) developing an action plan for implementing AFHS. Focus group discussions were held with various adolescent groups and parents, while key informant interviews were carried out with district/local leaders, service providers, planners and policy-makers. A review of documents on existing services, studies on adolescent sexuality and reproductive health needs, growth and development was undertaken; as well as observation at service delivery points, mapping of local services and resources, and problem ranking.

Generally, adolescents face many problems ranging from common and reproductive health diseases, including STDs and HIV/AIDS, early/unwanted pregnancies, early/forced marriages and their consequences such as unsafe abortions. They are also increasingly vulnerable to rape and defilement, especially in this era of HIV/AIDS. Currently a number of service delivery factors restrain adolescents from using existing services: the high cost of health care; long distances to health units; lack of transport; shortage of drugs; poor access to information; poor staffing at service points; and negative attitudes of health staff towards them. Adolescents also indulge in high-risk behaviours like substance abuse; sex in exchange for money; and living on the streets. Harsh socio-economic conditions lead to household poverty; unemployment; child labour and street children; and parental neglect, further giving rise to situations like dropping out of school and high illiteracy (especially among girls). Adolescents want integrated services that are accessible; where there is mutual trust; and prompt attention, with assured confidentiality. Most importantly, adolescents want to be involved in all stages of the development and implementation of their own services.

1. The authors thank UNICEF-Uganda for providing funding for the needs assessment presented in this chapter; the Ministry of Health (especially the Reproductive Health Division) for the idea and commissioning of the study; and the District Directors of the District Health Services of all the study districts, policy makers, community leaders, school heads and teachers, health providers, and most of all adolescents (both in-school and out of school)/young persons and their parents, for their invaluable assistance and participation.

Introduction

There is a growing worldwide concern about adolescent sexual and health and development problems. In order to address the problem, the 1994 Cairo International Conference on Population and Development (ICPD) Programme of Action called for governments and organizations to initiate or strengthen programmes to better meet the reproductive health needs of adolescents in particular (United Nations Population Information Network, 1994). The rapid bodily and psychosocial changes adolescents experience, coupled with the lack of information, guidance, counselling, and support from their environment often make them feel confused and embarrassed. Consequently, they often do not know whom to turn to when problems eventually arise. Considerable attention needs to be given to psychosocial and behavioural aspects of adolescents, especially in view of their risk-taking tendencies, and the assumption of unhealthy social habits such as smoking, drug use and violent behaviour. Many of the concerns have intensified in recent decades because of increased urbanization, increased exposure to media and high rates of unemployment, including, in some areas persistent homelessness and various forms of social upheaval. The advent of the HIV/AIDS pandemic, and the easy access to drugs and alcohol, have greatly added to the adolescents' problems of sexual and reproductive ill health (Senderowitz, 1997; WHO, 1998a; Mirembe, 1999).

The need for adolescent-friendly health services (AFHS) has emerged especially as a result of increased understanding and better definition of the life stages of adolescents. To that end efforts to meet their age-specific needs have emerged, including meeting their sexual and reproductive health needs. Such services were mainly reserved for older married women, whilst the special needs of younger married women were not considered because of their biological development and emotional maturity; unmarried young women and men were thus effectively excluded. However, now, more than ever before, young people need reproductive health care – especially through prevention – as a result of a longer period of non-marital sexual activity, related to earlier menarche, later marriage, greater economic opportunities for women, increased urbanisation, and liberalising attitudes, mainly influenced by modern mass communications. The emergence of the HIV/AIDS pandemic has equally brought this about, especially in view of increased and earlier sexual activity amongst adolescents and young adults. Studies have also indicated that adolescents are more concerned about provider characteristics than specific site or service characteristics for 'friendly' services. The provider characteristics mentioned include respect for adolescents, experience, and confidentiality (WHO, 1998a; Senderowitz, 1999; Mirembe, 1999).

In Uganda adolescents (or teenagers) are defined as people aged between 10–19 years, and young adults as those between 20 and 24 years. Altogether, they constitute about 32 per cent of the total population. For purposes of this study, the term adolescents or their equivalents may include young people who at the time of the study were slightly older than 19 years. This is a stage in life where a person is in transition from childhood to adulthood, and it is associated with a lot of experimentation, high incidence of sexually transmitted infections (STIs) including HIV/AIDS, early and unwanted pregnancies, alcohol and substance abuse, and female genital mutilation among some nationalities. Sexually transmitted diseases (STDs) are most frequent in young people aged 15–24 years, and half of all new HIV infections are of people in this age group (UNFPA, 1998). Uganda has one of the highest rates of teenage pregnancies in the world, estimated at about 43 per cent among the 13–15 years of age group (Uganda Demographic Health Survey, 1995).[1] These high rates contribute about one-third of maternal mortality in hospitals around the capital city of Kampala (Ministry of Health, 1998).

A number of studies and reports have shown that adolescents in Uganda now engage in sexual relations at an earlier age than before, and increasingly take on sexually risky behaviours, such as early/casual or unprotected sex. They also suffer the consequences of early or mistimed pregnancies, and are exposed to high prevalence of sexually transmitted infections and HIV/AIDS (Turyasingura, 1989; Bachou, 1992; National Council for Children, 1999; Statistic Department, 1996; Bohmer & Kirumira 1997; Kirumira et al., 1997). Other key problems affecting adolescents include unmet reproductive health needs; for example, resulting in low family planning usage, currently at only 7–8 per cent (Kyaddondo, 1994; Ministry of Health, 1998).

The appropriate use of health facilities by adolescents would contribute to reduction in exposure to risk and fewer adverse consequences of risk behaviour, but more often, adolescents do not use the existing health facilities. There are a number of reasons that they do not use the health facilities, one of which is that they are not treated in a "friendly" manner when they do go to facilities (Senderowitz, 1999). Currently, there are no specific programmes to address these adolescent sexual and reproductive

---

1. The Uganda Demographic Health Survey of 2000–2001 showed a substantial decline of teenage pregnancy to 31%.

needs (Ministry of Health, 1998; Mirembe, 1999). The Ugandan government does recognise this fact, hence, the Ministry of Health (MoH) has developed an adolescent health policy whose overall goal is to mainstream adolescent health concerns in the national development process in order to improve the quality of life and standard of living of young people in Uganda. Among the specific objectives of the policy are: (i) to create an enabling legal and socio-cultural environment that promotes provision of better health information services; (ii) to protect and promote rights of adolescents to health education, information and care; (iii) to promote the involvement adolescents in conceptualisation, design, implementation, monitoring and evaluation of their programmes (iv) to promote adequate development of responsible health-related positive behaviour; and (v) to provide legal and social protection, especially of the girl-child, against harmful traditional practices, and all forms of abuse, including sexual abuse, exploitation, trafficking and violence (Ministry of Health, 2004).

The policy sets out a number of strategies which include: providing guidelines for addressing adolescent health concerns; training and reorienting the health system to focus and meet special needs of adolescents; and creating awareness concerning adolescent health, especially among service providers, the community, and its leaders. The long-term expected outcomes of implementing the above adolescent health policy goals and objectives include: imparting accurate knowledge on health issues; improving health-seeking behaviour; the provision of user-friendly health services to adolescents and young people; and encouraging positive attitudes towards health among adolescents and young people. Besides the new policy, the MoH has prepared a training manual and a draft sensitisation package on adolescent user-friendly services. A National Technical Committee on Adolescent Health has also been instituted, and in 1999 in conjunction with international partners, the MoH developed a 'Sexual and Reproductive Health Minimum Package for Uganda'. These developments underscore the importance the government attaches to this area of service delivery. The package includes a specific component on adolescent sexual and reproductive health.

In Uganda, AFHS are defined as services that are geographically accessible, affordable, acceptable, welcoming and provide confidentiality for the adolescents (UNICEF/MoH, 1998). The proposed minimum package includes the following components: information on sexuality, growth and development, reproductive health services, counselling services, life-skills education and recreation services. The main goal of the needs assessment therefore, was to collect information that can assist the various key players in AFHS to plan, implement and monitor these services, and eventually to help chart the way forward for the whole country. The specific objectives were a) to provide an inventory and assessment of existing adolescent health services; b) to identify critical adolescent health and development unmet needs/gaps; and c) to develop an action plan for implementing AFHS. Among the key stakeholders are relevant sectors such as the ministries of health, gender, labour and social development, and education, as well as global bodies like UNICEF, non-governmental organisations; the districts and the lower local councils. In carrying out the needs assessment, it was also anticipated that the home, school, health centre, the media, youth groups, and gathering areas for adolescents and others related to them, are all potential avenues for promoting and providing AFHS. Such services should be integrated so as to build optimal utilisation, and referral to existing services and resources. The following four elements in particular, are considered to be very important for strengthening AFHS in Uganda:

– the provision of AFHS in health units, schools, youth clubs/groups and key gathering points for adolescents through peer education and counselling, life-skills education, confidential counselling and screening by adolescent-friendly staff;

– setting up a referral system for AFHS between health units, hospitals, schools, peer-educators, youth and adolescent organisations;

– increasing the demand for AFHS through participation of adolescents in planning, implementation and monitoring; and

– sensitising key stakeholders in the community, and promotion through the media (UNICEF/MoH, 1998).

Methodology

Design

A cross-sectional exploratory study was conducted using mainly qualitative data collection methods to obtain participants' views, opinions and attitudes to existing services for adolescent sexual and reproductive health.

Study districts

The study was carried out in five pilot districts of Kabale in the southwestern region; Kiboga in the central; Mbale in the east; Nebbi in the northwest;

and Rukungiri in the west. The districts were purposively selected on the basis of regional location; representing broad socio-cultural and economic variations, and on the basis of activities already begun, with focus on adolescent sexual and reproductive health services in particular. Two sub-counties and town councils from each of the five districts were purposively selected, based on predetermined criteria. Sub-counties/town councils were considered on the basis of rural/urban setting, under-served areas, cross-border activities, and presence of especially vulnerable groups like street children, disabled adolescents, or orphans.

Data collection

First, documents with information on adolescent services/programmes and related activities in the districts were reviewed, as well as the locally available literature on adolescents' sexual and reproductive health, and growth and development. Particular attention was paid to information concerning the planning process, opportunities for information, education and communication (IEC), reproductive health and counseling services available, resources, mobilization, recreation, life-skills efforts, and referral systems for adolescents. Where possible, copies of some of the documents reviewed were also collected.

Second, focus group discussions (FGDs) were held with adolescents both in and out of school, of various age groups/brackets (10–14, 15–19, 20–24); married adolescents were also included. Adolescents in school were selected according to age groups, by their teachers; while those out of school were identified by community members, through their local leaders. Others, including young adults (20–24), were purposively selected, according to the age categories they were in. Other focus groups were with parents of adolescents (female and male groups). Discussions were facilitated and moderated by experienced field supervisors, assisted by research assistants who spoke the local dialect or language. Tape recorders were used to record the information, to capture the mood of discussions and complement the written notes taken by the person recording. About 1,000 adolescents took part in focus group discussions.

Third, key informant interviews using topic guides were held with district and sub-county leaders; service providers (mainly teachers, health workers, probation/welfare and community development officers); community resource persons and leaders (traditional birth attendants, traditional healers, local councillors, women's leaders); and representatives of NGOs. A total of 191 key informant interviews were carried out.

Finally, to supplement the above data collection techniques, other participatory methods were used. These included observation at service delivery points, mapping of available services, and problem ranking, the aim of which was to observe service settings and/or any interactions of interest, particularly with adolescent clients, most of who happened to be teenage mothers or young adults. Twenty resource-maps were drawn, showing existing and other potential facilities for adolescents. Adolescents also ranked their problems according to their own perceived magnitude of the problems.

After data collection at each site, there was feedback to the community, and work plans for future programmes were drawn up. This helped in validation of the preliminary findings as well as sensitizing the stakeholders about the status and need for adolescent-friendly services, and the way forward. Key issues generated from discussions during the dissemination and planning sessions were integrated in the final district report.

Data analysis and report writing

The focus group discussions were transcribed and edited. All field notes were word processed for easy handling, categorized and developed for analysis. Texts were coded and clusters compiled along emergent or pre-defined themes and sub-themes for subsequent analysis. Using the thematic approach, data was then summarized using flow charts, matrices, as well as narrative texts; case studies were then prepared, based on the emerging themes. Key phrases, statements, or anecdotes expressing strong views on important events or feelings were quoted and integrated in the report in order to get the full meaning of the statements.

Results

This section presents key results of the study. The first section presents and describes what the adolescents reported their reproductive health and developmental problems were. The second and third sections give data on the status of the existing adolescent services in the five districts, and gaps in services or unmet needs, respectively.

Main sexual and reproductive health problems

The occurrence of HIV/AIDS and STDs was generally reported to be high (according to the adolescents themselves) due to unprotected sex, lack of information on sexual matters, absence of counseling services, limited or no condom supplies. However, there were generally no available or reliable data on the prevalence or exact number of HIV/AIDS cases in the districts. Despite the fairly high level of awareness about the dangers posed by STDs, and in particular HIV/AIDS, adolescents were still prone to engaging in high-risk behaviours, including indulging in unprotected sex. This was reported to be common, especially during ceremonies related to male circumcision (initiation) in Mbale district, where circumcision rites are an integral part of the growth and development (maturation) process of male adolescents. Elsewhere, district officials and service providers mentioned such happenings during other communal ceremonies and dances.

Early/unwanted pregnancies and marriages

Adolescents and other study participants in all districts in general reported a high rate of early pregnancies, which often result in early marriages before they are physically and emotionally ready. Illegal and unsafe abortions were reported by using herbs and drugs such as chloroquine and aspirin, and some of them reportedly resort to committing suicide out of desperation. For adolescent mothers, being pregnant, more often than not, means possible resentment from friends or at times harassment from their parents. Discussions with adolescent girls in three districts in the west, north and east indicated that parents encourage or 'force' girls to marry early, as they reportedly find it difficult to provide them with basic necessities, including feeding them. In Uganda, the statutory age of consent is 18, yet many girls are married off at 12 or 13 years.

Sexual abuse: rape and defilement cases

In Uganda, defilement age by law is below 18 years, and many cases of rape and defilement were reported to be common in all districts. In one district in particular, rape and defilement cases were reported to commonly occur during ceremonies related to traditional initiation (circumcision) rites. This often occurs especially when adolescents of one age-set are caught up in a frenzy of activities after initiation such as heavy drinking, during which many casual sexual encounters occur often resulting in unsafe sex. During circumcision-related ('*kadodi*') dances that are performed by young boys and girls, such incidences commonly take place (Kivumbi et al., 1999):

> *During this time of circumcision, it is difficult to control children. So, you just leave them to go their way. With this kind of freedom they (girls) mess up with men. She*

only comes home, starts falling sick, becomes thin, and dies. I wish there was a way to control this circumcision. [A mother, Mbale]

Girls are often lured by older men, who give them money or other material gifts, in exchange for sex; some parents noted that rape and defilement cases were common after discos, traditional dances, or video shows. In one district, 13 rape and 33 defilement cases were reportedly handled by the law courts and probation/welfare department during 1997/98, though it was readily acknowledged that many more cases would have gone unreported. An earlier study in the district had shown that 31 per cent of girls and 15 per cent of boys in secondary schools had been forced to have sex (Bagarukayo et al., 1993). In another district, rape and defilement cases were reportedly on the increase and during 1995 alone, the courts and probation and welfare department dealt with 105 defilement cases. In general, there is manifest leniency in dealing with the cases, since the law seems to be hardly enforced by the law enforcement, judicial agencies, and community. This seems to support the commonly held view that there is some kind of conspiracy of silence or collusion of interests at play, either because of the shame attached to such cases, or the possibility of receiving in-kind payments as settlement. In such instances, animals or cash payments are made to the parents or relatives of the girls, who often prefer settlement of cases outside the legal framework. A number of concerns were expressed about this apparent lack of sensitivity and non-enforcement of the law:

> *We have a Ugandan government law or regulation for defilement but it has failed. Parents, police and others tend to minimize it, for example when one is arrested in case of the girl, parents have gone ahead to tell their daughters to tell lies on oath, telling them she is above 19, above defilement age. Most if not all prefer to settle the case outside court. Some even bribe the officers in charge, so it is that bad. So many girls are suffering at the expense of their parents.* [Policy maker, Nebbi]

A common outcome of such 'mutual settlement' is that marriage may be forced on the two adolescents involved:

> *Sexual abuse is rampant and society is quiet about it…those who report the case to police are rare. They confuse the police that they should solve the problem at home or outside the court by both parents of the victims…* [Policy maker].

In one of the districts, cases of defilement end up in marriage after settlement of a fine, ranging from Uganda shillings 100,000/= to 500,000/= (US$ 60–300), or livestock; in rural areas it may be a bull or a few goats.

Usually parents take the money; but more often it is the father and not the mother; it is a kind of compensation, according to one policy maker.

Problems associated with delivery of services

Respondents in all the districts identified a number of health service delivery-related problems affecting the adolescents, like the high cost of health care due to cost-sharing charges (user-fees) in government units (cost-sharing has since been abolished), usually without getting the prescribed drugs. In private clinics/health units where treatment is relatively more expensive, depending on what the patient can afford to pay, most adolescents say they cannot afford it. Screening services for HIV/AIDS are generally not available, except in a few hospitals, where services are not readily accessible to adolescents in particular. There is no effective referral system, which in any case, is severely constrained by lack of efficient transport services, and related high costs for treatment. Other problems mentioned include understaffing of delivery points; the chronic shortage of drug supplies; lack of contraceptive and counseling services; shortage of health education (IEC) materials; and lack of clean water supply and sanitation facilities. In most schools visited, no school-based health services were available, and adolescent girls voiced their concern about the lack of sanitary kits (pads, soap, etc); parents are generally blamed for not providing them.

Negative attitudes and behaviour of health providers towards adolescents

Dissatisfaction among adolescents with health workers' behaviour was mentioned in all the districts, which according to them, negatively portrays the quality of care. Some health workers were reported to be openly rude, often barking at their adolescent clients, who in turn become reticent and might decline to ask or answer any questions:

> *Health workers are rude to us, especially when we have STDs, they discriminate against our age group and chase us away when we have no money.* [Male adolescents, Rukungiri]

> *If she asks and you don't answer, she barks at you instead of asking you in a good way.* [Female adolescents, Mbale]

Lack of confidentiality

Adolescents also say that they do not use family planning services due to lack of confidentiality, and the unprofessional behaviour of some service providers, who often betray their clients by for example, disclosing confidential information about them to other parties:

> *FP providers reveal those girls who ask for pills to the community. This leads to failure to get a partner for marriage because it is believed that you will not produce children.* [Local leaders/councilors]

Fear is often the most common experience of adolescents in their encounters with health workers:

> *We fear to approach the nurses as they ask us where we are taking the pills or condoms.* [Male adolescents, Rukungiri]

Heavy workload/shortage of staff

For their part, health personnel raised their concerns about how they work under very difficult circumstances; a matter also raised by some adolescents themselves and other key informants. They said it is difficult for them to cater to adolescents, saying the services are extra-demanding in terms of workload, and many adolescents may have to wait a long time before they are served due to shortage of staff:

> *There is long waiting time due to understaffing at health units, and sometimes the costs hinder adolescents from accessing these services.* [Service Provider, Rukungiri]

As a consequence of the heavy workload indicated, more often than not, some vital activities like health education are often not carried out:

> *We are supposed to carry out home visits, outreach programmes and health education for adolescents, but we are unable because we are very few. We are only four staff and are always busy. We need other health workers to assist us.* [Health worker, Mbale]

High-risk behaviour and related problems

Some socio-economic factors tend to lead adolescents to engage in high-risk behaviours such as substance abuse, sexual abuse (rape and defilement), sex in exchange for money with young adolescents (applicable mostly to girls), and problems associated with living on the street, primarily affecting young boys and in some cases girls as well. The consequences include unsafe abortions, STIs/HIV/AIDS, crime, prostitution, dropping out of school and so on. Reasons for these problems are explained or perceived differently by different people; for example: as due to 'idleness' (according to parents and some district officials); negative peer pressure; lack of recreation; the desire for money or material items; or absence of legal control/enforcement of the law. They are further exacerbated by a number of factors: inadequate information and lack of life skills, lack of education, poverty, unemployment, and a largely hostile and/or non-supportive environment, especially at home.

Many adolescents, especially street children, reportedly indulge in gambling, smoking marijuana (*bhang*) or opium, sniffing fuel, chewing *khat* (or *mairungi*), or drinking strong liquor (crude *waragi,* a local potent alcoholic drink); and they are often charged by the police for being 'idle and disorderly'. Many acts of rape, indulging in unprotected sex, fighting, accidents, and homicide, were reported in one district as a direct result of substance abuse (Kivumbi et al.,1998). Key informants, notably community leaders or policy-makers, attributed this mainly to what they consider to be 'idleness'. For their part, some of the adolescents, including street children said that when they are confronted with hard tasks like fishing and carrying heavy loads of coffee beans, they take strong stimulants to enable them to carry out the tasks, in other words to keep them busy, and not idle, as most adults tend to think. Such substances make them feel 'strong and courageous enough, even to do daring acts like fighting, stealing, or sexual assaults'. Despite being aware of the dangers e.g. committing crime, street children justified their use of strong drugs/substances, on the premise that the drugs made them feel good, strong, and able to defend themselves in the case of any danger. As one boy during a discussion with street children remarked:

Taking in glue and petrol is bad because you may look at one object as very many, but it gives us strength to defend ourselves. [Adolescent boy, Mbale]

Risky sexual behaviours also result from use of substances: whereas most cases of substance abuse are committed by adolescent boys, girls are more likely to end up indulging in acts like exchanging sex for payment from an early age. These behaviours are reportedly on the increase, particularly in the towns where there is an apparent lure and search for a 'better life', especially for those out of school. For most girls, their *aunties* (who are traditionally supposed to be protective and provide advice) may currently not be so protective; some of the *aunties* may actually be condoning or abetting such risky behaviours of the young girls:

> *Some girls who stay with aunties are exposed to high risk of being lured at any moment; for example, they indulge in commercial sex as a way of earning a living. Some are sent to sell beer, for example.* [School Head, Nebbi]

Poverty and related factors

Poverty at the household level was seen as a major contributing or underlying factor to most other problems both inside and outside the home as most people depend on subsistence farming, and other small-scale income-generating activities. Adolescents and their young adult counterparts were all concerned about the effects of poverty on the welfare of the family and the community at large. Adolescent girls in particular are disadvantaged in many respects due to poverty, and may fail to resist the urge to have unprotected sex in exchange for basic necessities of life:

> *Poverty is the leading cause of our problems because it makes us lack control over our lives, and we have to depend on other people for support; this may even force some girls into promiscuity in order to acquire the basic needs of life.* [Adolescent girls, (15–19) Rukungiri]

Unemployment is a serious problem among adolescents, and many are forced to do unsuitable work or labour with serious consequences to their health. Another problem mentioned was a lack of or shortage of land: in two of the districts where high population density is a problem, lack of land reportedly results in alienation of the adolescents, rendering them redundant and unable to participate in normal productive activities. As a result, many young adolescents are forced to migrate, often doing unsuitable work, especially in the towns.

Problems of poor education and illiteracy

Because of poverty, many adolescents and young people are reported to be out of school, some having dropped out because of their parents' failure to provide for their education; this has resulted in high levels of illiteracy among the adolescent population, especially girls. Lack of basic things or materials e.g. clothing, uniforms, sundries, and other scholastic materials may lead to leaving school; girls in particular drop out early, and end up marrying early. Poor health and lack of proper nutrition resulting in fatigue or lack of concentration are some of the problems mentioned affecting the education of adolescents, notably girls.

> *Basic education is a problem; that is, primary education is a problem among the youth of the district. The illiteracy rate is 53 per cent, which is high...* [Planner, Nebbi]

Socio-cultural and institutional change and quality of parenting

As a consequence of a breakdown in traditional institutions such as the system of clan leaders or elders, uncles and aunts, which used to play a role in preparing adolescents for responsible adulthood, many parents are not able to cope with the task of bringing up their adolescent children in a secure environment. Some adolescents in particular tend to get a raw deal from their parents in the home, as was observed here by a group of young adult student teachers:

> *Some parents don't care about the well-being of the adolescents, and as soon as they are of a certain age, they are left to fend for themselves. They are not given a second chance and are chased away.* [Trainee teachers (20–24 years), Nebbi]

In matters concerning sex or adolescent sexuality, parents acknowledge fearing to talk to their adolescent children, who more often than not are taken to be old enough to marry, even at the very tender age of 12:

> *Parents are not open to their children; they cannot or don't mention 'the real thing' to the children, yet they start having sex at the age of 12...actually, someone can love a boy or girl friend or even marry at that age.* [Policy Maker, Nebbi]

Many parents expect service providers like teachers to take on the role of discussing issues pertaining to adolescent growth and sexuality, and to give the adolescents answers. Teachers feel that parents have shifted their responsibility for providing information to adolescents to teachers:

> *The roles that used to be for parents are now left to teachers. Parents no longer talk to their children, leading to a lot of misbehaviour.* [Secondary School teachers, Kiboga]

Some parents on the other hand, blame the teachers for whatever is happening with the adolescents; it has become a question of shifting the responsibility:

> *These days teachers don't care about what happens to our children, yet they are with them (the teachers) most of the time.* [Parents, Kiboga]

Family breakdown

The changing family pattern and function, now typically depicted by family breakdowns, single headed households, and the frantic search for survival has made it very difficult for parents to support and monitor the growth and development of their adolescent children. For example, some respondents noted that the original role of the aunt, locally known as *Ssenga* in central Uganda and other areas, particularly in advising the adolescent girl, seems to be dying out. They no longer play a leading role; instead, that role is increasingly being assumed or replaced by adolescent peers or friends giving advice to fellow adolescents who themselves may not be well-informed, and are likely to give wrong information.

> *Girls used to talk to their aunts when they knew they were getting married and the boys to their uncles, but now mainly their friends or through peer information networks. Nowadays it is rare that girls interact with their aunts, who leave the problem to their mothers, who rarely talk to them. Very few parents talk to their children maybe because of fear or because they think they (adolescents) want to try out.* [District official, Nebbi]

Status of existing adolescent health services

Whilst findings indicate that there are generally no services specifically targeting adolescents in the five districts, a very small proportion of adolescents said they are able to utilize the existing health facilities and services for their health needs. Efforts by a number of government institutions and non-governmental organizations (NGOs) are evident in the districts. They include services run by the AIDS Information Centre (AIC); AIDS Communication Education and Training (ACET); and Uganda Women's Council (UWC) projects, all in one of the districts. Elsewhere, some services under the UNFPA-supported 'programme for enhancing adolescent reproductive life' (PEARL); and the World Vision, CARE, Youth Alive, and the Agency for Cooperation in Research and Development (ACORD) were in operation. The African Medical Research Foundation (AMREF), CARE-International, World Vision, The Red Cross, various church-based services, and FM radio stations, operate in two of the districts in western Uganda. Services available for adolescents include general curative and preventive services in health units, under the Directorates of District Health

Services (DDHS), as well as private, and NGO health facilities, which all operate under the district local administrations. Reproductive health services are generally provided in public health units, NGO or community-based facilities, and to a limited extent in some schools (contraceptive supplies, condoms, etc.).

Some IEC materials and supplies, though grossly inadequate, were available from the district health directorates, NGOs and Education Department. In the media, supplements for adolescents *'Straight Talk* and *'Young Talk'* from the Straight Talk Foundation, inserted in the leading daily, *The New Vision*, are distributed in schools, and local FM stations have some programmes discussing adolescent issues. NGOs like 'The AIDS Support Organisation' (TASO), 'AIDS Information Centre' (AIC), offered some counseling services in schools. In the schools, it is mainly senior women teachers (SWTs), or health/science teachers who advise the students on sexuality/reproductive health issues, especially menstruation, pregnancy problems, and HIV/AIDS. However, some adolescent girls expressed their misgivings about the benefits of senior women teachers who, according to them are adults (i.e. too old for them), who have fixed views about their (adolescent) sexuality, and therefore, were not the best to assist them:

> *Senior women teachers are mostly adults who have personal or religious views about sexuality that influence how they want to assist adolescents, they have difficulty seeing the situation from the point of view of the young person. So adolescents often hesitate to tell senior women/men teachers that they are sexually active and talk about contraception.* [Adolescent girls, (15–18) Kabale]

Adolescents getting by without specific services

Within their communities, adolescents said that they usually consult and get advice from other close people or providers, among them aunts, uncles, older siblings, elders, traditional healers, birth attendants, and friends about sexual/reproductive health related issues, especially in matters of sexual relationships and pregnancy. In the area of life-skills development, there are limited efforts by only a few NGOs, religious organizations/churches e.g. Youth Alive by the Catholic Church, schools, and UNICEF's basic education, child care and development (BECCAD) programme. Recreational services are barely available, mostly in the form of sports and games like football, netball in schools and other institutions. Debate, drama, music and dance are common activities in some schools, usually as extracurricular activities; in the communities they are also a major source of social entertainment. These are potentially useful, and often also used as a medium for communicating appropriate health education messages.

Rules and regulations are mostly institutional, such as school rules for good discipline or religious instructions for good moral behaviour. The home is no longer the sort of safety net that the adolescent boy or girl can fall back on. Many of the existing laws or statutes are either not well known or not enforced. Virtually no local by-laws have been initiated to regulate, prevent or control some of the serious offences that violate the sexual and reproductive rights of adolescents. The police and other agents who are supposed to deal with instances of substance abuse seem to be ineffective mainly due to lack of resources. There is need for appropriate protective laws on rights of adolescents and young people to be in place that should be widely disseminated and implemented.

According to the adolescents, factors that would encourage them to use existing services include *accessibility* (in terms of affordable cost, proximity, and having friendly providers); *trust* of service providers by the adolescents, and of adolescents by providers; *prompt attention; assured confidentiality;* and *good interpersonal interaction skills* of providers with clients. For instance, they said that kindness, receptiveness and showing an interest are among the qualities of a good provider who will make the services more accessible to them.

Existing gaps

Gaps or unmet needs in adolescent services are mainly due to the following: the absence of specific services for adolescents; service delivery problems; and absence of or inadequacy of a functioning referral system. Others include limited geographical coverage; insufficient IEC materials for reproductive health, family planning and contraceptive services; and, where available, they are not appropriately tailored for use by adolescents, or are not available in the local language.

As a consequence of a lack of trained personnel, guidance and counseling services for adolescents are not provided. There are no effective services for substance abuse prevention and control, and inadequate enforcement of laws dealing with cases of sexual abuse such as rape and defilement. Other gaps include poor education services, such as poor structures/classrooms, and teaching materials/facilities; high illiteracy; a lack of life-skills development activities; and the absence of, or inadequate, recreation facilities. Other factors that hinder utilization include socio-cultural and religious sanctions such as prohibiting the use of artificial contraceptive methods for birth control/child spacing or using condoms to prevent pregnancies, STIs and HIV/AIDS. A better understanding of the problems and gaps (see Table 1), should lead to setting up of facilities for offering friendly reproductive health services for the adolescents – such as the so-called teenage centres – which have now come to fill some of the gaps left by the conventional services, especially in public health facilities.

Discussion and conclusion

The needs assessment exercise has brought out a number of salient features about the situation of adolescent sexual and reproductive health services. Nevertheless, it was limited both in scope and coverage, and a number of limitations were inherent in the methodology. In particular, lack of information on the sexual and reproductive health needs of adolescents/young people from other countries in the region for comparison, was a major limitation.

The general situation of adolescents in Uganda (one of the countries hardest hit by the HIV/AIDS scourge) demonstrates that a large proportion of adolescents (especially girls) live at high risk. They are particularly vulnerable to unprotected sex and early pregnancies, often with serious consequences, including unsafe abortions, early marriages, prostitution, as well as other unhealthy risk behaviours such as alcoholism, smoking hard drugs, and increased exposure to injuries, violent behaviour, often resulting in death. They are also vulnerable to violent sexual assaults or abuses like rape and defilement, many of which are carried out by those known to them, such as close family members, or friends. Others include fellow adolescents, service providers like security personnel, teachers, health workers, and other persons in the community, including much older adults.

The study also shows that there is now a widening communication gap between adolescents and their parents, giving rise to an increasingly non-supportive economic and socio-cultural environment. There are also serious constraints in gaining access to services due to persisting negative socio-cultural and economic factors, as well as limited resources. Instances of parental neglect, negative socio-cultural norms and values towards adolescents like early and forced marriages, giving little or no education for girls causing high illiteracy, hostility or hard feeling towards them all constitute major bottlenecks. The high levels of poverty in most parts of the country, especially in the rural areas have had dire consequences on their health and welfare, and in meeting some of their most basic needs, including good nutrition and housing. Many adolescents drop out of school and become very vulnerable due to increased unemployment, and lack of opportunities for them to earn an income to support themselves.

The need for AFHS in Uganda has thus become urgent, particularly in view of the fact that adolescents are living at high risk of STIs/HIV/AIDS, early/unwanted pregnancies, unsafe abortions, and substance abuse, since they are neglected under the existing health service delivery system. However, the general mapping of the existing services in the study districts has provided an array of potential opportunities, including services at health units, schools, other social service sectors like probation and welfare services, community development, education, disability and special needs education, police and legal departments, as well as adolescent-focused community-based development activities carried out by a few non-governmental organizations, development agencies and religious or church-related programmes. Most services at the moment tend only to be concentrated in a few, mainly urban or town centres, without adequate coverage of the rural areas, which means that they do not reach the majority of the adolescent population. In addition, services are not affordable to the majority of adolescents, and they are not particularly 'welcoming' (friendly), or attractive to the adolescents, especially within the public health units.

The way forward suggests a serious need for listening to adolescents' views and concerns, and for involving them from the inception of planning any services designed for them. They should participate at every stage including the planning, implementation, monitoring, assessment and evaluation of the services. This will enable them to discover the right enabling environment, to meet their sexual and reproductive health and development needs. The services in question should enable adolescents to seek services and information freely without restriction, and encourage positive health-seeking behaviour on their part, as well as positive attitudes of the service providers. The starting point should be the adolescents' own, coupled with other stakeholders' recommendations highlighted during the discussions, which may include the following possibilities:

– setting up of one-stop centres for adolescents, within communities with appropriate structures, activities, and avenues for providing information (IEC), contraceptives, voluntary testing and counseling (VCT), screening services for HIV/AIDS, and treatment of STDs;

– integrating services at existing established service points to improve quality of care through specific skills training;

– employment of adolescent peer educators and young persons as counsellors;

– training and re-orienting of various cadres of health service providers, especially in areas like guidance skills, counseling, vocational skills, and life-skills development, to pass on to adolescents;

– setting up a multi-disciplinary and multi-sectoral team or coalition of parents, opinion leaders and service providers, which could include teachers, health workers, the police, and social workers; youth-friendly organizations, the mass media, local FM radio stations, and professional associations;

– enacting supportive and protective laws, local by-laws, social and welfare policies, and mechanisms for enforcing them to improve the quality of adolescent reproductive health; and;

– allocating the necessary funds and budgeting for programmes that will support adolescents' education and health.

Table 1. Summary of major gaps and constraints to adolescent friendly services

1. Health Care Delivery System
 – Inadequate drugs and supplies at health units
 – Lack of training and skills for staff to provide adolescent reproductive services
 – Unavailability of family planning/contraceptive services
 – Lack of specific information/reproductive health messages and IEC materials
 – Negative/hostile attitudes of health staff
 – Limited coverage: services mainly found in urban and main centers
 – Poor working conditions for existing health staff
 – Lack of skills e.g. in counseling and guidance
 – Lack of referral services

2. School/Education System
 – High illiteracy
 – Early dropping out of school, especially girls
 – Poor/lack of proper structures e.g. classrooms
 – Lack of school health education services and learning materials
 – Inadequate skills of teachers to handle adolescent growth and development problems
 – No suitable curriculum on sex education
 – Lack of extra-curricular activities e.g. for recreation and life-skills development
 – Lack of vocational education/skills for adolescents

3. Policy and Legislative Systems
 – Lack of technical/policy guidelines for use of health personnel
 – Inadequate/weak existing laws and absence of bye-laws
 – Non-enforcement of existing regulations/laws for offences e.g. rape and defilement for control of substance abuse
 – Lack of knowledge of relevant laws by appropriate organs/institutions

4. Home and Community Systems
 – Lack of knowledge about adolescent growth, sexual and reproductive health needs
 – Lack of cooperation and support between parents and service providers
 – Inadequate communication between parents and their adolescents; poor parenting skills
 – Weakening of traditional institutions and norms to guide adolescents
 – Lack of local planning/management capacities, especially at sub-county levels

5. Planning and Management Systems in Districts and Sub-Counties
 – Lack of planning, management, and monitoring capacities in districts and sub-counties
 – Shortage of trained staff in existing planning units
 – Inadequate funding and budgeting for AFHS

11. Quality of Care

Assessing Nurses' and Midwives' Attitudes towards Adolescents with Sexual and Reproductive Health Problems

Elisabeth Faxelid, Joyce Musandu, Irene Mushinge
Eva Nissen and Mathilda Zvinavashe

Abstract

This chapter gives a short overview of research in relation to quality of sexual and reproductive health (SRH) care for young people in sub-Saharan Africa. A pilot study has been conducted among 87 nurses and midwives (enrolled and registered) to develop an instrument, which included 69 statements to test nurses'/midwives' attitudes towards young people with sexual and reproductive health problems in Zambia, Zimbabwe and Kenya. Four scales were extracted from the instrument to elucidate positive and negative attitudes towards girls and boys respectively but the sample is small and the sampling method does not allow for any generalization. The results show, however, that it is necessary to reduce the number of statements and improve the precision of the instrument. When the attitudinal instrument described is well tested, it can be useful as a quick and simple tool to measure attitudes over time e.g. before and after training of communication skills. It could also be used during training in nursing and midwifery programmes as a starting point for discussions.

Introduction

Adolescence is defined as the period between 10 and 19 years of age (WHO, 1993). In sub-Saharan Africa, this age group constitutes at least 20–25% of the population (WHO 1993). Sexual and reproductive health problems are extremely prevalent among adolescents (Ahlberg et al., 1997; Webb, 1997; Blum & Nelson-Mmari, 2004). The International Conference on Population and Development held in Cairo in 1994 marked a major conceptual shift among population experts, from an emphasis on population control to reproductive health and the special needs and rights of adolescents (UN, 1995). Efforts to deal with adolescents' needs have also been prioritized within the health reforms in most sub-Saharan countries. One strategy to improve the health of young people is health promotion, and sex education/family life education (although controversial) is slowly being introduced in schools in several countries. However, many young people, girls in particular, are not in educational institutions. Furthermore, the consequences of the HIV/AIDS epidemic in sub-Saharan Africa have led to a growing number of orphans (UNAIDS, 2004) who are often outside the educational system, lack parental support and care (Baggaley & Needham, 1997; Drew et al., 1998; UNICEF, 2003). These children are in particular need of information and support in relation to SRH. The General Assembly adopted a political declaration on HIV/AIDS in 2006. In this declaration the member states commit themselves to address the rising rates of HIV infection in young people by implementing, among other things, youth specific HIV/AIDS education and provision of youth friendly services (UNGASS, 2006).

Sexual and reproductive health among adolescents

Studies indicate that sexual debut in East and Southern Africa is at 16–17 years of age in both sexes (Okumu & Chege, 1994; Mbizvo et al., 1995; Klepp et al., 1996; Zambia DHS, 2002; Kenya DHS, 2003). Furthermore, a study from Zambia showed that sex in exchange for money or gifts is common, while studies from southern and eastern Africa show that many young girls had experienced force during sexual encounters (Population Council, 1999; Kaiser Family Foundation/KLA 2000). This obviously exposes the young sexually active population, particularly girls, to early unwanted pregnancies, as well as sexually transmitted infections (STIs) including HIV (Matasha et al., 1998). Nyanza Province in Kenya has the highest rate of HIV infection in Kenya, 14 per cent among men and women aged 15–49 years. The HIV prevalence in adolescents aged 15–19 is about 2 per cent (Kenya DHS, 2003). In Zambia, it is estimated that the prevalence of HIV in the urban female population is around 10 per cent in the age range 15–19 years compared to 5 per cent among the boys (Zambia National AIDS Council, 2004).

Governmental policy, in both Kenya and Zambia is to provide all sexually active men and women with contraceptive services (NCPD 2003, WHO 1995) but in reality, adolescents have limited access to such services (Ahlberg et al., 2001; Mmari and Magnani, 2003). This leaves adolescents with periodic abstinence as their only protective option and adolescent pregnancy is a growing concern (Ahlberg et al., 2001). Girls are suspended from school, and there are high rates of illegal, often self-induced abortions (IPAS 2000). The desire to continue education was found to be the main reason why Zambian unmarried girls resorted to induced abortion. Although abortion is legal in Zambia, adolescents undergo illegal abortions because legal abortion services are inaccessible and unacceptable (Koster-Oyekan 1998). Findings from Western Province in Zambia revealed that one in 100 schoolgirls dies from abortion related complications. Hospital-based studies in Nairobi, Kenya have shown unsafe abortion accounts for about 35 per cent of maternal deaths (Rogo, 1993). In Zambia and Kenya, over 25 per cent of all teenage girls have started childbearing by the time they are 18 years (Kenya DHS 2003; Zambia DHS, 2002) .

SRH problems are thus extremely prevalent among young people. However, studies show that communicating about SRH is difficult both among young people and between adults and young people (Ahlberg & et al., 1997; Mngadi et al. 2003). Furthermore, many societies have different understandings and expectations of young women's and young men's sexuality and sexual conduct. Girls are told to abstain from sex before marriage while boys are left with almost total silence and no support at all from the adult community. At the same time, young people receive multiple and contradictory messages from churches, schools, peers, elders, and the media (Dowsett & Aggleton, 1999). Cultural norms and practices that traditionally controlled adolescent sexual behaviour in many communities have weakened (Caldwell & Caldwell, 1988; Ilinigumugabo, 1995). The traditional initiation rites that were supposed to inform and introduce young boys and girls into marriage and proper adulthood no longer play a main role. However, results from Zambia indicate that traditional values and stereotypical gender roles continue to influence Zambian boys' identity (Dahlbäck et al., 2006) The adult generation, which grew up with traditional rules, is not well prepared to counsel the younger generation on issues in relation to sexuality in a changing society. The failure of parents and other close adults to discuss sexual matters with their adolescents has forced adolescents to make sense of conflicting messages and information they receive from both print and electronic media. In the absence of guidance and counselling from parents, adolescents seek sex education from peers whose limited knowledge might misdirect and offer conflicting information to fellow adolescents (Akonga, 1988, Warenius et al., Accept 2006).

Many children who have lost their parents end up living on the streets. This is a particularly vulnerable group. They have a high risk of being sexually abused, and studies among street children in Dar es Salaam, Tanzania show that girls in particular, engage in highly risky sexual behaviour (Rajani & Kudrati, 1996). Eighty percent of the girls said that they had had an STD at least once, and many of them sold sex to earn their living. Although some children who spend their days on the streets return to their homes and families in the evening, many street children have no adults to guide them in issues related to sexuality. This is a problem that is increasing rapidly as the HIV/AIDS epidemic continues.

Health care providers' attitudes and youth friendly services

Public health services tend to be underutilised by young people due to factors such as shyness, lack of awareness, judgmental attitudes by staff, lack of privacy and high costs (Kim et al., 1997; Webb, 2000; Amuyunzu-Nyamongo et al., 2005). Studies in Zambia report that politeness, privacy, and confidentiality were reasons why young people turned to traditional healers for reproductive health problems (Ndubani, 1998; Muturi 2005; Dahlbäck et al., Accept 2007).

It is not uncommon that service providers have negative attitudes toward providing SRH services to youth. Furthermore, there are indications that clinicians miss important opportunities to promote the health of their adolescent patients (Masatu, 2001). Many providers also restrict access to family planning methods by age even though age restrictions are not part of the national guidelines. Studies conducted in Southern Africa show that patients are dissatisfied due to a number of different reasons such as poor availability of medicines and other supplies, lack of privacy, poor interpersonal communication and negative staff attitudes (Lule et al., 2000; Bediako et al., 2006; Phillips, 1996; Ndulo et al., 1995; Faxelid et al., 1997a). Communication is a major component of the patient-provider interaction, and effective communication is particularly important when dealing with sensitive issues such as sexuality (WHO, 1993). Lack of communication skills and negative attitudes among health care providers should be regarded as a serious problem since, in addition to being unethical, it may have a negative influence on access to health care particularly for young people (Abdool et al., 1992; Gilson et al., 1994; Wood & Jewkes, 1997). However, the problem of poor patient-provider relationships is complex and may also be related to organisational and administrational factors, for instance (Faxelid et al., 1997b; Jewkes et al., 1998).

In East and Southern Africa, nurses/midwives constitute the core of health care providers in SRH services. WHO and UNICEF have pronounced the need for stronger national and international support to midwifery in order to promote women's health (WHO 1987, 1992, 2004b). However, nurse-patient relationships have largely been neglected as a research topic. A study from Zimbabwe indicates that women see nurses as hard and indifferent, but nurses do not seem to recognise their own behaviour as a source of patient dissatisfaction (Bassett et al., 1997). In a study from South Africa, nurses were said to verbally abuse patients at obstetric services (Jewkes et al., 1998), and in a study from Uganda nurses showed more negative attitudes towards people with AIDS than did the physicians (Mungherera et al., 1997).

In several African countries such as Kenya, Tanzania, Uganda and Zambia, youth clinics/centres and youth friendly services funded by NGOs and other donors have been established (see Arube-Wani et al. 2008). The majority of these projects have been initiated in urban areas. An evaluation of multi-purpose youth centres in Ghana, Kenya and Zimbabwe found that these centres were only marginally effective in reaching girls and younger adolescents with SRH information and services (Population Council, 1999). Furthermore, adolescents stigmatized youth centres because they were considered places for those who are sexually active or for those with sexually transmitted infections. Youth centres have also been found to be an expensive strategy to reach young people. Considering the large number of adolescents in these countries and the cost involved in creating specific services for adolescents, it seems important to explore how already existing services can be organised in such a way that they are utilised and valued by the adolescents (WHO, 1998a). Study results show, however, that community acceptance of reproductive health services for youth may have a larger impact on adolescents' utilization of the services than youth friendliness as such (Mmari and Magnani, 2003).

It is thus of great importance to understand how adolescents perceive their needs in relation to SRH information and service, where and how they want this service to be provided, and how they perceive the current SRH service. This has partly been studied in Zambia (Warenius et al., Accept 2006). However, adolescents constitute a heterogeneous group and important differences which need to be considered include factors such as sex, age, school and work status. It is also important to increase our understanding of health care providers' attitudes and how they interact with young people seeking care. In order to develop a comprehensive study about nurses'/midwives' role in improving the quality of adolescent sexual and reproductive health care, a pilot study was conducted in Kenya, Zambia and Zimbabwe. The main purpose of the pilot study described in this chapter was to construct an instrument to test nurses'/midwives' attitudes and to pilot test the instrument in the three countries.

Methods

In the initial phase of this study, interviews concerning regulations and policies in relation to adolescents' SRH were held with key informants, such as chief nursing officers at hospital level. In each country, a matron who was the supervisor for the nurses and midwives at hospital level was interviewed. Topics covered hospital policies related to adolescents' SRH, if there was any training of staff in relation to adolescents' SRH, and if there were any specific services available for adolescents at the hospital. At urban and rural health centres the nurse/midwife in charge was interviewed about available services for adolescents and how the staff interacted with adolescents. Finally, a number of traditional birth attendants were interviewed about their interaction with adolescents. Appointments were made with each one of these persons a few days before the interview. Then an informal conversation took place.

Based on these interviews an instrument was constructed to identify positive as well as judgmental attitudes within the professional groups of nurses and midwives. An attitude is defined as a tendency to react favourably or unfavourably to a designated class of stimuli, such as a national or ethnic group (Anastasi & Urbina, 1997). Attitudes cannot be directly observed and must be inferred from overt behaviour. The concept of attitude may be said to connote response consistency with regard to certain categories of stimuli (Anastasi & Urbina, 1997). The instrument was based on the previous knowledge and understanding of attitudes prevailing in the countries under study in the research group, which consisted of midwives from Kenya, Zambia, Zimbabwe and Sweden.

Altogether the instrument included 69 statements covering a number of issues such as youth friendly or youth negative attitudes towards boys and girls with SRH problems, attitudes towards in and out of school adolescents, attitudes in regard to social status of the adolescent, and attitudes towards traditional practices. The instrument was designed with a modified Likert scale format with a four-point response format ranging from "disagree completely", "disagree", "agree", to "agree completely" in order to avoid the informants taking a "neither nor" position. A purposive sample of 92 enrolled nurses, enrolled midwives, registered nurses, and registered midwives was selected. The sample was selected to represent different working areas such as hospitals, health centres, and school clinics in rural and urban areas. Three nurses and two midwives did not respond to the attitude instrument, only to the background questionnaire, and were thus excluded from all analysis. In total, results from 87 nurses and midwives with experience from urban and rural areas were thus included in the analysis.

Data were then analyzed to determine discrimination among the responses to the statements by contingency tables. Thirty items regarding positive and negative attitudes towards girls and boys were put together in four scales. Internal consistency for these four preliminary scales was tested by Cronbach's alpha. Pearson regression coefficient was used to correlate attitude scales for boys and girls. To test differences in attitudes towards girls and boys, paired T-tests were used.

Results

Key informant interviews

The key informants interviewed in the three countries were not aware of any national policy on adolescent sexual and reproductive health. The current policy in Kenya deals with family planning issues only, stating that only those who have given birth or had an abortion should be allowed to use contraceptives. Both Kenya and Zambia have new national policies, but youth friendly activities still rely mostly on non-governmental organisations. The traditional birth attendants interviewed saw adolescents to a limited extent. Their contact with adolescents was mainly restricted to childbirth and occasionally they assisted in conducting abortions.

Nurses and midwives responding to the attitudinal questionnaire

The mean age of the 87 nurses and midwives who answered the attitude instrument ranged from 34 to 41 years for the three countries. All participants belonged to a Christian community. Fifty-four participants did not report what ethnic group they belonged to. In general, the participants considered their socio-economic status to be low, but a higher proportion of the enrolled nurses and enrolled midwives compared to the registered nurses and midwives considered their socio-economic status to be very low (p=0.02). Additional background information is presented in Table 1.

In Kenya, Zambia and Zimbabwe continuing education for nurses/midwives in relation to adolescents' reproductive health was considered to be largely lacking. Of the 87 nurses and midwives, 8 per cent enrolled nurses, 3 per cent enrolled midwives, 27 per cent registered nurses, and 24 per cent registered midwives reported at least one occasion they attended continuing education.

The registered nurses and the registered midwives considered their health facility to be well equipped, while the enrolled nurses and the enrolled midwives found their working place to be poorly equipped. In all three countries, a majority of participants in the four professional groups said that they attended to adolescents.

Attitudinal scale

Statements that could be categorised as youth friendly (9 statements referring to girls and 8 to boys) or youth negative (7 statements referring to girls and 6 to boys) were summarized into four separate scales, indicating positive and negative attitudes toward girls and boys respectively. Examples of statements included are given in Table 2 along with the internal consistency (Cronbach alpha values) for each scale.

The youth negative attitudes towards girls and towards boys correlated with each other (r=0.63; p=0.0001), as did youth friendly attitudes towards girls and boys (r=0.69; p=0. 0001). When comparing the scales by paired T-test, it was found that the professionals held stronger youth friendly attitudes towards girls than towards boys (p=0.036), but also more negative attitudes towards girls than towards boys (p=0.011).

Nurses and midwives in Zambia had more negative attitudes towards both boys and girls than did the nurses and midwives in Kenya (Table 3). When separate statements were compared country-wise, answers to a few statements differed. However, the sample sizes are too small to draw any conclusions.

Registered midwives tended to have a more open attitude to adolescents and found it easier to talk to adolescents, both boys and girls, compared to the other professional groups (p=0.007). A higher proportion of both enrolled and registered midwives, compared to the nurses, agreed with the statement "It is not necessary for a boy to be circumcised" (p=0.005). A majority of all categories of professionals, except for registered midwives, agreed with the statement "The adolescent boy should be taught the danger of masturbation" (p=0.031).

An attempt was made to construct a scale for checking attitudes in relation to in and out of school adolescents' behaviour. However, the statements were not put in a comparative way or the correspondence between the statements regarding boys and girls was not as feasible as for the others scales. Four statements assessing attitudes towards the social status of the adolescents were combined in a scale in order to investigate whether there were any differences by country or by profession. A tendency toward different judgements was found between Zambia and Kenya, indicating more judgmental attitudes in Zambia. However, these scales need to be further developed.

Finally, twelve statements were to be left out or rephrased on the basis of the informants' lack of understanding of these statements, or because the statements were perceived as being offensive or unclear. There were no differences between the countries in this regard.

Discussion

This pilot study demonstrates that the proposed instrument seems to be useful in order to assess nurses' and midwives' attitudes towards adolescents. Furthermore, the instrument is gender sensitive, and sensitive to the differences among health professionals. Registered midwives in our sample seemed to have a somewhat more open attitude toward adolescents, which might be a result of their more frequent exposure to adolescent SRH problems compared to the other groups. However, the sample is small, and the sampling method does not allow for any generalization.

The internal consistency was good for three of the scales whereas the fourth "youth negative attitude scale towards boys" had a lower internal consistency and needs to be improved. The instrument was shown to discriminate between positive and negative attitudes towards boys and girls.

Many respondents had a rather negative attitude towards both girls' and boys' sexuality. Interestingly, results on some statements showed that respondents had a more strict attitude towards girls' sexuality than towards boys' sexuality yet results on other statements showed that respondents had a friendlier attitude towards girls than towards boys. It is possible that this finding reflects a greater concern for girls than for boys. This is in line with other studies in Zambia (Dahlbäck et al., 2006; UNICEF 2004). Few differences between the countries were seen, which indicates that the same instrument can be used in all the three countries. Some differences between the professional groups were noted.

It is necessary to reduce the number of statements in order to decrease the number of internal and external dropouts, and to make the instrument easy to use. We also need to improve the precision of the instrument. The statements should be categorised in more categories than negative and positive. Furthermore, the precision can be further improved by employing a confirmatory factor analysis on a larger sample. In this way, more scales could be developed from the most relevant and precise statements and statements that do not contribute to the analysis of attitudes can be omitted.

The way forward

We believe it is extremely important to carry out a comprehensive study of health providers' attitudes since good interaction between the patients and their providers is fundamental in order for the providers to be able to establish rapport, transmit information, and influence patients' behaviour (Ngomuo et al., 1995; Joos & Hickam, 1990). When the attitudinal instrument described is well tested, it can be useful as a quick and simple tool to measure attitudes over time, for instance before and after the training of communication skills. It can also be used during training in nursing and midwifery programmes as a starting point for discussions. Thus, harmful attitudes could be targeted both during basic training and during continuing education. However, a more qualitative approach would be of great value to gain a deeper understanding of prevailing attitudes and the perceptions that lie behind them. Furthermore, there is need to study the quality of adolescent SRH care in general in order to identify strategies by which young people's health care can be improved. Such an intervention study should then build on applicable theories and include a long-term follow up of its impact.

Table 1. Background data. Number of participants from different professions and their experience of working in rural and urban areas

Profession	Zambia n=32	Kenya n=32	Zimbabwe n=23	Total sample n=87
Enrolled nurses	6	5	2	13
Enrolled midwives	8	4	0	12
Registered nurses	6	17	2	25
Registered midwives	12	6	19	37
Nurses' experience of work in:				
urban areas (years)	11±6.5	10,7±6.7	14±6.8	11.7±6.7
rural areas (years)	6±7.4	7.4±7.6	5,1±5	6.3±6.2
Midwives' experience of work in:				
urban areas (years)	8.3±4.2	9.7±7.2	9.9±7.8	9.4±6.6
rural areas (years)	5.1±3.8	5.6±6.2	4.8±4.8	5.2±5.2

Note: Mean years ± SD are reported country wise and for the total sample.

Table 2. Examples of positive and negative statements in relation to girls and boys

Examples of positive statements towards girls from the Youth friendly scale. (0.81)

– A girl who becomes pregnant should be allowed to continue school.
– Adolescent girls who are sexually abused should not be blamed.

Examples of positive statements towards boys from the Youth friendly scale. (0.85)

– Masturbation is a good way to prevent STD and HIV.
– Boys who want to know how to use a condom should be offered counselling in privacy.

Examples of negative attitudes towards girls from the Youth negative attitude scale. (0.78)

– Girls who get raped usually have themselves to blame.
– A 14-year-old out of school girl with a genital ulcer is likely to be promiscuous.

Examples of negative attitudes towards boys from the Youth negative attitude scale. (0.64)

– A school-boy who impregnates a girl should be expelled from school.
– A secondary school boy who has got a genital ulcer is likely to be irresponsible.

Note: Cronbach's alpha for each scale within brackets.

Table 3. Total scores by country of the four different scales[1]

Scale	Zambia n=32	Kenya n=32	Zimbabwe n=23	Total sample n=88
Youth friendly towards girls	2.8±0.4	2.8±0.7	2.9±0.6	2.8±0.5
Youth friendly towards boys	2.8±0.4	2.5±0.6	2.8±0.6	2.7±0.6
Negative towards girls	2.5±0.4[2]	2.1± 0.7	2.3±0.6	2.3±0.6
Negative towards boys	2.3±0.3[3]	2.0±0.5	2.1±0.7	2.2±0.5

[1]Maximum score is 4.The higher the scores on the youth friendly scale the more youth friendly is the attitude; the higher the score on the negative scales, the more negative is the attitude. Each scale has been divided by the number of items included in the scale to make the scales comparable.

[2]Comparisons between Zambia and Kenya showed significantly more negative attitudes towards girls in Zambia than in Kenya, $p < 0.05$.

[3] Comparisons between Zambia and Kenya showed significantly more negative attitudes towards boys than in Kenya, $p < 0.05$.

IV

Evaluation and Review of Interventions in Sub-Saharan Africa

12. Evaluating Adolescent Sexual and Reproductive Health Interventions in Southern and Eastern Africa

Alan J. Flisher, Wanjiru Mukoma and Johann Louw

Abstract

This chapter provides an overview of evaluations of sexual and reproductive health interventions targeting adolescents done in Southern and Eastern Africa since the mid-1980's. The studies are presented in terms of the major settings in which the interventions were delivered: schools, health facilities, youth centres, and media campaigns. From the review, a number of key impressions emerged: a relatively low number of evaluations, done mostly in South Africa; the importance of involving programme managers and staff in the evaluations to encourage the utilisation of findings; the usefulness of making explicit the theoretical assumptions of the programme; an absence of information about the resources required by the various programmes; the importance of an evaluation of process and output for purposes of accountability; and a relative lack of outcome research to indicate effectiveness.

Introduction

Programme evaluation is an applied field of study, with its roots in many disciplines. It distinguishes itself from these disciplines by the fact that its 'objects of study' are social programmes that are intended to bring about changes in a social problem. When a problem is identified, such as a rapid increase in the incidence of HIV infection among adolescents in a country, programmes can be mounted to address the problem. Such programmes are organised and systematic efforts are made to bring about social change.

As a result of having disparate types of programmes as its objects of study, programme evaluation is a diverse discipline, with many kinds of evaluations that are useful for different purposes. In a report which dealt with AIDS programmes and research, Turner et al. (1989, p. 317–318) gave a useful definition of evaluation through a series of questions:

> Evaluation is a systematic process that produces a trustworthy account of what was attempted and why; through the examination of results – the outcomes of intervention programmes – it answers the questions, 'What was done?' 'To whom, and how?' and 'What outcomes were observed?'" Well-designed evaluation permits us to draw inferences from the data and addresses the question: "What do the outcomes mean?"

Thus we need to know what services the programme delivered, as an examination of the programme itself. In evaluation terms, this is called a *process* evaluation. Normally one would examine the *inputs* of the programme (which refer to what resources are dedicated to the programme) and *outputs* in this regard (which are about the delivery and implementation of activities). These terms will receive further attention below (see Figure 1). But as the definition indicates, we also want to know about the programme's effectiveness: whether outcomes were observed, and whether these were attributable to the programme's efforts. This will be an *outcome* evaluation, which establishes whether the programme produced the intended social benefits.

Stated in the most general of terms, we can say that the most important reason for doing an evaluation of a programme is to improve the programme and its service delivery. A carefully conducted evaluation has the capacity to benefit the programme (it receives feedback on managing its activities, and on demonstrating its effectiveness), the target population (they receive the intended services efficiently), and the policy frameworks in the field (we build upon the lessons learnt from many evaluations). Of course, evaluation results provide only one of several sources for these decisions, and final decisions are always taken in a political context.

In this chapter, our aims are two-fold: first, to provide an impression of evaluations that have been done in Southern and Eastern Africa (SEA) in each major site of intervention (for example, the school, health facility, and media); and second, to address selected key issues that emerge from these evaluations.

Review of evaluated programmes

This review is confined to sexual and reproductive health programmes or interventions that have been exposed to an evaluation process (Table 1). Furthermore, for inclusion in the review the programme should focus explicitly on adolescents; programmes that include a wide age range, even if they include adolescents, have been excluded. While we have made every effort to unearth as many programmes as possible, we do not claim that the review is exhaustive. We have arranged the programmes according to the setting in which they are based.

Schools

In chapter 13 in this volume addressing the school as a setting for intervention programmes, Mukoma and Flisher provide a systematic review of evaluations of South African school-based AIDS prevention programmes. They located ten reports, in which eight specific programmes were evaluated. One report involved the respondents' impressions of and reactions to various programmes (Seydel, 1992), while two papers reported complementary aspects of the same programme (Mathews et al., 1995, 1996). Besides those in South Africa, we could locate only one additional evaluated programme in both Tanzania and Zimbabwe.

The Tanzanian intervention was conducted among primary school children in the Arusha and Kilimanjaro regions of Tanzania (Klepp et al., 1994, 1997, 1999). It was informed by the Theory of Reasoned Action (Fishbein and Middlestadt, 1989) and social learning theory (Bandura, 1989), and was developed by local health educators in collaboration with the investigators. It was evaluated by means of a randomised controlled community trial, in which schools were randomised to receive the intervention (n = 6) or control (n = 12) conditions. The investigators found that the programme produced positive effects both immediately after the programme (Klepp et al., 1994) and at follow-up 12 months after its completion (Klepp et al., 1997).

The Zimbabwean intervention was conducted among secondary school students in Mashonaland Central (Mbizvo et al., 1997; Rusakaniko et al., 1997). The intervention package consisted of lectures, videos and IEC materials in the form of leaflets and pamphlets. The intervention was offered at 11 schools, while three were selected as controls. Thus, it would appear that the schools were not randomly allocated to the intervention or control conditions. The main outcome of interest was knowledge, which was found to be improved both immediately after the intervention and five months later.

As we mentioned in the introduction to this chapter, one objective of programme evaluation is programme improvement. This objective is a priority in formative evaluations such as those by Bailie (1991) and Mathews et al. (1995). However, in the Tanzanian study, a revised intervention was developed taking into account the results of the evaluation. The teachers and local health workers who implemented the programme were intimately involved in this process. The revised intervention was then offered in the comparison schools, and subsequently pilot tested for use in secondary schools throughout Tanzania (Klepp et al., 1994, 1997, 1999).

Health facilities

The majority of the evaluation studies involving sexual and reproductive health services to adolescents have focussed on the perceptions and experiences of adolescents who receive the services. As outcomes, these are rather 'soft' indicators of the effectiveness of the programmes; in fact, they can be considered generally as process evaluations. Data were gathered by exit interviews or community surveys. Typical findings are that the health services are relatively inaccessible to many young people, especially the poor and those living in rural areas (Health Systems Development Unit, 1998); the services are characterised by a lack of confidentiality and privacy (Abdool Karim et al., 1992; Health Systems Development Unit, 1998); the health service personnel are rude, short-tempered, arrogant, and intrusive (Wood et al., 1997); and that there are many missed opportunities for intervention regarding sexual and reproductive health when young people attend health facilities for other reasons (Flisher et al., 1991, 1992).

All these studies evaluated health services that were provided by the South African public sector health services; all were conducted by researchers from outside these services; all relied on the health services having no knowledge that the evaluations were being carried out; and all were based on retrospective reports of service recipients or potential service recipients.

We were not able to locate any studies involving health facilities in SEA countries besides South Africa.

Youth centres

Youth centres generally offer sexual and reproductive health services integrated with other activities such as recreation, vocational activities and library facilities. The intention is to achieve a greater amount of "adolescent friendliness" than is possible with health facilities and to increase access through removal of many of the barriers that exist with health facilities. They generally target youth aged 10–24 years.

Two "sets" of evaluated youth centres were located. First, the Population Council has evaluated two youth centres under the auspices of the Family Planning Association of Kenya (Erulkar and Mensch, 1997) and three under the auspices of the Zimbabwe National Family Planning Council (Phiri and Erulkar, 1997). These centres had been in operation since the 1980s, but no evaluations had been conducted. The main findings of the evaluations are that youth centres are often stigmatised by the community and youth themselves; youth centres tend to be dominated by boys; young people visiting youth centres tend to be older youth or even adults; a low proportion come for reproductive health or family planning services; staff are highly knowledgeable but often judgmental; and confidentiality and judgementalism on the part of the provider are the main concerns of youth who receive counselling.

Second, staff and students of the University of Cape Town have evaluated training programmes for peer educators and lifeskills workshops that are based at the New Crossroads Youth Centre (Brener, 1996, 1997; Villa-Vicencio, 1998). These evaluations focus on one aspect of the activities of the youth centre, unlike the evaluations by the Population Council, which provided a more global evaluation of the youth centres in Kenya and Zimbabwe. In general, the youth enjoyed the interventions and felt that they profited from them. A number of specific problems were identified, such as high attrition rates, organisational problems and lack of mutual support.

These "sets" of evaluations can be regarded as process evaluations, and were characterised by methodological diversity, with the use of focus groups, exit interviews with youth, individual interviews and questionnaires. In both cases the core of the evaluations relied on qualitative methods. The evaluations conducted by the Population Council also carried out detailed inventories of the assets of the centres, in order to provide estimates of input.

Media

Media are powerful tools for transmitting messages to young people. In most of SEA, media interventions for young people are in the form of magazines, posters, radio, video and television productions. These are generally short-term interventions designed to influence the behaviour and attitudes of young people (Israel and Nagano, 1997).

We located one evaluated media project in each of Botswana (Meekers et al., 1997), Kenya (Kiragu, 1997) and Uganda (Kiragu et al., 1996). All involved, *inter alia*, the radio and print media and all were found to have achieved their desired impact on variables such as beliefs, knowledge and behaviour. The remaining three evaluated media projects were from South Africa. Reddy et al. (1994) found that a photo-novella increased the proportion that believed that using a condom was a good idea; decreased the proportion that found using condoms to be embarrassing; and increased knowledge. Preston-Whyte et al. (1995) reported that participation in a drama project (DramAidE) was experienced positively by the students and altered knowledge and attitudes about HIV/AIDS in a positive direction, but did not change reported sexual behaviour. CASE (1997) evaluated Soul City, which is a multimedia project in which television, radio and print media are used as vehicles to reach large numbers of youth. They found that Soul City reached 61 per cent of the South African population, of whom 95 per cent reported that they learned something; and there was an increase in the proportion that were considering limiting their sexual activity to one partner and that used condoms.

Selected issues

Number of evaluation studies

A relatively small number of evaluations were identified. Furthermore, they were not equally distributed between the countries in SEA. South Africa (and particularly Cape Town) was over-represented, and several countries were not represented at all.

Even though the review was not exhaustive or systematic, we have reason to believe that it is relatively comprehensive. First, we conducted computerised literature searches of databases such as MEDLINE and AIDSLINE. Second, as part of the activities of the Adolescent Reproductive Health Network (ARHNe), research assistants were employed to accumulate as much literature as possible (whether published or not) in the six countries in SEA represented in the network. It is unlikely that they would have failed to identify large numbers of relevant studies. All the relevant literature from this search was included in this chapter. Second, the list of references for this chapter was distributed to all ARHNe members, with the request that they inform us of any omitted work. Network members are generally well informed about work in their own countries.

There are a number of reasons for a reluctance to conduct evaluation studies. First, programme managers frequently invest a great deal of time and energy in their programmes. On a personal level, cognitive dissonance (Festinger, 1957) could occur in the face of evidence that the programme has been ineffective. This would force a recognition that their efforts have been in vain, which would be difficult to reconcile with the time and energy expended on the programme.

Second, programme managers frequently believe that their programmes have been successful on the basis of grateful clients and numerous examples of success. They may believe that the "face success" of the programme is so manifestly obvious that evaluations are redundant, and perhaps even a misallocation of resources that could have been allocated to the programme itself. The situation is exacerbated by the fact that funders and government agencies frequently refrain from insisting that an outcome evaluation is an integral part of the programme.

Finally, there are relatively few scientists in SEA that have the necessary training and experience to conduct evaluation research. These barriers can all be addressed by improved education of all those involved in programme funding, management and implementation. Several training programmes in fields such as public health and educational psychology have recently been established in the region. It is important for these programmes to include courses in evaluation, and for these courses themselves to be subjected to evaluation.

Involvement of programme managers

The overwhelming majority of the evaluations were carried out by postgraduate students or researchers that were based in universities or research agencies. Clearly, it is refreshing that such institutions are tackling issues of enormous social impact and not focusing exclusively on those that are divorced from the social contexts in which they exist. However, it is of crucial importance for the researchers to involve programme staff in all phases of the evaluation projects, including the initial phases of deciding on the aims of the evaluation. This contributes to capacity development of those involved in the development and implementation of programmes.

The chances of recommendations being implemented are increased if those who are well placed to do so have a sense of "co-ownership" of the evaluation process and hence its products. In a clinic-based study, it was found that there were a large number of missed opportunities for the provision of contraception services to young people (Flisher et al., 1992). Indeed, about a third of young people attending primary health care clinics in Cape Town did not receive any information about contraception, yet would have liked to do so. Managers from the health department were involved in the project from its inception. This facilitated the translation of these findings into practice changes. It is unfortunate that a subsequent evaluation was not completed to assess whether these changes resulted in reduction in the rate of missed opportunities for contraception counselling.

The ideal scenario from the point of view of implementation of evaluation research findings is present when programme managers request (and even pay for) an evaluation. An example of this is provided by the "set" of evaluations of the training programmes for peer educators and lifeskills workshops that were based at the New Crossroads Youth Centre in Cape Town (Brener, 1996, 1997; Villa-Vicencio, 1998). This youth centre comprises a project of the Planned Parenthood Association. Even though these evaluations were conducted by staff and students at the University of Cape Town, the fact that they were requested by the Planned Parenthood Association resulted in an immediate application of the findings to subsequent training programmes and lifeskills workshops. In the peer education workshops, for example, a number of problems were identified mid-way through the training, such as trainees dropping out of the training, lack of consensus about what is to be achieved, and lack of control over the proceedings of workshops. When this became clear through the monitoring of the training process, a team building exercise was arranged to allow planners and trainees to address these difficulties (Villa-Vicencio, 1998).

The role of theory

Only a minority of the interventions drew on an explicit theoretical framework in the design and implementation of the programmes. Of course, all social interventions are based on assumptions why certain activities would bring about changes in the social conditions they are designed to address. Most of the time these assumptions are implicit in the design of the intervention. For example, almost all of the evaluations in Table 1 had as one of their aims to increase knowledge about selected aspects of sexual and reproductive health. There is an assumption that this will lead to behaviour change. In most cases, the processes by which this would occur are not explicated. Indeed, these processes are generally considerably more complicated than common sense might suggest (Eaton and Flisher, 2001; Eaton et al., 2003; Flisher et al., 1999).

We would argue that there is great value in programmes making their theoretical assumptions explicit. We would then be in a better position to assess whether these assumptions are reasonable in terms of what the available research literature tells us about the effectiveness of the kinds of strategies based on such a theory. Under normal circumstances a prior body of evidence exists around a specific behavioural or other theory, and we can learn much from it. Thus it is possible to generalise (even if only in a limited way) from the success of one programme to the next.

Furthermore, an explicit theoretical base can provide a useful framework for negotiating with stakeholders about which outcomes to focus on. The theory normally gives an indication of what changes one can expect at different stages of programme delivery, and this enlightens us on what to measure when. This greatly assists programme managers, because it helps them to identify the outputs and outcomes which they have control over. It also tempers the often unrealistic expectations of politicians and senior managers.

Several of the school-based intervention programmes were based on explicit theoretical assumptions. The "Get Wise about AIDS" programme that was evaluated by Mathews et al. (1996), for example, included theoretical constructs from Freirian theories of learning (Freire, 1972), Bandura's theory of self-efficacy (Bandura, 1989), the Health Belief Model (Janz and Becker, 1984) and the Theory of Reasoned Action (Fishbein and Middlesstadt, 1989). As mentioned above, the Tanzanian intervention (Klepp et al., 1994, 1997, 1999) was informed by the Theory of Reasoned Action and social learning theory. The evaluations of these programmes measured some of the constructs comprising the theory. This can assist in interpreting the outcomes of an intervention. The programme evaluated by Mathews et al. (1996), for example, failed to change behaviour in the desired direction and also failed to increase self-efficacy. This suggests that one possible reason for the lack of the desired impact on behaviour was the lack of impact on self efficacy. Clearly, this hypothesis would need to be subject to empirical validation.

Lack of studies on inputs

As mentioned above, the inputs refer to the resources which are dedicated to the programme. These include, *inter alia*, the money, staff, number and nature of volunteers, staff qualifications and training, facilities, equipment that are used to run and support the activities that comprise the intervention. The programme itself requires this information for accountability reasons: it needs to monitor and report aspects such as how much money is received, how it is spent, and how staff spend their time. This is particularly important in places where there are few resources, since these need to be utilised in the most cost-effective manner.

There is another reason for describing and analysing the inputs into a programme, which goes beyond the needs and requirements of the programme itself. Other programme developers facing similar social conditions might be interested in adapting the programme for their situation. They will need to know whether they have the resources and capacity to do so. For example, if a programme requires four full time counsellors to provide counselling to teenagers, and the staff of a programme at a new site of intervention know that they will only be able to afford one counsellor, they may very well refrain from implementing the programme.

In this context, it is a cause for concern that only two of the intervention studies (Table 1) evaluated the inputs in a systematic manner (Erulkar and Mensch, 1997; Phiri and Erulkar, 1997). Both of these involved youth centres. Of course, in many of the other studies one can infer something about the inputs based on the information that is provided. However, one has no way of knowing how valid one's estimates are.

Documenting process

A programme is seldom delivered in the way it was designed. The evaluator therefore cannot assume that the actual delivery of services is done in the way it was planned, and will need a description of what happened in the delivery of the programme activities. One reason for documenting programme implementation is to provide accountability information, as it provides evidence that certain activities have indeed taken place. This may seem an obvious point, but there are too many examples of programmes not being implemented at all, or being completely corrupted in the way they were implemented. Another equally important reason for taking this aspect of the evaluation of programmes seriously, is to inform the evaluation of their outcomes. When an outcome evaluation shows that the programme brought about little or no change in the condition of its participants, one reason may be that it was not implemented properly. One answer to the question "Why did the programme fail?" therefore might be: "Because it was not implemented properly". It is clear that this is a very different answer from: "Because it is a poor (or weak) programme", and that it has very different consequences for the programme itself. In practical terms, we do not want to reject potentially effective programmes for the wrong reasons – before we can say that a programme is ineffective, it ought to have been given a proper opportunity to bring about the desired changes, by being implemented at full strength. This is a very real concern, as we know that weak implementation is often identified as a major cause for failure of programmes to bring about change.

Some of the studies conducted in health facilities can be regarded as process evaluations. If young people experience staff at health facilities as unfriendly and are concerned about issues of confidentiality (Abdool Karim et al., 1992; Wood et al., 1997) they are less likely to make use of such health facilities when they require contraceptive services. However, this does not imply that programmes based at health facilities are inherently ineffective. Rather, they were not implemented in an optimal manner.

Outputs

The outputs refer to the delivery and implementation of the activities. They reflect the measurable, direct products of a programme; for example, the number of classes taught, counselling sessions conducted, visits by a health worker, community meetings held, and participants served. In the programmes reviewed above, outputs have included the extent to which primary care facilities succeeded in the provision of contraceptive services (for example, Flisher et al., 1991, 1992), the penetration of media initiatives (for example, CASE, 1997), and who used youth centres (for example, Phiri and Erulkar, 1997).

Evaluations of this aspect of programmes provide a relatively short feedback loop on the efficacy of a programme. Thus, they provide information in a relatively short period of time about aspects such as whether it serves the population it intended to reach; whether it delivers the services it intended, and in the way they were intended; and whether its resources are expended as they were supposed to be. If evidence comes to the fore that there is a discrepancy between what was planned and what is delivered, the programme is able to take corrective action in midcourse. Without monitoring the outputs of the programme, programme staff might not be aware of a problem until it is too late to do anything about it. The study by Abdool Karim et al. (1992), for example, identified a number of barriers to the provision of condoms to teenagers who seek them from family planning services in Durban, South Africa. These included difficulty in locating the facilities, embarrassment by security staff, a lack of privacy, insufficient information about how to use the condoms, and insufficient availability. There are obvious and immediate steps that the family planning clinics could take to overcome each of these barriers.

Close monitoring of programme inputs and outputs is essential to develop highly effective and accountable organisations. Furthermore, it has a consequence that is frequently overlooked, namely that it builds the capacity of managers and staff to create and use ongoing evaluation information. This might entail the improvement of their planning and decision-making, the ability to anticipate and respond to problems, or justifying continued support for their programmes. However, in most of the examples of output evaluations (Table 1), these were conducted by people based in universities or research organisations. In these cases, the organisational benefits of the evaluations are unlikely to be realised.

Outcomes

Finally, we need to know how participants have benefited from the programme. Did they acquire new knowledge? Did they improve their skills in the area of interest? Did they change their attitudes? Effective programmes influence participants in a meaningful way on the outcome of interest.

We measure outcomes for a number of reasons. Service providers themselves, the staff and management of programmes, certainly want to be able to demonstrate that their efforts improve the social condition. More important perhaps, is the increasing tendency for governments, funders and even the general public, to require evidence that the resources expended on programmes actually produce benefits to the recipients of the services. This is another example of the accountability function of programme evaluation: we need to demonstrate that the programme makes a difference in the lives of people.

Outcomes may be short-term or long-term. Some will occur closer in time to the programme activities than others. In the school-based interventions reviewed above (Table 1), outcomes such as an increase in knowledge or more favourable attitudes to people living with AIDS were generally evident immediately after the programme. Some outcomes by their nature are removed in time from the programme in the sense that they can be expected to occur much later. An actual change in behaviour may be manifest some time after the programme because of a lack of opportunity to demonstrate the changed behaviour. For many adolescents, sexual intercourse is an infrequent event, and may thus occur some time after participation in an intervention programme.

Where possible, it is important to include both short term and long term outcome evaluations, as was the case in a subset of the school-based programmes. One hopes that a positive effect observed immediately after a programme will still be evident in the long term. This occurred in the Tanzanian school studies mentioned above, where positive outcomes in terms of subjective norms and behavioural intention that were evident immediately after the programme were still evident 12 months later (Klepp et al., 1994, 1997). However, a common scenario is that positive effects are attenuated or even disappear in the long term. An example of this is provided by Mitchell's (1994) evaluation. She found that changes in knowledge and attitudes in the desired direction were not present several weeks later. This serves to emphasise the importance of long term evaluations. Mitchell's evaluation also provides an example of the rather rare phenomenon of a "sleeper effect". She found that there were no programmemematic effects on self efficacy immediately after the programme, but there was a trend for such effects to be manifest at long term follow-up. Thus, the impact of the programme occurred some time after the programme. Further research is required to understand the reasons for such effects.

Examples of even more distal outcomes include a reduction in the incidence of sexually transmitted infections or unwanted pregnancy, or a change in social norms regarding attitudes to people living with AIDS. However, the more distal the outcome the more challenging it is to link the outcome to a specific intervention programme. In most cases, a large number of influences acting synergistically account for the more distal outcomes.

As with output measures, outcome measures provide a learning loop that feeds information back to the programme. However, the information collection occurs further down the line from the delivery of services than is the case with output measures. Nevertheless, this information is also used to adapt and improve the programme, on the basis of how effective it is in bringing about changes in behaviour.

If an evaluation shows that a programme ultimately achieves a positive outcome, it contributes to the formulation of policy in that area. Indeed, the importance of taking a longer view is sometimes overlooked in the day-to-day evaluations of individual programmes. We want to accumulate knowledge about effective programmes, about what works best under what conditions for which participants. We can only learn these kinds of bigger lessons if we also take a long-term outlook about programmes, and consolidate the lessons we have learned across a number of programmes and their evaluations. Such consolidation is facilitated by work that reviews the "state of the art", for example the reviews of HIV/STD interventions in developing countries by MacPhail and Campbell (1999) and of South African school-based programmes addressing sexual and reproductive health (Mukoma and Flisher, chapter 13, this volume).

Conclusions

Since each of the seven selected issues contained its own conclusions, there is little need here to re-visit these in detail. However, a number of them can be framed in terms of overall recommendations, and it is perhaps most useful to conclude the chapter with a few of the most outstanding ones.

– Given the relatively few evaluations we could identify, we recommend that more programmes conduct systematic evaluations of their work. These could be evaluations of input, process, output or outcome – anything that would strengthen service delivery and thus potential impact on the problem situation.

– Alternatively, if such evaluations were conducted but not reported, we strongly encourage programme staff to publish that information in one way or the other. If studies are done but not reported we lose an important opportunity to learn from the evaluation of other people's experiences.

– Given the low number of studies documented, and the relatively weak evidence on outcomes of these programmes, we recommend that the research community identify and document some success stories. It may be more fruitful at this stage of our knowledge base to study in depth one or more programmes where clear evidence exists that they were successful.

– Simultaneously, it would be necessary to conduct more pilot studies, before broad implementation of interventions. This would only enhance our understanding and efforts in this area, however, if they are carefully evaluated, along the lines we suggested here. Pilot studies in particular would be useful to identify potential harmful effects of the programme, before it is implemented on a wider scale.

– It is stating the obvious to say that we need more evaluation expertise locally, and that people working in the field, as well as educational institutions, assist in training more people.

– Finally, and perhaps the most discouraging conclusion we can come to, is that we know very little about tying these programmes to changes in HIV transmission. On the basis of the studies presented here, we simply do not know whether they contribute to this long term impact.

Table 1. Summary of programmes

Author(s)	Place	Setting	Main type(s) of evaluation
Abdool Karim et al., 1992	Durban, RSA	Health facility	Process Output
Baillie, 1991	Cape Town, RSA	School	Formative
Brener, 1996	Cape Town, RSA	Youth centre	Process Output Outcome
Brener, 1997	Cape Town, RSA	Youth Centre	Process Output Outcome
CASE, 1997	RSA	Media	Outcome Output
Erulkar and Mensch, 1997	Kenya	Youth centre	Input Process Output
Flisher et al., 1991	Cape Town, RSA	Health facility	Process Output
Flisher et al., 1992	Cape Town, RSA	Health facility	Process Output
Flisher et al., 2000	Atlantis, RSA	School	Process
Harvey et al., 2000	KwaZulu-Natal, RSA	School	Outcome
HSDU, 1998	Acornhoek, RSA	Health facility	Process Output
Kiragu, 1997	Media	Kenya	Output Outcome
Kiragu et al., 1996	Uganda	Media	Output Outcome
Klepp et al., 1994, 1997, 1999[1]	Arusha, Kilimanjaro, Tanzania	School	Outcome
Kuhn et al., 1994	Cape Town, RSA	School	Output
Mathews et al., 1995[2]	Cape Town, RSA	School	Formative
Mathews et al., 1996[2]	Cape Town, RSA	School	Outcome

Mbizvo et al., 1997[3]	Mashonaland, Zimbabwe	School	Outcome
Meekers et al., 1997	Botswana	Media	Output Outcome
Meyer, 1989	Soshanguve,, RSA	School	Outcome
Mitchell, 1994	Cape Town, RSA	School	Outcome
Page, 1990	Midrand, RSA	School	Outcome
Phiri and Erulkar, 1997	Zimbabwe	Youth centre	Input Process Output
Preston-Whyte et al., 1995	RSA	Media	Process Outcome
Reddy et al., 1994	Cape Town, RSA	Media	Outcome
Rusakaniko et al., 1997[3]	Mashonaland, Zimbabwe	School	Outcome
Villa-Vicencio, 1998	Cape Town, RSA	Youth centre	Formative
Visser, 1996	Various centres, RSA	School	Outcome
Wood et al., 1997	Northern Province, RSA	Health facility	Process Output

[1.] Reported the outcome at different times after the same programme.
[2.] Reported complementary aspects of the same programme.
[3.] Provided similar results for the same programme.

Figure 1. Evaluation logic

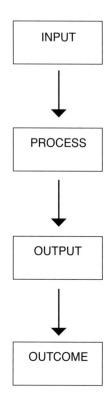

13. A Systematic Review of School-Based HIV/AIDS Prevention Programmes in South Africa

Wanjiru Mukoma and Alan J. Flisher

Abstract

In response to the high and rising rate of HIV infection among adolescents in South Africa, a number of school-based AIDS prevention programmes have been initiated by researchers and governmental and non-governmental structures. It is important to determine whether these programmes have achieved their aim of modifying sexual behaviour and other attributes such that the chances of contracting HIV infection are reduced. This chapter reviews evaluations of school-based HIV/AIDS education programmes in South Africa. The focus is on methodological aspects and effectiveness of the interventions. We identified twelve studies that reported evaluations of school-based AIDS prevention or sexual health and life skills programmes that included HIV/AIDS prevention. Seven are published journal articles, four post-graduate dissertations or theses and one report. The main results and conclusions from the review were as follows: (i) A small number of evaluated AIDS prevention programmes have been reported. The majority were conducted more than five years ago, were unevenly distributed through the country, and involved small numbers of students and schools. (ii) There is considerable diversity between the programmes, which limits the extent to which findings can be generalised. (iii) Almost all the evaluations were predominantly outcome evaluations, to the relative neglect of process and other types of evaluation. (iv) There was little in common between the evaluation instruments that were used, making it difficult to compare results across studies. (v) Few of the studies had designs that enable one to be confident that changes that appeared after the programme were caused by the programme. In general, the programmes demonstrated positive effects on knowledge, attitudes, and amount of communication about sexuality, and negative, few or no effects on perceptions of susceptibility to infection, self-efficacy and (most importantly) behavioural intention or behaviour. This review concludes that there is an urgent need to evaluate AIDS prevention programmes in South African schools. Rigorous evaluation designs are also required if noted changes are to be confidently attributed to the interventions.

Introduction

The 2004 national HIV and syphilis antenatal prevalence survey reported a 29.5% HIV prevalence among pregnant women (Department of Health, 2004). This is a statistically significant increase from the prevalence levels in 2002 and 2003. The report reiterated the higher risk of HIV among older teenagers and women in their twenties. The prevalence rates among women under 20 increased from 14.8% in 2002 to 16.1% in 2004 (Department of Health, 2004). These increases have occurred despite the ever-increasing zeal with which the government, private sector, business, NGOs and various other institutions, organisations and individuals have stepped up efforts to combat HIV/AIDS. Adolescents and youth are thus important segments of the population to target for intervention purposes. Most youth under 20 years old are still in school, making it one of the most important settings for interventions that aim to reach large numbers of young people.

Of the South African adolescent population, 97% of those aged 10–14 years and 83% of those aged 15–19 years attend school (National Institute for Economic Policy, 1995). It is thus an important setting for adolescent and youth development. This is where many spend a substantial part of their time, and where they learn, love, work and play. The 1993 World Bank Development Report identified school-based programmes as one of the most cost-effective approaches to health and development (World Bank, 1993). Some schools in South Africa have taken steps to incorporate the principles of health promotion into their policies and to transform into "health promoting schools" (Flisher et al., 2000; Flisher & Reddy, 1995; Vergnani et al., 1998).

In South Africa today, the question is no longer whether sex education should be provided in schools, but rather how it should be provided. Life skills and AIDS education programmes that specifically target youth have been developed under the auspices of the Department of Health. The two overarching goals of these programmes are: (i) to prevent the spread of HIV through changing behaviour, treating STDs and providing condoms; and (ii) to reduce the impact of the epidemic through providing comprehensive, co-ordinated care services, building acceptance and support for people living with HIV (or PLHA) and providing welfare support.

Most of the country's primary and secondary schools have therefore implemented HIV/AIDS education as one of the focus areas in the life orientation curriculum. Life orientation is currently a compulsory but non-examinable subject in all public schools in the country. Teachers have been trained to facilitate the programmes. By 1998, 9,034 teachers and 840 master trainers had been trained to provide life skills and HIV/AIDS education programmes in South African schools (Flisher et al., 1999). In the Western Cape, for example, a total of 816 teachers had been trained in 433 secondary schools (Karim, 1999), and the programme has been implemented in 241 secondary schools. However there is great diversity in the implementation of the curriculum. There are also a number of short-term school-based sex and AIDS education programmes that have been initiated by researchers and non-governmental organisations (Flisher et al., 1999).

The most important question, however, is whether these interventions have been effective in modifying behaviour and practices, preventing the spread of HIV and promoting the health of adolescents and youth. If they are effective, how can they be improved? And if they are not, why have they not been so?

Evaluation is thus an integral part of school-based AIDS interventions. Evaluations are important to highlight whether the programmes are appropriate and acceptable, and whether they are achieving their objective and reducing the magnitude of the problem. For adolescents and youth, who are at a critical phase of life, effective programmes should aim to shape the development of sexual behaviour, practices, and attitudes and to promote health.

This chapter aims to review evaluations that have been conducted on school-based sex/AIDS education programmes. Specifically, we aim to: (a) document selected methodological aspects of the evaluations; (b) investigate whether the existing programmes are meeting their aims, and, if not, why not; and (c) extract implications for the development of school-based HIV/AIDS prevention programmes in South Africa.

Methods

We searched the AIDSLINE, MEDLINE, NEXUS, Social Sciences Index, Index to South African Periodicals and Psychlit databases for articles in English using the following keywords singly or in combination: "evaluation", "sex education", "sexuality education"; "HIV/AIDS", "South Africa", "school", "adolescent", "youth", "teenagers", "health promotion", and "AIDS education". We obtained unpublished literature, such as dissertations and reports, through telephone, email or fax communication with researchers and organisations, library catalogues, visits to resource centres within reach of the authors, and perusal of the data base of the Adolescent Reproductive Health Network (ARHNe). We scanned the reference lists of all the items for references to additional literature. All published and unpublished evaluations were included in this review if they evaluated a school-based AIDS prevention or sexual or reproductive health promotion programme.

Results and discussion

We located twelve studies that satisfied the inclusion criteria. These are summarised in Table 1.

Description of programmes

There were considerable differences between the programmes in terms of who designed and implemented them. Five studies evaluated programmes that were designed and implemented by government departments, namely Departments of Health and Education (Bailie, 1991; Magnani et al., 2005; Meyer, 1989; Visser, 1996; Visser et al. 2004). These programmes were developed nationally or provincially for inclusion in the school timetables, but schools were at liberty as far as implementation was concerned. Three programmes were designed using a participatory method, in which students, parents and teachers were involved in the design and implementation of the programme (Kuhn et al., 1994; Mathews et al., 1995, 1996). One of these (Mathews et al., 1995), was a formative evaluation undertaken to develop a socially and culturally appropriate classroom AIDS education resource. Two programmes were designed by independent professionals (Mitchell, 1994; Page, 1990). In one of these, the intervention was in the form of a Drama Approach to AIDS Education ("DramAide"), delivered by qualified actors, teachers and nurses, with participation of students (Harvey et al., 2000). The programme consisted of drama, song, poetry, dance and posters, while comparison schools were provided with a booklet in Zulu containing information about HIV/AIDS. The remaining study did not evaluate any specific programme but inquired about sex education received at school (Seydel, 1992).

Also, there were large differences in the duration and intensity of the programmes. The programme with both the shortest duration and greatest intensity was implemented for ten hours over two teaching days (Mitchell, 1994). At the other extreme in terms of duration is the programme evaluated by Mathews et al. (1996) that was of nine months duration, while at the other extreme in terms of intensity was the programme described by Bailie (1991) which consisted of only one or two lessons per year. Harvey (2000),

Meyer (1989) and Seydell (1992) did not provide any details of intensity or duration of the programmes they evaluated. The duration and intensity of the programmes evaluated by Magnani et al. (2005) and Visser et al. (2004) is not clear as there was great variation in implementation across schools.

The fact that these variations between the programmes exist implies that there are limitations in the extent to which findings from the evaluations can be generalised to other existing programmes. If, for example, it was found that a particular programme failed to demonstrate a positive effect on an outcome of interest, this could be ascribed to a number of factors. Such factors could include the way the programme was designed, and the duration and intensity of the programme. Conversely, if all the programmes shared certain characteristics, and some differed from the others in terms of effect on outcome variables, it would be possible to attribute differences in the effect on outcome variables to non-shared programme characteristics.

Finally, in the light of the extent of the public health challenge posed by the HIV epidemic among South African adolescents, it is certainly a cause for concern that we were able to locate such a small number of evaluations of school-based AIDS prevention programmes. Of course, this could reflect the fact that a small number of programmes exist, or that a small proportion of those that do exist have been evaluated.

There are three factors that amplify concern about the low number of evaluations of school-based AIDS prevention programmes. First, only two of the evaluations have appeared in the past five years. Second, a relatively small number of schools and students were included in the evaluations. Of the ten studies that were based at schools, seven involved three or fewer schools. Third, five of the evaluations were carried out at schools in the Western Cape. Some provinces in the country have not had any evaluations of school-based AIDS prevention programmes. Only one study drew its sample of schools from different rural and urban regions in the country, representing the different language and population groups (Visser, 1996).

Description of evaluations

Type of evaluations

One can divide evaluations into the following types:[1]
- Formative: attempts to document the development of a programme;

---

1. See chapter 12 in this volume for a more elaborated discussion of these terms.

- Input: provides information about the people and resources that were allocated to a programme;
- Process: describes the actual implementation of a programme;
- Output: addresses the issues of whether the programme was delivered and programme coverage; and
- Outcome: investigates whether the desired outcomes were observed, and whether these were attributed to the programme.

Bailie (1991) and Mathews et al. (1995) presented formative evaluations. Bailie's (1991) study aimed at gaining greater understanding of pupils' attitudes to sexuality and the sexuality education programme they were receiving. Mathews et al. (1995) presented a formative evaluation of a programme developed in partnership with students, teachers and parents in a predominantly working class Muslim community in Cape Town. This was followed by an outcome evaluation to determine whether this programme was appropriate for a different cultural setting (Mathews et al., 1996). Thus, they examined the effect of the programme on factors such as knowledge, attitudes, and communication with significant others. Although Visser et al. (2004) conducted outcome evaluation to investigate programme effectiveness this was mainly a detailed process evaluation to assess the implementation of the programme and barriers to implementation. The remaining studies were all outcome evaluations. However, some studies included formative (Kuhn et al., 1994; Mitchell, 1994) or process (Visser, 1996) evaluations as a secondary component of the evaluation. While outcome evaluations are clearly crucial, it is important not to neglect the other types of evaluation for reasons that are addressed in chapter 12 in this volume.

Evaluation instruments

The majority of the studies conducted their evaluations principally by self-administered questionnaires. Focus group discussions were the only source of data in the evaluation by Bailie (1991). Although a quantitative survey was conducted in an earlier phase of the study reported by Mathews et al. (1995), the formative evaluation was conducted using focus groups and free attitude interviews. Face-to-face interviews were the principal data collection method in the evaluation by Magnani et al. (2005). Only one study combined both qualitative and quantitative methodologies in the form of interviews, focus group discussions and self administered questionnaires (Visser et al., 2004).

Two studies used a questionnaire comprising both closed- and open-ended questions (Kuhn et al., 1994; Mathews et al., 1996); one used a questionnaire comprising mainly questions that required the respondents to choose between three options ("yes", "no" and "don't know") as well as seven open questions (Visser, 1996); and the remaining studies employed a questionnaire comprising mainly closed-ended questions or precoded statements to which only one response in the range of categories provided could be selected. The fact that each study used a questionnaire that was not used by any of the other studies makes it difficult to compare the results of different evaluation studies. Even though two of the most recent studies we located, (Magnani et al., 2005; Visser et al., 2004) both evaluated programmes developed under the auspices of the National Departments of Education, Health and Welfare, there is no suggestion that a similar questionnaire was employed. The validity of self-report closed-ended questionnaires is sometimes problematic, as they tend to overestimate the respondents' knowledge. If possible, we would suggest that future studies attempt to introduce some uniformity in terms of the instruments that are used.

Study design

Of the twelve studies, one relied exclusively on qualitative methods (Bailie, 1991). Mathews et al. (1996) undertook a quantitative survey in the first phase of the study, followed by qualitative methods, while Seydel (1992) based her report on a one-off questionnaire administered to female adolescents attending a reproductive health clinic. Harvey et al. (2000) undertook a randomized community intervention trial, and Magnani et al. (2005) conducted 2 panel surveys, in 1999 and 2001. The evaluation by Magnani et al. (2005) also employed econometric approaches to address the potential bias emanating from non-random exposure to the life skills education. The remaining six studies employed a design that involved a pre-test and post-test. This is important since one is thus able to draw conclusions about whether there was a change in the outcomes of interest between the two assessments. However, it is not possible to attribute any changes that are detected to the programme. Other factors, such as passage of time or completion of the assessment instruments, may have contributed to any observed changes. In order to be able to attribute changes to the programme with greater confidence, control groups are necessary. However, only four studies employed a control group (Harvey et al., 2000; Kuhn et al., 1994; Meyer, 1989; Mitchell, 1994). Greater importance can be attached to the results of these three studies compared to the studies that did not employ control groups.

For studies that employed a pre- and post-test design, there was variation in the time period after the programme when the post-test evaluations were completed. Two studies conducted the post-test immediately after the programme (Kuhn et al., 1994; Visser, 1996); two studies both immediately after the programme, and again 5 weeks (Page, 1990) and 6.5 weeks (Mitchell, 1994) later; three studies did not test subjects immediately after the intervention, but two weeks, six months and 1 year later respectively (Mathews et al., 1996; Harvey et al., 2000; Visser et al., 2004); while another conducted daily assessments (Meyer, 1989). Clearly, the longer after the programme the post-test is conducted the more confident one can be that any positive effects of the programme will have a meaningful influence on sexual behaviour. This is exemplified by Mitchell's (1994) study. A significant increase in knowledge and understanding was observed in the intervention group relative to the control group immediately after the programme. However, at delayed follow-up, these differences between the two groups had disappeared. It is thus a source of concern that apart from the studies by Harvey et al. (2000) and Visser et al. (2004), the other longest period before follow-up was only 6.5 weeks. This can be attributed partly to the demands of funding agencies for rapid completion of projects, and partly to the tight time frames under which many dissertation and thesis students conduct their studies.

Key findings from evaluations

Knowledge and attitudes

With the exception of the studies by Bailie (1991) and Mathews et al. (1995), all the studies investigated the effects of the programmes on knowledge. This included knowledge of HIV, AIDS, other sexually transmitted infections, condoms and other methods of preventing diseases or pregnancy. For studies that assessed attitudes, some addressed attitudes towards people with AIDS (Kuhn et al., 1994; Mitchell, 1994; Visser, 1996), attitudes towards the use of condoms or contraceptive methods (Meyer, 1989; Visser et al., 2004), premarital sex (Page, 1990) or both people living with AIDS (PWA) and behaviour that is protective against infection (Harvey et al., 2000; Mathews et al., 1996). Page (1990) also investigated attitudes towards STDs, and one study investigated attitudes towards abortion and sexual abuse (Seydel, 1992).

Most of the studies that had pre-tests found that levels of knowledge were low and attitudes unfavourable before the programme (Harvey et al., 2000; Kuhn et al., 1994; Meyer, 1989; Mitchell, 1994; Page, 1990; Visser et al., 2004). Marked improvements were noted after the intervention. A typical finding regarding knowledge is that the number of respondents who knew that HIV cannot be transmitted through touching increased from 44.0% at pre-test to 71.7% at post-test, whilst for the control group the corresponding figures were 46.1% and 45.1% respectively (Kuhn et al., 1994). Likewise, a typical finding regarding attitudes is that 48.0% of the students were not afraid of a person with AIDS before the programme, compared to 68.0% after the programme (Visser, 1996). Visser et al. (2004) reported statistically significant changes in knowledge and attitude towards HIV/AIDS and preventive behaviour while modest gains in knowledge were reported in the study by Magnani et al. (2005). Providing literature only as an intervention did not seem to have any effect on attitudes (Harvey et al., 2000). While mean percentage scores on attitudes increased from 38.1 to 50.5 in schools that received the drama intervention, there was no evidence of change in schools that received a booklet intervention only (Harvey et al., 2000).

It is encouraging that the programmes were able to increase levels of knowledge, even though many of the studies have methodological shortcomings as outlined above. Negative findings would have been a cause for concern. If, for example, a study without a control group had failed to detect a positive effect following the programme, a study with a control group among the same population would be most unlikely to demonstrate a positive effect.

The importance of follow-up assessments some weeks after the programme is illustrated by the results reported by Mitchell (1994). The programme had significant positive effects on both knowledge and attitudes when assessed immediately after the programme. However, these effects were not evident several weeks later. Besides the evaluation by Visser et al. (2004) which was conducted a year after the intervention, the other studies cited above did not have evaluations some weeks after the programme, and we thus have no way of knowing whether the short-term effects of the programme dissipated or not. The study by Visser et al. (2004) however, shows that programmes can have longer-term effects. Modest but significant increases in knowledge were reported a year after the intervention. Similarly, Harvey et al. (2000) reported knowledge gains. in the intervention schools receiving the drama programme "DramAide" six months after the intervention.

There were two studies where the expected positive changes did not occur. Seydel (1992) did not detect changes in attitudes or knowledge after exposure to intervention programmes. However, she asked respondents to indicate whether or not they received sex education at school. If they had, they were asked whether, in their opinion, it had any effect on knowledge or attitudes. Thus, there were no objective data about the impact of the programmes.

The second exception was the study by Mathews et al. (1996). Their respondents, who attended a suburban, middle-class school in Cape Town, had very high knowledge levels before the programme. Over 90%, for example, knew that AIDS could be transmitted vertically and that sex without a condom is risky. There was no increase in knowledge for those items for which the students had a high level of knowledge before the programme. However, for other items for which the levels of knowledge were low before the programme, there was an increase in levels of knowledge after the programme. The percentage who knew why people with a sexually transmitted infection have a higher risk of getting infected with HIV increased significantly from 6.4% to 20.8%. In the same study, the programme had no impact on attitudes towards people with HIV or behaviour that is protective against infection. However, attitudes were very positive before the programme, again suggesting that programmes have less potential to exert a positive impact when conditions are favourable prior to the programme.

This suggests that the level of knowledge and the extent to which attitudes are positive needs to be taken into account when planning the programme. It would not be a sensible use of resources to attempt to increase very high levels of knowledge even further, or to induce already favourable attitudes to be even more favourable. Rather, one should focus on areas where the pre-programme knowledge levels or attitudes are unfavourable, when there is the scope to demonstrate positive effects.

Susceptibility to HIV infection

A person's perception of their personal risk of contracting HIV is an important determinant of their sexual behaviour. People who believe that they can contract HIV and who feel anxious about the risk, are more likely to change their behaviour than those who feel immune or do not perceive a personal risk (Flisher et al., 1999). Whilst improvements were reported on most knowledge scales by a majority of the studies, only Harvey et al.

(2000) reported an increase (49% to 54%) in the proportion of sexually active students in the *"DramAide"* intervention group who thought they could get HIV. No significant differences were reported with regard to susceptibility in the other studies that addressed this issue (Kuhn et al., 1994; Visser, 1996). The majority of respondents in the study by Kuhn et al. (1994) considered that only particular groups were at risk of contracting HIV infection, such as "prostitutes" and "women who sell their bodies". Furthermore, AIDS was characterised as a "white disease". Only 16% of the students in this study stated explicitly after the programme that AIDS could affect anyone. In Visser's (1996) study, there was a non-significant increase (from 43 to 59%) in the proportion of students who believed that AIDS did not only affect only certain population groups. Also, *more* students were sure that they were not at risk of contracting AIDS after the intervention (66% versus 53%). The two most recent evaluations (Magnani et al., 2005; Visser et al., 2004) did not address this issue. It is likely that with increased visibility of people of diverse backgrounds living with HIV, these perceptions may have changed during the last decade.

These results suggest that programmes should prioritise increasing the insight of the programme participants into their susceptibility to infection by the HIV. Of course, this challenge may be easier to meet since the incidence rates have increased sharply among South African adolescents, as indicated in the introduction to this chapter. Not only has this led to increased media coverage of the HIV epidemic, but it is becoming increasingly more likely that adolescents participating in programmes would themselves know of people their own age who are living with, or have died from, AIDS. It is reasonable to assume that these factors will result in an increase in the perceived susceptibility of South African adolescents to AIDS.

Self-efficacy

Self-efficacy refers to people's perception that they will be able to carry out a behaviour, such as wearing a condom (or persuade a partner to do so) in a sexual encounter. It is the perception of mastery that is relevant here; whether they will in fact be able to carry out the behaviour is another matter. The extent of self-efficacy is correlated with the probability that a person will be able to carry out a behaviour (Bandura, 1989).

Four studies included this variable in their evaluations. Mitchell (1994) investigated self-efficacy with respect to avoiding HIV infection and reducing sexual transmission of the virus. She found that there was no evidence of an increase in self-efficacy immediately after the programme. However,

at follow-up 6.5 weeks later, there was a trend for improvement in both domains. Thus, a failure to demonstrate an impact immediately after the programme does not imply that longer term effects are absent.

Harvey et al. (2000) found an increase in percentage of students in the
drama intervention schools who thought they would be able to tell their
girlfriend/boyfriend to use a condom during intercourse (46 versus 64%).
Percentage decreases were found in the booklet intervention group (53 versus 45%). As was the case for knowledge and attitudes, the students in the
study by Mathews et al. (1996) displayed favourable self-efficacy before the
programme in some respects; for example, over 85% of the students believed
that they would be able to show their partner love without having sex, and
that they would be able to insist on their using a condom during sex even
if their partner did not want to do so. The programme did not increase the
levels of self-efficacy for those behaviours for which self-efficacy was high
before the programme. However, 56% of the sexually active students believed that it was difficult to refuse when their partner wanted sex. This
proportion decreased to 44% after the programme. Even though this difference was not statistically significant, it was in the desired direction. Again,
these findings underline the importance of tailoring the programme to fit
the characteristics of the students at baseline.

Magnani et al. (2005) investigated perceived self-efficacy to obtain and
use condoms. At the second phase of the study, 84% of respondents were
confident in their ability to obtain condoms when needed, compared to
70% at the first phase of the study. Gains were also observed in self-efficacy
to use condoms effectively at the second phase, although only 62% were
"very confident" that they could use a condom. Gender and age differences
were observed, with younger females displaying lower levels of self-efficacy
compared to males and older youth (Magnani et al., 2005).

Communication about sex/sexuality

Four studies investigated whether communication with family, friends and/
or girl- or boyfriends about sexuality changed as a result of programmes
(Kuhn et al., 1994; Meyer, 1989; Page, 1990; Seydel, 1992). In general, the
programmes did have a positive effect on the amount of communication
about sexuality. An exception is the study by Page (1990), which found
that there was an increase in communication with friends, no change in
communication with girl- or boyfriends, and a decrease in communication with parents. However, this study was conducted at a boarding school,

where one would expect that there would in any case be minimal contact with parents.

Although the amount of communication increased, none of the studies addressed the content of the communication. An increase in communication is not necessarily a good thing. It is possible, for example, that there was an increase in communication about sexuality with (say) parents, but the communication was characterised by conflict and recrimination. In this case, an increased amount of communication would be unlikely to exert a positive effect on sexual behaviour. We recommend that future evaluations include additional details regarding the content of the communication and the emotional atmosphere in which it occurred.

Behaviour

Three studies investigated the effects of the programme on behavioural intention (Kuhn et al., 1994; Page, 1990; Visser, 1996). None of these studies reported a positive effect on behavioural intention to use condoms (Kuhn et al., 1994), change their sexual behaviour (except use of condoms more frequently) (Page, 1990) or undergo a blood test or have sexual relationships (Visser, 1996).

Four studies asked about actual behaviour as opposed to behavioural intention. Harvey et al. (2000) reported an increase in condom use amongst students in the "DramAide" intervention schools. There was no evidence of an increase of sexual activity following either intervention, but the proportion of students under the age of 18 years that were sexually active fell slightly in both groups. Mathews et al. (1996), Magnani et al. (2005) and Visser et al. (2004) found that significantly more students became sexually active at the second point of assessment. However, this is not a surprising finding, particularly in the studies by Magnani et al., and Visser et al., given that the youth were one and two years older at the time of the second survey. Visser et al. (2004) also attribute this to more honesty in completing the questionnaire post-test. The practice of secondary abstinence by older youth in this study also increased significantly, especially amongst females. Also, of those students who were sexually active at the first survey, Magnani et al. (2005) reported an increase in secondary abstinence. The programme evaluated by Mathews et al. (1996) had no effect on the prevalence of condom use at last intercourse, and a significantly negative change on the proportion who had a condom. However, as Mathews et al. (1996) concede, the absence of a control group in these studies makes it impossible to distinguish changes that can be attributed to the programmes from changes that would have occurred in the absence of a programme. Some of these findings are disappointing, and underline the importance of conducting evaluations of intervention programmes (Flisher et al., chapter 12 in this volume). There are several possible explanations for the failures of the programmes to affect behaviour or behavioural intention, such as the limited duration of the programmes, the fact that they were not embedded in a theoretical framework, did not address skills such as decision-making and assertiveness or the programmes were not properly implemented as intended (Kuhn et al., 1994; Visser et al., 2004). This last point is particularly well illustrated in the process evaluation by Visser et al. (2004). The study found that the HIV/AIDS programme was not successfully implemented in the majority of the schools to facilitate change in the behaviour patterns of learners. The main barrier to implementation was structural and organisational factors within the school system, such as lack of resources and support from principals. However, even in schools where some implementation occurred, the teachers failed to build learners' life skills and capacity, focussing rather on awareness and education (Visser et al., 2004).

Seydel's (1992) study, in which attendees at a reproductive health clinic were asked about their experience of school-based sex education programmes, did indicate that there were differences between those who has received "some" and "much" sex education. Those that had received "much" sex education were more likely to choose condoms (32 vs. 13%), and less likely to use the pill (32 vs. 52%) as their preferred method of contraception. Among those who had "no" sex education, 5% chose the condom as their preferred method of contraception whereas 43% chose the injection. It is difficult to interpret these results as they refer to a number of sex education programmes and it is unclear whether choice of contraception reflects behavioural intention or actual behaviour. Also, the focus was on contraception as opposed to AIDS prevention, which has a bearing on the reasons that a particular method of contraception was chosen.

Involving communities in developing AIDS education programmes

Two studies reported the involvement of school communities in developing the intervention (Kuhn et al., 1994; Mathews et al., 1995). The programme by Kuhn et al. (1994) was initiated through a process of consultation and training with teachers, parents, school nurses, students and the educational authorities. The aim was to utilise existing resources, and give primary responsibility for the programme to the school community.

Mathews et al. (1995) conducted a formative evaluation aimed at exploring religious and cultural beliefs, and understanding students' sexual experiences and sexual health needs so as to develop culturally and socially appropriate classroom AIDS resources. The approach was based on Paulo Freire's theory of education and empowerment. By involving the school community, the researchers' realised that their assumptions about AIDS education were not shared and were challenged. What they thought to be public health imperatives were in conflict with the acceptable religious and cultural values of the community. For example, during the piloting stage of the programme, teachers were faced with the question of whether precautions against HIV should include safer sex and acceptance of PLWA, in a community in which Muslim religious teaching forbids premarital sex and homosexuality. The teachers' concern was that the programme should respect and uphold the religious values of the community. On the other hand, students were experimenting with sex, and many spoke of experiencing desire and pressure to have sex. The essential conflict between the parents' and teachers' needs to promote religious values, and students' needs to cope with experiences of sexuality and to protect themselves in high risk situations was evident in the discussions. While Visser et al. (2004) do not report on community involvement in designing the programme, process evaluation data gathered from the trained teachers was used to inform further interventions aimed at encouraging implementation in the schools. However, one of the barriers to implementation was lack of support from principals and other staff members who did not view the non-examinable programme as important (Visser et al., 2004)

These studies suggest strongly the need for researchers and programme designers to undertake formative evaluation to inform programme development. It is also important that the school community is involved in the development of the evaluation. Some of the implementation barriers reported by Visser et al. (2004), for example, might have been minimised if principals were involved in developing the programme and supporting its implementation. As mentioned earlier in this chapter, it is important to involve the target audience in the process so that researchers and educators do not impose but rather take into consideration the social and cultural context of the community. The study by Mathews et al. (1995) highlights the moral, religious, cultural and personal conflicts facing AIDS education in a multicultural context. The researchers conceded that they had failed through not taking sufficient heed of the reservations and uneasiness voiced by teachers in the first few discussions. Findings from this formative evaluation were used to develop a photo novella using the students' experiences, and also to inform the development of the AIDS education programme in partnership with teachers. Qualitative methods are shown to be useful in understanding in depth the social and cultural factors related to adolescent sexuality.

Respondents' evaluations of the programmes

In general, respondents provided positive evaluations of the programmes. This was manifest, for example, in requests for more information on HIV and AIDS (Bailie, 1991; Kuhn et al., 1994; Mitchell, 1994; Mathews et al., 1996; Seydel, 1992; Visser, 1996). However, in some studies (Bailie, 1991; Mathews et al., 1996; Visser, 1996) respondents indicated that they would have preferred a greater emphasis on visual and participatory methods as opposed to lectures and other passive methods. For example, Bailie's (1991) formative evaluation of a programme offered by the National Health Department reported that the programme should:

- include more imaginative and stimulating teaching methods;
- promote more trusting relationships between programme facilitators and students;
- increase the use of small discussion groups and role plays;
- address issues of concern to them;
- involve parents and the community members to a greater extent; and
- offer easier access to the students for individual counselling.

The suggestion for more visual and participatory methods is supported by evidence from the study by Harvey et al. (2000) in which longer-term positive effects were reported. The "DramAide" intervention schools in the study had higher scores of improvement in knowledge and attitude compared to the schools receiving information literature only.

Conclusion

The key points that emerge from this review are that:

- there is considerable diversity in the AIDS education programmes, which limits the extent to which findings can be generalised;

- there were a small number of evaluated AIDS prevention programmes, only one of which was reported in the last five years;
- the evaluations involved small numbers of students and schools, and were unevenly distributed throughout the country;
- almost all the evaluations were predominantly outcome evaluations, to the relative neglect of process and other types of evaluation;
- there was little in common between the questionnaires that were used to evaluate the programmes, which makes it difficult to compare results across studies;
- few of the studies had designs that enable one to be confident that changes that were manifest after the programme were caused by the programme; and
- in general, the programmes demonstrated positive effects on knowledge, attitudes, and amount of communication about sexuality, and little or no negative effects on susceptibility to infection, self-efficacy and (most importantly) behavioural intention or behaviour.

In conclusion, there is an urgent need for evaluated AIDS prevention programmes in South African schools. Such efforts should build on the lessons that the programmes reviewed above have provided. In particular, the programmes should have sufficient duration and intensity to produce positive outcomes that will be evident at follow-up both immediately after the programme and some time later. They should draw on the emerging international consensus about the necessary conditions for successful programmatic outcomes. These include, *inter alia*, the need for interventions to be securely grounded theoretically; to increase skills (such as assertiveness) and self efficacy; to address social and material barriers to the practice of safer sex; and to recognise that unsafe sexual behaviour cannot be understood in isolation from other risk behaviours (Flisher et al., 1996; Varga, 1997; WHO, 1999b). Evaluations should also pay attention to process evaluation as this has important implications for observed outcomes. Finally, the evaluations should be of sufficient methodological sophistication to enable confident conclusions about whether the programmes have achieved their desired objectives both immediately after the programme and thereafter.

Table 1. Evaluations of school-based reproductive health promotion programmes in South Africa

Author	Description of programme	Sample	Details of evaluation	Factors investigated	Summary of results
Bailie, 1991	Developed by National Health Department. Presented by trained advisors. 1 or 2 lessons per year.	3 high schools in Cape Town. Grades 6–12 12–19 years. Purposive sampling N=60.	Formative evaluation. 6 focus groups with learners.	Knowledge of STIs & reproductive anatomy Knowledge & attitude to contraception Sexual attitudes Students' opinions of the programme	Higher levels of knowledge reported amongst std 9–12 compared to lower grades. Superficial knowledge of contraceptive methods; fear of negative effects of contraception. Students expressed dislike for lectures, issues addressed are not of concern to repsondents. Need for more visual and creative presentations.
Harvey et al., 2000	For intervention group, a 3-phase programme. Phase I: a play presented by qualified actors, teachers and nurses. Phase II: drama workshops for teachers & students. Phase III: a 'school open day' presented by students. For control group, a 10-page booklet information in Zulu.	2 pairs of schools from 5 districts (4 rural, 1 urban) in kwaZulu Natal. Std. 8 pupils. N=1080 at pre-test, 699 at post-test. Mean age = 17.6 years at pre-test, 18.3 at post-test.	Outcome evaluation. Randomized community intervention trial. Pre- and post-intervention self administered questionnaire survey with closed questions.	Knowlede of HIV/AIDS Attitudes towards HIV/AIDS and PWA Behaviour	Increase in men % score on knowledges from 48.3 to 59.1 in "DramAide" schools and 50 to 51.8 in booklet intervention schools. Decrease in men % score on attitudes in "DramAide" schools. No change in the booklet intervention schools. Only three behaviour questions were analysed. Increase in men % score on behaviour for sexually active students in "DramAide" schools. No change in booklet intervention schools.
Kuhn et al., 1994	Developed through brainstorming with staff & students. Attempted to reach out to parents. Presented by trained teachers. Intense high-profile focus on AIDS for 2 weeks.	A high school in a socio-economically disadvantaged area of Cape Town. 2 classes from each standard. Control school, N = 336 at pre-test, 276 at post-test. Programme school, N = 231 at pre-test, 206 at post-test Mean age = 18 (range 12–30)	Formative and outcome evaluations. Questionnaire with closed & open-ended questions.	Knowledge Attitudes to PWA Susceptability Communication with parents, peers, teachers, sexual partners and nurses. Condom use	Significantly higher increase in knowledge in prog. group. Low but increased acceptance of PWA in programme group. No increase in % of students who thought AIDS was everyone's problem. Dramatic impact on communication with parents, friends, teachers, nurses and sexual partners. Small, statistically significant change in intention to use condoms. A range of negative attitudes towards condoms were reported.

Author	Description of programme	Sample	Details of evaluation	Factors investigated	Summary of results
Magnani et al., 2005	A life skills curriculum overseen by the National Project Committee of the Departments of Health and Education. Each province followed committee guidelines to design and implement the programme.	N=2222 in KwaZulu Natal Probability sample of households in 2 magisterial districts. Multi-stage cluster sampling of households with youth 14–22 years.	2 panel surveys, 1999 & 2001. Impact measure: net dose-response relationship between life skills exposure and outcomes. Interviews with youth and adults. Interviews with principals.	Exposure to life skills education. Impact on: Sexual debut, Secondary abstinence, Number of sexual partners, Condom behaviour.	Substantial increase in exposure to life skills education from 1999–2001. Significant but modest gains in knowledge of aspects of reproductive health, STIs, HIV/AIDS, and perceived condom efficacy. Larger effects on condom use at first and last sex. No consistent effects on age at first sex. Increase in secondary abstinence. Increase in proportion of sexually active youth. No significant change with regard to number of sexual partners in the last 4 weeks. Increase in self-efficacy to obtain and use condoms .
Mathews et al, 1995	Qualitative research aimed at developing culturally appropriate resources for AIDS education with input from teachers and students.	Teachers and students in a high school in a Muslim community in Cape Town. Purposive selection of students.	Formative evaluation using focus groups and free attitude interviews.	The cultural meaning and social context of sexuality and sexual behaviour.	Researchers' assumptions about AIDS education were in conflict with cultural and religious values. Students experienced conflict between their sexual desires and societal and religious values. Findings informed the AIDS education programme later developed.
Mathews et al., 1996	Designed by students, teachers and parents. Classroom-based activities, video, photo comic. Taught by two guidance teachers. 9 months duration.	1 high-school in an affluent area of Cape Town Grade 10 N = 232. Mean age = 15 Females – 49% Christians – 84% Moslems – 7% 79.2% never had sex	Pre-tests and post-tests Direct observation 2 interviews with guidance teachers 2 focus groups Students' diaries	Knowledge of HIV & AIDS Attitude towards PWA Self-efficacy Behaviour Student opinions of the programme	High accurate knowledge levels at pretest. No change. No significant changes in attitude towards PWA. Significant increase in the proportions that would use a condom. More students became sexually active during the inte vention. Request for more in-depth information on Catholicism, homosexuality and living with HIV. Teachers found the programme manual easy to use.

Author	Description of programme	Sample	Details of evaluation	Factors investigated	Summary of results
Meyer, 1989	Developed by National Health Department. Use of flashcards, audio-visual equipment, group discussions, role playing.	2 high-schools in Soshanguve. 30 students in intervention and 30 comparison groups. Random selection.	Pre-test, post-test with control group Daily assessment. Self-administered questionnaire	Knowledge of STDs, physiological development and contraceptive methods Interpersonal communication Respondents' evaluation	Improvements in knowledge of STDs, physiological development & contraceptive methods in programme group. Improvement in communication with parents & friends. Request for further information on topics discussed.
Mitchell, 1994	Professionally designed and delivered 10 hrs over 2 full teaching days.	Private multiracial Anglican boys secondary school in Cape Town. N = 60, 30 in intervention and control group. Ages 16–18 Random sampling	Pre-test (1 experimental 1 control). Post-test (4 groups). Post-test immediately & 61/2 weeks later. Self administered questionnaire	Knowledge & understanding of HIV & AIDS Attitude towards PWA Perceived social norms Self efficacy	Significant increase in knowledge and understanding relative to the comparison group at immediate follow-up. At delayed follow-up – no significant changes in knowledge. Self-efficacy improved at 61/2 weeks follow-up. No details of changes in other outcomes at follow-up.
Page, 1990	Presented by 5 trained volunteer counsellors 1 hour weekly for 4 weeks.	Private boarding school in Midrand. Convenience sampling 35 male, 18 female Black students Mean age 17.7, range 16–18 years 61% of males and 22% of females had had sexual intercourse.	Pre-test, post-test Repeated measures Subjective/outcome evaluation	Knowledge of contraception, STDs and sexual knowledge. Attitude towards pre-marital sex. Behaviour Communication	Significant increase in knowledge. No change in attitudes towards pre-marital sex. Clearer sexual values. Students would be more comfortable with using contraception after the intervention. No effect on sexual behaviour Increase in communication with friends. Less communication with parents. No change in communication with boy/girlfriend.

Author	Description of programme	Sample	Details of evaluation	Factors investigated	Summary of results
Seydel, 1992	No specific programme	Attendees at reproductive health clinic in Western Cape. N = 67 English speaking, sexually active females Ages 12-19 No sex education N = 21, some N = 21, much N = 25	Self-administered questionnaire No control group	Knowledge of contraception and biological facts about reproduction. Attitude towards abortion and sexual abuse.	37.3% had "comprehensive" sex education at school. No increases in knowledge. No changes in attitude. No differences in the "no sex education", "some sex education" & "much sex education" groups.
Visser, 1996	Developed by the National Health Department. Presented by counselling teachers. 8–18 periods 6 weeks	11 urban and rural schools in different provinces. N = 339 Grades 8–11 All races	Process and outcome evaluation Before-and-after design Self report questionnaire 2 focus groups per school Interviews with presenters	Knowledge of STDs, HIV transmission and prevention of AIDS. Attitude towards PWA Perception of condom use Behavioural intentions	Significant increase in all knowledge scales except susceptibility; e.g. knowledge that: AIDS could not be cured – pretest 69%, posttest 82%; condoms prevent AIDS – pretest 48%, posttest 59%. Increase in positive attitude towards PWA. No significant difference in perceptions of condom use . No significant differences on behavioural intention.
Visser, et al., 2004	Developed by the National Departments of Education, Health and Welfare, and helping organisations. Implemented by trained teachers.	24 high schools in 2 urban educational districts. Convenient sampling of classes in 5 schools. N=873 at pretest; 794 at posttest Age range-19 47% male, 53% females	Conducted over 2 years Process evaluation: interviews with teachers and principals; focus groups with learners. Outcome evaluation: self administered questionnaire. Pre- and posttest design with one year between.	Outcomes: knowledge of HIV/AIDS and attitude towards HIV/AIDS and condom use. Psychological wellbeing; feelings of personal control Sexual behaviour Process: impact of training on teachers' ability to present HIV/AIDS education; teachers' experience of implementation; perceived outcomes.	Statistically significant changes in knowledge of HIV/AIDS amongst learners and teachers. No significant changes in learners' attitudes toward condom use, psychological wellbeing and feelings of personal control. Increased high risk behaviour. No implementation of the programme in the majority of the schools. In most schools, no time allocated to HIV/AIDS education.

Bibliography

Aarø, L.E., B. Wold, L. Kannas and M. Rimpelä, 1986, "Health behaviour in schoolchildren. A WHO cross national survey. A presentation of philosophy, methods and selected results of the First Survey", *Health Promotion*, 1(1):17–33.

Aas, H. and K-I. Klepp, 1992, "Adolescents Alcohol-Use Related to Perceived Norms", *Scandinavian Journal of Psychology*, Vol. 33, Nr. 4, pp. 315–25.

Abdella, A., 1996, "Demographic characteristics, socioeconomic profile and contraceptive behaviour in patients with abortion at Jimma Hospital, Ethiopia", *East African Medical Journal*, 73:660–64.

Abdool Karim, Q., E. Preston-Whyte and S.S. Abdool Karim, 1992, "Teenagers seeking condoms at family planning services", Part 1, A user's perspective, *South African Medical Journal*, 82:356–69.

Abdool Karim, S.S., Q. Abdool Karim, E. Preston-Whyte and N. Sankar, 1992, "Reasons for lack of condom use among high school students", *South African Medical Journal*, 82:107–10.

Abeja-Apunyo, C., 1999, *Utilising pilot projects to develop reproductive health programmes in Uganda*. CARE International (obtained from their website).

Abraham, C., P. Sheeran and M. Johnston, 1998, "From health beliefs to self-regulation: Theoretical advances in the psychology of action control", *Psychology and Health*, 14(4):569–91.

Abraham, C. and P. Sheeran, 2005, "The Health Belief Model", in M. Conner and P. Norman (eds), *Predicting Health Behaviour*. Buckingham: Open University Press.

Abraham, S.C.S, T.K. Rubaale and W. Kipp, 1995, "HIV-preventive cognitions amongst secondary school students in Uganda", *Health Education Research*, 10:155–62.

Adih, W.K. and C.S. Alexander, 1999, "Determinants of condom use to prevent HIV infection among youth in Ghana", *Journal of Adolescent Health*, 24:68–72.

Adomako, A.A., 1997, "Costs and Rewards–Exchange in Relationships. Experiences of Some Ghanaian Women", in E. Evers-Rosander (ed), *Transforming Female Identities. Women's organizational forms in West Africa*. Seminar Proceedings No. 31. Uppsala: Nordiska Afrikainstitutet.

Agha, S., 2002, "An Evaluation of the Effectiveness of a Peer Sexual Health Intervention among Secondary School Students in Zambia", *AIDS Education and Prevention*, 14(4):269–81.

Agha, S. and R. Van Rossem, 2004, "Impact of a School-Based Peer Sexual Health Intervention on Normative Beliefs, Risk Perceptions, and Sexual Behavior of Zambian Adolescents", *Journal of Adolescent Health*, 34:441–52.

Ahlberg, B.M., 1991, *Women, sexuality and the changing social order. The impact of government policies on reproductive behavior in Kenya.* International Studies in Global Change, 1. Philadelphia: Gordon and Breach Science.

Ahlberg, B.M., E. Jylkäs and I. Krantz, 2001, "Gendered construction of sexual risks: implications for safer sex among young people in Kenya and Sweden", *Reproductive Health Matters,* 9(17):26–36.

Ahlberg, B.M., V. Kimani, I. Krantz and G. Persson, 1997, "The Mwomboko research project: breaking the silence on adolescent sexuality", *African Sociological Review,* 1(1):66–81.

Airhihenbuwa, C.O., R. Obregon, 2000, "A critical assessment of theories/models used in health communication for HIV/AIDS", *Journal of Health Communication,* 5:5–15.

Ajayi, A.A., L.T. Marangu, J. Miller and J.M. Paxman, 1991, "Adolescent sexuality and fertility in Kenya. A survey of knowledge, perceptions, and practices", *Studies in Family Planning,* 22:205–16.

Ajzen, I., 2001, "Nature and operation of attitudes", *Annual Review of Psychology,* 52:27–58.

Ajzen, I., 1996, "The directive influence of attitudes on behavior", in P.M. Gollwitzer and J.A. Bargh (eds), *The psychology of action. Linking cognition and motivation to behavior.* New York: The Guilford Press, pp 385–403.

Ajzen, I., 1991, "The Theory of Planned Behavior", *Organizational Behavior & Human Decision Processes,* 50:179–211.

Ajzen, I., 1988, *Attitudes, personality, and behavior.* Buckingham: Open University Press.

Ajzen, I. and M. Fishbein, 1980, *Understanding Attitudes and Predicting Health Behaviour.* Englewood Cliffs, NJ: Prentice Hall Inc.

Ajzen, I. and M. Fishbein, 1977, "Attitude-behavior relations: A theoretical analysis and review of empirical research", *Psychological Bulletin,* 84:888–918.

Ajzen, I. and M. Fishbein, 1970, "The prediction of behaviour from attitudinal and normative beliefs", *Journal of Personality and Social Psychology,* 6:466–87.

Akonga, J., 1988, "Adolescent fertility and policy implications in Kenya". Paper presented at the Institute of African Studies, University of Nairobi, Kenya.

Allen, L, 2004, "'Getting off' and 'going out': Young people's conceptions of (hetero)sexual relationships", *Culture, Health & Sexuality,* Vol. 6, Nr. 6, pp. 463–81.

Amuyunzu-Nyamongo, M., A.E. Biddlecom, C. Ouedraogo and V. Woog, 2005, *Qualitative evidence on adolescents' views of sexual and reproductive health in sub-Saharan Africa.* Occasional Report No. 16. Guttmacher Institute.

Anarfi, J. and C. Fayorsey, 2000, "Male protagonists in the commercialization of aspects of the female life cycle in Ghana", in C. Bledsoe, S. Lerner and J.I. Guyer (eds), *Fertility and the Male Life-Cycle in the Era of Fertility Decline.* Oxford/New York: Oxford University Press.

Anastasi, A. and S. Urbina, 1997, *Psychological testing,* 7th ed., New Jersey: Prentice Hall.

Anate, M., O. Awoyemi, O. Oyawoye and O. Petu, 1995, "Procured abortion in Ilorin, Nigeria", *East African Medical Journal*, 72, pp. 386–90.

Ankomah, A., O.C. Aloo and M. Chu, 1997, "Manlagnit A: Unsafe abortions: Methods used and characteristics of patients attending hospitals in Nairobi, Lima, and Manila", *Health Care for Women International*, 18, pp. 43–53.

Apila, H.M., 2001, "Children's psychological problems associated with parental illness and death due to HIV/AIDS. A case study of orphans supported by the "AIDS Widows Orphans Family Support Organisation (AWOFS), Kampala, Uganda". Field report, Research Centre for Health Promotion, University of Bergen, Norway.

Arinaitwe, L. and A. Kabali, 1999, *A needs assessment for adolescent-friendly health services in Kabale District*. Kampala: Child Health and Development Centre, Makerere University.

Arube-Wani, J. and L. Mpabulungi, 1999, *A needs assessment for adolescent-friendly health services in Nebbi District*. Kampala: Child Health and Development Centre, Makerere University.

Bachou, H., 1992, *Adolescent mothers and their children: a case study of needs, resource availability, and constraints to care in a rural area of Uganda*. Kampala: Department of Paediatrics and Child Health, Makerere University.

Backett-Milburn, K. and S. Wilson, 2000, "Understanding Peer Education: Insights from a Process Evaluation", *Health Education Research*, 15(1):85–96.

Badura. A.S., M. Millard, E.A. Peluso and A. Ortman, 2000, "Effects of peer education training on peer educators: Leadership, self-esteem, health knowledge and health behaviors", *Journal of College Student Development*, 41:471–78.

Bagachwa, M.S.D., 1992, "Background, evolution, essence and prospects of current economic reforms in Tanzania", in M.S.D. Bagachwa, A. Mbelle, B. Van Arkaide (eds), *Market reforms and parastatal restructuring in Tanzania*. Economics Department of the Economic Research Bureau, University of Dar es Salaam.

Bagarukayo, H. D. Shuey and J.K. Babishangare, 1993, *An Operational study relating to sexuality and AIDS prevention among primary school students in Kabale District of Uganda*. Kampala: AMREF.

Baggaley, R.C. and D. Needham, 1997, "Africa's emerging AIDS-orphans crisis", *Canadian Medical Association Journal*, 156:873–75.

Bailie, R.S., 1991, "'We have it we sit on it': A formative evaluation of a high school sexuality education programme". Unpublished M.Phil. dissertation, University of Cape Town.

Bajos, N. and J. Marquet, 2000, "Research on HIV sexual risk: Social relations-based approach in a cross-cultural perspective", *Social Science & Medicine*, 50:1533–46.

Balyagati, D., D. Luhamba, S. Nnko, V. Nyonyo and D. Schapink, 1995, "HIV/AIDS and STD Health Promotion in Tanzanian Fishing Villages", *AIDS STD Health Promotion Exchange*, 2:3–7.

Bandawe, C.W. and D. Foster, 1996, "AIDS-related beliefs, attitudes and intentions among Malawian students in three secondary schools", *AIDS Care*, 8:223–32.

Bandura, A., 2004, "Health promotion by social cognitive means", *Health Education and Behavior,* 31 (2):143–64.

Bandura, A., 1998, "Health promotion from the perspective of social cognitive theory", *Psychology and Health,* 13:623–49.

Bandura, A., 1989, "Perceived self-efficacy in the exercise of control over AIDS infection", in V.M. Maya, G.W. Albee, S.F. Schneider (eds), *Primary Prevention of AIDS: Psychological Approaches.* Newbury Park CA: Sage Publications, pp. 89–116.

Bandura, A., 1986, *Social foundations of thought and action: A social cognitive theory.* Englewood Cliffs, NJ: Prentice Hall.

Bandura, A., 1977, *Social learning theory.* Englewood Cliffs, NJ: Prentice-Hall.

Bandura, A., 1969, *Principles of behavior modification.* New York: Holt, Rinehart & Winston.

Bangkok Charter of Health Promotion in a Globalized World, 2005, World Health Organization, http://www.who.int/healthpromotion/conferences/6gchp/ bangkok_charter/en/print.html

Baranowski, T., 1997, "Families and health actions", in D.S. Gochman (ed), *Handbook of health behavior research. Vol. I. Personal and social determinants.* New York/ London: Plenum Press, pp 179–206.

Barker, G.K. and S. Rich, 1992, "Influences on adolescent sexuality in Nigeria and Kenya: Findings from recent focus-group discussions", *Studies in Family Planning,* 23, 199–210.

Barnett, B. with J. Schueller, 2000, *Meeting the Needs of Young Clients: A Guide to Providing Reproductive Health Services to Adolescents.* Research Triangle Park, NC: Family Health International.

Bartholomew, L.K., G.S. Parcel, G. Kok and N. Gottlieb, 2006, *Planning health promotion programmes: An Intervention Mapping approach.* San Francisco, CA: Jossey-Bass.

Bartholomew, L.K., G.S. Parcel, G. Kok and N. Gottlieb, 2001, *Intervention Mapping: A process for designing theory- and evidence-based health education programmes.* Mountain View, CA: Mayfield.

Basen-Engquist, K. and G. Parcel, 1992, "Attitudes, norms and self-efficacy: A model of adolescents' HIV-related sexual risk behavior", *Health Education Quarterly,* 19:263–77.

Bassett, M.T., L. Bijmakers and D.M. Sanders, 1997, "Professionalism, patient satisfaction and quality of health care: experiences during Zimbabwe's structural adjustment programme", *Social Science & Medicine,* 45:1845–52.

Becker, M.H., 1988, "AIDS and behaviour change", *Public Health Reviews,* 16, pp. 1–11.

Becker, M.H., 1974, "The health belief model and personal health behavior", *Health Education Monographs,* 2:324–73.

Becker, M.H., D.P. Haefner and L.A. Maiman, 1977, "The Health Belief Model in the prediction of dietary compliance: a field experiment", *Journal of Health and Social Behaviour,* 1977; 18: 348–366.

Bediako, M.A., M. Nel and L.A. Hiemstra, 2006, "Patients' satisfaction with government health care and services in the Taung district, North West Province", *Curationis*, 29:12–15.

Bem, D.J., 1972, "Self-Perception Theory", in L. Berkowitz (ed.), *Advances in experimental social psychology.* Vol. 6. New York: Academic Press, pp. 1–62.

Bem, D.J., 1967, "Self-perception. An alternative interpretation of cognitive dissonance phenomena", *Psychological Review,* 74:183–200.

Berer, M., 2003, "Integration of sexual and reproductive health services: A health sector priority", *Reproductive Health Matters,* 11(21):6–15.

Bergjsø, P., R.M.S. Olomi, A. Talle and K-I. Klepp, 1995, "Bar workers as health educators: Prevention of sexually transmitted diseases in high risk areas", *Tanzanian Medical Journal,* 10, (1):14–18.

BEST, 2005, Basic Statistics in Education in Tanzania – 1995–2005. National Data, Ministry of Education and Culture, United Republic of Tanzania, Government Printer, Dar es Salaam.

BEST, 1997, Basic Statistics in Education in Tanzania – 1991–1995. National Data, Ministry of Education and Culture, United Republic of Tanzania, Government Printer, Dar es Salaam.

BEST, 1994, Basic Education Statistics in Tanzania – 1989–1993. National Data, Ministry of Education and Culture, United Republic of Tanzania, Government Printer, Dar es Salaam.

BEST, 1991, Basic Education Statistics in Tanzania, 1985–1989, National Data, Ministry of Education and Culture. United Republic of Tanzania, Government Printer, Dar es Salaam.

Bhutta, Z.A., 2002, "Ethics in international health research: A perspective from the developing world", *Bulletin of the World Health Organization,* 80, (2):114–120.

Bigsten, A. och A. Danielson, 2001, *Tanzania: Is the ugly duckling finally growing up. A report for the OECD project "Emerging Africa".* Research report no. 120. Uppsala: Nordiska Afrikainstitutet, 22–26.

Bjørgo, R., 2001, "HIV positive mothers in Uganda: What do they tell the children about illness, death and the children's future as orphans – and how do the children experience this?" A pilot study of "The memory project" of "The National Community of Women Living with HIV/AIDS" (NACWOLA) in Kampala, Uganda. Thesis written for professional psychology degree. University of Bergen.

Bledsoe, C.H., 1980, *Women and Marriage in Kpelle Society.* Stanford: Stanford University Press.

Bledsoe, C., S. Lerner and J.I. Guyer (eds), 2000, *Fertility and the Male Life-Cycle in the Era of Fertility Decline.* Oxford/New York: Oxford University Press.

Bledsoe, C. and G. Pison (eds), 1994, *Nuptiality in Sub-Saharan Africa. Contemporary Anthropological and Demographic Perspectives.* Oxford: Clarendon Press.

Bledsoe, C.H. and B. Cohen (eds), 1993, *Social dynamics of adolescent fertility in Sub-Saharan Africa.* Washington DC: National Academy Press.

Bleek, W., 1988, "A field work experience from Ghana", *Population and Development Review*, 13, 314–22.

Bleek, W., 1976, *Sexual Relations and Birth Control in Ghana. A Case Study of a Rural Town*. Amsterdam: Universitet van Amsterdam.

Blum, R.W. and K. Nelson-Mmari, 2004, "The health of young people in a global context", *Journal of Adolescent Health*, 35:402–18.

Boddy, J., 1989, *Wombs and alien spirits: Women, men, and the Zar cult in northern Sudan*. Madison WI: University of Wisconsin Press.

Bohmer, L. and E. Kirumira, 1997, *Access to reproductive health services: participatory research with Ugandan adolescents*. Los Angeles and Kampala: Pacific Institute for Women's Health and Child Health Development Centre, Makerere University.

Boler, T., R. Adoss, A. Ibrahim and M. Shaw, 2003, *The Sound of Silence: Difficulties in Communicating on HIV/AIDS in Schools*. London: ActionAid.

Bond, G.C., J. Kreniske, I. Susser and J. Vincent (eds), 1997, *AIDS in Africa and the Caribbean*. Boulder, CO: Oxford, Westview Press.

Borgia, P., C. Marinacci, P. Schifano and C.A. Perucci, 2005, "Is peer education the best approach for HIV prevention in schools? Findings from a randomized controlled trial", *Journal of Adolescent Health*, 36(6):508–16.

Bosompra, K., 2001, "Determinants of condom use intentions of university students in Ghana: An application of the theory of reasoned action", *Social Science & Medicine*, 52:1057–69.

Brabin, L., J. Kemp, O.K. Obunge, J. Ikimalo, N. Dollimore, N.N. Odu, C.A. Hart and N.D. Briggs, 1995, "Reproductive tract infections and abortion among adolescent girls in rural Nigeria", *The Lancet*, 345:300–4.

Bracht, N. (ed.), 1999, *Health Promotion at the Community Level–New Advances*. 2nd edition. Newbury Park, CA: Sage Publications.

Brener, L., 1997, "The New Crossroads Youth Information and Contraceptive Service: An Evaluation of the Sexuality and Reproductive Health Workshops for Youths: Report No. 2". Unpublished report submitted to the Planned Parenthood Association of South Africa, Western Cape.

Brener, L., 1996, "The Adolescent Sexuality Research Project of the Planned Parenthood Association of South Africa Western Cape. An Evaluation: Report No. 1". Unpublished report submitted to the Planned Parenthood Association of South Africa, Western Cape.

Brieger, W.R., G.E. Delano, C.G. Lane, O. Oladepo and K.A. Oyediran, 2001, "West African Youth Initiative: Outcome of a Reproductive Health Education Program", *Journal of Adolescent Health*, 29:436–46.

Brislin, R., 1993, *Understanding culture's influence on behavior*. Fort Worth, TX: Harcourt Brace College Publishers.

Brislin, R.W., 1986, "The wording and translation of research instruments", in W.J. Lonner and J.W. Barry (eds), *Field methods in cross-cultural research*. Newbury Park, CA: Sage Publications.

Brown, B., 1971, "Muslim Influence on Trade and Politics in the Lake Tanganyika Region", *African Historical Studies,* Vol. 4, No. 3:617–29.

Brummelhuis, H. and G. Herdt (eds), 1995, *Culture and Sexual Risk: Anthropological Perspectives in AIDS.* New York: Gordon and Breach.

Buga, G.A., D.H. Amoko and D.J. Ncayiyana, 1996, "Sexual behaviour, contraceptive practice and reproductive health among school adolescents in rural Transkei", *South African Medical Journal,* 86:523–27.

Buller, D.B., C. Morrill, D. Taren, M. Aickin, L. Sennott-Miller, M.K. Buller, L. Larkey, C. Alatorre and T.M. Wentzel, 1999, "Randomized Trial Testing the Effect of Peer Education at Increasing Fruit and Vegetable Uptake", *Journal of the National Cancer Institute,* 97 (17):1491–1500.

Bureau of Statistics, 1997, *Tanzania Demographic and Health Survey 1996.* Calverton, Maryland, Bureau of Statistics and Macro International.

Bureau of Statistics, 1992, *1988: Population Census Basic Demographic and Socio-Economic Characteristics.* Planning Commission United Republic of Tanzania, Dar es Salaam.

Caldwell, J.C. and P. Caldwell, 1988, "Marital status and abortion in Africa". Paper presented at the international union for the scientific study of population seminar on nuptiality in sub-Saharan Africa: Current changes and impact on fertility, Paris, November 14–17, 1988.

Campbell, C., 2003, *'Letting them die' - Why HIV/AIDS prevention programmes fail.* Oxford: The International African Institute in cooperation with James Currey (Oxford), Indiana University Press (Bloomington) and Double Storey (Cape Town).

Campbell, C., C.A. Foulis, S. Maimane and Z. Sibiya, 2005, "The Impact of Social Environments on the Effectiveness of Youth HIV Prevention: A South African Case Study", *AIDS Care,* 17(4):471–78.

Campbell, C. and C. MacPhail, 2002, "Peer education, gender and the development of critical consciousness: Participatory HIV prevention by South African youth", *Social Science & Medicine,* 55:331–45.

Campbell, C. and Z. Mzaidume, 2001, "Grassroots Participation, Peer Education, and HIV Prevention by Sex Workers in South Africa", *American Journal of Public Health,* 91, (12):1978–86.

CASE (Community Agency for Social Enquiry), 1997, *Soul City Evaluation Report.* Series II. Unpublished Report.

Chabal, P., 1996, "The African Crisis: Context and interpretation, in R. Werbner and T. Ranger (eds), *Postcolonial Identities in Africa.* London/New Jersey: Zed Books Ltd.

Chacha, C.M., 1994, "The growing incidence of youth unemployment: Strategy and policy options", *Journal of Social Work,* 2: 26–37.

Chambers, R., 1994, "Poverty and Livelihoods: Whose reality counts?" Paper presented at the United Nations Development Programme's Stockholm Roundtable Conference on Global Change: "Change: Social Conflict or Harmony?" New York, United Nations Development Programme.

CIA, 2005, *The World Fact Book Tanzania.* Washington, DC: Central Intelligence Agency, August 2005.

Cialdini, R.B., R.R. Reno and C.A. Kallgren, 1990, "A focus theory of normative conduct: Recycling the concept of norms to reduce littering in public places", *Journal of Personality and Social Psychology,* 58:1015–26.

Cohen, A., 1955, *Delinquent Boys: The culture of the gang.* New York: The Free Press.

Conner, M.T., 1993, "Pros and cons of social cognition models in health behaviour", *Health Psychology Update,* 14: 24–31.

Conner, M. and P. Norman, 2005, *Predicting health behaviour.* Second Edition. Buckingham: Open University Press.

Conner, M. and P. Norman, 1996, *Predicting health behaviour.* Buckingham: Open University Press.

Conner, M. and P. Sparks, 1996, "The Theory of Planned Behaviour and health behaviours", in M. Conner and P. Norman, *Predicting health behaviour.* Buckingham: Open University Press, pp 121–62.

Cooksey, B., G. Malekela and J. Lugalla, 1993, *Parents' attitude towards education in rural Tanzania.* Tanzania Development Research Group (TADREG) report, no. 5, Dar es Salaam.

Corsar, W.A., 1997, *The Sociology of Childhood.* Thousand Oaks, CA: Pine Forge Press.

Crewe, E. and E. Harrison, 1998, *Whose Development? An Ethnography of Aid.* London: Zed Books.

Cruise O' Brien, D.B., 1996, "A lost generation? Youth identity and state decay in West Africa", in R. Werbner and T. Ranger (eds), *Postcolonial Identities in Africa.* London/New Jersey: Zed Books Ltd.

Dahlbäck, E., M. Maimbolwa, L. Kasonka, S. Bergström, A-B. Ransjö-Arvidson, 2007, "Unsafe induced abortions among adolescent girls in Lusaka", *Health Care for Women International,* 28(7):654–76.

Dahlbäck, E., P. Makelele, C.B. Yamba, S. Bergström and A-B. Ransjö-Arvidson, 2006, "Zambian male adolescents' perceptions about premarital sexual relationships", *African Journal of AIDS Research,* 5(3):257–65.

de Quadros, C.A., 1985, *Immunization, Health and Family Planning Components of Community Based Distribution Projects.* Boulder: West View Press.

De Vries, H., M. Dijkstra and P. Kuhlman, 1988, "Self-efficacy: The third factor besides attitude and subjective norm as a predictor of behavioural intentions", *Health Education Research,* 3(3): 273–82.

Department of Health, Republic of South Africa, 2004, *National HIV and syphilis antenatal sero-prevalence survey in South Africa 2004.* Pretoria: National Department of Health.

Department of Health, Republic of South Africa, 2001, *National Policy Guidelines for Adolescent and Youth Health.* Pretoria: Government Printers.

Department of Health, Republic of South Africa, 1997, *White Paper on the Transformation of the Health System in South Africa.* Pretoria: Government Printers.

Deutsch, C., B. Michel and S. Swartz, 2003, "Peer education as a rigorous technology for South Africa", *AIDS Bulletin,* 12(2):8–10.

Deutsch, C. and S. Swartz, 2002, *Towards Standards of Practice for Peer Education in South Africa.* Pretoria: Department of Health.

Dowsett, G. and P. Aggleton, 1999, "Young people and risk-taking in sexual relations", in *Sex and youth: contextual factors affecting risk for HIV/AIDS. A comparative analysis of multi-site studies in developing countries.* Geneva: UNAIDS.

Dressler, W.W. and K.S. Oths, 1997, "Cultural determinants of health behavior" in D.S. Gochman (ed.), *Handbook of health behavior research. Vol. I: Personal and social determinants.* New York/London: Plenum Press, pp. 359–78.

Drew, R.S., C. Makufa and G. Foster, 1998, "Strategies for providing care and support to children orphaned by AIDS", *AIDS Care,* 10 (suppl.1):S9–15.

Dundas, C., 1968 (1924), *Kilimanjaro and Its People.* London: Frank Cass & Co.

Dunkle, K.L. et al., 2004, "Gender-based violence, relationship power, and risk of HIV infection in women attending antenatal clinics in South Africa", *The Lancet,* 363:1415–21.

Eagly, A.H. and S. Chaiken, 1993, *The psychology of attitudes.* Fort Worth, TX: Harcourt.

Eakin, J.M., 1997, "Work-related determinants of health behaviour", in D.S. Gochman (ed.), *Handbook of health behavior research. Vol. I. Personal and social determinants.* New York/London: Plenum Press, pp. 337–57.

Eaton, L. and A.J. Flisher, 2001, "Why do young people engage in unsafe sex?", *South African Journal of Psychiatry,* 7:55–58.

Eaton, L., A.J. Flisher and L. Aarø, 2004, "Unsafe sexual behavior in South African youth", in Y.K. Djamba (ed.), *Sexual behavior of adolescents in contemprary sub-Saharan Africa.* Lewiston/New York: Edwin Mellen Press, pp. 65–109.

Eaton, L., A.J. Flisher and L. Aarø, 2003, *Unsafe sexual behaviour in South African youth, Social Science & Medicine,* 56(1):149–65.

Ebreo, A., S. Feist-Price, Y. Siewe and R.S. Zimmerman, 2002, "Effects of Peer Education on the Peer Educators in a School-Based HIV Prevention Program: Where Should Peer Education Research Go from Here?", *Health Education and Behavior,* 29 (4):411–23.

Ekwempu, C.C., D. Maine, M.B. Olurukoba, E.S. Essien and M.N. Kisseka, 1990, "Structural adjustment and health in Africa", *The Lancet,* pp. 336–57.

Elden, M. and M. Levin, 1991, "Cogenerative learning: Bringing participation into action research.", in W.F. Whyte (ed.), *Participatory action research.* Newbury Park, CA: Sage Publications.

Erulkar, A.S. and B.S. Mensch, 1997, *Youth Centres in Kenya: Evaluation of the Family Planning Association of Kenya Programme.* Nairobi: Population Council.

ESAURP (Eastern and Southern African Universities Research Programme Publication), 1996, *Tanzania's Tomorrow.* Dar es Salaam: Tema Publishers Company Ltd.

Fals Borda, O., 1998, *People's Participation. Challenges Ahead.* London: The Apex Press, New York and Intermediate Technology Publications.

Faxelid, E., B. Ahlberg, S. Freudenthal, J. Ndulo and I. Krantz, 1997a, "Quality of STD care in Zambia. Impact of training in STD management", *International Journal for Quality in Health Care,* 9:361–66.

Faxelid, E., B. Ahlberg, M. Mainbolwa and I. Krantz, 1997b, "Quality of STD care in an urban Zambian setting: the providers' perspective", *International Journal of Nursing Studies,* 34:353–57.

Feldman, D.A., P. O'Hara, K.S. Baboo, N.W. Chitalu, and Y. Lu, 1997, "HIV prevention among Zambian adolescents: developing a value utilization/norm change model", *Social Science & Medicine,* Feb, 44(4):455–68.

Festinger, L., 1957, *A theory of cognitive dissonance.* Stanford, CA: Stanford University Press.

Figa, T.I., T.A. Sinnathuray, K. Yusof, C.K. Fong, V.T. Palan, N. Adeeb, P. Nylander, A. Onifade, A. Akin, M. Bertan, G. Santiago, K. Edstrom, O. Ayeni and A. Belsey, 1986, "Illegal abortion: An attempt to assess its cost to the health services and its incidence in the community", *International Journal of Health Services,* 16, 375–89.

Fishbein, M., 2000, "The role of theory in HIV prevention", *AIDS Care,* 12:273–78.

Fishbein, M. and I. Ajzen, 1975, *Belief, attitude, intention and behaviour. An introduction to theory and research.* Reading, MA: Addison-Wesley.

Fishbein, M., A. Bandura, H.C. Triandis, F.H. Kanfer, M.H. Becker and S.E. Middlestadt, 1991, "Factors influencing behavior and behavior change". Report from a workshop, Washington DC, October 3–5, 1991. Bethesda, Maryland, National Institute of Mental Health (NIMH).

Fishbein, M. and S.E. Middlestadt, 1989, "Using the Theory of Reasoned Action as a framework for understanding and changing AIDS-related behaviours", in V.M. Mays, G.W. Albee and S.F. Schneider (eds), *Primary Prevention of AIDS: Psychological Approaches.* Newbury Park, CA: Sage Publications, pp. 93–110.

Fisher, J.D., W.A. Fisher, A.D. Bryan and S.J. Misovich, 2002, "Information-Motivation-Behavioural Skills Model-Based HIV Risk Behavior Change Intervention for Inner-City High School Youth", *Health Psychology,* 21(2):177–86.

Flisher, A.J., 1998, "Epidemiological research in adolescent risk behaviour in the Department of Psychiatry at the University of Cape Town", *Southern African Journal of Child and Adolescent Mental Health,* 10:140–54.

Flisher, A.J., K. Cloete, B. Johnson, A. Wigton, R.Adams and P. Joshua, 2000, "Health promoting schools: Lessons from Avondale Primary School", in D. Donald, A. Dawes, and J. Louw, *Addressing Childhood Adversity: Psychosocial Interventions in South Africa.* Cape Town: David Phillip, pp. 113–30.

Flisher, A.J., C. Cruz , L. Eaton, W. Mukoma and Y. Pillay, 1999, "Review of Research Involving Health of South African Youth". Report submitted to the Youth Development Trust, Department of Psychiatry, University of Cape Town.

Flisher, A.J., N. Du Toit, and F. Moolla, 1991, "The potential for prevention of risk-taking behaviour by youth at primary health care level: A pilot study", *Southern African Journal of Child and Adolescent Psychiatry,* 3:20–22.

Flisher, A.J., C. Mathews, S. Guttmacher, F. Abdullah and J.E. Myers, 2005, "AIDS prevention through peer education", Editorial, *South African Medical Journal*, 95,(4): 245–48.

Flisher, A.J., W. Mukoma and J. Louw, 2008, "Evaluating adolescent sexual and reproductive health interventions in Southern and East Africa", in K-I. Klepp, A.J. Flisher, and S. Kaaya (eds), *Promoting Adolescent Sexual and Reproductive Health in East and Southern Africa.* Uppsala: The Nordic Africa Institute.

Flisher, A.J. and P. Reddy, 1995, "Towards health promoting schools in South Africa", *South African Medical Journal*, 85:629–30 (editorial).

Flisher, A.J., M.M. Roberts and R. Blignaut, 1992, "Youth attending Cape Peninsula day hospitals: Sexual behaviour and missed opportunities for contraception counselling", *South African Medical Journal*, 82:104–06.

Flisher, A.J., C.F. Ziervogel, D.O. Chalton, P.H. Leger and B.A. Robertson, 1996, for a syndrome of adolescent risk behaviour", *South African Medical Journal*, 86:1090–93.

Flisher, A.J., C.F. Ziervogel, D.O. Chalton, P.H. Leger and B.A. Robertson, 1993, "Risk taking behaviour of Cape Peninsular high-school students. Part VIII. Sexual behaviour", *South African Medical Journal*, 83:495–97.

Foucault, M, 1998, *The Will to Knowledge: The History of Sexuality.* Volume 1. Harmondsworth: Penguin Books Ltd.

Fox, R, 2000, "Tanzanian AIDS project works towards 'good things for young people'", *The Lancet*, 355, 9216:1703.

Freire, P., 1970, *Pedagogy of the Oppressed.* New York: Seabury Press.

Freire, P., 1972, *Pedagogy of the Oppressed.* Harmondsworth: Penguin.

Fuglesang, M, 1997, "Lessons for life–past and present modes of sexuality education in Tanzanian society", *Social Science & Medicine*, 44, 1245–54.

Gage, A.J. and C. Bledsoe, 1994, "The Effects of Education and Social Stratification on Marriage and the Transition to Parenthood in Freetown, Sierra Leone", in C. Bledsoe and G. Pison (eds), *Nuptiality in Sub-Saharan Africa. Contemporary Anthropological and Demographic Perspectives.* Oxford: Clarendon Press.

Geisler, G., 2000, "Women are women, or how to please your husband: Initiation ceremonies or the politics of 'tradition' in Southern Africa", in V.A. Goddard (ed.), *Gender, Agency and Change: Anthropological perspectives.* London: Routledge.

Gianetti, V.J., J. Reynolds and T. Rihen, 1985, "Factors which differentiate smokers from ex-smokers among cardiovascular patients: A discriminant analysis", *Social Science & Medicine*, 20:241–45.

Giles, M., C. Liddell and M. Bydawell, 2005, "Condom use in African adolescents: The role of individual and group factors", *AIDS Care*, 17(6):729–39.

Gilles, P., "The contribution of social and behavioral science to HIV/AIDS prevention", in J.M. Mann and D. Tarantola (eds), *AIDS in the world II.* New York: Oxford University Press, pp. 131–58.

Gillmore, G.D. and M.D. Campbell, 1996, *Needs assessment strategies for health education and health promotion.* Madison, WI: Brown and Benchmark.

Gilson, L., M. Alilio and K. Heggenhougen, 1994, "Community satisfaction with primary health care services: An evaluation undertaken in the Morogoro region of Tanzania", *Social Science & Medicine*, 39:767–80.

Gochman, D.S., 1997, *Handbook of health behavior research. Vol. I: Personal and social determinants.* New York/London: Plenum Press.

Goddard, V.A. (ed.), 2000, "Gender, Agency and Change: Anthropological perspectives". London/New York: Routledge, Taylor and Francis Group.

Godin, G. and G. Kok, 1996, "The Theory of Planned Behavior: A review of its applications to health-related behaviors", *American Journal of Health Promotion*, 11:87–98.

Gollwitzer, P.M., 1999, "Implementation intentions: Strong effects of simple plans", *American Psychologist*, 54:493–503.

Goody, J. and S.J. Tambiah, 1973, *Bridewealth and dowry.* Cambridge: Cambridge University Press.

Green, L.W. and M.W. Kreuter, 2005, *Health promotion planning: An educational and ecological approach.* San Francisco, CA: McGraw-Hill.

Gulbrandsen, Ø., 1986, "To Marry—or Not to Marry. Marital Strategies and Sexual Relations in a Tswana Society", *Ethnos*, Vol. 51:1:7–28.

Hamilton, N.E., E.G. Belzer and H.J. Thiebaux, 1980, "An experimental evaluation of the KAP model for health education", *International Journal of Health Education*, 23(3):156–61.

Haram, L., 1995, "Negotiating sexuality in the times of economic want: The young and modern Meru woman", in K-I. Klepp, P.M. Biswalo and A. Talle (eds), *Young people at risk: Fighting AIDS in Northern Tanzania.* Oslo: Scandinavian University Press, pp. 31–48.

Harcourt, W. (ed.), 1997, *Power, Reproduction and Gender: The Intergenerational Transfer of Knowledge.* London and New Jersey: Zed Books.

Harrison, J.A., P.D. Mullen and L.W. Green, 1992, "A meta-analysis of studies of the Health Belief Model with adults", *Health Education Research*, 7:107–16.

Harvey, B., J. Stuart and T. Swan, 2000, "Evaluation of a drama-in-education programme to increase AIDS awareness in South African high schools: A randomized community intervention trial", *International Journal of STD and AIDS*, 11:105–11.

Hayes, R.J., J. Changalucha, D.A. Ross, A. Gavyole, J. Todd, A.I.N. Obasi, M.L. Plummer, D. Wight, D.C. Mabey and H. Grosskurth, 2005, "The *MEMA kwa Vijana* Project: Design of a community randomized trial of an innovative adolescent sexual health intervention in rural Tanzania", *Contemporary Clinical Trials*, 26:430–42.

Hazlewood, A., 1989, *Education, work and pay in East Africa.* Oxford: Clarendon Press.

Health Systems Development Unit (HSDU), 1998, *Adolescent sexuality and reproductive health in the Northern Province.* Johannesburg: Department of Community Health, University of the Witwatersrand.

Heggenhougen, H.K., 1984, "Will Primary Health Care Efforts Be Allowed to Succeed?", *Social Science & Medicine*, 19(3):217–24.

Hegna, K. and W. Pedersen, 2002, *Sex for overlevelse eller skyggebilder av kjærlighet?: om ungdom under 18 år som selger seksuelle tjenester.* Rapport 5/02. Oslo: Norsk institutt for forskning om oppvekst, velferd og aldring (NOVA).

Helgesson, L., 2001, "Halfway through the first COBET cycle. The progress of COBET in Masasi and Kisarawe districts". A consultant report submitted to the Ministry of Education and Culture, Actionaid Alliance.

The Helsinki Declaration, 1996, http://www.etikkom.no/NEM/REK/declaration96. html.

Hinman, L.M., 2001, *Ethics Updates. Glossary.* http://ethics.acusd.edu/Glossary.html.

Holcomb, D.R. and R.W. Seehafer, 1995, "Enhancing Dating Attitudes through Peer Education as a Date Rape Prevention Strategy", *Peer Facilitator Quarterly,* 12, (4):16–20.

Honwana, A. and F. De Boeck (eds), 2005, *Makers and Breakers. Children and Youths in Postcolonial Africa.* Dakar: CODESRIA.

Hope, K.R., 2003, "Promoting Behavior Change in Botswana: An Assessment of the Peer Education HIV/AIDS Prevention Program at the Workplace", *Journal of Health Communication,* 8:267–81.

Horton, R., 2006, "Reviving reproductive health", *The Lancet,* 369(4):1549.

Hughes-d'Aeth, A., 2002, "Evaluation of HIV/AIDS Peer Education Projects in Zambia", *Evaluation and Program Planning,* 25:397–407.

Human Rights Watch, 2001, *Scared at School: Sexual Violence against Girls in South African Schools.* Washington: Human Rights Watch.

Huygens, P., E. Kajura, J. Seeley and T. Barton, 1996, "Rethinking methods for the study of sexual behavior", *Social Science & Medicine,* 42:221–31.

Iliffe, J., 1979, *A Modern History of Tanganyika.* Cambridge: Cambridge University Press.

Illinigumugabo, A., K.O. Rogo and P.W. Njau, 1995, *Socio-cultural and medical consequences of adolescent pregnancies among out of school adolescent girls in four rural communities in Kenya.* Nairobi: Centre for African Family Studies.

IPAS, 2000, "Initiatives in Reproductive Health Policy", 3:1–12.

Israel, R.C. and R. Nagano, 1997, *Promoting Reproductive Health for Young Adults through Social Marketing and Mass Media: A Review of Trends and Practices.* Washington DC: FOCUS on Young Adults (Research Series).

Janz, N. and M. Becker, 1984, "The health belief model: A decade later", *Health Education Quarterley,* 11:1–47.

Jenkins, R.J. and L.M. Jenkins, 1987, "Making peer tutoring work", *Educational Leadership,* 44,(6):64–68.

Jewkes, R., N. Abrahams and Z. Mvo, 1998, "Why do nurses abuse patients? Reflections from South African obstetric services", *Social Science & Medicine,* 47:1781–95.

Jewkes, R.K., S. Fawcus, H. Rees, C.J. Lombard and J. Katzenellenbogen, 1997, "Methodological issues in the South African incomplete abortion study", *Studies in Family Planning,* 28, 228–34.

Johnson, B.R., S. Ndhlovu, S.L. Farr and T. Chipato, 2002, "Reducing unplanned pregnancy and abortion in Zimbabwe through postabortion contraception", *Studies in Family Planning*, 33(2):195–202.

Joos, S.K. and D.H. Hickam, 1990, "How health professionals influence health behavior: patient-provider interaction and health care outcomes", in K. Glanz, F.M. Lewis and B.K. Rimer (eds), *Health behavior and health education. Theory, research and practice*. San Francisco: Jossey-Bass Publishers.

Justesen, A., S.H. Kapiga, Haga van Asten, 1992, "Abortions in a hospital setting: Hidden realities in Dar es Salaam, Tanzania", *Studies in Family Planning*, 23, 325–29.

Kaaya, S., W. Mukoma, A.J. Flisher and K-I. Klepp, 2002a, "School-based sexual health interventions in sub-Saharan Africa: A review", *Social Dynamics*, 28:64–88.

Kaaya, S., A. Flisher, J. Mbwambo, H. Schaalma, L.E. Aarø and K-I. Klepp, 2002b, "Sexual behavior in school populations of sub-Saharan Africa: A review of studies conducted between 1987–1999", *Scandinavian Journal of Public Health*, 30:148–60.

Kaaya, S., M.T. Leshabari, G.I. Van den Bergh and K-I. Klepp, 2005, "Contextual aspects in relation to reproductive health information among school youth in Rombo District, Tanzania", in K.H. Heggenhougen and J.L.P. Lugalla (eds), *Social Change and Health in Tanzania*. Dar es Salaam: Dar es Salaam University Press Ltd., pp 47–68.

Kaiser Family Foundation (KLA), 2000, *South African Youth Survey*.

Kalichman, S., 1988, *Preventing AIDS: A sourcebook for behavioural interventions*. New Jersey: Lawrence Erlbaum Associates Inc.

Kalipeni, E., S. Craddock, J.R. Oppong and J. Ghosh (eds), 2005, *HIV and AIDS in Africa. Beyond Epidemiology*. Oxford: Blackwell Publishing.

Kamm, M., "The Problem of Youth and School Leavers in the Youth", 1977, in *Report of the Child Study in Tanzania–Age 7 to 15*. Tanzania National Scientific Research Council, Dar es Salaam, pp. 175–203.

Kapiga, S.H., D.J. Hunter and G. Nachtigal, 1992, "Reproductive knowledge, and contraceptive awareness and practice among secondary school pupils in Bagamoyo and Dar-es-Salaam, Tanzania", *Central African Journal of Medicine*, 38(9):375–80.

Kariem, S., 1999, "Update. HIV AIDS Programme". Read at Workshop of the Faculty of Health Sciences, University of Cape Town.

Kasen, S., R.D. Vaughan and H. Walter, 1992, "Self-efficacy for AIDS-preventive behaviors among tenth-grade students", *Health Education Quarterly*, 19:187–202.

Kasule, J., M.T: Mbizvo, V. Gupta, S. Fusakaniko, R. Mwateba, W. Mpanju-Shumbusho, S.H. Kinoti and J. Padachy, 1997, "Zimbabwean teenagers' knowledge of AIDS and other sexually transmitted diseases", *East African Medical Journal*, 74:76–81.

Kelly, J.A., 2004, "Popular opinion leaders and HIV-prevention peer education: Resolving discrepant findings, and implications for the development of effective community programmes", *AIDS Care*, 16(2):139–50.

Kenya Demographic and Health Survey (DHS), 2003, Nairobi: National Council for Population and Development, Central Bureau of Statistics, Office of the Vice President and Ministry of Planning Ministry.

Kerrigan, D., 1999, *Peer Education and HIV/AIDS: Concepts, uses and challenges.* Geneva: UNAIDS.

Kilonzo, G.P. and S. Kaaya, 1994, "The family and substance abuse in the United Republic of Tanzania", *Bulletin on Narcotics*, Vol. XLVI, No. 1.

Kim, Y.M., C. Marangwanda and A. Kols, 1997, "Quality of counselling of young clients in Zimbabwe", *East African Medical Journal*, 74:514–18.

Kiragu, K., 1997, "A dialogue with young people through radio, the Youth Variety Show, a component of the Kenya Youth Initiative Project". Presented at Johns Hopkins University, Population Communication Services.

Kiragu, K., N. Lewicky, C. Lettenmaier, J. Sengendo and A. Gamurorwa, 1996, "'Hits for Hope', Delivery of Improved Services for Health (DISH) Project, Uganda". Presented at Johns Hopkins University, Centre for Communication Programmes.

Kirby. D. and R.J. DiClemente, 1994, "School-based interventions to prevent unprotected sex and HIV among adolescents", in R.J. DiClemente and J.L. Peterson (eds), *Preventing AIDS–Theories and Methods of Behavioral Interventions.* New York: Plenum Publishing Co., pp. 117–41.

Kirby, D., B.A. Laris and L. Rolleri, 2006, *The Impact of Sex and HIV Education Programmes on Sexual Behaviors of Youth in Developing and Developed Countries.* Research Triangle Park, NC: Fam Health Int.

Kirumira, E., A. Katahoire, A. Aboda and K. Edstrom, 1997, *Study on sexual and reproductive health in Ugandan women.* Washington: World Bank Washington.

Kivumbi, G.W. and L. Mpabulungi, 1999, *A needs assessment of adolescent-friendly services in Mbale District.* Kampala: Child Health and Development Centre, Makerere University.

Klepp, K-I., P.W. Biswalo and A. Talle (eds), 1995, *Young People at Risk. Fighting AIDS in Northern Tanzania.* Oslo: Scandinavian University Press.

Klepp, K-I. and A.J. Flisher, 2008, "Comprehensive school-based health promotion: Focus on sexual health and related risk behaviours", in K-I. Klepp, A.J. Flisher and S. Kaaya (eds), *Promoting Adolescent Sexual and Reproductive Health in East and Southern Africa.*

Klepp, K-I., A. Halper and C.L. Perry, 1986, "The efficacy of peer leaders in drug abuse prevention", *Journal of School Health*, 1986; 56, (9): 407–411.

Klepp, K-I. and W.L. Lugoe, "AIDS education in Tanzania: Focus on school children", *The AIDS Reader*, 9(4):276–81.

Klepp, K-I., S.S. Ndeki, M.T. Leshabari, P.J. Hannan and B.A. Lyimo, 1997, "AIDS Education in Tanzania: Promoting Risk Reduction among Primary School Children", *American Journal of Public Health*, 87(12):1931–36.

Klepp, K-I., S.S. Ndeki, A.M. Seha, P. Hannan, B.A. Lyimo, M.H. Msuya, M.N. Irema and A. Schreiner, 1994, "AIDS Education for primary school children in Tanzania: An evaluation study", *AIDS,* 8(8):1157–62.

Klepp, K-I., S.S. Ndeki, F. Thuen, M. Leshabari and A.M. Seha, 1994, "Predictors of intentions to be sexually active among Tanzanian school children", *East African Medical Journal,* 73:218–24.

Koawo, E., 1999, "Some aspects of the adolescent sexual behaviour", *IFE-Psychol,* 7:128–37.

Kok, G., 1992, "Quality of planning as decisive determinant of health education", *Hygie,* 11:58.

Kok, G., 1991, "Health education theories and research for Aids prevention", *Hygie,* 10:32–39.

Kok, G., H. De Vries, A.N. Mudde and V.J. Strecher, 1991, "Planned health education and the role of self efficacy: Dutch research", *Health Education Research,* 6(2):231–38.

Kok, G., H. Schaalma, H. De Vries, G. Parcel and T. Paulussen , 1996, "Social psychology and health education", in W. Stroebe and M. Hewstone (eds*)*, *European Review of Social Psychology,* vol. 7. Chichester: John Wiley and Sons, pp. 210–40.

Komba, D., 1995, *Declining Enrolment and Quality of Primary Education in Tanzania Mainland: An Analysis of Key Data and Documentation and Review of Explanatory Factors.* A Report of a Study Initiated by Ministry of Education and Sponsored by UNICEF. Dar es Salaam, Tanzania.

Komba-Malekela, B., R. Liljeström, 1994, "Looking for Men", in Z. Tumbo-Masabo and R. Liljeström (eds), Chelewa, *Chelewa: The Dilemma of Teenage Girls.* Uppsala: Nordiska Afrikainstitutet, pp. 133–49.

Konde-Lule, J., S.F. Berkley and R. Downing, 1989, "Knowledge, attitudes and practices among AIDS in Ugandans", *AIDS,* 3:513–18.

Konje, J.C. and K.A. Obisesan, 1991, "Septic abortion at University College Hospital, Ibadan, Nigeria", *International Journal of Gynecology and Obstetrics,* 36:121–25.

Korukiiko, L. and C. Ampaire, 1999, *A needs assessment for adolescent-friendly health services in Rukungiri District.* Kampala: Child Health and Development Centre, Makerere University.

Koster-Oyekan, W., 1998, "Why resort to illegal abortion in Zambia? Findings of a community-based study in Western province", *Social Science & Medicine,* 46(10):1303–12.

Kuhn, L., M. Steinberg and C. Mathews, 1994, "Participation of the school community in AIDS education: An evaluation of a high school programme in South Africa", *AIDS Care,* 6:161–71.

Kuper, A., 1982, *Wives for Cattle : Bridewealth and Marriage in Southern Africa.* London: Routledge & Kegan Paul.

Kyaddondo, D., F. Nangendo and T. Barton, 1994, *Availability and accessibility of family planning services to adolescents.* Kampala: Child Health and Development Centre, Makerere University.

Kyaddondo, D. and J. Nassuna, 1999, *A needs assessment for adolescent-friendly health services in Kiboga District.* Kampala: Child Health and Development Centre, Makerere University.

La Fontaine, J, 1985, *Initiation. Ritual Drama and Secret Knowledge across the World.* Harmondsworth: Penguin.

Landau, L.B., 2000, "The Humanitarian Hangover: Transnationalization of governmental practice in Tanzania's refugee-populated areas", *New Issues in Refugee Research,* Working Paper No. 40. UNHCR, 2000: http://www.unhcr.ch/refworld/pub/wpapers/ wpno40.pdf

Larsen, C.J. and W. Pedersen, 2005, *Bytte, kjærlighet, overgrep. Seksualitet blant ungdom i randsonen.* Oslo: NOVA Rapport 10/05.

Lary, H., S. Maman, J. Mbwambo and M. Katebalila, 2004, "Working with young men to address violence and HIV in Tanzania", *Sexual Health Exchange,* 3–4:5.

Lau, R.R., K.A. Hartman and J.E. Ware, 1986, "Health as a value: Methodological and theoretical considerations", *Health Psychology,* 5:25–43.

Laukamm-Josten, U., B.K. Mwizarubi, A. Outwater, C.L. Mwaijonga, J.J. Valadez, D. Nyamwaya, R. Swai, T. Saidel and K. Nyamurekung'e, 2000, "Preventing HIV infection among truck drivers and their sexual partners in Tanzania, 1990–1993", *AIDS Care,* 12, (1):27–40.

Leach, F., 2004, "Conspiracy of silence–Why is gender violence so common in schools? Why is so little action taken to tackle it?", *Gender Violence in Schools,* March, 1–2.

Leach, F., V. Fiscian, E. Kadzamira, E. Lemani and P. Machakanja, 2003, *An Investigative Study of the Abuse of Girls in African Schools.* DFID Educational Research No. 54, London: DFID.

Lema, V.M., K.O, Rogo and R.K. Kamau, 1996, "Induced abortion in Kenya: Its determinants and associated factors", *East African Medical Journal,* 73:164–68.

Leonard, L., I. Ndiaye, A. Kapadia, G. Eisen, O. Diop, S. Mboup and P. Kanki, 2000, "HIV prevention among male clients of female sex workers in Kaolack, Senegal: Results of a peer education program", *AIDS Education and Prevention,* 12,(1):21–37.

Leshabari, M.T., S.F. Kaaya and F. Kawau, 1997, "Reproductive Health Knowledge, Premarital Sex and Other Problem Behaviour among School Youth in Rombo District, Kilimanjaro Region, Tanzania". Research report submitted to the Ford Foundation, Institute of Public Health, Muhimbili University College of Health Sciences, Dar es Salaam.

Leshabari, M.T., S.F. Kaaya, J. Nguma and S. Kapiga, 1996, "Household and community responses to HIV/AIDS in Kyela district, Mbeya". Research report submitted to WHO, Geneva.

Leshabari, M.T. and S.F. Kaaya, 1997, "Bridging the information gap: Sexual maturity and reproductive health problems among youth in Tanzania", *Health Transition Review,* 7:29–44.

Levi-Strauss, C., 1969, *The Elementary Structures of Kinship.* Boston: Beacon Press.

Ligate, E.N., 1982, "Early Child Bearing and Education in Tanzania", in *Project for Youth,* Seminar Report on Adolescent Fertility Management. American

Home Economics Association, International Family Planning Project and the Responsible Parenthood Education for the Youth (EMAU), Dar es Salaam.

Locke, E.A. and G.P. Latham, 1990, *A theory of goal setting and task performance.* Englewood Cliffs, NJ: Prentice Hall.

Lugalla, J.L.P., 1997, "Where do the majority live in urban Tanzania?", in Green, C. (ed.), *Globalisation and survival in the black diaspora: The new urban challenge.* Albany State: University of New York Press.

Lugalla, J.L.P., 1995, *Adjustment and poverty in Tanzania.* Bremer Afrika-Studien Bd. 12. Munster: Lit Verlag, pp. 49–61.

Lugalla, J.L.P., 1993, "Structural adjustment policies and education in Tanzania", in P. Gibbon (ed.), *Social Change and Economic Reform in Africa.* Uppsala: Nordiska Afrikainstitutet.

Lugoe, W. and J. Rise, 1999, "Predicting intended condom use among Tanzanian students using the Theory of Planned Behaviour", *Journal of Health Psychology,* 4:497–506.

Lugoe, W.L., K-I. Klepp, J. Rise, A. Skuttle and P.M. Biswalo, 1995, "Relationship between sexual experience and non-sexual behaviours among secondary school students in Arusha, Tanzania", *East African Medical Journal,* 72: 635–40.

Lule, G.S., J. Tugumisirize and M. Ndekha, 2000, "Quality of care and its effect on utilisation of maternity services at health centre level", *East African Medical Journal,* 77:250–55.

Lwihula, G., K. Nyamuryekunge and J.B. Hamelmann, 1996, "Baseline survey of sexual and reproductive health knowledge, perceptions and behaviour among school youth in Kinondoni District, Dar es Salaam". Report submitted to the African Medical Research Council (AMREF), Dar es Salaam.

Machungo, F., G. Zanconato and S. Bergstrom, 1997, "Socio-economic background, individual cost and hospital care expenditure in cases of illegal abortion in Maputo", *Health and Social Care in the Community,* 5:71–76.

MacNeil, J.M. and J. Hogle, 1998, "Applying social, behavioral and evaluation research to developing country HIV prevention programs", *AIDS,* 12 (suppl 2): S99–S108.

MacPhail, C. and C. Campbell, 1999, "Evaluating HIV/STD interventions in developing countries: Do current indicators do justice to advances in intervention approaches?", *South African Journal of Psychology,* 29:149–65.

Madebo, T. and T. Tsadic, 1993, "A six month prospective study on different aspects of abortion", *Ethiopian Medical Journal,* 31:165–72.

Magnani, R., K. McIntyre, A.M. Karim, L. Brown and P. Hutchinson, 2005, "The impact of life skills education on adolescent sexual risk behaviours in KwaZulu-Natal, South Africa", *Journal of Adolescent Health,* 36:289–304.

Mahe, T. and K. Travers, 1997–98, "Evaluation of a peer health education project in The Gambia, West Africa", *International Quarterly of Community Health Education,* 17, (1):43–56.

Main, D.S., 2002, "Commentary: Understanding the Effects of Peer Education as a Health Promoting Strategy", *Health Education and Behavior,* 29, (4):424–26.

Mair, L., 1969, *African Marriage and Social Change*. London: Frank Cass & Company Limited.

Malangalila, F., 1998, "The quantity of education versus the quality of teaching in Tanzania", *Sunday Observer*, 26 July, p. 6.

Maliamkono, T. and P. Msekwa, 1979, *The Experiment: Education policy reform before and after the Arusha Declaration*. Dar es Salaam: Black Star Agencies.

Maman, S., J. Mbwambo, M. Sweat, N. Hogan and G.P. Kilonzo, 2002, "HIV positive women report more lifetime partner violence: Findings from a voluntary counselling and testing clinic in Dar Es Salaam, Tanzania", *American Journal of Public Health*, 92, (8):1331–37.

MAP (Monitoring the AIDS Pandemic), 1997, The status and trends of the HIV/AIDS/STD epidemics in sub-Saharan Africa. Official satellite symposium of the Xth International Conference on STD and AIDS in Africa. Abidjan December, 1997.

Marlatt, G.A. and J.R. Gordon, 1986, *Relapse prevention: Maintenance strategies in the treatment of addictive behaviors*. New York: Guilford.

Masatu, M.C., 2001, "Promoting reproductive health of Tanzanian young people. Intervention opportunities". PhD thesis at Centre for International Health, University of Bergen, Norway.

Masatu, M.C., G. Kvale and K- I. Klepp, 2003, "Frequency and perceived credibility of reported sources of reproductive health information among primary school adolescents in Arusha, Tanzania", *Scandinavian Journal of Public Health*, 31:216–23.

Mascarenhas, O. and M. Mbilinyi, 1983, *Women in Tanzania: An analytical bibliography*. Uppsala: Nordiska Afrikainstitutet.

Maswanya, E.S., K. Moji, I. Horiguchi, K. Nagata, K. Aoyagi, S. Honda and T. Takemoto, 1999, "Knowledge, risk perception of AIDS and reported sexual behaviour among students in secondary schools and colleges in Tanzania", *Health Education Research*, 14(2):185–96.

Matasha, E., T. Ntembelea, P. Mayaud, W. Saidi, J. Todd, B. Mujya and L. Tendo-Wambura, 1998, "Sexual and reproductive health among primary and secondary school pupils in Mwanza, Tanzania: need for intervention", *AIDS Care*, 10(5):571–82.

Mathews, C., C. Everett, J. Binedell and M. Steinberg, 1995, "Learning to listen: Formative research in the development of AIDS education for secondary school students", *Social Science & Medicine*, 41:1715–24.

Mathews, C., C. Everett, C. Lombard and S. Swanevelder, 1996, "Students get wise about AIDS: The acceptability, feasibility and impact of an AIDS education programme in a suburban school in Cape Town", *South African Medical Journal*, 86:1494–98.

Mathews, C., K. Everett, J. Binedell and M. Steinberg, 1995, "Learning to listen: formative research in the development of AIDS education for secondary school students", *Social Science & Medicine*, 41:1715–24.

Mathews, C., S. Guttmacher, A. Hani, I. Antonetti and A.J. Flisher, 2001, "The identification of student opinion leaders for an HIV prevention programme in Cape Town high schools", *International Quarterly of Community Health Education*, 20:369–79.

Mauss, M., 1990, *The gift: The form and reason for exchange in archaic societies.* London: Routledge.

Mbelle, A.V.Y., 1996, "Can Structural Adjustment Programmes Deliver the Goods in Tanzania? A Programme of Action", in *Tanzania's Tomorrow: An Eastern and Southern Africa Universities Research Programme Publication.* Dar es Salaam: Tema Publishers Company Ltd., pp. 6–20.

Mbelle, A.V.Y. and J. Katabaro, 2003, *School Enrolment, Performance and Access to Education in Tanzania.* Research Report No. 03.1. Research on Poverty Alleviation (REPOA). Dar es Salaam, Mkuki na Nyota Publishers.

Mbizvo, M.T., J. Kasule, V. Gupta, S. Rusakaniko, J. Gumbo, S.N. Kinoti, W. Mpanju-Shumbusho, A.J. Sebina-Zziwa, R. Mwateba and J. Padayachy, 1997, "Effects of a randomized health education intervention on aspects of reproductive health knowledge and reported behaviour among adolescents in Zimbabwe", *Social Science & Medicine*, 44:573–77.

Mbizvo, M.T., J. Kasule, V. Gupta, S. Rusakaniko, J. Gumbo, S.N. Kinoti, W. Mpanju-Shumbusho, A.J. Sebina-Zziwa, R. Mwateba and J. Padayachy, 1995, "Reproductive biology knowledge and behaviour of teenagers in East, Central and Southern Africa: The Zimbabwe case study", *Central African Journal of Medicine*, 41:346–54.

Mbunda,W.M., 1988, *Adolescent Fertility in Tanzania: Knowledge, Perceptions and Practices.* Chama cha Uzazi na Malezi Bora (UMATI), Dar es Salaam.

McCurdy, S., 2000, *Transforming Associations: Fertility, Therapy and the Manyema Diaspora in Urban Kigoma, Tanzania, 1850–1993.* Dr. Ph. Thesis. New York: Columbia University.

McFadden, P., 1992, "Sex, Sexuality and the Problems of AIDS in Africa", in R. Meena (ed.), *Gender in Southern Africa: Conceptual and Theoretical Issues.* Harare: SAPES Books.

McGuire, W.J., 1985, "Attitudes and attitude change", in M. Lindsay and E. Aronson (eds), *The Handbook of Social Psychology*, Vol. 2. New York: Random House, pp. 233–346.

McGuire, W.J., 1964, "Inducing resistance to persuasion", in L. Berkowitz (ed.), *Advances in Experimental Social Psychology*, Vol. 1. New York: Academic, pp.191–229.

Mead, M., 1949, *Coming of Age in Samoa. A Study of Adolescence and Sex in Primitive Societies.* London: Penguin.

Meekers, D. and G. Ahmed, 2000, "Contemporary patterns of adolescent sexuality in urban Botswana", *Journal of Biosocial Science*, Vol. 32, No. 4, 467–85.

Meekers, D. and M. Klein, 2002, "Determinants of condom use among youth in urban Cameroon", *Studies in Family Planning*, 33:335–46.

Meekers, D., G. Stallworthy and J. Harris, 1997, *Changing Adolescents' Beliefs about Protective Sexual Behavior: The Botswana Tsa Programme.* Working Paper No. 3. Wasgington, DC: Population Services International.

Megafu, U. and B.C. Ozumba, 1991, "Morbidity and mortality from induced illegal abortion at the University of Nigeria Teaching Hospital, Enugu: A five year review", *International Journal of Gynecology and Obstetrics*, 34:163–67.

Meghji, Z.H., 1996, "Implementation of Cost-Sharing and Options Available to Improve Health Services for the Poor and Vulnerable Groups in Tanzania", ESAURP, Dar es Salaam, Tema Publishers Company Ltd.

Meillasoux, C., 1981, *Maidens, meal and money: Capitalism and the domestic economy.* Cambridge: Cambridge University Press.

Mellanby, A.R., R.G. Newcombe, J. Rees and J.H. Tripp, 2001, "A comparative study of peer-led and adult-led school sex education", *Health Education Research*, 16, (4):481–92.

Mellanby, A.R., J.B. Rees and J.H. Tripp, 2000, "Peer-led and Adult-led School Health Education: A Critical Review of Available Comparative Research", *Health Education Research*, 15, (5):533–45.

Meyer, A.J., 1989, *An exploratory study to establish the effectiveness of a sex education programme which was undertaken in Soshanguve.* Pretoria: Human Sciences Research Council.

Mgalla, Z., D. Schapink, T. Boerma, B. Mlemya, M. Maswe, I. Veldhuijzen, V. Justine, K. Senkoro, B. Muyaya and V. Kamba, 1997, *Sexual exploitation of school girls in Africa: Findings from operational research in Tanzania.* TANESA Working Paper No.17. Mwanza: Tanzania-Netherlands Project to support HIV/AIDS Control in Mwanza Region (TANESA).

Milburn, K., 1996, *Peer Education-Young People and Sexual Health: A critical review.* HEBS Working Paper No. 2. Edinburgh: Health Education Board for Scotland.

Ministry of Gender, Labour and Social Development, Uganda, 1999, *The National Action Plan on Women.* Kampala.

Ministry of Health (MoH), Tanzania, 2000, *National Package of Essential Reproductive and Child Health Interventions in Tanzania.* Dar es Salaam.

Ministry of Health (MoH), Tanzania, 1994a, *National Policy Guidelines and Standards for Family Planning Service Delivery and Training.* Programme for International Training in Health. Dar es Salaam.

Ministry of Health (MoH), Tanzania, 1994b, *Proposals for Health Sector Reform.* Dar es Salaam.

Ministry of Health (MoH), Uganda, 2004, *National Health Policy for Uganda.* Kampala.

Ministry of Health (MoH), Uganda, 1998, *Reproductive Health Activities in Uganda, Entebbe.* Kampala: Maternal and Child Health and Family Planning.

Ministry of Health (MoH), Zambia, 1997, *Reproductive Health Policies, Strategies and Guidelines.* Lusaka, December 1997.

Ministry of Labour and Youth Development, Tanzania, 1996, *National Youth Development Policy.* Dar es Salaam.

Ministry of Labour and Youth Development, Tanzania, 1990, *National Youth Development Policy.* Dar es Salaam.

Mirembe, F., 1999, "Reproductive health needs of the population with emphasis on adolescents". Paper presented at Regional Workshop on Reproductive Rights and Legislation for Parliamentarians in Eastern and Southern Africa, Kampala.

Mitchell, G.V., 1994, "An evaluation of the impact of a ten hour HIV/AIDS prevention programme on male adolescents' HIV/AIDS-related knowledge, attitudes and beliefs". Unpublished M.Ed. dissertation, University of Cape Town.

Mmari, K.N. and R.J. Magnani, 2003, "Does Making Clinic-based Reproductive Health Services More Youth-friendly Increase Service Use by Adolescents? Evidence from Lusaka, Zambia", *Journal of Adolescent Health*, 33:259–70.

Mngadi, P.T., I.T. Zwane, B.M. Ahlberg and A.B. Ransjö-Arvidson, 2003, "Family and community support to adolescent mothers in Swaziland", *Journal of Advanced Nursing*, 43:137–44.

Molassiotis, A., I. Saralis-Avis, W. Nyirenda and N. Atkins, 2004, "The Simalelo Peer Education Programme for HIV Prevention: A Qualitative Process Evaluation of a Project in Zambia", *African Journal of AIDS Research*, 3(2):183–90.

Mollel, O., R. Olomi, J. Mwanga and B. Mongi, 1995, "Peer education in Mererani mining settlement", in K-I. Klepp, P. Biswalo and A. Talle (eds), *Young People at Risk: Fighting AIDS in Northern Tanzania*. Oslo: Scandinavian University Press, pp.196–203.

Mpangile, G.S., M.T. Leshabari, S.F. Kaaya and D.J. Kihwele, 1996, "The Role of Male Partners in Teenage Induced Abortion in Dar es Salaam", *African Journal of Fertility, Sexuality and Reproductive Health*, 1, 29–37.

Mpangile, G.S., M.T. Leshabari and D.J. Kihwele, 1993, "Factors Associated with Induced Abortion in Public Hospitals in Dar es Salaam, Tanzania", *Reproductive Health Matters*, 2, 21–31.

Mrumbi, K., 2006, *Parental illness and loss to HIV/AIDS as experienced by AIDS orphans aged between 12 and 17 years from Temeke District, Dar es Salaam, Tanzania.* Research Centre for Health Promotion, University of Bergen.

Muhondwa, E.P.Y., 2000, "Towards Defining and Assessing the Sexual and Reproductive Health Needs of Adolescents in Tanzania". Literature Review and Research Agenda compiled for Reproductive and Child Health Section. Dar es Salaam: Ministry of Health, Institute of Public Health, Muhimbili University College of Health Sciences.

Mukoma, W. and A.J. Flisher, 2008, "A systematic review of evaluations of school-based AIDS prevention programmes in South Africa", in K-I. Klepp, A.J. Flisher and S. Kaaya (eds), *Promoting Adolescent Sexual and Reproductive Health in East and Southern Africa*. Uppsala: Nordiska Afrikainstitutet.

Mungherera, M., A. van der Straten, T.L. Hall, B. Faigeles, G. Fowler and J.S. Mandel, 1997, "HIV/AIDS-related attitudes and practices of hospital-based health workers in Kampala, Uganda", *AIDS*, 11(supplement 1):S79–85.

Munthali, A.C., A.M. Moore, S. Konyani and B.B. Zakeyo, 2006, *Qualitative Evidence of Adolescents' Sexual and Reproductive Health Experiences in Selected Districts of Malawi.* Occasional Report No. 23, June 2006. http://www.guttmacher.org/pubs /2006/06/01/or23.pdf

Mutalemwa, D., P. Noni and S. Wangwe, 1998, "Managing the transmission from aid dependence: The case of Tanzania". Paper presented at the AERC/ODC Aid Dependence Workshop, Nairobi, December, 1998.

Muturi, N.W., 2005, "Communication for HIV/AIDS prevention in Kenya: social-cultural considerations", *Journal of Health Communication,* 10:77–98.

Mwakagile, D., E. Mmari, C. Makwaya, J. Mbwana, G. Biberfeld, F. Mhalu, and E. Sandström, 2001, "Sexual behaviour among youth at high risk for HIV-1 infection in Dar es Salaam, Tanzania", *Sexually Transmitted Infections,* 77(4):255–59.

Mwateba, R., R. Goergen, A. Mlay and B. Pfander, 1999, "Adolescent Reproductive Health Needs Assessment. New Methodologies and New Findings". The Paper Slip Method field tested in Lindi Region. Report, November 1999.

Narotzky, S. and F.P. Moreno, 2002, "Reciprocity's dark side: Negative reciprocity, morality and social reproduction", *Anthropological Theory,* 2 (3):281–305 (25).

National AIDS Control Programme (NACP), 2005, *Surveillance of HIV and syphilis infections among antenatal clinic attendees 2003/4.* Dar es Salaam: Ministry of Health, United Republic of Tanzania.

National AIDS Control Programme (NACP), 2004, *Behavioural surveillance surveys among youth, 2002.* Dar es Salaam: Ministry of Health, United Republic of Tanzania.

National Bureau of Statistics (NBS) [Tanzania] and ORC Macro, 2005, *Tanzania Demographic and Health Survey 2004–05.* Dar es Salaam: National Bureau of Statistics and ORC Macro.

National Bureau of Statistics [Tanzania] and Macro International Inc., 2000, *Tanzania Reproductive and Child Health Survey 1999.* Calverton, Maryland: National Bureau of Statistics and Macro International Inc.

National Council for Children (and the Government of Uganda), 1999, *Equity and vulnerability: a situation analysis of women, adolescents and children in Uganda, 1994.* Kampala: Child Health and Development Centre/UNICEF.

National Council for Population and Development (NCPD), 2003, *Adolescent and Reproductive Health Development Policy, Kenya.* Nairobi: NCPD.

National Institute for Economic Policy, 1995, *Children, Poverty and Disparity Reduction: Towards Fulfilling the Rights of South Africa's Children.* Pretoria: Reconstruction and Development Programme, Office of the Deputy President.

National Programme of Action Steering Committee, 1996, *National Programme of Action for Children in South Africa: Framework.* Pretoria: National Programme of Action Steering Committee.

Ndeki, S.S., K-I. Klepp, M.N. Irema, B.A. Lyimo, Msuya M.H. Ngao, 1995, "AIDS education for primary school children", in K-I. Klepp, P.M. Biswalo and A. Talle (eds), *Young people at risk. Fighting AIDS in Northern Tanzania.* Oslo: Scandinavian University Press, pp. 133–48.

Ndeki, S.S., K-I. Klepp and G.R.Z. Mliga, 1994, "Knowledge, perceived risk of AIDS and sexual behaviour among primary school children in two areas of Tanzania", *Health Education Research,* 9(1):133–38.

Ndhlovu, M., 1999, *Nurses' experiences of abortion in South Africa and Zambia.* University of the Western Cape, South Africa.

Ndubani, P., 1998, "Sexually transmitted diseases in rural Zambia: Knowledge, perceptions and practices among young males and traditional healers". Licentiate thesis. Stockholm: Karolinska institutet, IHCAR.

Ndulo, J., E. Faxelid and I. Krantz, 1995, "Quality of care in sexually transmitted diseases in Zambia: Patients' perspective", *East African Medical Journal,* 72:641–44.

Nelson, N., 1987, "'Selling her Kiosk': Kikuyu notions of sexuality and sex for sale in Mathare Valley, Kenya", in P. Caplan (ed.), *The Cultural Construction of Sexuality.* London: Tavistock Publications.

Ng'weshemi, J., T. Boerma, J. Benett and D. Schapink (eds), 1997, *HIV prevention and AIDS care in Africa: A district level approach.* Royal Tropical Institute–The Netherlands. Amsterdam: KIT Press.

Ngaina, R.R., 2002, "A Study on AIDS Orphans' and Caregivers' Perceptions of Needs and of Support Offered to AIDS Orphans: A case study of MKUKI Centre, Himo Village in Kilimanjaro, Tanzania". Research Centre for Health Promotion, University of Bergen.

Ngallaba, S., S.H. Kapiga, I. Rogobya and J.Y. Boerma, 1993, *Tanzania Demographic Health Survey 1991/92.* Dar es Salaam: Planning Commission, Bureau of Statistics.

Ngomuo, E.T., K-I. Klepp, J. Rise and K.S. Mnyika, 1995, "Promoting safer sexual practices among young adults: a survey of health workers in Moshi Rural District, Tanzania", *AIDS Care,* 7:501–7.

Ngugi, E., D. Wilson, J. Sebstad, F. Plummer and S. Moses, 1996, "Focused peer-mediated educational programs among female sex workers to reduce sexually transmitted diseases and Human Immunodeficiency Virus transmission in Kenya and Zimbabwe", *Journal of Infectious Diseases,* 174, (2):S240–47.

Nnko, S. and R. Pool, 1997, "Sexual discourse in the context of AIDS: Dominant themes on adolescent sexuality among primary school students in Magu, Tanzania", *Health Transition Review,* (7), S3:85–90.

Norman, P., C. Abraham and M. Conner (eds), 2000, *Understanding and changing health behaviour: From health beliefs to self-regulation.* Amsterdam: Harwood Academic Publishers.

Norman, P., M. Conner, 1996, "The role of social cognition models in predicting health behaviours: Future directions", in M. Conner and P. Norman (eds), *Predicting health behaviour.* Buckingham: Open University Press, pp. 197–225.

Nsamenang, A.B., 1993, "Psychology in Sub-Saharan Africa", *Psychology and Developing Societies,* 5, (2):171–84.

Ntukula, M., 1994, "The Initiation Rite", in Z. Tumbo-Masabo and R. Liljeström (eds), *Chelewa Chelewa – The dilemma of teenage girls.* Uppsala: Nordiska Afrikainstitutet.

Nyerere, J.K., 1968, *Education for Self-Reliance.* Dar es Salaam: Government Printers.

Obasi, A.I., B. Cleophas, D.A. Ross et al., 2006, "Rationale and design of the MEMA kwa Vijana adolescent sexual and reproductive health intervention in Mwanza Region, Tanzania", *AIDS Care,* 18:311–22.

Obbo, C., 1982, "Strategies for Urban Survival", in C. Obbo, *African Women: Their Struggle for Economic Independence.* London: Zed Press, pp. 101–121.

Okonofua, F.E., P. Coplan, S. Collins, F. Oronsaye, D. Ogunsakin, J.T. Ogonor, J.A. Kaufman and K. Heggenhougen, 2003, "Impact of an intervention to improve treatment-seeking behavior and prevent sexually transmitted diseases among Nigerian youth", *International Journal of Infectious Diseases,* 7:61–73.

Okumu, M. and I. Chege, 1994, *Female adolescent health and sexuality in Kenya secondary schools. A survey report.* Nairobi: African Medical and Research Foundation.

Oldenburg, B. and G. Parcel, 2002, "Diffusion of innovations", in K. Glanz, F.M. Lewis and B.K. Rimer (eds), *Health behaviour and health education: Theory, research and practice,* 3rd ed. San Francisco: Jossey-Bass, pp. 312–34.

Oliff, M., P. Mayaud, R. Brugha and A.M. Semakafu, 2003, "Integrating reproductive health services in a reforming health sector: The case of Tanzania", *Reproductive Health Matters,* 11, 37–48.

Omale, J., 2000, "Tested to Their Limit: Sexual Harassment in Schools and Educational Institutions in Kenya", in J. Mirsky and M. Radlett (eds), *No Paradise Yet: The World's Women Face the New Century.* London: The PANOS Institute and Zed Books.

Omari, C.K., 1977, "Family structure and the child", in *Report on a Study of the young child in Tanzania from age 7–15 years.* Dar es Salaam: Tanzania National Scientific Council.

Omari, I.M., 1995, "Conceptualising quality in primary education in Tanzania", *Papers in Education and Development* (a journal of the Faculty of Education, University of Dar es Salaam), 16, 25–48.

Onyango-Ouma, W., J. Aagaard-Hansen, B.B. Jensen, 2005, "The Potential of Schoolchildren as Health Change Agents in Rural Western Kenya", *Social Science & Medicine,* 61:1711–22.

Orlandi, M.A., C. Landers, R. Weston and N. Haley, 1990, "Diffusion of health promotion innovations," in K. Glanz, F.M. Lewis and B.K. Rimer (eds), *Health behaviour and health education: Theory, research and practice,* 2nd ed. San Francisco: Jossey-Bass, pp. 288–313.

Orobaton, N., 2000, "Dimensions of Sexuality among Nigerian Men: Implications for Fertility and Reproductive Health.", in C. Bledsoe, S. Lerner and J.I. Guyer (eds), *Fertility and the Male Life-Cycle in the Era of Fertility Decline.* Oxford: Oxford University Press, pp. 207–30.

Osler, M. and M. Kirchhoff, 1995, "Smoking behaviour in Danish adults from 1982 to 1992", *Public Health,* 109(4):245–50.

Ottawa Charter for Health Promotion: World Health Organization,1986, Health and Welfare Canada, Canadian Public Health Association. Ottawa, Ontario, Canada.

Ottawa Charter: Charter developed by the WHO/Health and Welfare Canada/ Canadian Public Health Association. Health Promotion, 1996; 1: iii-iv.

Øye, C, 1995, "You Can't Control Nature – Seksualitetsutforming i en urban multietnisk setting i Kenya", Unpublished Cand. Polit. thesis. Department of Social Anthropology, University of Bergen.

Ozer, E.J., R.S. Weinstein, C. Maslach and D. Siegel, 1997, "Adolescent AIDS prevention in context: The impact of peer educator qualities and classroom environments on intervention efficacy", *American Journal of Community Psychology,* 25, (3):289–323.

Page, N.P., 1990, "Effectiveness of a sex education programme in changing sexual knowledge, attitudes and behaviour of black adolescents". Unpublished dissertation, University of the Witwatersrand.

Parnell, B., G. Lie, J.J. Hernandez and C. Robins, 1996, *Development and the HIV Epidemic. A forward-looking evaluation of the approach of the UNDP HIV and Development Programme.* New York: United Nations Development Programme.

Pattullo, A.L.S., M. Malonza, G.G. Kimani, A. Muthee, P.A.O. Otieno, K. Odhiambo, S. Moses and F.A. Plummer, 1994, "Survey of knowledge behaviour and attitudes relating to HIV infection among Kenyan secondary school students", *AIDS Care,* 6:173–81.

Paulme. D., 1963, *Women in Tropical Africa.* Berkerley: University of California Press.

Paulussen, T.G.W., G.J. Kok and H.P. Schaalma, 1994, "Antecedents to adoption of classroom-based AIDS education in secondary schools", *Health Education Research,* 9:485–96.

Pearlman, D.N., L. Camberg, L.J. Wallace, P. Symons and L. Finison, 2002, "Tapping Youth as Agents for Change: Evaluation of a Peer Leadership HIV/AIDS Intervention", *Journal of Adolescent Health,* 31:31–39.

Pedersen, W., 1993, "The Majority Fallacy Reconsidered", *Acta Sociologica,* Vol. 36, 4, 343–55.

Pedersen, W., S.O. Samuelsen, and L. Wichstrom, 2003, "Intercourse Debut Age: Poor Resources, Problem Behavior, or Romantic Appeal? A Population-Based Longitudinal Study", *The Journal of Sex Research,* Vol. 40.

Peersman, G. and J. Levy, "Focus and effectiveness of HIV-preventive efforts for young people", *AIDS,* (12) Suppl. A:191–96.

Peltzer, K., 1999, "Factors affecting condom use in an urban adult community of the Northern Province, South Africa", *Journal of Psychology in Africa,* 9:66–77.

Perry, C.L., 1999, *Creating health behaviour change: How to develop community-wide programmes for youth.* London: Sage Publications.

Perry, C.L., M. Grant, G. Ernberg, R.U. Florenzano, M.C. Langdon, A.D. Myeni, R. Waahlberg, S. Berg, K. Andersson, K.J. Fisher, D. Blaze-Temple, D. Cross, B. Saunders, D.R. Jacobs and T. Schmid, 1989, "WHO Collaborative Study on Alcohol Education and Young People: Outcomes of a four-country pilot study", *International Journal of Addictions,* 24, (12):1145–71.

Perry, C.L., K.I. Klepp, A. Halper, K.G. Hawkins and D.M. Murray, 1986, "A process evaluation study of peer leaders in health education", *Journal of School Health,* 56, (2):62–67.

Petty, R.E. and D.T. Wegener, 1997, "Attitude change: Multiple roles for persuasion variables", in D.T. Gilbert, S.T. Fiske and G. Lindzey (eds), *The handbook of social psychology,* 4th ed. Boston: McGraw Hill, pp. 323–90.

Pfander, B., 2000, *Survey on Knowledge, Attitude and Practice of Adolescents with Regard to Reproductive Health and Sexually Transmitted Infections, including HIV/AIDS.* Ministry of Health, United Republic of Tanzania – RCHS. GTZ.

Phillips, D., 1996, "Medical professional dominance and client dissatisfaction", *Social Science & Medicine,* 42:1419–25.

Phiri, A. and A.S.S. Erulkar, 1997, *A situation analysis of the Zimbabwe National Family Planning Council's youth centres.* Nairobi: Population Council.

Piaget, J. 1977, *The Development of Thought: Equilibration of Cognitive Structures.* New York: Viking Press.

Pillay, Y., 1999, "Researching public policy", in M. Terre Blanche and K. Durheim (eds), *Research in Practice: Applied methods for the social sciences.* Cape Town: University of Cape Town Press.

Population Council, *Programme Briefs. Operation Research. Technical assistance. Africa Project II.* http://www.popcouncil.org/pdfs/pb/adolescence.pdf.

Preston-Whyte, E., M. Du Toit and L. Dalrymple, 1995, "DramAidE – Is DramAidE making a difference? " Unpublished evaluation of the DramAidE programme.

Prochaska, J.O., C.A. Redding and K.E. Evers, 2002, "The transtheoretical model and stages of change", in K. Glanz, B.K. Rimer and F.M. Lewis (eds), *Health behaviour and health education: theory, research and practice,* 3rd ed. San Francisco: Jossey-Bass, 99–120.

Rajani, R. and M. Kudrati, 1996, "The The Varieties of Sexual Experience of the Street Children of Mwanza, Tanzania", in S. Zeidenstein and K. Moore (eds), *Learning about Sexuality: A practical beginning.* New York: The Population Council International Women's Health Coalition.

Rasch, V., S. Massawe, Y. Mchomvu and S. Bergstrom, 2004, "Acceptance of contraceptives among women having unsafe abortion in Dar es Salaam", *Tropical Medicine and International Health,* March 9(3):399–405.

Rasch, V., V. Mmary, E. Urassa and S. Bergstrom, 1999, "Sexual history and contraception among women with induced and spontaneous abortion in Dar es Salaam", *African Journal of Health Sciences,* 6, 33–39.

Rasch, V., H. Muhammad, E. Urassa and S. Bergstrom, 2000a, "The problem of induced abortion – Results from a hospital-based study conducted at district level in Dar es Salaam", *Tropical Medicine and International Health,* 5, 495–502.

Rasch, V., M.Silberschmidt, Y. Mchumvu and V. Mmary, 2000b, "Adolescent Girls with Illegally Induced Abortion in Dar es Salaam: The Discrepancy between Sexual Behaviour and Lack of Access to Contraception", *Reproductive Health Matters,* 8:52–62.

Rasch. V., H. Muhammad, E. Urassa and S. Bergstrom, 2000c, "Self-Reports of Induced Abortion: An Empathetic Setting Can Improve the Quality of Data", *American Journal of Public Health,* 90, 1141–44.

RDP Office (Reconstruction and Development Programme), 1996, *Children, Poverty and Disparity Reduction: Towards fulfilling the rights of South Africa's children.* Pretoria: RDP.

Reddy, P., K. Everett, C. Mathews and C. Lombard, 1994, "The evaluation of an AIDS photo-comic developed for South African youth", Tenth International Conference on AIDS, Tokyo, Japan.

Reddy, P., A. Meyer-Weitz, B. Van den Borne and G. Kok, 2000, "Determinants of condom-use behaviour among STD clinic attenders in South Africa", *International Journal of STDs & AIDS,* 11:521–30.

Regional Education Officer, 2001, *Regional Summary, 2001–2002.* Mpango wa Uboreshaji wa Elimu ya Msingi. Muhtasari wa Mkoa. Maoteo. Regional Education Office. United Republic of Tanzania, Kigoma.

Rehle, T., T. Saidel, S. Mills and R. Magnani (eds), 2001, *Evaluating Programmes for HIV/AIDS Prevention and Care in Developing Countries. A Handbook for Programme Managers and Decision Makers.* Research Triangle Park, NC: Family Health International. (http://www.fhi.org/en/aids/impact/impactpdfs/ evaluationhandbook.pdf)

Reproductive and Child Health Section, Ministry of Health, Tanzania, *National Reproductive and Child Health Communication Strategy for 2001–2005.*

Republic of South Africa, 2000, *Implementation of the Convention on the Rights of the Child: South Africa's supplement to the initial country report, January 2000.* Pretoria: The Door Communication.

Richards, A, 1982, *Chisungu. A Girl's Initiation Ceremony among the Bemba of Zambia.* London: Tavistock Publications.

Rivers, K. and P. Aggleton, 2004, *Adolescent sexuality, gender and the HIV epidemic. UNDP, HIV and Development Programme.* Institute of Education, University of London Read on: http://www.undp.org/hiv/publications/gender/adolesce.htm

Rogers, E.M., 1983, *Diffusion of innovations*, 3rd edition. New York: The Free Press.

Rogo, K., 1993, "Induced abortion in Kenya", Paper prepared for the International Planned Parenthood Federation. Nairobi: Centre for the Study of Adolescence.

Rosenstock, I., 1990, "The health belief model: Explaining health behavior through expectancies", in K. Glanz, F.M. Lewis and B.K. Rimer (eds), *Health behavior and health education. Theory, research, and practice.* San Francisco: Jossey-Bass, pp. 39–62.

Rosenstock, I.M., 1974, "The Health Belief Model and preventive health behavior", *Health Education Monographs,* 2:354–86.

Rosenstock, I.M., V.J. Strecher and M.H. Becker, 1994, "The Health Belief Model and HIV risk behavior change", in R.J. DiClemente and J. Peterson (eds), *Preventing AIDS: Theories and methods of behavioral interventions.* New York: Plenum Press, pp. 5–24.

Rosenstock, I.M., V.J. Strecher and M.H. Becker, 1988, "Social Learning Theory and the Health Belief Model", *Health Education Quarterly,* 15:175–83.

Rosenthal, S.L., K.A. Burklow, F.M. Biro, L.C. Pace and R.F. DeVellis, 1996, "The reliability of high-risk adolescent girls' reports of their sexual history", *Journal of Pediatric Health Care,* 10, 217–20.

Ross, L. and R.E. Nisbett, 1991, *The person and the situation.* New York: McGraw-Hill.

Royston, E. and S. Armstrong, 1989, *Preventing maternal deaths.* Geneva: WHO.

Rubin, G., 1975, "The Traffic in Women: Notes on the 'Political Economy' of Sex", in R. Reiter (ed.), *Toward an Anthropology of Women.* New York: Monthly Review Press.

Ruiter, R.A.C., C. Abraham and G. Kok, 2001, "Scary warnings and rational precautions: A review of the psychology of fear appeals", *Health Psychology,* 16:614–30.

Rusakaniko, S., M.T. Mbizvo, J. Kasule,V. Gupta, S.N. Kinoti, W. Mpanju-Shumbushu, J. Sebina-Zziwa, R. Mwateba and J. Padayachy, 1997, "Trends in reproductive health knowledge following a health education intervention among adolescents in Zimbabwe", *Central African Journal of Medicine,* 43:1–6.

Rutter, D. and L. Quine, 2002, *Changing health behaviour.* Buckingham: Open University Press.

Sarbin, T.R. and V.L. Allen, "Role Theory", in G. Lindzey and E. Aronson (eds), *The Handbook of Social Psychology,* Vol. 1, 2nd edition. Reading, MT: Addison-Wesley, pp. 488–567.

Sawyer, R.G., P. Pinciaro and D. Bedwell, 1997, "How peer education changed peer sexuality educators' self-esteem, personal development, and sexual behavior", *Journal of American College Health,* 45, (5):211–17.

Sax, B., 2002, "Brief report: New roles for tutors in an online classroom", *Journal of College Reading and Learning,* 33, (1):62–66.

Schaalma, H. and S.F. Kaaya, 2008, "Health Education and the promotion of reproductive health: Theory- and evidence-based development and diffusion of intervention programs", in K-I. Klepp, A.J. Flisher, and S. Kaaya (eds), *Promoting Adolescent Sexual and Reproductive Health in East and Southern Africa.* Uppsala: The Nordic Africa Institute.

Schaalma, H., G. Kok, S.C.S. Abrahams, H.J. Hospers, K-I. Klepp and G. Parcel, 2002, "HIV Education for Young People. Intervention Effectiveness, Programme Development, and Future Research", *Prospects,* 32:187–206.

Schaalma, H., G. Kok and L. Peters, 1993, "Determinants of consistent condom use by adolescents: The impact of experience of sexual intercourse", *Health Education Research,* 8(2):255–69.

Schaalma, H., J. Reinders, M. Masatu, S. Kaaya and K-I. Klepp, 2004, "When the researchers have gone home to write their articles. Diffusion and implementation of school-based HIV-prevention programmes in Tanzania", *East African Journal of Public Health,* 24–32.

Schapink, D., J. Hema and B. Mujaya, 1997, "Youth and HIV/AIDS Programmes", in J. Ng'weshemi, T. Boerma, J. Bennet and D. Schapink (eds), *HIV prevention and AIDS care in Africa: A district level approach.* Amsterdam: Royal Tropical Institute, pp. 163–84.

Scheper-Hughes, N. and C.F. Sargent (eds), 1999, *Small Wars: The Cultural Politics of Childhood.* Berkeley: University of California Press.

Scherer, J.H., 1965, *Marriage and Bride-Wealth in the Highlands of Buha (Tanganyika)*. Department of Cultural Anthropology, Faculty of Social Sciences Rijksuniversiteit te Utrecht.

Schoepf, B. Grundfest, 1998, "Inscribing the Body Politic: Women and AIDS in Africa", in M. Lock and P.A. Kaufert (eds), *Pragmatic Women and Body Politics*. Cambridge: Cambridge University Press.

Perspectives in AIDS. New York: Gordon and Breach.

Schoepf, B.G., 2001, "International AIDS research in anthropology: Taking a critical perspective on the crisis", *Annual Review of Anthropology*, Vol. 30:335–61. (doi:10.1146/annurev.anthro.30.1.335)

Schoepf, B.G., 1995, "Culture, sex research and AIDS prevention in Africa", in H. Brummelhuis and G. Herdt (eds), *Culture and Sexual Risk: Anthropological Schopper, D., S. Doussantousse and J. Orav, 1993, "Sexual behaviors relevant to HIV transmission in a rural African population", *Social Science & Medicine*, 37:401–12.

Schwarzer, R., 1992, "Self-efficacy in the adoption and maintenance of health behaviors: Theoretical approaches and a new model", in R. Schwarzer (ed), *Self-efficacy: Thought control of action*. London: Hemisphere, pp. 217–43.

Seha, A.M., K-I. Klepp and S.S. Ndeki, 1994, "Scale reliability and construct validity: A pilot study among primary school children in Northern Tanzania", *AIDS Education and Prevention*, 6(6):524–34.

Senderowitz, J., 1999, *Making reproductive health services youth friendly*. Washington: FOCUS on Young Adults (Research Series).

Senderowitz, J., 1997, *Health facility programs on reproductive health for young adults*. Washington: FOCUS on Young Adults (Research Series).

Senderowitz, J., 1995, *Adolescent health: reassessing the passage to adulthood*. Washington: The World Bank (Discussion Paper 275).

Setel, P., 1999, *A plague of paradoxes: AIDS, culture and demography in Northern Tanzania*. Chicago: University of Chicago Press, pp. 89–150.

Setel P., 1996, "AIDS as a Paradox of Manhood and Development in Kilimanjaro, Tanzania", *Social Science & Medicine*, 43, (8):1169–78.

Setel, P., 1995, "The social context of AIDS education amongst young men in Northern Tanzania", in K-I. Klepp, P.M. Biswalo and A. Talle (eds), *Young people at risk: Fighting AIDS in Northern Tanzania*. Oslo:, Scandinavian University Press, pp. 49–68.

Seydel, K., 1992, "The influence of sex education on sexual knowledge and attitudes of sexually active adolescent schoolgirls". Unpublished M.A. dissertation, University of Stellenbosch.

Sheeran, P., 2001, "Intention-behaviour relations: A conceptual and empirical review", in W. Stroebe and M. Hewstone (eds), *European Review of Social Psychology*, Vol. 12. Chichester: Wiley.

Sheeran, P. and C. Abraham, 1996, "The Health Belief Model", in M. Conner and P. Norman (eds), *Predicting health behaviour*. Buckingham: Open University Press, pp. 23–61.

Sheeran, P., C. Abraham and S. Orbell, 1999, "Psychosocial correlates of heterosexual condom use: a meta-analysis", *Psychological Bulletin,* 125:90–132.

Sheeran, P. and S. Tylor, 1999, "Predicting intentions to use condoms: A meta-analysis and comparison of the Theories of Reasoned Action and Planned Behavior", *Journal of Applied Social Psychology,* 29:1624–75.

Shiner, M. and T. Newburn, 1999, *Young People, Drugs, and Peer Education: An Evaluation of the Youth Awareness Program (YAP).* London: Policy Studies Institute.

Shiner, M., 1999, "Defining Peer Education", *Journal of Adolescence,* 22:555–566.

Shuey, D.A., B.B. Babishangire, S. Omiat and H. Bagarukayo, 1999, "Increased sexual abstinence among in-school adolescents as a result of school health education in Soroti district, Uganda", *Health Education Research,* 14:411–19.

Shuma, M. and R. Liljestrom, 1998, "The erosion of the matrilineal order of the Wamwera", in M. Rwebangira and R. Liljeström (eds), *Haraka Haraka... Look before you leap: Youth at the Crossroad of Custom and Modernity.* Uppsala: Nordiska Afrikainstitutet.

Silberschmidt, M. and V. Rasch, 2001, "Adolescent girls, illegal abortions and 'sugar-daddies' in Dar es Salaam: Vulnerable victims and active social agents", *Social Science & Medicine,* 52:1815–26.

Silversin, J.B., 1979, "Strategies for improving your community's oral health", in P.M. Lazes (ed.), *The handbook of health education.* Germantown: Aspen Systems, pp. 77–91.

Sjöstrand, M., V. Quist, A. Jacobson, S. Bergstrom and K.O. Rogo 1995, "Socio-economic client characteristics and consequences of abortion in Nairobi", *East African Medical Journal,* 72, 325–32.

Sloan, N. and J. Myers, 2004, "Evaluation of HIV peer education in a South African workplace", *HIV/AIDS in the Workplace: Symposium Procedings,* University of the Witwatersrand.

Solo, J., D.L. Billing, C. Aloo-Obunga, A. Ominde and M. Makumi, 1999, "Creating linkages between incomplete abortion treatment and family planning services in Kenya", *Studies in Family Planning,* 30, 17–27.

Speizer, I.S., R.J. Magnani and C.E. Colvin, 2003, "The Effectiveness of Adolescent Reproductive Health Interventions in Developing Countries: A Review of the Evidence", *Journal of Adolescent Health,* 33:324–48.

Speizer, I.S., B.O. Tambashe and S.P. Tenang, 2001, "An evaluation of the "Entre Nous Jeunes" peer-educator program for adolescents in Cameroon", *Studies in Family Planning,* 32(4):339–51.

Stakic, S., R. Zielony, A. Bodiroza and G. Kimzeke, 2003, "Peer Education within a Frame of Theories and Models of Behavior Change", in *Does Peer Education Work in Europe? Entre Nous,* The European Magazine for Sexual and Reproductive Health. No. 56, WHO.

Stanton, B.F., A.M. Fitzgerald, X. Li, H. Shipena, I.B. Ricardo, J.S. Galbraith, N. Terreri, J. Strijdom, V. Hangula-Ndlovu and J. Kahihuata, "HIV risk behavior, intentions and perceptions among Namibian youth as assessed by a theory-based questionnaire", *AIDS Education and Prevention,* 11:132–49.

Statistics Department [Uganda] and Macro International Inc, 1996, *Uganda demographic and health survey, 1995.* Calverton: Statistics Department, Entebbe, Uganda.

Story, M., L.A. Lytle, A.S. Birnbaum and C.L. Perry, 2002, "Peer-Led, School-Based Nutrition Education for Young Adolescents: Feasibility and Process Evaluation of the TEENS Study", *Journal of School Health,* 72, (3):121–27.

Strebel, A. and A. Perkel, 1991, *"Not our problem": AIDS knowledge, attitudes, practices and psychosocial factors at UWC.* Psychology Resource Centre Occasional Paper Series, 1991, No. 4. Cape Town: University of the Western Cape.

Strecher, V.J., V.L. Champion and I.M. Rosenstock, "The Health Belief Model and health behavior", in D.S. Gochman (ed.), 1997, *Handbook of health and behavior research I: Personal and social determinants.* New York: Plenum Press, pp. 71–91.

Stroebe, W., 2000, *Social psychology and health.* Buckingham: Open University Press.

Strömquist, N.P., 1999, "The Impact of Structural Adjustment Programmes in Africa and Latin America", in C. Heward and S. Bunwaree (eds), *Gender, Education and Development: Beyond Access to Empowerment.* London: Zed Books, pp. 17–32.

Sundby, J., 2006, "Young people's sexual and reproductive health rights", *Elsevier. Best Practice & Research Clinical Obstetrics and Gynaecology,* Vol. 20, 3, pp. 355–68.

Sutherland, E., 1947, *Principles of Criminology,* 4th ed. Philadelphia: JB. Lippincott Company.

Sutton, S., 2002, "Using social cognition models to develop health behaviour interventions: Problems and assumptions.", in D. Rutter and L. Quine (eds), *Changing health behaviour.* Buckingham: Open University Press, pp. 193–208.

Svenson, G. and other collaborators, 1998, *European Guidelines for Youth AIDS Peer Education.* Brussels: European Commission.

Swantz, M.L., 1985, *Women in Development: a creative role denied? The case of Tanzania.* London: C. Hurst.

Talle, A., 1994, "The Making of Female Fertility: Anthropological perspectives on a bodily issue", *Acta Obstetricia et Gynecologica Scandinavica,* 73:280–83.

Tankoano, F., 1994, "Children take the lead in peer education in Burkina Faso villages", *AIDS Analysis Africa,* 4, (5):4.

Tanzania Commission for AIDS (TACAIDS), National Bureau of Statistics (NBS) and ORC Macro, 2005, *Tanzania HIV/AIDS Indicator Survey 2003–04.* Calverton: TACAIDS, NBS, and ORC Macro.

Tengia-Kessy, A., G.I. Msamanga and C.S. Moshiro, 1998, "Assessment of behavioural risk factors associated with HIV infection among youth in Moshi rural district, Tanzania", *East African Medical Journal,* 75:528–32.

Therkildsen, O., 2000, "Contextual issues in decentralization of primary education in Tanzania", *International Journal of Educational Development,* 20:407–21.

Thorne, B., 1993, *Gender play: Girls and boys in school.* Buckingham: Open University Press.

Todd, J., J. Changalucha, D.A. Ross, F. Mosha, A.I.N. Obasi, M. Plummer, R. Balira, H. Grosskurth, D.C.W. Mabey and R. Hayes, 2004, "The sexual health of pupils in years 4–6 of primary schools in rural Tanzania", *Sexually Transmitted Infections,* 80:35–42.

Tones, K. and S. Tilford, 1994, *Health education. Effectiveness, efficiency and equity.* London: Chapman & Hall.

Tumbo-Masabo, Z. and R. Liljestrom (eds), 1994, *Chelewa, Chelewa – The Dilemma of Teenage Girls.* Uppsala: Nordiska Afrikainstitutet.

Turner, C.F., H.G. Miller and L.E. Moses (eds), 1989, *AIDS, sexual behavior, and intravenous drug use.* Washington, DC: National Academy Press.

Turner, G. and A. Shepherd, 1999, "A Method in Search of a Theory: Peer Education and Health Promotion", *Health Education Research: Theory and Practice,* 12, (2):235–47.

Turyasingura, G., 1989, "Sexual behaviour and contraceptive use among youth of Jinja District". A dissertation in fulfillment of the Master of Arts Degree in Demography. Institute of Statistics and Applied Economics, Makerere University, Kampala.

US Department of Health and Human Services, 1994, *Preventing Tobacco Use among Young People.* A report of the Surgeon General. Atlanta, Georgia, Department of Health and Human Services, Public Health Service, Centers for Disease Control and Prevention, National Center for Chronic Disease Prevention and Health Promotion, Office on Smoking and Health.

UNAIDS, 2006, *Report on the global AIDS epidemic.* Geneva: UNAIDS.

UNAIDS, 2006, Joint United Nations Programme on HIV/AIDS, 2006, *Report on the global AIDS epidemic.* Read on: http://www.unaids.org/en/HIV_data/ 2006GlobalReport/default.asp.2006

UNAIDS, 2004 and 2000, Joint United Nations Programme on HIV/AIDS/WHO World Health Organisaton, *Epidemic Update: Sub-Saharan Africa*

UNAIDS, 2004, *Children on the brink 2004. A joint Report of New Orphan Estimates and a Framework for Action.* UNICEF, July, 2004.

UNAIDS, 2004, *AIDS epidemic update 2004.* Geneva: UNAIDS.

UNAIDS, 2004a and 2000, *Epidemiological fact sheet: Africa.*

UNAIDS, 2004e, *Epidemiological fact sheets on HIV/AIDS and sexually transmitted infections.* Malawi Update.

UNAIDS, 2002, Joint United Nations Programme on HIV/AIDS/ WHO World Health Organisation, http://www.unaids.org/youngpeople/YPposter_en.pdf.

UNAIDS, 2000–2001, http://www.unaids.org/.

UNAIDS, 2000, *Report on the global HIV/AIDS epidemic.* Joint United Nations Programme on HIV/AIDS, Geneva.

UNAIDS, 2000 and 2004, *AIDS Epidemic Update:* December. UNAIDS Information Centre. Geneva. Switzerland.

UNAIDS, 2000a, *Epidemiological fact sheets on HIV/AIDS and sexually transmitted infections.* Botswana Update.

UNAIDS, 2000b and 2004b, *Epidemiological fact sheets on HIV/AIDS and sexually transmitted infections*. South Africa Update.

UNAIDS, 2000c, *Epidemiological fact sheets on HIV/AIDS and sexually transmitted infections*. Zimbabwe Update.

UNAIDS, 2000d (revised) and 2004c, *Epidemiological fact sheets on HIV/AIDS and sexually transmitted infections*. Tanzania Update.

UNAIDS, 2000e, *Epidemiological Fact sheets on HIV/AIDS and sexually transmitted infections*. Uganda Update.

UNAIDS, 1999, *Sexual behavioural change for HIV: Where have theories taken us?* Geneva: UNAIDS.

UNAIDS, 1997a, *Impact of HIV and sexual health education on the sexual behaviour of young people: A review update*. Geneva: UNAIDS.

UNAIDS, 1997b, *Learning and teaching about AIDS at school*. Geneva: UNAIDS.

UNAIDS, 1996a, UNFPA – HIV/AIDS and reproductive Health. UNAIDS website, p. 10.

UNAIDS, 1996b, *UNICEF Helping Namibian Youth to Avoid HIV.* UNAIDS website, pp. 12–13.

UNFPA, 2006, State of world population 2005. The promise of equality: Gender equity, reproductive health and the MDGs. Youth and HIV/AIDS fact sheets. http://www.unfpa.org/swp/2005/presskit/factsheets/facts_youth.htm#ftn1. Online 2006.

UNGASS, 2006, *Political Declaration on HIV/AIDS,* 60/262.

UNICEF, 2004, *Breaking Silence. Gendered and sexual identities and HIV/AIDS in education*. Available at www.unicef.org

UNICEF, 2003, *Fact sheet,* 21st October.

UNICEF, 2000, *State of the World's Children 2000*. URL: http://www.inicef.org/sowc00/

UNICEF, 1998, *The state of the world's children*. Oxford: United Nations Children's Fund.

UNICEF and Ministry of Health, Uganda, 1998, *A guide to establishing adolescent-friendly health services*. Kampala: United Nations Children's Fund and Ministry of Health.

UNICEF, 1994, *Safe motherhood in Zambia: a situation analysis*. Lusaka: UNICEF.

UNICEF, 1990a, *Convention on the Rights of the Child*. www.unicef.org/crc

UNICEF, 1990b, *First Call for Children: World Declaration and Plan of Action from the World Summit for Children and Convention on the Rights of the Child*. Pretoria: UNICEF.

United Nations, 2006, The *Millennium Development Goals Report 2006*. New York. http://unstats.un.org/unsd/mdg/Resources/Static/Products/Progress2006/MDGReport2006.pdf

United Nations, Economic Commission for Africa, 2000, *African Development Forum 2000: AIDS: the Greatest Leadership Challenge*. Addis Abeba, Ethiopia, 3–7 December 2000.

United Nations, Population Division, 1998, *World Population Prospects: The 1998 Revision.* New York.

United Nations Fourth World Conference on Women, 1995, *Report of the Fourth World Conference on Women,* Beijing, 4–15 September 1995.

United Nations Fund for Population Activities, 1998, *The state of the world population.* New York: United Nations Fund for Population Activities.

United Nations International Conference on Population and Development, 1994, *Programme of Action of the UNICPD,* Cairo, 5–13 September 1994.

United Nations Population and Development, 1995, "Programme of action adopted at the International Conference on Population and Development", Cairo, 5–13 September 1994. UN: Department for Economic and Social Information and Policy Analysis.

United Nations Population Information Network (UNPIN): UN Population Division, Department of Economic and Social Affairs, with support from UN Population Fund (UNFPA), 1994, *Report of the International Conference on Population and Development (ICPD),* Cairo, 5–13 September 1994. A/Conf. 171/13. 18 Oktober 1994.

United Republic of Tanzania, 1997a, *Bureau of Statistics: Tanzania Demographic and Health Survey 1996.* Dar es Salaam: Planning Commission and Calverton: Macro International.

United Republic of Tanzania, 1997b, Regional Educational Officer, *Kigoma: Takwimu Za Watoto Watoro, Mkoa wa Kigoma, Standard IV – Standard VII, 1997 na 1998.* Prepared by Msuya, Regional Academic Officer.

United Republic of Tanzania, 1998, The Planning Commission Dar es Salaam and Regional Commissioner's Office: *Kigoma Region. Socio-Economic Profile.* December, 1998

Van Aswegen, E., 1995, "Aids-related knowledge: attitudes and behavioural practices among high-school pupils", *S.A. Family Practice,* May 1995:307–18.

Van den Bergh, G., forthcoming, "From Blessing to Burden: Coping with the Fertile Body in times of AIDS: Adolescent girls in Western Tanzania at the turn of the millennium". Thesis submitted in partial fulfilment of the requirements for the degree of Doctor Rerum Politicarum. Department of Social Anthropology, University of Bergen.

Van den Bergh, G., 2006, *Preventing unwanted pregnancy, preventing HIV infection? The challenges of contraceptive technology, illegal abortion and youth-friendly services in Tanzania.* AIDS 2006. XVI International AIDS Conference 13-18 August 2006. Toronto: Abstract Book, Volume I.

Van den Bergh, G., 1996, "Sexual Relations in the Making: The Case of School Adolescents in Rombo District, Kilimanjaro Region". Unpublished Master of Science in Health Promotion Thesis, Faculty of Psychology, University of Bergen.

Van den Bergh, G., 1995, "Difference and Sameness: A socio-cultural approach to disability in Western Tanzania". Unpublished M.Phil. Thesis. Faculty of Social Sciences, University of Bergen.

Van Rossem, R. and D. Meekers, 2000, "An evaluation of the effectiveness of targeted social marketing to promote adolescent and young adult reproductive health in Cameroon", *AIDS Education and Prevention,* 12, (5):383–404.

Van der Straten, A, 1998, "Sexual coercion, physical violence and HIV infection among women in steady relationships in Kigali, Rwanda", *AIDS and Behaviour,* 2:61–73.

Van Sambeek, J., 1949, *Croyances et Coutumes des Baha,* Premiere Partie (hectographed manuscript) Kabanga.

Van Wijck, B., 1994, "The dynamics of HIV transmission amongst a group of school-going adolescents in South Africa". Unpublished honours project. Cape Town, University of Cape Town.

The Vancouver Convention, 1997, (updated October 2001): http://www.icmje.org/

Varga, C.A., 1997, "Sexual decision-making and negotiation in the midst of AIDS: Youth in Kwa Zulu/Natal, South Africa", *Health Transition Review,* 7 (Supplement 3):45–67.

Vaz, R.Gg, S. Gloyd and R. Trindade, 1996, "The effects of peer education on STD and AIDS knowledge among prisoners in Mozambique", *International Journal of STD and AIDS,* 7, (1):51–54.

Venier, J.L., M.W. Ross and A. Akande, 1998, "HIV/AIDS-related social anxieties in adolescents in three African countries", *Social Science & Medicine,* 46:313–20.

Vergnani, T., A.J. Flisher, S. Lazarus, P. Reddy and S. James, 1998, "Health promoting schools in South Africa: Needs and prospects", *Southern African Journal of Child and Adolescent Mental Health,* 10:44–58.

Villa-Vicencio, T., 1998, "A Formative Evaluation of the Peer Education Programme on Sexuality and Reproductive Health: A Planned Parenthood Association Initiative in New Crossroads". Unpublished Report.

Visser, M., 1996, "Evaluation of the First AIDS Kit, the AIDS and lifestyle education programme for teenagers", *South African Journal of Psychology,* 26:103–13.

Visser, M., J.B. Schoeman and J. Perold, 2004, "Evaluation of HIV/AIDS prevention in South African schools", *Journal of Health Psychology,* 9(2):263–80.

Vygotsky, L.S., 1978, "Internalization of Higher Cognitive Functions", in M. Cole, V. John-Steiner, S. Scribner and E. Souberman (eds. & transl.), *Mind in Society: The Development of Higher Order Psychological Processes.* Cambridge: Harvard University Press, pp. 52–57.

Wagner, L., 1982, *Peer teaching: Historical perspectives.* Westport, CT: Greenwood Press.

Walker, D., 2003, "Cost and cost-effectiveness of HIV prevention strategies in developing countries: Is there an evidence base?", *Health Policy and Planning,* 18, (1):4–17.

Walker, S.A. and M. Avis, 1999, "Common reasons why peer education fails", *Journal of Adolescence,* 22:573–77.

Wallston, K.A. and B. Wallston, 1981, "Health locus of control scales", in H. Lefcourt (ed.), *Research with the locus of control construct* (Vol.1). New York: Academic Press.

Wallston, K.A. and B.S. Wallston, 1982, "Who is responsible for your health? The constuct of health locus of control", in G.S. Sanders and J. Suls (eds), *Social psychology of health and illness*. Hillsdale: Erlbaum, pp. 65–95.

Walt, G., 1994, *Health Policy: An introduction to process and power*. Johannesburg: Witwatersrand University Press.

Ward, C.L., A.J. Flisher and L. Kepe, in press, "Preventing negative mental health consequences of forensic mortuary work: A pilot study", *Journal of Traumatic Stress*.

Ward, J., G. Hunter and R. Power, "Peer education as a means of drug prevention and education among young people: An evaluation", *Health Education Journal*, 56:251–63.

Warenius, L., K. Odberg Pettersson, E. Nissen, B. Höjer, P. Chishimba and E. Faxelid, 2006, Vulnerability of sexual and reproductive health in young people – A study among Zambian secondary school students. Accept Culture, Health and Sexuality 2006.

Warwick, I. and P. Aggleton, 2004, "Building on Experience: A Formative Evaluation of a Peer Education Sexual Health Project in South Africa", *London Review of Education*, 2(2):137–53.

Webb, D., 1997, *Adolescence, sex and fear. Reproductive health services and young people in urban Zambia*. Lusaka: Central Board of Health and UNICEF.

Webb, D., 2000, "Attitudes to 'Kaponya Mafumo': the terminators of pregnancy in urban Zambia", *Health Policy and Planning*, 15:186–193.

Whiting, J.W.M., 1990, "Adolescent rituals and identity conflicts", in J.W. Stigler, R.A. Shweder and G. Herdt (eds), *Cultural psychology. Essays on comparative human development*. Cambridge: Cambridge University Press, pp. 357–65.

Wicker, A.W., 1969, "Attitudes versus actions: The relationship of verbal and overt behavioral responses to attitude objects", *Journal of Social Issues*, 25:41–78.

Wilson, D., I. Dubley, S. Msimanga and L. Lavelle, 1991, "Psychosocial predictors of reported HIV-preventive behaviour change among adults in Bulawayo, Zimbabwe", *Central African Journal of Medicine*, 37:196–202.

Windsor, R.A., T. Baranovski, N. Clark and G. Cutter, 1994, *Evaluation of health promotion, health education, and disease prevention programmes*, 2nd edition. Mountain View: Mayfield.

Wolf, R.C. and K.C. Bond, 2002, "Exploring similarity between peer educators and their contacts and AIDS-protective behaviors in reproductive health programmes for adolescents and young adults in Ghana", *AIDS Care*, 14(3):361–73.

Wolf, R.C. and J. Pulerwitz, 2003, "The Influence of Peer versus Adult Communication on AIDS-Protective Behaviors among Ghanaian Youth", *Journal of Health Communication*, 8:463–74.

Wolf, R.C., L. Tawfik and K. Bond, 2000, "Peer Promotion Programs and Social Networks in Ghana: Methods for Monitoring and Evaluating AIDS Prevention and Reproductive Health Programs among Adolescents and Young Adults", *Journal of Health Communication*, 5:61–80.

Wood, K. and R. Jewkes, 1997, "Violence, rape and sexual coercion: Everyday love in a South African township", *Gender and Development,* 5:41–46.

Wood, K., J. Maepa and R. Jewkes, 1997, *Adolescent sex and contraceptive experiences: Perspectives of teenagers and clinic nurses in the Northern Province.* Pretoria: Medical Research Council.

World Bank, 2003, Education and HIV/AIDS: A Sourcebook for HIV/AIDS Prevention. Programs. Washington, DC: World Bank, 2003.

World Bank, 2002, *Education and HIV/AIDS: A window of hope.* Washington DC: World Bank.

World Bank, 2000, *Poverty* Net: http://www.worldbank.org/poverty/data/trends/aids. htm.

World Bank, 1998, *World Development Report.* Washington DC: World Bank.

World Bank, 1993, *Investing in health: World development report.* Oxford: Oxford University Press.

WHO, 2004a, *Adolescent health and development in nursing and midwifery education.* Geneva: WHO.

WHO, 2004b, *Unsafe abortion.* Global and regional estimates of incidence of and mortality due to unsafe abortion, with a listing of available country data, 2000. Geneva: WHO.

WHO, 2001, *Mental Health Policy Project. Policy and Service Guidance Package. Executive Summary.* Geneva: WHO.

WHO, 1999a, *Monitoring Reproductive Health: Selecting a short list of national and global indicators.* Geneva: WHO.

WHO, 1999b, *Programming for Adolescent Health and Development.* Technical Report Series 886. Geneva: WHO.

WHO, 1998a, *Coming of age: from facts to action for adolescent sexual and reproductive health.* Geneva: WHO.

WHO, Division of Reproductive Health, 1998b, *Unsafe abortion.* Global and regional estimates of incidence of and mortality due to unsafe abortion, with a listing of available country data, 1998. Geneva: WHO.

WHO, 1995, *An assessment of the need for contraceptive introduction in Zambia.* Geneva: WHO.

WHO, 1993, *The health of young people.* Geneva: WHO.

WHO, 1992, *Strengthening nursing and midwifery in support of strategies for health for all.* Report by the Director General. Geneva: WHO.

WHO, 1987, *Women's health and the midwife. A global perspective.* Geneva: WHO.

World Health Organisation (WHO), UNDP, UNIFEM, UNICEF, UNFPA, UNAIDS, 2007, *Step up the pace of HIV prevention in Africa.* 2006–The year to accelerate HIV prevention in Africa: read on http://www.who.int/hiv/ mediacentre/AFRO-prevention_f s.pdf

Zambia Demographic and Health Survey (DHS), 2001/2002, 2002, Lusaka, University of Zambia, Central Statistical Office.

Zambia National AIDS Council, 2004, *Joint review of the national HIV/AIDS/STI/TB intervention strategic plan (2002–2005) and operations of the national ADS Council.* 30th June, 2004.

Zulu, E.M., F.N-A. Dodoo and A.C. Ezeh, 2005, "Urbanization, Poverty and Sex: Roots and Risky Sexual Behaviours in Slum Settlements in Nairobi, Kenya", in E. Kalipeni, S. Craddock, J.R. Oppong and J. Ghosh (eds), *HIV and AIDS in Africa.* Beyond Epidemiology. Oxford: Blackwell Publishing.

Contributors

Editors:

Alan J. Flisher is a child and adolescent psychiatrist. He is currently Professor and Head of the Division of Child and Adolescent Psychiatry at the University of Cape Town (UCT), South Africa, and Red Cross War Memorial Children's Hospital, Professor II at the Research Centre for Health Promotion at the University of Bergen in Norway, Director of the Adolescent Health Research Institute at UCT, and Honorary Senior Research Fellow at the Health Systems Research Unit at the Medical Research Council. His principal research interests are adolescent health and mental health services research.

Sylvia. F. Kaaya is a Psychiatrist, Senior Lecturer and Head of the Department of Psychiatry and Mental Health of the School of Medicine at Muhimbili University of Health and Allied Sciences in Dar es Salaam, Tanzania. She has research interests in adolescent risk behaviours; including sexual and drug use behaviours. She also has conducted research on women's mental health with a focus on understanding depression occurring in the peri-natal period and strengthening services for the psychosocial support of pregnant women living with HIV/AIDS.

Knut-Inge Klepp, Ph.D., M.P.H. is a professor in public health nutrition and health promotion and head of the Centre for Prevention of Global Infections at the Faculty of Medicine, University of Oslo, Norway. His research is primarily concentrated on studies investigating the development and change of health-related behavior among children and adolescents and evaluations of interventions to promote health. He has carried out a number of studies on reproductive health and HIV/AIDS prevention targeting adolescents in Sub-Sahara Africa. Klepp has served as a member of WHO's Steering Committee on Child and Adolescent Health and Development. He is currently Director of the Public Health and Welfare Division of the Norwegian Directorate for Health and Social Affairs.

Authors:

Leif E. Aarø is professor of social psychology at the Research Centre for Health Promotion, University of Bergen, Norway. His research has focused on determinants of health behaviour as well as large-scale evaluations of health education and health promotion programmes. Aarø has been a member of a number of expert panels and committees for the World Health Organization, the International Union for Health Promotion and Education, the Norwegian Research Council, and the Norwegian Ministry of Health. He is at present on the editorial board of Health Promotion International. He is also coordinator of a EU-funded research project that aims at developing and evaluating an HIV/AIDS health education programme for school students in Tanzania and South Africa.

John Arube-Wani, currently a public health specialist, has a B.A. from Makerere University, Kampala, Uganda, an MPhil from St. Andrews, Fife, U.K., and an M.P.H from Glasgow University, U.K. He was trained as a nurse initially and prior to teaching served as a medical/psychiatric social worker in Uganda's two leading teaching and referral general and psychiatric hospitals, Mulago and Butabika, respectively. He is a former lecturer at the Department of Paediatrics and Child Health at Makerere University Medical School.

Sheri Bastien is a PhD candidate at the Faculty of Education, University of Oslo, Norway. She holds a B.A/BEd from the University of Lethbridge, Canada and an MPhil in Comparative and International Education from the University of Oslo.

Elisabeth Faxelid with a background as nurse/midwife is associate professor in international health at Division of International Health (IHCAR), Department of Public Health Sciences, Karolinska Institutet, Stockholm, Sweden. She also holds a position as senior lecturer at Division of Reproductive and Perinatal Health Care, Department of Women and Child Health at Karolinska Institutet. Her main research area is sexual and reproductive health with a focus on adolescents and she is the principle investigator in the Nurses/Midwives Adolescent Reproductive Health Project in Kenya and Zambia.

Jessica Jitta (Dr) holds an MBChB and a M. Med. (Paediatrics) from Makerere University, Kampala, Uganda. She is a paediatrician and senior lecturer at the Department of Paediatrics and Child Health and also the director of the Child Health and Development Centre at Makerere University Medical School. She is a former lecturer and consultant paediatrician at Kenyatta National Hospital in Nairobi, Kenya.

Melkizedeck T. Leshabari is an Associate Professor in Behavioural Sciences and the Dean of the School of Public Health and Social Sciences, Muhimbili University College of Health Sciences, Dar es Salaam, Tanzanina. He has been doing research on adolescent health in Tanzania since 1985 and he has published several papers in collaboration with his network of researchers in the field of youth reproductive health.

Gro Th. Lie, Social and Community Psychologist, PhD, is Professor of Development Related Health Promotion at the Department of Education and Health Promotion and the Research Centre for Health Promotion (HEMIL), University of Bergen, Norway. She has worked for 18 years in joint Tanzanian–Norwegian research projects with the University of Dar es Salaam on HIV/AIDS related challenges in selected Tanzanian communities. Currently she is the head of a multidisciplinary thematic research group "Multicultural Venues of Empowerment in Health and Education: Applying Local Cultural Perspectives on Global Social Challenges" working with 10 African countries and the Middle East.

Johann Louw is a professor of psychology at the University of Cape Town. He has a PhD from the University of Amsterdam, and teaches programme evaluation at postgraduate level.

Catherine Mathews is a researcher in the Health Systems Research Unit of the South African Medical Research Council. She is also an honorary lecturer in the School of Public Health and Family Medicine, University of Cape Town, South Africa. Her interests are adolescent sexual and reproductive health and HIV prevention.

Wanjiru Mukoma is currently a HIV/AIDS programme manager at the Children's Institute, University of Cape Town, South Africa. Her research interests are HIV/AIDS, adolescent risk behaviours, school-based interventions, and programme evaluation.

Joyce Musandu is a registered community health nurse and midwife with a PhD degree from the American World University (through distance learning) from 2004. She has a MScN from Boston University, USA and a Diploma in

Advanced Nursing from the University of Nairobi, Kenya. Currently she is working as a Senior Lecturer at the Department of Nursing Sciences at the University of Nairobi. She is Co-Researcher in the Nurse/Midwives Adolescent Reproductive Health Project.

Irene Mushinge worked as a lecturer at Kitwe School of Nursing, Zambia, and was responsible for the design of the Nurse/Midwives Adolescent Reproductive Health Project in Zambia. Sadly she passed away in 2004. Friends, colleagues, and relatives miss Irene enormously.

Eva Nissen has a PhD from Karolinska Institutet, Stockholm, Sweden. She is at present working as a university lecturer at the Department of Woman and Child Health, Division of Reproductive and Perinatal Health Care, Karolinska Institutet, and at the School of Life Sciences, the University of Skövde, Sweden. Her research interest is in perinatal care and in health promotion in the field of sexual and reproductive health.

Anne Nordrehaug Åstrøm is professor in odontology at the Centre for International Health, University of Bergen, Norway Her research has focused on epidemiology, public health and behavioural research, primarily within the field of dentistry. Nordrehaug Åstrøm has a long standing cooperation regarding research and competence building with University of Addis Ababa in Ethiopia, Muhimbili the University College of Health Sciences in Tanzania and Makerere University in Uganda. She is coordinator of the research program "Oral health in a global perspective" and co-researcher of EU and NUFU funded projects of East African origin. She has been member of the editorial board for the Journal of Community Dentistry and Oral Epidemiology.

Yogan Pillay is currently chief director responsible for strategic planning in the National Department of Health, South Africa. He has a doctorate in public health from the John Hopkins University's School of Public Health, Baltimore, USA. In addition, he qualified as a clinical psychologist and practiced and taught on various aspects of clinical psychology between 1984 and 2005. He serves on the boards of several non-governmental organizations in the field of health, as well as on the steering committee of multi-country research projects.

Vibeke Rasch, MD, PhD is an Associate Professor at the Department of International Health, the University of Copenhagen, Denmark. She has extensive experience within the field of sexual and reproductive health and rights. Her research activities have mainly focused on contraceptive behaviour, unsafe abortion and post-abortion care in low income countries, more specifically East Africa. This work has resulted in a number of published papers in peer reviewed journals. She has also been involved in abortion research in Denmark, with a special focus on immigrant women's reproductive behaviour and choice of induced abortion.

Lillian Ssengooba Mpabulungi holds a B.A. in Sociology from Makerere University, in Kampala, Uganda, and an M.A (Medical Anthropology) from the University of Amsterdam,the Netherlands. She is currently a project officer on adolescent sexual and reproductive health with CARE International in Kampala.

Herman Schaalma is associate professor at the Department of Experimental Psychology, Maastricht University, the Netherlands. His main research interests are related to the design, evaluation and implementation of HIV/Aids prevention programs targetting migrant populations and youth in the Netherlands and developing countries. Schaalma's scientific specializations are the application of psychological theory in research and health promotion program design, and the application of Intervention Mapping, a protocol for designing theory and evidence-based health promotion programs. Schaalma holds the endowed chair for 'Aids Prevention and Health Education' for the Dutch Aids Foundation.

Margrethe Silberschmidt holds a doctoral degree in social anthropology from the University of Copenhagen, Denmark. Her principal research interests include sexual and reproductive health and behavior with particular emphasis on gender and sexuality, gender focused methodologies and policy issues. In relation to her research she has conducted long term field studies in rural and urban East Africa. She is an associate professor at the department of Women and Gender Research in Medicine, Institute of Public Health, the University of Copenhagen.

Anna Tengia-Kessy is Public Health Specialist and a Lecturer in the Community Health Department, Muhimbili University College of Health Sciences, Dar es Salaam, Tanzania. She has been working and researching on adolescent health including youth sexual health. She has also published in the same field.

Graziella Van den Bergh is assistant professor at Bergen University College, Norway. She holds a BA in Physiotherapy from Belgium, a MPhil in Social Anthropology and a MPhil in Health Promotion from the University of Bergen. She is pursuing her PhD in Social Anthropology at the same university. Her main research interests are in gender, sexual and reproductive health, disability / rehabilitation and comparative health and social systems research.

Mathilda Zvinavashe has a PhD degree in Nursing Science from the University of Michigan, Ann Arbor, USA. Currently she holds a position as lecturer at the Department of Nursing Science at the Medical School, University of Zimbabwe, Harare. She was instrumental in the early development of the Nurse/Midwives Adolescent Reproductive Health Project.

Index